Sue Stewart, Fiona Warburton and John D. Smith

Cambridge International AS and A Level

Travel and Tourism

Coursebook

Second edition

CAMBRIDGE
UNIVERSITY PRESS

University Printing House, Cambridge CB2 8BS, United Kingdom

One Liberty Plaza, 20th Floor, New York, NY 10006, USA

477 Williamstown Road, Port Melbourne, VIC 3207, Australia

314–321, 3rd Floor, Plot 3, Splendor Forum, Jasola District Centre, New Delhi – 110025, India

103 Penang Road, #05-06/07, Visioncrest Commercial, Singapore 238467

Cambridge University Press is part of the University of Cambridge.

It furthers the University's mission by disseminating knowledge in the pursuit of education, learning and research at the highest international levels of excellence.

Information on this title: education.cambridge.org

© Cambridge University Press 2017

First published 2014
Second edition 2017

20 19 18 17 16 15 14 13 12 11 10 9 8

Printed in Italy by Rotolito S.p.A.

A catalogue record for this publication is available from the British Library

ISBN 978-1-316-60063-4 Paperback

Additional resources for this publication at cambridge.org/9781316600634

The questions, answers and annotation in this title were written by the authors and have not been produced by Cambridge International Examinations.

In an examination, the marks granted might differ from the ones given to the answers found in this material.

Contents

Introduction   v
Acknowledgements   vii
How to use this book   x

1 Features of the travel and tourism industry   1
   Introduction   2
1.1 The nature of travel and tourism   3
1.2 Scale of the travel and tourism industry   12
1.3 Factors affecting tourism   17
1.4 The structure of the travel and tourism
   industry   33
1.5 Subsectors of the travel and tourism
   industry   39
   Summary   56
   Exam-style questions   57

2 Principles of customer service   59
   Introduction: The principles of customer
   service   60
2.1 Customers and their needs   61
2.2 Meeting external customer needs   61
2.3 The impacts of quality customer service   69
2.4 Assessing the quality of customer service in travel
   and tourism organisations   70
2.5 Setting organisational, functional area
   and individual customer service standards   73
2.6 Delivery of customer service   75
2.7 General customer feedback   78
   Summary   84
   Exam-style questions   85

3 Destination marketing   86
   Introduction   87
3.1 Defining the tourism market   87
3.2 The aims of market research and analysis   87
3.3 Market research: advantages and disadvantages
   of each research method   95
3.4 Market analysis tools and techniques   100
3.5 Market segmentation (target customers)   105
3.6 Visitor profiling   107
3.7 Product positioning   110
3.8 Review the marketing mix   112
3.9 Building a destination brand   119
3.10 Characteristics of an effective destination
   brand   122
3.11 Creating a brand identity   126

3.12 Marketing activities for launching the brand   129
3.13 Implementing the destination brand   132
3.14 Communication methods used to raise
   awareness of the destination's brand identity   134
3.15 Considerations for selection of communication
   methods   138
3.16 Different media used to communicate the
   destination's brand identity   139
3.17 Difficulties in implementing the destination
   brand   140
3.18 Challenges in branding destinations   140
3.19 Methods used to monitor costs and marketing
   activities   143
3.20 Key performance indicators (KPIs)   144
   Summary   148
   Exam-style questions   148

4 Destination management   151
   Introduction   152
4.1 Organisations involved in destination
   management, their roles and priorities   153
4.2 Objectives of tourism development and
   management   159
4.3 Destination management activities   163
4.4 Encouraging responsible tourist behaviour
   through education   165
4.5 Destination branding and marketing: mass
   and specialised markets   168
4.6 Partnerships of commercial and
   non-commercial organisations   168
4.7 Regular environmental impact auditing   169
4.8 Community involvement, community projects,
   education training and employment of locals   171
4.9 Impacts of tourism development   172
4.10 Socio-cultural impacts of tourism   178
4.11 Environmental impacts of tourism   182
4.12 Changes in the evolution of destinations   190
   Summary   195
   Exam-style questions   196

**5 Planning and managing a travel and
tourism event**   200
   Introduction   201
5.1 Assessment   202
5.2 Stages in the event   202
5.3 Forming – storming – norming – performing   203
5.4 Autocratic leadership   204

iii

Contents

5.5 Democratic leadership 205

5.6 Bureaucratic leadership 205

5.7 The team performance curve 206

5.8 Staffing for the event 206

5.9 Investigate potential travel and tourism events and undertake feasibility studies 207

5.10 Technology in the travel and tourism market 209

5.11 Aims and objectives for the chosen event 212

5.12 Marketing the event 213

5.13 Use of appropriate resources 216

5.14 Finance 217

5.15 Financial documents used whilst organising an event 219

5.16 Business plan 220

5.17 Evaluation 225

Summary 229

Index 230

Introduction

Travel and tourism is the world's largest service industry and in 2015 had a global economic contribution of US$7.6 trillion. It is an exciting and dynamic industry responsible for one in every 12 jobs in the world. Tourism is also one of the fastest growing industries and is seen by many as the key to socio-economic progress.

Undoubtedly, travel and tourism can be susceptible to global influences, however its business volume exceeds many other established industries such as food and oil production. This trend feeds into the mind-set of governments and policy makers where travel and tourism is seen to produce economic and employment benefits. With many traditional industries in decline, travel and tourism can offer a diverse and sustainable option, perhaps one that can offer not only economic benefits but environmental and socio cultural ones too.

There are consistently popular tourism destinations in the world, such as France, USA and Italy; however, there are many emerging, less well-known destinations that are keen to benefit from the economic advantages of this massive industry. This Cambridge International AS and A Level Travel and Tourism coursebook has been designed and written to reflect the changes in the industry and cover the Cambridge International AS and A Level syllabus 9395 for first teaching from 2017.

About the syllabus

Through the study of the syllabus learners will be able to develop:

- An understanding of the importance of the travel and tourism industry to host destinations, to communities, to the economy, globally, nationally and locally
- An understanding of the positive and negative impacts of travel and tourism and the importance of sustainability
- An appreciation of the importance of the customer in the travel and tourism industry
- An understanding of how the travel and tourism industry responds to change, including technological advances
- Their own values and attitudes in relation to travel and tourism industry issues
- Problem solving, decision making and communication skills.

- Appreciate the scale and importance of the travel and tourism industry
- Learn that the travel and tourism industry is dynamic in nature and how the industry responds to change, e.g. external factors such as changing consumer needs and expectations and developments in information technology
- Recognise the positive and negative impacts the industry may have on people, environments and economies.

The syllabus also allows learners to develop in four Assessment Objectives:

AO1 Knowledge and understanding

AO2 Application of knowledge and understanding

AO3 Analysis and research

AO4 Evaluation and decision-making

In a few places this coursebook refers to theories outside of the syllabus remit, but which are useful for enrichment purposes. These instances have been marked with a vertical coloured bar in the margin next to the relevant text.

Key concepts

The key concepts on which this syllabus is built are set out below. These concepts can help learners to make links between topics and develop a deep overall understanding of the subject. They key concepts are:

1 Global and growing

The travel and tourism industry is a global industry. Changes in political and socio economic circumstances and technological developments contribute to the continuing growth of the travel and tourism industry and its importance to many national economies.

2 Change and development

A key feature of the industry is its dynamic nature. The only constant is change. Exciting new enterprises, products or services are often developed in response to economic, political, social or technological change.

3 Customer focus

Travel and tourism organisations provide products, services and facilities to meet customer's needs. In order for travel and tourism providers to be successful, they must adopt a strong customer focus. This means they must really understand who their customers are and how they can best meet their needs.

4 Sustainability and responsibility

The Travel and Tourism industry has close links to destinations and so has a vested interest in ensuring environmental and sociocultural impacts are managed. Responsible management means that any developments must maximise the positive, and minimise the negative impacts of tourism.

The syllabus covered in this coursebook, encourages learning in practical and technical skills, including industry complex situations and problems. The textbook can be used in conjunction with visits to appropriate travel and tourism organisations and destinations.

Emphasis is given to the use of realia. As a vocational subject area this is vital for allowing learners to see and use authentic industry material.

Key features of this book

* A key feature of this textbook is the inclusion of **case study materials**. The many references to the case studies, data and examples from countries all around the world supports practical and interactive learning styles.

* There is an **international perspective** which allows areas for discussion and links to tourism applications through the different activities provided in each chapter.
* **Learning objectives are identified** and clearly linked to content and concepts covered in each chapter.
* The **text is clearly laid out**, with easy to use sections.
* Emphasis is given to the use of current **realia.**
* The **Key concept approach** demonstrates the global nature and linking patterns of the travel and tourism industry. It allows for integration of thought processes and development of critical thinking.
* **Key terms** are given throughout each chapter to assist with understanding.
* A variety of **'In-chapter' activities** are supplied to offer opportunity to practice applying what is being learned, using evidence and data taken from current real life situations.
* **Examination-style questions** with expected answers are provided to test the skills, knowledge and understanding of the syllabus.
* Opportunity for learners to **develop their higher order skills** in application through analysis, evaluation and assessment techniques.
* **Resource links** to current industry providers.

Sue Stewart, 2016.

Acknowledgements

The authors and publishers acknowledge the following sources of copyright material and are grateful for the permissions granted. While every effort has been made, it has not always been possible to identify the sources of all the material used, or to trace all copyright holders. If any omissions are brought to our notice, we will be happy to include the appropriate acknowledgements on reprinting.

Print Book

Cover image: Pablo Scapinachis/Shutterstock; Chap. 1 opener Petko Danov/Getty Images; Fig 1.1 Flip Nicklin/Minden Pictures/Getty Images; Fig. 1.2 Jean-Pierre Pieuchot/Getty Images; Fig. 1.3 JIJI PRESS/AFP/Getty Images; Fig. 1.4 Mark Williamson/Getty Images; Fig. 1.5 Li Wei/VCG via Getty Images; Fig. 1.6 Sergey Dzyuba/Shutterstock; Fig. 1.7 Trips of EU residents by month of departure(^{1}) and duration, EU-28(^{2}), 2013 (Millions) http://ec.europa.eu/eurostat/statisticsexplained/ index.php/Seasonality_in_tourism_demand © European Union, 1995-2013; Fig. 1.8 jenifoto/Getty Images; Fig. 1.9 Marco Simoni/Getty Images; Fig. 1.10 Matteo Colombo/Getty Images; Fig. 1.11 Christian Aslund/Getty Images; Fig. 1.12, 1.13 © UNWTO 92844/24/16 Source: World Tourism Organization (2015), International tourist arrivals up 4% in the first four months of 2015, press release PR15048 9 July 2015, UNWTO, Madrid (online), available at: www.unwto.org; Fig. 1.19 david franklin/Getty Images; Fig 1.20 Brian Jannsen/Alamy Stock Photo; Fig. 1.21 TOM MARESCHAL/Alamy Stock Photo Fig. 1.22 Klaas Lingbeek- van Kranen/Getty Images; Fig. 1.23 Manuel ROMARÍS/Getty Images; Fig. 1.24 moodboard/Getty Images; Fig. 1.26 Jordan Mansfield/Getty Images; Fig. 1.27 the Mauritius Tourism Promotion Authority (MTPA); Fig. 1.28 United Nations World Tourism Organization; Fig. 1.29 Regional Tourism Organisations New Zealand (RTONZ) with permission; Fig. 1.30 Iain Masterton/ Alamy Stock Photo, Fig. 1.32 (plane) Stephen Strathdee/Getty Images; Fig. 1.32 (cruise ship) NAN728/Shutterstock; Fig. 1.34 (train) Julian Elliott Photography/Getty Images; Fig. 1.35 (coach) Ralf Hettler/Getty Images; Fig. 1.37 Travelasia/Getty Images; Fig. 1.37, 1.38 Brittany Ferries; Fig. 1.40 Education Images/UIG via Getty Images; Fig. 1.41 Pawel Libera Images/Alamy Stock Photo; Fig. 1.43 John Warburton-Lee Photography/Alamy Stock Photo; Fig. 1.45 dpa picture alliance archive/Alamy Stock Photo; Fig. 1.47 fotostorm/Getty Images; Fig. 1.48 Piero M. Bianchi/Getty Images; Fig. 1.49 Jonny Abbas/Alamy Stock Photo; Fig. 1.50 Trinette Reed/Getty Images; Fig. 1.52 Greg Balfour Evans/Alamy Stock Photo; Fig. 1.53 adapted from 'The 50 most popular tourist attractions in the world in 2014' by Love Home Swap, with permission; (Niagara Falls) Hans-Peter Merten/Getty Images; (Union Station) Travelpix Ltd/Getty Images; (Central Park) Yiming Chen/Getty Images; (Time Square) @by Feldman_1/Getty Images; (Las Vegas) PhotoStock-Israel/Getty Images; Fig. 1.54 EDU Vision/Alamy Stock Photo; Chap. 1 exam-style question 3 adapted from Mail & Guardian Africa; Chap. 2 opener Michael Blann/Getty Images; Fig. 2.1 Steve Back/Getty Images; Fig. 2.3 Izzet Keribar/Getty Images; Fig. 2.4 Chris Mellor/Getty Images; Fig. 2.6 Digital Vision/Getty Images; Fig. 2.7 Walter Bibikow/Getty Images and accompanying text © Copyright 2016 FRHI, all rights reserved; Fig. 2.10 Zero Creative/Getty Images; Fig. 2.12 VIEW Pictures Ltd/Alamy Stock Photo; Fig. 2.13 Ikonoklast Fotografie/ Shutterstock; Fig. 2.15 Echo/Getty images; Fig. 2.16 by Opella Hospitality; Fig. 2.17 Dirk Renckhoff/Alamy Stock Photo; Fig. 2.18 Malcolm Park London events/Alamy Stock Photo; Fig. 2.19 David Brabiner/Alamy Stock Photo; Fig. 2.20 Bateaux Dubai; Fig. 2.21 comment card from Bateaux Dubai; Chap. 3 opener M.M./Shutterstock; Fig. 3.1 Sayid Budhi/Getty Images; Fig. 3.2 Herve Gyssels/Getty Images; Chap. 3 Case Study 1 extract from the ITB World Travel Trends Report 2014/2015; Table 3.2 adapted from 'Toward a Sociology of International Tourism' by Erik Cohen, *Social Research*, vol. 39, no. 1, 1972; Fig. 3.4 Erich Schmidt/Getty Images; Fig. 3.5 Juergen Ritterbach / Alamy Stock Photo; Chap. 3 Case Study 2 from Myanmar Tourism Master Plan 2013-2020, published by the Ministry of Hotels and Tourism for the Republic of the Union of Myanmar; Fig. 3.7 tourism destination questionnaire used by permission of the Ministry of Economic Development and Technology Directorate for Tourism and Internationalisation, Slovenia; Chap. 3 Case Study 4 text and Fig. 3.11 Magical Kenya brand logo used with permission of Euromonitor International Ltd; Fig. 3.12 Ozkan Bilgin/Anadolu Agency/Getty Images; Fig. 3.15 Tetra Images/Getty Images; Chapter 3 Case Study 5 2020 summary of Tourism Australia's India Strategic Plan used by permission of

Supplementary Case Studies

Pierre Klemas/Getty Images; CS11 adapted from Visit Britain, image Caiaimage/Sam Edwards/Getty Images; CS12 adapted from eTurboNews with permission from eTN Corporation, image Nilanjan Sasmal/Getty Images; CS13 adapted from madamtussauds.com, image Fred Duval/FilmMagic/Getty Images; CS14 adapted from eTurboNews with permission from eTN Corporation, image Hagen Hopkins/Getty Images; CS15 with permission of Fáilte Ireland, image Trish Punch/Getty Images; CS16 adapted from eTurboNews with permission from eTN Corporation, image Danita Delimont/Getty images; CS17 text and image by permission of Mas Vidrier; CS18 with permission from Morro Bay's City Manager, image John D. Smith; CS19 adapted from fcbarcelona.com, image John D. Smith; CS20 adapted from eTurboNews, image John D. Smith; CS21 adapted from Cape Town Magazine, image John D. Smith

How to use this book

In this section of the syllabus you will learn about:

- the nature of travel and tourism, including the main types of tourism, types of destination, the main reasons why people travel and characteristics of the industry
- the scale of the travel and tourism industry
- factors affecting tourism
- the structure of the travel and tourism industry
- the subsectors of the industry.

Learning Objectives
Set the scene of each chapter, help with navigation through the book and give a reminder of what's important about each topic.

> 🔑 **KEY TERMS**
>
> **Destination:** any geographical area consisting of all the services and infrastructure necessary to support tourism i.e. the basic physical and organisational structures and facilities (e.g. buildings, roads, power supplies).

Key terms
Clear and straightforward explanations are provided for the most important words in each topic.

> **ACTIVITY 3**
>
> Choose **two** different destinations. Research and compare the range of built and natural attractions offered in each destination. Which destination would you recommend to a leisure visitor? Give reasons for your recommendation.

Activities
Chapter activities offering students the opportunity to practice applied learning using varied evidence, data and situations.

- Drive to maturity: growth should be self-sustaining, having spread to all parts of the country, and leading to an increase in the number and types of industry. During this stage more complex transport systems and manufacturing expand as transport develops, rapid urbanisation occurs, and traditional industries may decline. This has been the experience of many of the 'Tiger' and 'BRIC' economies with sustained GDP growth and rising per capita income levels.
- Age of mass consumption: rapid expansion of tertiary industries occurs alongside a decline in manufacturing. This is the situation in most MEDC nations where GDP levels are high but growth is slow. Per capita incomes are high and large sections of the population have significant levels of disposable income to consume a variety of goods and services.

Enrichment/Extension material
Theories outside of the syllabus remit.

Key Concept
Indicate to students and teachers where specific areas of the text meet the key concepts of the syllabus.

>  **KEY CONCEPTS**
>
> **Change and development**
>
> The Rostow Model epitomises the concept of change and development within destinations. It maps out how a destination evolves over time, linked to economic development.

CASE STUDY 3

Pollution

Haze affecting Thai tourism industry – October 2015

After engulfing Singapore, and parts of Malaysia and Indonesia, thick haze is also causing severe pollution in southern Thailand, and impacting the nation's crucial tourism sector. Caused by forest fires in Indonesia, the thick smog, which has already shrouded parts of Malaysia and Singapore for two months, has also reached hazardous levels in the five southern Thai provinces of Songkhla, Satun, Pattani, Surat Thani and Yala, making the areas dark and foggy. In fact, the pollution index recently hit a record-high reading of 365 in Thailand. (A reading of 101–200 is unhealthy; 201–300 is very unhealthy and above 300 is hazardous.) The next provinces up the peninsula, Narathiwat, Phuket and Phangnga, have dust levels within acceptable margins, but are coming close to the limit. As a result, the tourism industry is starting to feel the impact of the prolonged haze as Phuket and Surat Thani boast pristine tropical beaches which are popular among tourists. December is a crucial peak season for the Thai tourism industry, and if the haze continues during November, it could affect tourism bookings as tourists try to avoid the haze-affected tourism destinations in Southeast Asia. In fact, some tour operators have already complained about several flights packed with tourists being delayed or diverted due to unsafe conditions, as well as about holiday plans being cancelled. Tourism is a crucial part of the Thai economy, contributing around 10% of GDP, taking into account output and employment multiplier effects throughout the economy. And with the Thai economy already weak due to the impact of political turmoil during 2014, the haze conditions could further damage the tourism sector.

Case Studies
Real life examples and data from the tourism industry around the world to support students with practical and interactive learning.

Exam-style questions

Question 1

a   Explain, using examples, the difference between mass tourism and specialised tourism. **[4 marks]**

b   Analyse the relationship between the reasons why people travel and the types of destinations they visit. **[6 marks]**

c   Evaluate why LEDCs often find it difficult to attract tourists. **[9 marks]**

Question 2

The Seychelles islands are becoming an increasingly popular tourist destination after a 15% increase in arrivals was recorded between January and April 2015, when compared with the same period the previous year.

During 2014, the number of visitors who came to the Indian Ocean archipelago of 115 islands were almost the same compared with 2013, recording only a 1% increase. However, 2015 seems likely to have been a good year for the Seychelles tourism industry.

According to the National Bureau of Statistics (NBS), the months of March and April of 2015 recorded the highest number of visitors since January 2009 with 25 129 and 25 038 visitor arrivals respectively; a very promising figure for the small island state with a population of 90 000.

Tourism is the main pillar of the Seychelles economy. The island nation, which is situated in the Indian Ocean, east of the African Coast and northeast of Madagascar, is known for its white-sand beaches, turquoise sea water and its unique, well-preserved environment.

http://www.seychellesnewsagency.com

Refer to the information about tourism in the Seychelles.

a   Describe **two** reasons for the appeal of the Seychelles as a destination. **[4 marks]**

b   Analyse the data relating to tourist arrivals for the Seychelles and explain why these figures are important for the destination. **[6 marks]**

c   Discuss how ecological factors such as climate change might affect the future of tourism for an island destination such as the Seychelles. **[9 marks]**

Exam-style questions
Final questions to test student skills and their comprehension of the syllabus.

Summary
To review what the student will have learnt in the chapter.

Summary

We have seen how all aspects of the travel and tourism industry overlap and interrelate in creating the overall visitor experience. The component subsectors all depend on each other. All component subsectors will have some form of relationship with most of the other destination features. For example, the development of a new tourist attraction at a destination will have an effect on transport, the demand for accommodation and catering facilities, tour operators may want to organise tours to the new attraction and the local or regional tourism board will help to promote it.

For this section, you should be able to:

- give relevant examples of the current structure of the industry
- explain key organisations that make up the structure and their products, services, values and objectives
- analyse information and data relating to the structure of travel and tourism
- make appropriate judgements about the relationships between organisations within the industry.

Chapter 1
Features of the travel and tourism industry

In this section of the syllabus you will learn about:

- the nature of travel and tourism, including the main types of tourism, types of destination, the main reasons why people travel and characteristics of the industry
- the scale of the travel and tourism industry
- factors affecting tourism
- the structure of the travel and tourism industry
- the subsectors of the industry.

Introduction

The past 70 years have seen a remarkable growth in tourism-related activities. For example, the number of international arrivals shows an evolution from a mere 25 million international arrivals in 1950 to nearly 12 billion in 2015, corresponding to an average annual growth rate of over 6%. Today travel and tourism is one of the world's largest industries, it was responsible for 9.8% of world GDP (US$7.6 trillion) in 2014, 5.4% of total exports and now supports nearly 277 million people in employment, which equates to 1 out of every 11 people, in both the advanced and emerging economies. Furthermore, growth in tourism is expected to continue at a rate of 4% each year with tourists expected to continue spending more per trip and to stay longer on their holidays in the next ten years.

The Cambridge International AS and A Level syllabus introduces candidates to the dynamic nature of the travel and tourism industry and to the various ways in which it responds to change. This gives the readers a broad understanding of one of the world's fastest growing industries. This book investigates the reasons for the rapid growth in the modern travel and tourism industry and shows why it is described as 'the world's biggest industry'. Readers will learn that the international travel and tourism industry consists of a wide variety of commercial and non-commercial organisations that work together to supply products and services to tourists. During your studies, you will develop an appreciation of the values and attitudes of different organisations and the significance of travel and tourism to the economies of many countries.

To help introduce you to the content here are a few simple starter activities. You may or may not have studied the travel and tourism industry before but you will know something about it. Complete the following holiday survey, based on your most recent experience, with as many details as you can remember about the trip.

Holiday Features	Details
destination	
length of stay	
transport	
accommodation	
excursions/visits	
activities	
food & drink	
type of booking	

Table 1.1

The details you provide will be valid illustrations of aspects of the Travel and Tourism syllabus content. The destination you visited determines whether you would be classified as a domestic or an outgoing tourist. The destination, if abroad, may have been long haul or short haul; at home it may have been a short break or you were visiting friends and relatives, which is known as VFR.

ACTIVITY 1

1   You should be able to identify and provide examples of the main Travel, Tourism and Hospitality component activities present in your **local** area. You should be aware that it is possible to place these into categories. Name **three** examples in your local area of each of the following:

   - places of entertainment
   - travel service providers (travel agents etc.)
   - transport services (air, rail and road)
   - catering facilities
   - accommodation types
   - sport and leisure venues/providers
   - other visitor attractions.

2   These are all examples of the things that help to make tourism come alive not just in your local area but in all types of destination. You will have paid money and been a customer in some of them.

If you went to primary school in your local area you will have seen lots of changes over the last decade. Think and write about some illustrations of the following:

   - new building developments
   - new events
   - new attractions.

3   Have you been a guest at a wedding reception or some other similar event? Where was it held and what did the event involve as far you can remember? Your answers to all these questions will show that you have some basic familiarity with the products, services and facilities provided by travel and tourism organisations.

The accommodation used during your trip may have been serviced or self-catering, such as a four star hotel or a camp site, and you may have had half board or an all-inclusive meal plan. Whilst on holiday you may have visited natural and/or built tourist attractions and used the services of a local Tourist Information Centre (TIC) or guide. The holiday, or some of its components, may have been booked through a travel agency or direct with a tour operator. Different methods of transport by land, sea and air may have made up parts of the holiday.

There will be some aspects of your local area that will qualify it as being a tourist destination. Destinations are places where tourism develops. Tourist destinations are themselves influenced by the prevailing social, cultural, environmental, economic and political conditions. It is fundamental to the concept of the tourist destination that tourism is generally not the sole economic activity or function within the area identified as a destination.

1.1 The nature of travel and tourism

Travel, tourism and hospitality are old concepts and history is full of examples of explorers travelling to distant lands. Today, people around the world travel for many reasons and international travel by road, rail, sea and air transport has become common. However, should all people who travel to a particular destination be regarded as tourists? It is worthwhile now to consider the definition of the word 'tourist'. In 1995, the World Tourism Organization (UNWTO) provided the following clarification:

'Any person who travels to a country other than that in which s/he has his/her usual residence, but outside his/her usual environment for a period of at least one night but not more than one year and whose main purpose of visit is other than the exercise of an activity remunerated from within the country visited. This term includes people travelling for leisure, recreation and holidays, visiting friends and relatives, business and professional health treatment, religious pilgrimages and other purposes.'

'This definition of what being a tourist actually involves helps us to define the word tourism with a good degree of accuracy and one of the more straightforward definitions is that used by the UK Tourism Society:'

'Tourism is the temporary short term movement of people to destinations outside places where they normally live and work, and their activities during their stay at these destinations.'

'In other words, tourism comprises the activities of persons travelling to and staying in places outside their usual environment for not more than one consecutive year for leisure, business and other purposes. We can now have a look at some of the different types of tourism and consider the main reasons why people travel.'

Main types of tourism
Domestic tourism

Tourism is classified as **domestic** when the trip or holiday takes place within a person's home country. If a traveller crosses one or more national borders, this becomes **international** tourism and they will be classified as an international arrival in their destination country. An American citizen flying from Los Angeles (LAX) to Auckland (AKL) would be an **outbound** tourist from the USA and an **inbound** tourist to New Zealand. International tourist arrivals and international tourist receipts are the most commonly accepted measures of a country's international tourism industry. Tourism is a key driver of New Zealand's economy and it attracts people from around the world. Tourism's direct contribution to New Zealand's GDP was NZ$8.3 billion or 4.0% in 2014.

Domestic tourism in New Zealand continues to grow. Domestic tourism is popular with some people because it is convenient in many respects. For example, there are no difficulties speaking the language, using the currency and no passport or visa is required for travel. During 2013 domestic tourism increased by 4% to reach 19 million trips. 2013 domestic trip growth was, however, lower than the 9% growth seen in 2012. The more moderate growth in 2013 was perhaps due in part to the appreciation of the New Zealand dollar between 2012 and 2013, which made outbound travel more attractive. The number of domestic trips is expected to reach 21 million trips by 2018. Domestic travel spending generated 56.3% of direct travel and tourism GDP in 2014 in New Zealand compared with 43.7% for visitor exports (foreign visitor spending or international tourism receipts). Domestic travel spending is expected to reach the value of NZ$15.9 billion by 2025.

Inbound tourism involves overseas residents visiting a country and in 2014 New Zealand received 2 857 400 international visitors, up 5.1% on the previous year. International visitors contributed more than NZ$9.6 billion to New Zealand's economy. Figure 1.1 shows one of New Zealand's attractions for inbound tourists.

Outbound tourism refers to residents leaving their home country to travel overseas, usually for a holiday. In 2011, New Zealand residents made 2.2 million trips abroad, up 1% on the previous year.

Type of domestic trip	Number of trips (millions)	Annual growth (%)
day trips	31.5	14.6
overnight trips	16.6	4.1
total nights	49.1	2.8

Table 1.2 Tourism is a key driver of New Zealand's economy

Figure 1.1 Whale watching in New Zealand

KEY CONCEPTS

Global and growing

The New Zealand study shows the growth rate of tourism for one country, but the patterns shown can be found around the world, highlighting the importance of this industry on a global scale.

Key market	Number of trips (millions)	Annual growth (%)
Australia	1 156 426	+3.3
UK	230 316	-1.7
USA	184 714	-2.6
China	145 524	+18.6
Japan	68 963	-21.4

Table 1.3 International visitors in New Zealand

Mass tourism

Mass tourism is a form of tourism that involves a large number of tourists coming to one destination. There is usually a particular reason to visit a particular location for mass tourism purposes, such as skiing in a mountain resort or sunbathing at a beach location. This form of tourism can involve tens of thousands of people travelling to the same destination, often at the same time of year. It has been the most popular form of tourism since mass tourism holiday products were introduced in the 1970s as it is often the cheapest way to go abroad on holiday. A traditional package holiday is an example of mass tourism.

Specialised tourism

Tourism has changed in recent times to reflect the changing tastes and preferences of visitors. To meet the needs, wants and expectations of a more adventurous population, the travel and tourism industry has responded over the last decade with the rapid growth of **specialised tourism** geared towards particular interests such as hiking, painting or culinary activities. According to the World Tourism Industry (UNWTO), specialised tourism can be defined as that which involves individual or group tours by people who wish to develop their given interests or visit places with a connection to their specific interest. Sports tourism and medical tourism are two examples. We will look at a broad range of different forms of specialised tourism later in the chapter.

Independent and packaged tourism

Another innovation that has affected the travel and tourism industry in recent years is the way in which travel and tourism products are packaged. The rapid development of online services have changed how travellers book holidays. This has led to the creation of **independent tourism**. An independent holiday is one in which the traveller organises and books transport and accommodation from separate sources rather than purchasing them together as part of an organised package. **Packaged tourism**, on the other hand, is defined as the simultaneous sale of at least two elements of a holiday to the traveller, such as fares on public transport (e.g. flights) and commercial accommodation (e.g. a hotel or self-catering apartment). Other elements, such as meals or excursions, are not essential to the definition of a holiday package, but may also be included.

Types of destination

KEY TERMS

Destination: any geographical area consisting of all the services and infrastructure necessary to support tourism i.e. the basic physical and organisational structures and facilities (e.g. buildings, roads, power supplies).

Simply then, destinations are the places to which people travel in order to take part in leisure and tourism activities. Because people travel for different reasons, different aspects or features of a destination may appeal to different people. Destinations can be categorised under the following types.

Resort

The word 'resort' is often used to describe a tourism destination. These are places in which a high proportion of the jobs and businesses are connected to tourism. Resorts have a range of accommodation and include a number of attractions and other tourist facilities. For example **beach resorts** are on the beach and the main amenities and activities for visitors are linked to the beach, as in Benidorm and Alicante, which are in the Costa Blanca area of Spain. Resorts can also be **purpose built** such as Center Parcs or Disneyland Paris. These offer accommodation, food and beverages, activities and amenities designed around a certain theme and were carefully planned and developed to attract certain customer groups. **Integrated resorts** are a relatively new, mixed development concept which are large scale and purpose built. An integrated resort offers a broad range of leisure and conference facilities as well as a casino. There are two integrated resorts in Singapore, which opened in 2010. Resorts World Sentosa is a family-centred attraction, and includes the region's first Universal Studios theme park, S.E.A. Aquarium (one of the world's largest aquariums), Adventure Cove Waterpark and Dolphin Island. Other attractions include a Maritime Experiential Museum, an award-winning destination spa, a casino, six unique hotels, the Resorts World Convention Centre, celebrity chef restaurants and specialised retail outlets. Marina Bay Sands (see Figure 1.2) is a luxury resort complex, offering a 2 561-room hotel, a convention-exhibition centre, The Shoppes at Marina Bay Sands boutique shopping centre, a museum, two large theatres, seven 'celebrity chef' restaurants, a skating rink and the world's largest atrium casino with 500 tables. Other countries also offer integrated resorts, which are popular especially in Asia.

Figure 1.2 The Marina Bay Sands Integrated Resort, in Singapore

Town, city, country

Any geographical location can be a destination if it has the ability to attract visitors to it, no matter the size or scale of the area. Small medieval **towns**, historic **city** centres, even whole regions such as the Loire Valley in France or the Shanxi province in China are all destinations with charm, curious traditions, popular festivities and delicious local foods to attract tourists. **Countries** can be described as destinations too: Thailand or Kenya are both popular.

Urban and rural

Urban destinations are those with a relatively high population density so these are mainly large towns and cities. Day trips are popular to urban destinations as the transport infrastructure is usually well developed to complement a wide range of other facilities for tourists. Tourists usually go there for business purposes, to go shopping, for entertainment venues or to visit museums, churches and other built attractions. New York is an example of an urban destination. **Rural destinations**, also known as **countryside destinations**, are those in more remote and less densely populated areas. Tourists visit rural destinations to enjoy natural attractions such as lakes, mountains and forests. An example of a rural destination is the Fjords of Norway.

Coastal and island

Coastal destinations as the term suggests are towns and villages that attract visitors because they are located on the coast. Visits here are also known as seaside tourism and these types of destination are popular with families. Coastal destinations form an important part of the traditional 'Sun, sea and sand' package holiday. Calangute is a coastal destination in Goa, India. **Island destinations** attract visitors with their exotic images of white sandy beaches, activities such as snorkeling amongst the coral reefs and their strong cultural heritage. Jamaica is an island destination in the Caribbean.

More Economically Developed Countries (MEDCs) and Less Economically Developed Countries (LEDCs)

This is an important means of classifying destinations. Traditionally MEDCs have played an important role as destinations, acting as tourist receiving areas because they have the most developed infrastructure to support visitor numbers. Typical MEDCs are in the northern hemisphere and include countries in Western Europe, North America, Australia and Japan. By nature LEDCs are poor countries, and do not have stable economies. Their infrastructure is not well developed and there are sometimes political problems. All of these factors have made them unsuitable as tourist destinations in the past. Examples of LEDCs include Ethiopia, Cambodia and Haiti. However, over the last decade or so, many LEDCs have realised that there are many benefits to be gained from tourism and therefore some of these countries are emerging as destinations, attracting increasing numbers of visitors. Many LEDCs have been able to promote and exploit their natural landscapes and wildlife, from safaris in Tanzania and Kenya, gorilla trekking in Rwanda, to rainforest trekking in Costa Rica and glacier tours in Argentina. Other countries have relied on historical and cultural attractions such as Mexico and Egypt with their pyramids, Cambodia with the Angkor Wat temples and Peru with the Inca ruins of Machu Picchu. Newly industrialised countries (NICs) including Brazil, India and China are also gaining importance as destinations.

KEY CONCEPTS

Change and development

Emerging destinations are an example of how the travel and tourism industry can cause positive change and enable destinations and economies to develop.

KEY TERMS

Tourism generating area: places where the majority of tourists originate.

Tourism receiving area: main areas to which the majority of tourists travel.

Reasons why people travel

People travel for a variety of reasons and the most commonly used sub-divisions are as follows.

Leisure travel

Very simply, leisure travel is travel for pleasure and enjoyment. Leisure tourists visit a destination to see an attraction, take part in activities and to experience a break from their usual daily routines. The important point about leisure travel is that people are travelling to engage in some leisure-related activity during their free time and that they are using their own money in order to do so. Their travel plans are not work-related (although it is common for some individuals to combine business with pleasure) and to all intents and purposes such travellers are on holiday. Furthermore, these leisure travellers can be sub-divided into categories such as day trippers, overnight visitors or those on a particular type of holiday such as a short break.

Business travel

Business travel is an important part of the global travel and tourism industry and it is frequently referred to as MICE (Meetings, Incentives, Conferences and Exhibitions). People travelling for work-related purposes are business tourists. A particular business traveller may be going to meet with colleagues, they might be a delegate at a conference or an attendee at an exhibition or they might be travelling as a reward for past job performance. A characteristic feature of business travel is the fact that the employer will meet a significant proportion of the cost of travel and so business travellers tend to spend more than leisure travellers both in terms of transport and accommodation.

Visiting friends and relatives (VFR)

There is a trend in both the More Economically Developed Countries (MEDCs) and the Less Economically Developed Countries (LEDCs) for international travel for the purpose of visiting friends and relatives. In many cases, migration has resulted in large numbers of people working overseas while their families remain at home. This means that there will be a regular flow of expatriate workers travelling for home visits throughout the year, but particularly at holiday and festival times. VFR tourists usually spend money on transport and activities, but not on accommodation.

However, the travel and tourism industry is very dynamic and changes in the types of tourism people prefer have encouraged tour operators to offer specialised holidays catering for specific requirements. These focus on interests and activities which appeal to a particular sector of the tourist market.

KEY CONCEPTS

Customer focus

By adapting to the specific wants and needs of customers, the travel and tourism industry can definitely be described as customer-focused.

This has given rise to a variety of key specialised markets and travel motivations based on the particular reasons for travel such as:

- medical tourism: medical packages which offer cheaper general or cosmetic surgery abroad, followed by a period of recuperation
- religious tourism: religious journeys or pilgrimages to destinations such as Jerusalem, Lourdes and Mecca
- adventure tourism: such as trekking in the jungles of Borneo or the mountains of Nepal
- cultural tourism: heritage tours visiting historical and cultural sites, often in cities such as Rome, Athens, Florence and Venice
- ecotourism: trips to experience the unspoilt natural environment and wildlife in destinations such as Amazonia or Antarctica
- sports tourism: trips to see a cricket or rugby team in a competition abroad or attending the FIFA World Cup or the Olympic Games
- health and spa tourism: visits to spa resorts which offer health therapy and beauty treatments in luxurious, relaxing surroundings such as found at Kamalaya Koh Samui in Thailand.

Special interest tourism, including **dark tourism:** trips to the locations of former conflicts, such as battlefields or concentration camps such as Auschwitz and Dachau; **slum tourism:** organised excursions to informal settlements and impoverished areas as a more realistic form of experiencing a country, by getting in touch with real people and the local culture. An example is Favela Da Rocinha in Rio De Janeiro in Brazil; and **film tourism:** a specific form of cultural tourism which reflects the growing interest and demand for locations which become popular due to their appearance in films and television series. Film

tourism is particularly big in New Zealand following the success of *The Hobbit*.

ACTIVITY 2

To help you get a clearer idea about tourism in your own country, undertake some research and complete Table 1.4.

Purpose of tourism in your chosen country for last year				
	Your country residents		Overseas visitors	
	No. of trips	Spending	No. of visits	Spending
Leisure				
Business				
VFR				
Other				
Total				

Table 1.4

You could then compare and contrast these figures with those given in Table 1.1 and attempt to explain any differences.

Characteristics of destinations and attractions which appeal to visitors

A broad range of features exist within each destination which attract visitors or play an important part in their decision to visit. The following section explores a number of these reasons.

Accessibility

The provision of safe, convenient and economical transport and other tourism-related infrastructure is a key factor for the success of tourism in any destination. Visitors must have easy and affordable access to a destination in order to want to travel there. Having a good international airport, served by a number of international airlines from around the world makes a destination more accessible. Good local infrastructure, with good public transport networks and a variety of well-connected public amenities also attracts more visitors.

Built and natural attractions

When choosing where to visit, tourists will consider what attractions there are on offer. An ideal destination will have a broad mix of built and natural attractions as this creates the broadest appeal to visitors. Built attractions include churches, museums, castles, theme parks, zoos, art galleries, theatres and cinemas. Natural attractions include National Parks, lakes, beaches, forests etc.

ACTIVITY 3

Choose **two** different destinations. Research and compare the range of built and natural attractions offered in each destination. Which destination would you recommend to a leisure visitor? Give reasons for your recommendation.

Climate

The climate affects people's motivation to travel. Favourable climatic conditions at destinations are key attractions for tourists, especially in beach destinations. Most tourists seem to like to travel to destinations where it is mainly warm and dry. Mountain tourism or winter sports are also highly dependent on specific climate and weather conditions, for example fresh snow for skiing.

Culture

Culture refers to a way of life of a group of people, the behaviours, beliefs, values and symbols that they accept, that are passed along by communication and imitation from one generation to the next. Culture is of huge importance as a characteristic of a destination that draws visitors in. There are many different cultural aspects that appeal to visitors who want to experience something different from what can be experienced in their place of residence.

Traditions

These are the long-established customs that people from different cultures continue to practise. For example, ancient Māori cooking techniques practised by the indigenous people in New Zealand use natural cooking pools within the geothermal hot springs. Visitors are invited to witness the local people preparing food in this way.

Language

Language reflects the nature and values of society. Some countries have two or three languages. Tourists may often only choose to travel to destinations in which there is no communication barrier because of the languages commonly spoken in that country. English is without a doubt the actual universal language in tourism terms. It is the world's second largest native language and is the official language in 70 countries. This will help reassure many tourists as they can use English to communicate with local people, even if it is not the native tongue for either the visitor or the local person.

Gastronomy

Some tourists will choose a destination where the local food and beverages are the main motivating factors for travel. Travelling to taste the local speciality food and beverages tends to be a domestic tourism activity, with visitors travelling to places to eat and drink specific, local produce. For example in Barcelona, cultural tourists can book onto the Gastronomic Treasure Hunt. Participants will be asked to perform different, fun tests to develop their senses of taste and smell and their abilities to cook in a light-hearted way while they discover the secrets and curiosities of Catalan and Spanish gastronomy.

Dress

For people from certain cultures, the dress code within a destination is an important factor. For example, public bathing in bikinis is not acceptable within all cultures, therefore visitors from certain cultural backgrounds might choose not to visit beach resorts where this is commonly practised.

Handicrafts

Crafts reflect the artistic sense, feelings and cultural characteristics of a destination. People often choose destinations which offer traditional handicrafts, although this is unlikely to be a main travel motivation; combined with other cultural 'pulls' it might be one of a number of reasons why tourists visit a particular destination. In Turkey, for example, weaving materials from wool, mohair, cotton and silk are popular forms of handicrafts, which tourists often observe during their visit and purchase as souvenirs.

Figure 1.3 An exhibit at The Setouchi Art Festival in Japan

Events

These are an important reason why visitors choose certain destinations at particular times of the year. There are many different types of events held around the world each year, which draw in large numbers of visitors. They include: **art events** such as The Setouchi Art Festival in Japan, which brings artists, architects and designers together to display artwork in a range of different media (see Figure 1.3); **music events** including international music festivals such as the Montreux Jazz Festival, which celebrated its 50th year in 2016. More than just a jazz festival, Montreux has seen top names from pop, rock and hip hop music perform each year to more than 200 000 visitors. A **festival** is the name given to a period of celebration typically for religious reasons but nowadays also used to refer to an organised series of concerts, plays, or films held annually in the same place. Festivals appealing to tourists range from the Monkey Buffet Festival held in Thailand each year to pay respect to the macaque monkey population in Lopburi, to La Tomatina. The industrial town of Buñol in Valencia, Spain welcomes 20 000 visitors to throw tomatoes at one another every August. **Sporting events** attract visitors to specific destinations. Some are fixed year after year such as the Wimbledon Tennis Championships. Other major sporting events change location, such as the Olympic Games or the UEFA Champions League football matches. Fans of such sports will plan their visit to see their teams perform around the world.

History

Historical attractions play an important part in tourists' decisions to visit a destination. Cities often offer a choice of many different historical attractions, for example in Rome visitors can visit the Colosseum, the Roman Forum and the Pantheon. Or there are the Elephanta Caves located in western India, which is a UNESCO World Heritage site (see Figure 1.4).

Figure 1.4 The Elephanta Caves in western India

Architecture

Some visitors are drawn to destinations with interesting and unique architecture, such as Dubai, with the Burj Khalifa, the world's tallest building and the sail-shaped Burj Al Arab hotel, the world's first seven star hotel.

Leisure activities

For many tourists, it is the range of leisure activities available within a destination that influence the decision to visit. For example, the 'Discover the best of Mauritius' website lists kite surfing, swimming with dolphins, canyoning, underwater walking, mountain biking and golf as just some of the leisure pursuits that the island offers to its visitors. Or for some, the travel motivation is the availability of one particular leisure activity within a destination, for example, visiting the Bifengxia Panda Reserve in Ya'an, in the Sichuan Province of China (Figure 1.5).

Figure 1.5 Pandas playing at the Bifengxia Panda Reserve in Ya'an, in the Sichuan Province of China

Range and type of accommodation, including grading

A destination will appeal to a wide customer base if there is a large variety of different types of accommodation on offer, ranging from camp sites and simple hostel accommodation to attract budget travellers through to luxurious five star hotel accommodation.

It is important to understand that the types of accommodation used by tourists can be either serviced or non-serviced. In serviced accommodation the price charged to customers reflects the fact that members of staff are available on site to provide guests with services such as cleaning, meals and room service. Non-serviced means that the customer is purchasing sleeping accommodation that is being offered to guests furnished on a rental basis. Frequently used types of non-serviced accommodation include self-catering apartments, holiday cottages and caravans.

Many countries have devised official grading schemes and in Europe there has been an attempt to harmonise hotel grading criteria in an attempt to clarify standards for international travellers.

Religion

Some tourists will wish to travel to destinations in which the same religion as their own is widely practised. This might include visiting destinations for the purpose of pilgrimage. Others will deliberately choose to visit destinations in which a different religion is practised as part of a cultural experience.

Challenges of the travel and tourism industry
Seasonality

Depending on where you are in the world, the demand for various tourism products and services will vary throughout the year, often reflecting the local seasonal climatic conditions. Figure 1.6 shows an important French attraction.

Figure 1.6 Eiffel Tower, Paris in autumn

Tourism in countries within the European Union (EU) shows the effect of seasonality very clearly in terms of:

*   the pattern of tourism demand
*   participation in tourism by EU residents
*   the number of trips they made
*   the number of nights spent on those trips.

Seasonal variation applied to all aspects of trips made, regardless of whether they were spent in tourist accommodation (such as hotels or camp sites) or in less formal and often unpaid types of accommodation (such as owned dwellings or accommodation provided for free by friends or relatives). Research and analysis published in 2014 by the EU (Figure 1.7) clearly illustrates seasonal variation.

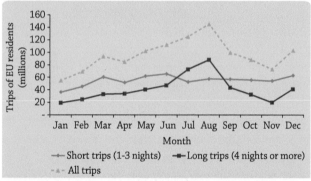

(^{1}) Trips which started in 2013 and ended in 2014, are included in the corresponding of departure of 2014 (f.i. a trip that started in November 2013 and ended in January 2014 is included in November 2014).
(^{2}) EU-28 aggregate estimated for this publication, not including Sweden, including 2013 dara for the United Kingdom.

Figure 1.7 Distribution of nights spent in the four quarters of 2014

Key findings of this European research were:

*   Nearly one in four trips by EU residents were made in July or August.
*   In August, 12.6% of all trips were taken and 10.9% in July.
*   The number of trips in the peak month (August) was 2.6 times higher than the number of trips in the lowest month (January).
*   When taking into account the duration of the trips, the seasonal pattern was even more pronounced, with EU residents having spent one in three nights away in these two months, August (17.2%) and July (16.1%).
*   The number of nights spent in the peak month (August) was four times higher than the number of nights spent in the lowest month (January).
*   In August 2013, EU residents made more than 88 million long trips of at least four overnight stays. This represents 18% of all long trips made through the entire year.

- The distribution of short trips over the year was more even. June was the most popular month for trips between one and three overnight stays, closely followed by December, May and March Figures 1.8 – 1.11, below show typical examples of popular destinations.
- Business trips are less season dependent, with business trips representing nearly 12% of all trips made by EU residents. This ranged from over 17% in November to 5% in the main holiday month of August.
- Nearly 40% of all tourism nights spent outside the summer peak months (July and August) were spent by Europeans aged 55 or more (the grey market).

Figure 1.10 Beautiful Venetian scenery

Figure 1.8 Traditional Dutch windmills with vibrant tulips

Figure 1.9 London Bridge at night

Figure 1.11 Skiers in mountains on a ski lift, Switzerland

Seasonality causes problems for suppliers of travel and tourism products and services because demand levels fluctuate throughout the year. An empty hotel room does not generate revenue if it remains unoccupied and empty seats on a flight cannot be sold once the aircraft takes off. Many travel and tourism products cannot be stored for future use. Thus, suppliers seek to minimise the impacts caused by seasonal nature of demand by reducing prices in the shoulder months when demand is traditionally lower. If you look at any holiday brochure you will see that prices vary throughout the year and many consumers take advantage of 'low season' offers.

KEY TERMS

Shoulder months: the travel season between peak and off-peak seasons, especially spring and autumn, when fares tend to be relatively low.

Intangibility

Travel and tourism is a service industry. The service product is intangible when it cannot be easily evaluated or demonstrated in advance of its purchase. For example, a travel agent cannot provide for the testing or sampling of a tourism product such as a package holiday. On the other hand, a car or a computer game can be tested prior to purchase, and clothing can be tried on. Much of the selling of travel, tourism and hospitality is related to the promise of safe and timely delivery of any given product or service at an agreed location. The problem may be overcome by distributing a wide range of sales literature, by producing videos and giving virtual tours or by offering the product at discounted rates in an attempt to increase tangibility.

Perishability

Perishability simply means that travel and tourism service products, unlike other products such as manufactured goods, cannot be stored for sale on a future occasion. For example, a hotel bed or an airline seat unsold, or a convention centre left empty, represents lost revenue that can never be recouped. This illustrates the high-risk nature of the tourism industry. Marketers in the tourism and hospitality sectors have to devise complex pricing and promotion policies in an attempt to sell 'off-season' periods. The reaction to perishability is for marketers to try to smooth out demand curves by careful use of

the marketing mix – for example, cheaper tickets for matinee shows. There is also a concentration on the use of computerised reservation systems in order to forecast the need for tactical action if demand is believed to be below expected levels. Yield management strategies are employed based on understanding, anticipating and influencing consumer behaviour in order to maximise revenue or profits from a perishable product.

1.2 Scale of the travel and tourism industry

Travel and tourism is a truly global economic activity, taking place in destinations across the world, from leading capital cities and smaller towns and villages in rural and coastal areas, to some of the remotest points on the planet. It is one of the world's largest industries, or economic sectors, contributing trillions of dollars annually to the global economy, creating jobs and wealth, generating exports, boosting taxes and stimulating capital investment.

KEY CONCEPTS

Global and growing

The new record of more than 1 billion tourists shows the scale of the industry. Predictions indicate that tourism will continue to grow at similar rates over the coming years, despite fears of terrorism, outbreaks of diseases and other such impacts.

International tourism hit new records in 2015 despite the challenging economic, social and political conditions that have existed now for a number of years. International tourist arrivals were up 4% to reach a record 1.2 billion travellers worldwide in 2015.

Figure 1.12 clearly indicates that the global travel and tourism industry is now directly responsible for 9% of the world's GDP.

Figure 1.12 clearly indicates that the scale of the travel and tourism industry varies between countries. The scale of New Zealand's tourism industry has already been considered when illustrating the differences between inbound and domestic tourism. We can now look at the scale of the industry in some other countries.

Figures 1.13 and 1.14 show some aspects of world travel and tourism at the start of 2012.

Figure 1.12 Why tourism matters

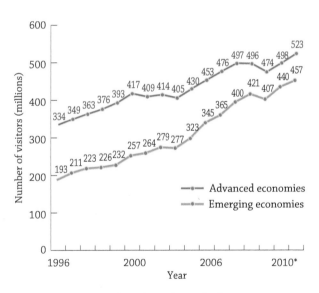

Figure 1.13 International tourist arrivals

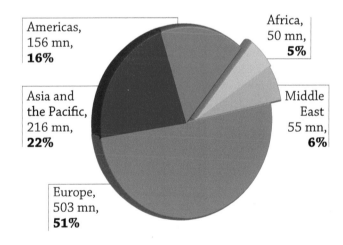

Figure 1.14 World inbound tourism 2011 (measurements shown in millions/mn)

Maldives tourism industry

Figure 1.15 shows clearly that the volume of international tourist arrivals has fluctuated over a 5-year period, with arrivals down significantly in 2009 following the global recession, and picking up again considerably in 2010 with a 20.75% total increase. Figures were affected in 2012 following a period of political unrest in the area.

However, 2013 saw a total of 1.125 million international tourists visit the Maldives, an all-time high, and this represented a 17.4% increase compared to the previous year.

	2009		2010		2011		2012		2013	
	Arrivals	Growth %	Arrivals	Growth %	Arrivals	Growth %	Arrivals	Growth %	Arrivals	Growth %
January	61531	−4.8	67478	9.7	79493	17.8	96146	20.9	88869	−7.6
February	58520	−13.9	77063	31.7	87392	13.4	83252	−4.7	104745	25.8
March	62127	−13.3	74975	20.7	80732	7.7	76469	−5.3	99498	30.1
April	57186	−8.8	60742	6.2	79947	31.6	79288	−0.8	90636	14.3
May	13154	−11.5	58324	35.2	64456	10.5	63534	−1.4	79426	25.0
June	36205	−10.1	44050	21.7	55947	27.0	59379	6.1	76493	28.8
July	44332	−7.0	57232	29.1	72516	26.7	76966	6.1	87972	14.3
August	52388	1.1	66315	26.6	76828	15.9	79768	3.8	98338	23.3
September	50396	−0.6	62524	24.1	71861	14.9	76806	6.9	92298	20.2
October	62432	10.8	74707	19.7	91059	21.9	92391	1.5	107331	16.2
November	61986	6.9	74252	19.8	85501	15.1	82311	−3.7	94584	14.9
December	65595	4.8	74255	13.2	85601	15.3	91717	7.1	105012	14.5
Total	655852	−4.0	791917	20.7	931333	17.6	958027	2.9	1125202	17.4

Source: Ministry of Tourism
Data provided by: Department of Immigration & Emigration

Figure 1.15 Tourist arrivals in the Maldives 2009–2013

Tourism has for a long time been the major source of foreign exchange earnings for the Maldives. Tourism is an important contributor to employment generation and the economic growth of the country. The contribution of tourism to the country's GDP has fluctuated between 25.8% and 28.5% in the five year period from 2009 to 2013, as shown in Figure 1.16.

Two additional indicators that reflect the health of the industry are occupancy rate of resorts and the average length of stay. The average duration of stay of tourists to the Maldives has declined from 8.6 nights in 2009 to 6.3 nights in 2013. Resort occupancy has been fairly consistent, ranging between 69.5% in 2010 to 74.0% in 2013.

Rank 2013	Country	2013		2012		Rank 2012
		Arrivals	Market share (%)	Arrivals	Market share (%)	
1	China	331719	29.5	229551	24.0	1
2	Germany	93598	8.3	98351	10.3	2
3	United Kingdom	85869	7.6	91776	9.6	3
4	Russia	76479	6.8	66378	6.9	4
5	Italy	57854	5.1	62782	6.6	5
6	France	54328	4.8	56775	5.9	6
7	Japan	39463	3.5	36438	3.8	7
8	India	38014	3.4	31721	3.3	9
9	Switzerland	34102	3.0	35457	3.7	8
10	Korea	30306	2.7	23933	2.5	10
Total		841732	74.8	733162	76.5	
Total arrivals to the Maldives		1125202		958027		

Source: Ministry of Tourism

Figure 1.16 Maldives top ten tourist markets 2013

Key patterns in local, national and global tourism (including data interpretation and manipulation)

The travel and tourism industry is measured through the collection of statistics and data. Many organisations are involved in the collection, collation and interpretation of huge sets of data relating to the size, scale and significance of the travel and tourism industry worldwide. Much of this data can be grouped under the following headings:

Number of tourist arrivals in key destinations

'International tourist arrivals up 4% in the first four months of 2015.

International tourism demand continued to be robust between January and April 2015 with tourist arrivals increasing 4% worldwide according to the latest UNWTO World Tourism Barometer. Almost all regions enjoyed strong growth. Prospects for the May–August period remained upbeat, with close to 500 million tourists expected to travel abroad during these four months.

Destinations worldwide received some 332 million international tourists (overnight visitors) between January and April 2015, 14 million more than the same period the previous year, corresponding to an increase of 4%. This result followed an increase of 4.3% in 2014 and consolidated the upward trend of international tourism in the previous few years (+4.5% international tourist arrivals a year on average since 2010).

By region, the Americas (+6%) led growth, followed by Europe, Asia and the Pacific and the Middle East, all recording 4%–5% more arrivals. By sub-region, Oceania and South America boasted the strongest increase (both +8%), followed by the Caribbean and Central and Eastern Europe (both +7%), the latter rebounding from the previous year's decline. In Africa, demand weakened in 2014 after years of solid growth, affected mainly by the Ebola outbreak among other challenges. Limited data currently available for January–April 2015 points to a 6% decline, as African destinations struggle to recover from misperceptions affecting the continent (source: http://media.unwto.org/press-release/ 2015-07-08/international-tourist-arrivals-4-first-four-months-2015).'

The earlier 'Maldives tourism industry' press release indicates the type of data analysis available in measuring the scale of international tourism. The World Tourism Organisation (UNWTO) and the World Travel and Tourism Council (WTTC) are two key sources of tourist arrival data.

Key tourism generating areas and receiving areas (see 1.1 for the definitions of MEDCs and LEDCs)

Traditionally MEDCs such as the United States, Canada, Western European countries and Australia produce the most tourists, although things are starting to change with the change in distribution of wealth. China and India are also likely to be major source markets for tourism in the coming years. Similarly MEDCs have traditionally played the part of tourism receivers, because of their advanced infrastructure and tendency towards political stability. Nowadays, tourists are prepared to travel further afield, take greater risks and see life in less well developed countries. This has given rise to emerging destinations in former LEDCs, such as Botswana which officially became a developing nation in 1994 and the Maldives which officially became developing in 2011. Tourists also visit LEDCs, often seeking to experience areas that are relatively untouched by tourism development.

 KEY CONCEPTS

Change and development

The statistics show the trend for emerging destinations and how tourism helps develop LEDCs. This is a fundamental benefit of tourism.

Future Predictions

The UNWTO's Tourism 2020 Vision projects that international arrivals are expected to reach nearly 1.6 billion by 2020. Of these worldwide arrivals in 2020, 1.2 billion will be intraregional and 0.4 billion will be long-haul travellers. East Asia and the Pacific, South Asia, the Middle East and Africa are forecast to grow at over 5% per year, compared to the world average of 4.1%. More mature regions – for example, Europe and the Americas – are anticipated to show lower than average growth rates. Europe will maintain the highest share of world arrivals, although this share will decline from 60% in 1995 to 46% in 2020. The total tourist arrivals by region shows that by 2020 the top three receiving regions will be Europe (717 million tourists), East Asia (397 million) and the Americas (282 million), followed by Africa, the Middle East and South Asia.

Visitor spending in travel and tourism

International tourism receipts earned by destinations worldwide have grown from a total of US$2 billion in 1950 to US$104 billion in 1980, US$415 billion in 1995 and US$1.25 trillion in 2014. Table 1.5 shows which countries spent the most on international tourism in 2014. While less than 6% of China's population holds a passport, the number of Chinese citizens taking trips abroad is growing. According to the World Tourism Organisation, this is in part down to an increase in disposable income, and appreciating currency, and an easing of restrictions on foreign travel. Chinese tourists are the biggest spenders overseas – accounting for 13% of global tourism receipts (http://www.weforum.org).

According to research carried out by the international credit card company, Mastercard, in 2012, visitors spent on average US$1 884 in the US, US$1 253 in Germany and US$1 249 in the UK. Visitors to Macau, the south-east Asian destination known for its casinos, spent a staggering US$3 213 each.

The Hawaii Tourism Authority released the following set of figures showing the relationship between visitor numbers, average length of stay and visitor spending on the islands in 2014.

Total visitor arrivals	8 282 680
Average length of stay	9.12 days
Average per person per day spending	US$195.3
Average per person per trip spending	US$1 780.50

Table 1.5 Data released by the Hawaii Tourism Authority in 2014

The data was affected by nearly 125 000 arrivals by cruise ship; these visitors stayed in Hawaii for less time (an average of 5.3 days) and spent much less on average than other visitors to the islands (US$63 per day or US$334 per trip).

http://www.hawaiitourismauthority.org

Number of people employed directly and indirectly in the industry

Front offices in hotels, restaurants, travel agencies, tourism information offices, aircrafts, cruise lines, resorts or shopping outlets provide **direct employment** because their employees are in contact with tourists and cater for tourist demand. Tourism also supports **indirect employment** in activities like restaurant suppliers, construction companies that build and maintain tourist facilities, as well as necessary infrastructure, aircraft

manufacturers, various handicrafts producers, marketing agencies and accounting services.

According to the World Travel and Tourism Council, in terms of employment, the importance of travel and tourism is pronounced. With 105 million people directly employed in 2014, travel and tourism directly employs:

- seven times more than automotive manufacturing
- five times more than the global chemicals industry
- four times more than the global banking industry
- four times more than the global mining industry
- double that of the global financial services industry.

With a total impact of 9.4% of world employment, travel and tourism is one of the leading job creators in the world. Travel and tourism sustained 277 million jobs in 2014. As stated earlier in the chapter, this equates to 1 in every 11 jobs worldwide being linked to travel and tourism.

KEY CONCEPTS

Global and growing

These employment figures show the importance of the industry on a global scale. Without this growth, many people would lose their livelihood and standards of living would fall. Governments will continue to encourage this global growth of tourism because of the benefits it brings to local economies.

Trends in travel and tourism, including occupancy rates, duration of stay, method of transport

Because of the dynamic nature of the industry, travel and tourism providers constantly use market research to try and understand the changing needs of their customers. Statistical data collated by national and international tourism agencies and authorities plays an important part in being able to understand the trends in travel and tourism. Data relating to load factors for transport providers, occupancy rates for accommodation providers and usage rates for tourist attractions gives a clear indication of how popular the products and services of these organisations are. Destinations will look at how long people choose to stay on average, and the methods that tourists use to travel to the destination, as all of this information helps travel and tourism providers make adjustments to their products and services to better meet the needs of their customers. It also helps with tourism forecasting, to ensure the industry is operating as efficiently and as profitably as possible.

ACTIVITY 4

Investigate the scale of the travel and tourism industry in your country. As a starting point in your research, find your country's report as listed by the World Travel and Tourism Council at http://www.wttc.org/research/.

1.3 Factors affecting tourism

Development of the modern travel and tourism industry

In the MEDCs, tourism has evolved from an elite, minority activity some 200 years ago into a mass participation activity, accessible to and enjoyed by the majority of the population. This is a revolution that needs to be explained because it is a change which is gradually impacting upon a range of LECDs and is a fairly reliable barometer of economic growth and maturity within a country.

Today, between 70% and 85% of the population of most western European and other developed countries participate in tourism, domestic or international – this is known as the tourism participation rate. By contrast, comparable figures for the world's poorest nations are in low single digits (2%–5%). Tourism participation in South Korea, Taiwan, Malaysia and Singapore have increased very significantly during the past 20 years, reflecting the major changes that have occurred within the economies of those countries. The participation rates in countries such as China and India are growing rapidly and, in real terms, the numbers involved with just a 5% increase in tourism in either country, means in excess of 50 million additional tourists seeking destinations to visit, accommodation to stay in and things to do.

A range of factors can affect the travel and tourism industry, and we can now look at some of the most important ones.

Economic factors: changes to the national economy and GDP

Economic factors relate to changes such as costs and prices of goods, interest rates, wage rates, exchange rates and the rate of inflation. These all affect the ability of tourism businesses to generate profits and tourists being able to afford to travel. All countries experience change in their economies during the development process and one way to examine the relationship between economic growth and a population's standard of living over time

is through the Rostow Model of Development. Rostow proposed that economic growth occurs in five basic stages, of varying length, as shown in Figure 1.17.

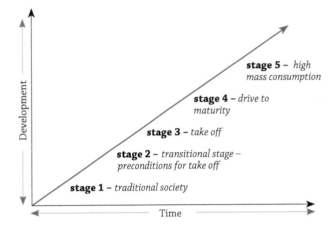

Figure 1.17 Rostow Model of Development

KEY TERMS

Gross domestic product (GDP): a monetary measure of the value of all final goods and services produced in a period (quarterly or annually). GDP estimates are commonly used to determine the economic performance of a whole country or region, and to make international comparisons. Gross National Product (GNP) is similar to GDP but GNP includes the value of all goods and services produced by nationals whether in the country or not.

Rostow described these stages as having particular characteristics:

- Traditional society: this is defined as subsistence economy based mainly on farming with very limited technology or capital to process raw materials or develop services and industries and so both GDP and per capita income levels are low. This is the situation in many of the world's poorest nations.
- Preconditions for take-off: are said to take place when the levels of technology within a country develop and the development of a transport system encourages trade. There is an increase in GDP and per capita incomes start to rise.
- Take-off: manufacturing industries grow rapidly, airports, roads and railways are built, and growth poles emerge as investment increases. GDP rises quickly as do per capita incomes for an increasingly large section of the population. These conditions characterise many LEDC nations at present as they actively pursue development policies.

17

- Drive to maturity: growth should be self-sustaining, having spread to all parts of the country, and leading to an increase in the number and types of industry. During this stage more complex transport systems and manufacturing expand as transport develops, rapid urbanisation occurs, and traditional industries may decline. This has been the experience of many of the 'Tiger' and 'BRIC' economies with sustained GDP growth and rising per capita income levels.

- Age of mass consumption: rapid expansion of tertiary industries occurs alongside a decline in manufacturing. This is the situation in most MEDC nations where GDP levels are high but growth is slow. Per capita incomes are high and large sections of the population have significant levels of disposable income to consume a variety of goods and services.

Changes in the national economy in terms of GDP clearly have a direct influence on income levels among the population. Thus, as national economies develop over time, there will be a rise in per capita incomes and this will usually be accompanied by an increase in disposable income levels. This, in turn, increases a person's propensity to travel.

KEY CONCEPTS

Change and development

The Rostow Model epitomises the concept of change and development within destinations. It maps out how a destination evolves over time, linked to economic development.

Levels of disposable income

To examine the relationship between economic development and disposable income levels, we can now look at how change has taken place in a selection of countries at different stages of the Rostow Model. Table 1.6 shows how disposable income per household has tended to change in the period 1995–2010 in various parts of the world.

These changes are very significant for the travel and tourism industry. The main variable that definitely influences tourist movements positively is growth in GNP. GNP growth increases disposable income and hence the willingness and ability to consume various goods and services, including an increase in tourist demand, whether

such a demand refers to number of arrivals and number of nights spent or to amounts of tourist foreign exchange.

Country	1995	2010	Percentage growth
Brazil	11 985.5	16 373.3	37.3%
China	1 456.6	4 809.8	230.2%
India	1 597.9	3 140.2	96.5%
Malaysia	11 297.2	17 509.9	55.0%
New Zealand	26 622.4	30 361.1	14.0%
Singapore	48 637.7	64 888.2	33.4%
South Africa	10 391.0	12 252.9	17.9%
United Kingdom	31 957.5	39 987.3	25.1%
USA	53 914.5	61 028.4	13.2%
Vietnam	1 043.0	2 392.0	129.3%

Table 1.6 Disposable income US$ per household 1995–2010

The current situation is illustrated in Figure 1.18.

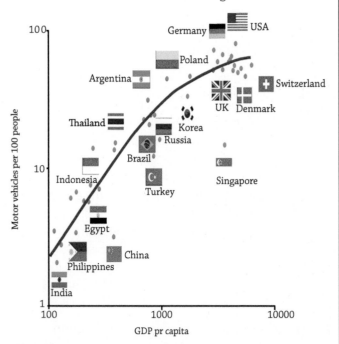

Figure 1.18 GDP per capita against motor vehicles per 100 people

Change in distribution of wealth

Global inequality is growing, with half the world's wealth now in the hands of just 1% of the population, according to a new report. The middle classes have been squeezed at the expense of the very rich, according to recent research, which also finds that for the first time, there are more individuals in the middle classes in China (109 million people) than the 92 million people in the United States. Since the 1970s, the gap in wealth between the highest and lowest brackets of earners has grown, with 2% of the population previously owning a majority of global wealth and the bottom half of the population owning less than 1% of global wealth in the year 2000. At the end of the 20th century, wealth was concentrated among the G8 nations (France, Italy, Germany, Japan, the United Kingdom, the United States, Canada and Russia) and Western industrialised nations, along with several Asian and OPEC (Organization of Petroleum Exporting Countries) nations.

Economists suggest that the BRIC countries (Brazil, Russia, India and China) hold the key to economic growth for the future. It is believed that China and India will, by 2050, become the world's dominant suppliers of manufactured goods and services respectively, while Brazil and Russia will become similarly dominant as suppliers of raw materials. Due to lower labour and production costs, many companies also consider the BRIC as a source of foreign expansion opportunity, and promising economies in which to invest.

Changes in employment opportunities

Global employment rates affect tourism, as those who are unemployed do not necessarily have sufficient income with which to travel. The unemployment rate varies significantly as Table 1.7 shows:

Country	Percentage of working age population not in employment as of December 2014
Bahamas	15.4
Botswana	27.9
Brazil	6.8
China	4.7
Greece	26.3
India	3.6
Maldives	11.6
Qatar	0.3
Russia	5.1
South Africa	25.1
Spain	24.7
United States	6.2

Table 1.7: Unemployment rates in different countries in 2014

With the advance in technology, many traditional jobs in manufacturing and agriculture have become automated. This has resulted in more people being employed in the tertiary or service industries, of which tourism offers significant employment opportunities.

Changes in currency exchange rates

Most major economies operate a floating exchange rate system, which means the currency's value is allowed to fluctuate in accordance with the foreign exchange market. Currency rates are influenced by a broad range of other economic factors including differences in interest rates, economic performance, supply and demand of currencies and inflation. The relative strength of the dollar against other major currencies will dictate whether tourists are likely to gain value for money when travelling overseas.

Travellers to foreign countries have to convert funds to that particular country's currency so they can spend money at hotels, restaurants and other attractions. When the dollar appreciates against major world currencies, U.S. tourists travelling to other countries will be able to enjoy more because the exchange rate will favour them when they exchange their dollars for the local currency. Airports might have currency exchange boards similar to the one shown below in Figure 1.19.

Figure 1.19 Currency exchange board

Infrastructure development and improvement

The development of tourism anywhere very much relies on the development of appropriate infrastructure, which service the needs of tourists and encourages investment in the sector. Infrastructure such as accommodation, restaurants, built attractions, tours and transport are primarily developed by the private sector. Private investors would be unwilling to invest in tourism facilities, however, without good airport and road infrastructure and the availability of affordable basic services such as water, sewerage, electricity, health facilities and telecommunications, for which the public sector is responsible. Governments recognise that infrastructure is a major stimulus to achieve economic growth, and to attract more visitors. This is why many governments around the world invest significantly in infrastructure development and improvement.

> **KEY TERMS**
>
> **Private sector:** usually composed of organisations that are privately owned and not part of the government.
>
> **Public sector:** usually composed of organisations that are owned and operated by the government. These includes national, federal, provincial, state or municipal governments.

Social factors

Social factors, such as religion, family or wealth, affect lifestyle. Tastes and fashions constantly change. Social factors also include changes in demography such as increased life expectancy or changes in the birth rate.

Ageing population

According to United Nations (2012) projections, the number of people aged 60 years or above will grow from 810 million in 2012 to nearly 2 billion by 2050, which means that every fifth person will be in this age group. Such a dramatic change in the age structure is already having major impacts on the world's economy and over the time it will be more and more evident. A demographic shift towards the older generation will change the needs of the average consumer and will thus affect global markets, in turn causing an overall change in the demand for products and services. Increased life expectancy and better pension provision has led to an increased number of wealthier older people with a disposable income. As a result, seniors ('the grey market') have become a broad and important group for the travel and tourism industry.

These impacts will certainly influence the tourism industry since the 'grey market' have better health, more available income, no family obligations and more free time, which

CASE STUDY 2

Air traffic in India is projected to triple to 570 million passengers by 2025 from the current 190 million. Investments of $40–50 billion are required to expand/upgrade airport infrastructure across the country to meet the demands for increased capacity. The government of India, recognising that it had neither the capital nor the expertise to embark upon an airport modernisation programme on this scale, initially proposed to develop and improve efficacy at four airports at Chennai, Kolkata, Jaipur and Ahmedabad through a public-private partnership. There are now plans to privatise airport operations at two of these airports, which will transfer the burden of investment away from the public sector. New terminals have been commissioned at Bengaluru and Mumbai, which together will add a capacity of more than 19 million passengers each year. Almost 70% of the population of India currently does not have air connectivity. Large numbers of people residing in smaller towns can afford to fly by air. The government is therefore taking initiatives to improve regional connectivity by planning more no-frills airports. The design and location for five such no-frills airports has been finalised, and construction began by the end of 2014. As a part of the strategy to encourage airlines to fly to smaller towns, the government plans to offer financial incentives to Indian carriers, including waiving of landing charges for aircrafts with a maximum certified capacity of less than 80 seats operating from non-metro airports. Officials said the government is also considering upgrading some airports in smaller cities into international airports. Airports at Bhopal, Indore and Raipur will soon be declared as International Airports. This will lead to more international flights arriving in smaller towns and will cut costs for fliers. This will spread inbound tourist footfall to a larger geographic area in India and open new destinations and products.

Figure 1.20 A traditional Mediterranean coastal resort.

allows them to travel more often and for longer periods of time. All of these characteristics will turn this growing segment into a very profitable target market, which gives tourism providers the opportunity to develop specific products and services for them. Traditional Mediterranean coastal resorts (see Figure 1.20) such as Malta are currently investigating expanding their traditional beach holiday tourism by increasing the heritage element of their package to appeal to the older generation.

Leisure time

Today's use of leisure time and likely future trends are very different from the patterns established in the 1960s when economic developments in Europe and North America triggered the beginning of the modern era of tourism. The future development of tourism will depend on how the industry manages to compete with increasingly attractive options for spending leisure time. Until quite recently it was widely assumed, particularly in the richer countries, that working hours were steadily reducing, the amount of leisure time increasing and that these trends would continue. Many people looked forward to a golden age of leisure. However, changes in the world economy in recent years have made the situation much more complex. Currently, working conditions which specifically affect leisure time such as shorter working days, shorter working weeks, longer holidays with pay and age of retirement have taken on more significance. In some countries, increased life expectancy has led to an increase in pension age. For example, women's retirement age has traditionally been five years earlier than men in European countries at 60 rather than 65, but from 2016, this has been increased in line with the retirement age for men. By 2018 in the UK the pension age of both men and women will be 67, as it already is in other parts of the world. This will have a negative effect on leisure time. Generally, however, leisure time has increased in the past 50 years or so because of the following:

- Increasing the flexibility of working hours provided benefits to employees in terms of greater freedom to choose when to go on holiday. This is important for tourism as leisure time will be increasingly shaped by the terms of new, more flexible working hours.

- Paid leave in countries within the European Union was underpinned by the 1993 Working Time Directive which gave a right to four weeks' paid holiday from 1999 onwards.
- Although the leisure time of the retired has been modified by changes in retirement age and pensions, many individuals continue to retire younger and fitter than previous generations and have more leisure interests.
- The leisure of the younger generation is constrained by limited incomes rather than time but many young people take the opportunity to travel before embarking on their careers and the changing pattern of employment, with less emphasis on lifetime careers, encourages some to take further breaks between periods of work.

Overall, the consumer behaviour is changing in response to these economic and social developments. Despite the squeeze on leisure time, the market response is not weakened, but a changing pattern of tourism demands towards shorter, more frequent and more intensive breaks. Increasingly flexible working hours including, in many countries, the substantial rise in those working at weekends, is changing the rhythm of leisure time. The work and leisure time of individuals, through the week and through the year, has become increasingly variable.

However, young people and the retired will be the groups with most leisure time available for travel. Leisure time availability continues to be shaped by hours of work, public holidays, paid leave entitlements and retirement arrangements, all of which vary widely between countries. Each country tends to have its own national values and traditions in terms of the importance attached to leisure.

These changes have resulted in the segmentation of people in terms of their leisure behaviour.

Today, it is common to see reference being made to the following groups of travellers:

- Money rich, time poor: interested in a wide range of high style, high fashion, short breaks – city culture, total relaxation, the exotic. Their time is more valuable to them than their money. They expect excellent products that can be tailored to their tight schedules.
- Money and time rich: these include the affluent retired, free to travel throughout the year. Many will be sophisticated and demanding travellers, open to enjoying several widely different holidays each year, including luxury cruising and long haul travel but with

many home – and perhaps second home – based interests competing for their time.
- Money and time poor: interested in a wide range of affordable holidays, often in the domestic market. Work pressures will incline them to get away for short breaks when they can, often at short notice.
- Money poor and time rich: often retired, interested in extended but inexpensive trips, including winter sun breaks, preferably with plenty of associated activities and, particularly for the young, backpacking.

Rising middle classes in the East, declining in the West

This links to the section on changes in the distribution of wealth under economic factors. This century, the wealth of the middle class has grown strongly in all regions and in almost all countries. Throughout the world, the size, health and resources of the middle class are seen as key factors in determining the speed and sustainability of economic development. Wealth is still predominantly concentrated in Europe and the United States. However, the growth of wealth in emerging markets has been steady, including China, which now accounts for a fifth of the world population, while holding nearly 10% of the global wealth. The Chinese middle class has now reached 109 million adults, well ahead of the 92 million adults who are part of the American middle class. Globally, 14% of the adult population belonged to the middle class in 2015 – 664 million adults in total. Forecasts predict that the middle class will continue to expand in emerging economies overall, with the bulk of that growth to occur in Asia.

New family structures

According to the World Family Map report on key indicators of family structures, although two parent families are becoming less common in many parts of the world, they still constitute a majority of families around the globe. Children under the age of 18 are more likely to live in two parent families than in other family forms in Asia and the Middle East, compared with other regions of the world. Children are more likely to live with one or no parent in the Americas, Europe, Oceania, and Sub-Saharan Africa than in other regions.

Marriage rates are declining in many regions. Adults are most likely to be married in Africa, Asia, and the Middle East, and are least likely to be married in South America, with Europe, North America and Oceania falling in between. Cohabitation (living together without marriage) is more common among couples in Europe, North America, Oceania and especially in South America.

Childbearing rates are declining worldwide. The highest fertility rates are in Sub-Saharan Africa. A woman gives birth to an average of 5.5 children in Nigeria, down from close to seven in the 1980s, but still high by world standards. Moderate rates of fertility (2.3–3.1) are found in the Middle East, and levels of fertility that are sufficient to replace a country's population in the next generation (about 2.1) are found in the Americas and Oceania. Below replacement-level fertility is found in East Asia and Europe.

For tourism, these changes to family structures means there are more single travellers, that is, those who travel without family members and more travellers without children. In the same way the ageing population creates a new market segment for tourism, so too does the new family structure, in catering to the needs of the single traveller and for the couples market.

Increased awareness of health

Travel is a strong force in the emergence of disease since the migration of humans has been the pathway for spreading infectious diseases throughout recorded history and will continue to shape the emergence, frequency and spread of infections in geographic areas and populations. Travellers may encounter serious health risks that may arise in areas where accommodation is of poor quality, and where hygiene and sanitation are inadequate. The recent change towards international tourists visiting less developed region will cause increased exposure for tourists to diseases endemic in those regions. Travellers can easily carry person-to-person transmitted infections to any part of the world as has been seen recently with the Ebola virus and was also the case with SARS and H1N1 in recent years.

Increased media coverage of such epidemics has highlighted the risks associated with travelling. People are generally more conscious of health these days, probably because of increased access to information via the internet. Health conscious travellers will avoid areas with specific risks of disease. Similarly the health conscious will also avoid travelling to areas with contaminated beaches or areas with poor air quality. Warning signs such as the one shown below in Figure 1.21 may be seen on some beaches.

Figure 1.21 Warning signs on a Spanish beach

CASE STUDY 3

Pollution

Haze affecting Thai tourism industry – October 2015
After engulfing Singapore, and parts of Malaysia and Indonesia, thick haze is also causing severe pollution in southern Thailand, and impacting the nation's crucial tourism sector. Caused by forest fires in Indonesia, the thick smog, which has already shrouded parts of Malaysia and Singapore for two months, has also reached hazardous levels in the five southern Thai provinces of Songkhla, Satun, Pattani, Surat Thani and Yala, making the areas dark and foggy. In fact, the pollution index recently hit a record-high reading of 365 in Thailand. (A reading of 101–200 is unhealthy; 201–300 is very unhealthy and above 300 is hazardous.) The next provinces up the peninsula, Narathiwat, Phuket and Phangnga, have dust levels within acceptable margins, but are coming close to the limit. As a result, the tourism industry is starting to feel the impact of the prolonged haze as Phuket and Surat Thani boast pristine tropical beaches which are popular among tourists. December is a crucial peak season for the Thai tourism industry, and if the haze continues during November, it could affect tourism bookings as tourists try to avoid the haze-affected tourism destinations in Southeast Asia. In fact, some tour operators have already complained about several flights packed with tourists being delayed or diverted due to unsafe conditions, as well as about holiday plans being cancelled. Tourism is a crucial part of the Thai economy, contributing around 10% of GDP, taking into account output and employment multiplier effects throughout the economy. And with the Thai economy already weak due to the impact of political turmoil during 2014, the haze conditions could further damage the tourism sector.

Political factors

Global politics are an important factor in **international** travel. As regions undergo change, uncertainty or in some cases violence and war, travel and tourism can slow or cease altogether.

Terrorism, war, civil unrest, crime and other factors affecting social harmony

Political change can either increase or decrease a country's attractiveness for tourism, depending on what the change is. If a country is perceived as unsafe before the change and the change results in a feeling of increased stability, then the country can slowly recover to a natural state of tourism. But if the country is perceived as unstable as a result of the political change, such as is the case now with Egypt, tourism will plummet.

There are many such instances of political unrest in the world today. We have never really recovered from the shock of 9/11. And there have been so many dreadful instances of acts of terrorism that have impacted on tourism around the world: Luxor in Egypt where 62 people, mostly tourists, were killed at the Egyptian archaeological site in 1997; the Indonesian island of Bali, where 202 people were killed and 209 injured in a 2002 bombing attack on nightclubs; Sharm el-Sheikh in Egypt, where 88 people were killed in an attack on the Egyptian resort in 2005. Since late 2011, Kenya has seen an upsurge in violent terrorist attacks and lost a quarter of its visitors in the first five months of 2015. The number of foreign tourists visiting Tunisia also dropped by about a million by the end of 2015 after two headline-hitting terrorist attacks. A gunman killed 38 people at a hotel in Sousse on the Mediterranean coast in June, three months after 21 tourists were killed by gunmen attacking the Bardo National Museum in the capital Tunis. In November 2015, there were seven coordinated terror attacks in Paris carried out by political activists, killing 130 people.

Civil and/or political unrest can be in the form of violent demonstrations, uprisings and riots. Such incidents have caused major declines in tourism demand in various parts of the world. Whether it is a coup d'état in Fiji, violent demonstrations against the Group of Seven nations (G7) in several different venues, the uprising of the Palestinians in the West Bank and Gaza or riots in Egypt, the effects have been the same. Such incidents have paralysed or severely impacted the local tourism industry due to trip cancellations and a shift of bookings to safer alternative destinations.

Crime rates typically increase with the growth of mass tourism. The presence of large numbers of tourists with a lot of money to spend, often carrying valuables such as cameras and jewellery, increases the attraction for criminals and brings along activities like robbery and drug dealing. The number of foreign tourists arriving in India dropped by 25% in 2013, with the number of women tourists falling by more than 35%, following negative media coverage about attacks on women in the country.

Changes to security measures, visa regulations and entry controls

Safety and security have always been important conditions for travel and tourism. It is a sad fact that safety and security issues have gained a much bigger importance in the last two decades in tourism. Recent events have highlighted the vulnerability of tourism both on a global and a local scale. Perceived or real threats to visitor safety have immediate impacts on a destination's reputation and can dramatically affect the number of visitors it receives. As a result of recent security breaches, Egypt is introducing a series of new security measures at its holiday resorts including installing additional closed circuit television (CCTV) camera systems in the Red Sea resorts of Sharm el-Sheikh and Hurghada. The government is also buying new scanning and detection equipment and increasing the number of security personnel and sniffer dogs for resorts. An additional 250 million Egyptian pounds (US$32 million) will be allocated for security.

Airport security has changed significantly over the past 20 years, with many new processes being introduced to protect passengers and airline crew. One way is to screen all airport workers every time they enter secure areas. This has happened in the UK since the early 1990s, with the European Union deciding to do the same in 2004. All European airport staff have to go through checks every time, however often they leave and re-enter secure areas, in the same way as passengers. There isn't the same system in place in the US and many other countries, which leaves air travel vulnerable. One thing that has undoubtedly improved over the last few years is the technology available to airport security. Electronic scanners are now able to detect explosive materials. Once staff are alerted, they use scanners to look for other suspicious items carried by the person or their companions.

Other measures have come in in response to particular incidents. In December 2001 a passenger tried to blow up an American Airlines flight from Paris to Miami using explosives in his shoe. This led to checks on people's footwear. In 2006 a planned attack on seven transatlantic planes using liquid explosives was overcome. In the aftermath, strict limits were placed on the amounts of liquids passengers could take on board. In recent years, full body scanners have been used at most airports. Security measures in current use are:

- Check-in: Strict regulations exist about what can be carried. No sharp objects or liquids in containers larger than 100 ml. Maximum size for hand luggage is typically 56 cm × 45 cm × 25 cm.
- Hand luggage: Scanned for illegal items with an X-ray machine. Sniffer dogs and chemical hand swabs may be used to detect explosives. Passengers may be asked to prove electronic and electrical devices in their hand luggage are sufficiently charged to be switched on.
- Body scanner: Passengers pass through a metal detector and or body scanners, which produce an outline image showing items concealed beneath clothing or on the body.
- Passport control: Biometric passports used by some countries use facial recognition technology to compare passengers' faces to the digital image recorded in their passport. Details are then automatically checked against Border Force systems and watch lists. Iris recognition is also used at some airports.
- Boarding pass check: Final check before getting onto the aircraft is usually the boarding pass control. Most airports have automatic readers that verify the pass to confirm the passenger is boarding the flight that is carrying their checked-in luggage.
- Baggage check: Checked baggage passes through large-scale X-ray machines and may be checked by sniffer dogs. All bags are kept completely separate from passenger areas in the terminal.

Visa requirements and entry controls

In order to fully reap the socio-economic benefits international tourism can generate for a country, it is necessary to put in place conditions that make the country competitive, the most important of which is to make destinations easy to visit. Visa policies are among the most important governmental formalities influencing international tourism. Visas perform several essential functions. They serve to ensure security; to control immigration and limit the entry, duration of stay or activities of travellers.

According to the UNWTO's Visa Openness Report in 2015, destinations around the world still require on average approximately two-thirds of the world's population to obtain a traditional visa prior to departure. Some 18% of the world's population is able to enter a destination without a visa, while another 15% can receive a visa on arrival and 6% is able to obtain eVisas. Globally there is a big variety in visa policies, from countries allowing almost any citizen to enter freely to countries requesting visas indiscriminately.

Changes to legislation

Very few countries in the world have what can be termed as tourism legislation such as consumer protection, employment law, anti-discriminatory practices on tourism providers. In most of the countries there are various laws that have a bearing on tourism operations and activities. The various types of tourism related laws, enacted in different countries, relate to protection of tourists, border controls, quality of services, protection of environment, conservation of historical sites and monuments, tourism industry regulations and the relationship between the various segments of the travel and tourism industry.

The role of tourism legislation is to formulate a legal and regulatory framework for the sustainable development and management of tourism, protection and conservation of natural and cultural resources and the facilitation of the involvement of private sector and local communities in tourism development activities. Tourism legislation will reflect the roles and responsibilities of all stakeholders; ensure the rights of international/local tourists and will ensure the rights and obligations of participating businesses, inbound-outbound tour operators and all others concerned in the tourism sector.

The legislation in each country will differ, in accordance to national government's priorities within that country. For example, in South Africa, the Tourism Act (1993) promotes tourism to and within South Africa, regulates and rationalises the tourism industry, standardises measures to maintain and enhance facilities and services available to tourists and coordinates the activities of people and businesses that are active in the tourism industry. Similarly under the Philippines' Tourism Act of 2009 'The State declares tourism as an indispensable element of the national economy and an industry of national interest and importance, which must be harnessed as an engine of socio-economic growth and cultural affirmation to generate investment, foreign exchange and employment, and to continue to mold an enhanced sense of national pride for all Filipinos.'

Many countries will legislate the provision of tourism services through licensing of approved operators. For example, in Mauritius a Tourist Enterprise Licence is issued to an establishment or activity that provides services or goods to tourists for reward, whether monetary or otherwise. This includes running a hotel or guesthouse, providing whale-watching boat tours or working as a tour guide.

Consumer protection measures can include regulatory (e.g. legislation) and non-government measures, including self-regulatory and co-regulatory procedures (e.g. codes of conduct or accreditation schemes). All such measures are intended to protect the interests of and promote better outcomes for consumers via protection from unfair or unjust conduct or unsafe/defective goods; to provide assistance when loss is suffered and to assist in making better purchasing decisions. Consumer laws have been developed in many countries; European countries offer protection under European law; Australia has in place the Australian Consumer Law (ACL), passed in 2011 and South Africa created the South African National Consumer Protection Act (CPA), which came into force in 2011. All of these pieces of legislation will offer protection to tourists for the goods and services they purchase from travel and tourism providers. There are still some countries which do not offer the same level of peace of mind to people spending large sums of money on holidays and this may influence a person's decision to purchase from operators in countries where no such protection exists.

KEY CONCEPTS

Customer focus

Providing consumer protection for tourists is a clear way in which the travel and tourism industry can prove it is customer-focused as well as being market driven.

Employment law may affect tourism provision because of directives about the number of hours employees are permitted to work, regulations about health and safety at work and so on. This may be costly for small and medium sized enterprises to implement, which make up a large share of travel and tourism businesses.

Anti-discriminatory legislation varies from country to country. Most countries now operate laws criminalising all forms of discrimination on the grounds of religion, caste, creed, doctrine, race, colour or ethnic origin. Many also protect the rights of fair access to products and services for disabled travellers. However, attitudes towards same sex marriages and gay, lesbian, bisexual and transgender visitors differ enormously from country to country. Tourists must ensure they understand a country's legal and social standing towards homosexuality before travelling to a destination.

Technological developments

Hand in hand with the socio-economic changes have been a variety of technological developments and we now consider how these have exerted an influence on the ways in which the modern travel and tourism industry has developed over recent years.

Developments in transport technology

Transport technology has two components: there are the actual conveyances designed for water, dry land, steel rails or the open sky, and there is what is called the infrastructure needed to run them. For conveyances such as trains, ships and motor vehicles, infrastructure of some sort must exist wherever they go: tracks, navigable waterways and road networks. Cruise ships and aircraft similarly require port and terminal facilities to allow them to operate effectively in serving their passenger markets. Since the 1960s, passenger transportation systems have expanded as new technologies are developed to make travel more efficient and comfortable for the travelling public some examples are shown in Figures 1.22, 1.23 and 1.24. Thus, during the 20th century, transport technology has allowed the spread of mass tourism to a widespread array of destinations, which were previously not reachable by rail or ship. Manufacturers are constantly developing the capabilities of vehicles. Such developments influence places which can be reached, in terms of social and cost constraints. In general terms this has created more choice for tourists, making travel faster and cheaper and giving easier access to destinations much further away.

From the international travel point of view, all of the following technological innovations have helped to reduce the frictional effect of distance.

- The development of wide-bodied long-haul planes such as the Boeing 747 jumbo jet has made a big difference to air travel times and affordability since 1968.
- The Airbus A380 super jumbo is able to accommodate between 544 and 850 passengers, depending on the seating configuration, and cover a range of 14 200 km. This in turn has made travel for tourists even more accessible.

- New generation cruise ships are able to cater for 3000 passengers and increase operating economies of scale stimulating demand.
- Fast trains, such as the French TGV and the Japanese Shinkasa (bullet train) allow for travel up to 300 km/hour through the countryside, reducing journey times, and have become attractions in their own right.
- Tunnel technology (Channel, Alps etc.) has increased road and rail traffic within Europe and elsewhere.

Figure 1.22 Desert safari

Figure 1.23 Classical auto rickshaw

Figure 1.24 Various passenger transportation systems

Developments in information technology

The availability of new technologies led to the development of new skills, new materials new services and new forms of organisation. This is especially true for the last two decades where the role of technological innovation was crucial. In tourism, technology created a new form of business called e-tourism, which today is the biggest force in e-commerce.

Most travel and tourism organisations have adopted developments in ICT to aid the efficient running of their business operations. The last ten years have seen the rapid expansion of internet-based service provision and this 24/7 availability has transformed customer interaction with hotels and other types of service provider. Many hotels make use of new technology to streamline their operating procedures within and between various departments and these have resulted in improvements to both customer service and profitability. There is a range of technological applications and, depending on the nature of the particular department, it is common to see the following aspects used by most providers.

The internet has opened up a whole host of different information sources to potential customers. Travellers can research and compare products and services from tourism providers around the world. The information is available around the clock, with no need for displacement.

A website for a travel and tourism organisation allows online booking and acts as a marketing tool. Similarly the use of databases aids direct marketing and finance systems and helps to streamline payments, accounts and stock control. Such applications increase efficiency in both front and back of house situations and allow organisations to become more competitive. This benefits customers as well as staff. A majority of customers like the ease and convenience of using the internet for booking travel arrangements. In particular they like the instant reservation/payment confirmation and the 24/7 availability of the service. The adoption of new technology has had great benefits for both producers and consumers.

Today the travel marketplace has become a global arena where millions of buyers (travel agents and the public) and sellers (hotels, airlines, car rental companies and so on) work together to exchange travel services. Among the 'shelves', on which buyers search for travel services, are the world's global distribution systems and the internet distribution systems. These systems have become electronic supermarkets linking buyers to sellers and allowing reservations to be made quickly and easily.

Nowadays, more travel is sold over the internet than any other consumer product. The internet is a perfect medium for selling travel as it brings a vast network of suppliers and a widely dispersed customer pool together into a centralised market place.

Recent advances in mobile technology mean that there are now more users of smartphones and tablets than traditional laptops and PCs in the world. This has allowed innovations in how travel and tourism providers communicate with their customers. Destinations management organisations, aware of visitor behaviour, are developing mobile applications in order to cater for tourism demands.

KEY CONCEPTS

Change and development

The way in which travel and tourism has used advances in technology to improve the products and services it offers customers is symptomatic of the industry being driven by the key concepts of change and development.

Social media has made a huge impact on the tourism industry. Consumers engage with social networking sites to research trips, make informed decisions about their travels and share their personal experiences of a particular hotel, restaurant or airline. TripAdvisor in particular has had a wide-reaching effect on the industry. It has 50 million unique monthly visitors who are actively seeking out travel information and advice from the sources they trust the most: other tourists and holidaymakers. This style of user-generated content is seen by the online community as more credible and authentic and for many hotels, restaurants and visitor attractions, if they are not listed in the top five spots, they are losing out to their competitors. With more than 200 million reviews and opinions posted on TripAdvisor to date, and more than 800 million active users on Facebook posting updates and sharing images, social media is dominating the industry.

Virtual tours are among the most cost effective online marketing tools. Panoramic virtual tours let potential customers literally see for themselves what is on offer. Not only do virtual tours add more impact to a website and engage the viewer with interactivity but virtual tours are far more convincing and credible than just a photograph. Research suggests that a site with a 360-degree virtual tour and interactive media will receive

40% more views than a competitor's site that is lacking the same media.

Online check-in is another way in which airlines are harnessing technology to benefit customers. While e-tickets form an integral part of the booking process, the actual procedure of arriving at the airport and getting on a flight has been made much quicker through alternative check-in methods. Most airlines offer online check-in as part of an effort to make the process more efficient. This involves the passenger being able to log onto the airline's website and print off their own boarding pass. The benefits to the customer are numerous; they can select the seat they want for the flight in advance and then go straight to the baggage drop-off point at the airport, bypassing the long queues associated with airport check-in.

Another important part of the general online world for tourism is the use of e-passports. These are normal passports with a small chip implant in the back cover. This chip contains the same data displayed in the passport itself and also has an additional digital photo for biometric identification purposes.

Ecological factors
Protection of the environment and conservation of natural/cultural heritage

For many destinations, the natural environment is one of the main attractions for leisure visitors, offering a wide range of recreational, activity based, educational and/or cultural activities and experiences. The development of natural areas for tourism requires a careful balance between providing adequate visitor experiences and services, protecting the ecological and cultural values of the area and ensuring the long-term sustainability of the site. Tourism has the potential to increase public appreciation of the environment and to spread awareness of environmental problems when it brings people into closer contact with nature and the environment. This association with nature may increase awareness of the value of preserving the environment and lead to more environmentally conscious behaviour and activities.

Tourism can significantly contribute to environmental protection, conservation and restoration of biological diversity through the creation of national parks and wildlife parks. The need to act sustainably now impacts tourism provision significantly, with many governments exercising control over developments and activities within destinations.

KEY CONCEPTS

Sustainability and responsibility

Learning that tourism practices need to conserve and protect the natural and built environments in which activities take place as well as the local heritage of host populations is part of the key concept of managing tourism through sustainable and responsible practices.

The threat posed by climatic change, including global warming and natural disasters

Climate scientists now generally agree that the Earth's surface temperatures have risen steadily in recent years because of an increase in the so-called greenhouse gases in the atmosphere, which trap heat from the sun. One of the most significant of these gases is carbon dioxide (CO_2), which is generated when fossil fuels, such as coal, oil and natural gas are burned (e.g. in industry, electricity generation and vehicles) and when there are changes in land use, such as deforestation. Global and regional temperatures are rising. 1998 was the hottest year of the millennium and the 1990s the warmest decade. Climate models suggest a future warming of 0.2–0.3 °C per decade and sea levels are expected to rise at a rate of 4–10 cm per decade.

The impacts of global warming and other climate changes on tourism are likely to manifest themselves in a number of ways according to local conditions. The threat of climate change puts tourism at risk in many destinations and important market changes could result. Many of these impacts will develop indirectly through increased stresses placed on environmental systems. The most serious impacts will result from the effects of sea level rise on small island states. For example, the Maldives, which is a popular tourist destination, are particularly vulnerable to sea level rise. Climate change is expected to increase the risk of illness in several parts of the world and consequently discourage tourism. More frequent periods of extreme heat will cause discomfort in many resorts of the Eastern Mediterranean, where the number of days above 40 °C is estimated to increase. Decreasing cloud cover in Australia will increase exposure to the sun's harmful rays and malaria is likely to re-emerge in Spain. The potential impacts of climate change have significant considerations for planning in the tourist industry from the prevention of coastal flooding and erosion to the conservation of water resources, the control of forest and bush fires and the conservation of vulnerable flora and fauna.

Coastal and island destinations are most vulnerable to direct and indirect impacts of climate change (such as storms and extreme climatic events, coastal erosion, physical damage to infrastructure, sea level rise, flooding, water shortages and water contamination), given that most infrastructure is located within short distance of the shoreline. The serious issue of seasonality of beach tourism has to be taken into consideration, as it can be made worse by climate change. In many beach destinations the high tourist season often coincides with low water regimes in dry seasons, negatively affecting water management and environmental issues.

The impacts of climate change and global warming will vary greatly in different coastal regions, and might bring opportunities as well as problems for tourism. For example, in traditional summer beach destinations (like the Mediterranean) shoulder seasons might lengthen, and the winter season might become more appealing to tourists, providing opportunities to reduce seasonality and expand the tourism product. Northern coastal areas might benefit from warmer summers, attracting more tourists and lengthening the summer season.

Mountain regions are also important destinations for global tourism. Snow cover and pristine mountain landscapes, the principal attractions for tourism in these regions, are the features that are most vulnerable to climate change. Besides the negative impacts, climate change can also bring opportunities in mountain areas. While the winter season might shorten, the summer season might lengthen, providing opportunities for other types of outdoor activities and tourism business to supply them (e.g., trekking, hiking, mountain biking and so on).

The impact of natural disasters has been more profound during recent years and this can be attributed to the changing weather patterns around the world as well as the increased number of tourist spots. Today, more and more natural reserves and areas that were once uninhabitable are being made accessible to attract tourists. Though this gives a boost to the local tourism, it also increases the impact of natural disasters. In fact, natural disasters cause many tourist destinations to lose their beauty, culture and economy for a temporary or extended period of time. The scale of the damage depends to a large extent on the scale of the natural disaster. For example, the 2004 tsunami caused widespread devastation for communities on island destinations in the Indian Ocean. Islands reliant on tourism and fishing, such as the Maldives, have had to rebuild their industries. It is usually the developing countries that are more affected by natural disasters than the developed ones, due to cheaper/weaker infrastructures. Catastrophes like floods, earthquakes, wildfires, volcanoes, avalanches, drought and diseases can have a serious effect on inbound and domestic tourism and thus on local tourism industries. Additionally, natural disasters more often than not cause an increase in tourists' concerns about security and safety in destinations.

About 150 major natural disasters affected millions of people worldwide in 2015. Asia again bore the brunt of these disasters reported globally. Floods continue to be the most frequently occurring natural disasters and also affect the most people worldwide. A magnitude 7.8 earthquake struck Nepal on April 25, killing more than 8800 people. It damaged or destroyed nearly 900 000 buildings, created avalanches in the Himalayas, and left almost 1 million children out of school. Major aftershocks, including a magnitude 7.3 tremor three weeks later, slowed recovery efforts and added to the devastation. In 2015, India suffered the longest heat waves in years, which claimed 2000 lives in Andhra Pradesh and Telangana states. In May, temperatures climbed to as high as 47.7 °C in the worst affected areas of Telangana, which included the major city of Hyderabad.

Diminishing oil reserves: seeking new travel forms

Most geologists estimate that 2 trillion barrels of oil were formed in the earth over millions of years. To date, we have pumped out half of this supply. British Petroleum (BP) predicts there are 40 years of oil supplies left. But the implications of this forecast are not straightforward. As world demand grows and supply diminishes, prices will soar. Governments are conscious of the problems that a shortage of oil will cause. Energy conservation measures are more wide spread now than ever before. This has led to the development of better aircraft that are more fuel efficient and the use of alternative energy sources.

The most obvious strategy to deal with diminishing oil will be replacement of petroleum with other fuels. There is unquestionable need for research and investment with regard to such fuels. However, every one of the likely replacements has one or more serious drawbacks. All are currently very limited in quantity and will require considerable time and investment to achieve a scale of production equal to that of petroleum today. Renewable biofuels such as ethanol, wood methanol and biodiesel are well suited to running existing engines. The main drawback is their requirement for arable land for growing crops such as corn, sugar cane or rapeseed, hence the

inevitability of an eventual trade-off between food and fuel. Solar, wind, tidal, hydro, wave and geothermal technologies all produce electricity. Thus most renewable energy sources other than biofuels will be suitable for running only electric vehicles and as yet hybrid cars are in an early stage of adoption.

Electric vehicles are a long way from being able to cope with the demands of mass tourism. After years of research on all types of electric vehicles, solar flight has developed a plan for the next generation aircraft. Promising to be as quiet as a glider and with the speed and utility of a light aircraft, test flights have been carried out, but we are in the very early stages of solar-powered air transportation, with the biggest solar powered aircraft currently offering only six seats. The obvious long-term replacement for air transport would be increasing reliance on transport by rail and ship, both of which enjoy much higher fuel efficiencies. In the case of trains, there is the option, at least for relatively short routes, of operation by electric rather than diesel motors. In countries such as the United States and Canada, where the existing passenger rail infrastructure is incapable of absorbing a substantial increase in riders, considerable time and investment will be required to increase capacity. Within cities there are more options for transport modes between cars at one extreme and the bicycle at the other; these primarily consist of electric buses, surface electric light rail (trolleys or trams) and electric underground rail systems.

⊚ **KEY CONCEPTS**

Sustainability and responsibility

Travel and tourism providers are conscious of the need to act responsibly and to find sustainable ways of offering products and services. Finding different means of powering transport is just one environmentally friendly practice promoted by the industry. Using renewable sources for building and using local products and services are now common practices for hotels and tourist attractions.

Changing consumer needs and expectations

Today's travel and tourism marketplace is saturated with products aimed at a wide variety of consumer types that together make up the world's travelling public. The development of holiday products has come a long way since Vladimir Raitz, the cofounder of the Horizon Holiday Group, pioneered the first mass package holidays abroad in 1950 with charter flights between Gatwick airport in the UK and Corsica. By the late 1950s and 1960s, these cheap package holidays, which combined flight, transfers and accommodation, provided the first chance for most people in the UK to have affordable travel abroad. However, by 2005 a growing number of consumers were avoiding package holidays and were instead travelling with budget airlines and booking their own accommodation. The trend for package holiday bookings saw a comeback in 2009, as customers sought greater financial security in the wake of a number of holiday and flight companies going bust, and as the hidden costs of 'no-frills' flights increased.

Market driven

The travel and tourism industry has always been market driven; this means that tourism providers try to cater for the changing tastes and demands of tourists by segmenting their customers into largely homogenous groups for which they then develop products that averagely suit everyone. Being market driven means that many tourism providers are controlled and guided by commercial considerations; that is, generating income, making profit and gaining competitive advantage, rather than being customer driven and considering the individual needs of each and every customer.

Change in attitudes and tastes

There has been a trend in tourism over recent years, especially in Europe, where international travel for short breaks is common. Tourists have a wide range of budgets and tastes, and a wide variety of resorts and hotels have developed to cater for them. For example, some people prefer simple beach vacations, while others want more specialised holidays, quieter resorts, family-oriented holidays or niche market-targeted holiday products. Furthermore, the growing concern worldwide over global warming and climate change combined with rising oil prices, the energy crisis and the economic slowdown has led to dramatic changes in consumer attitudes, travel seasonality and other travel patterns and trends. It is influencing individual choices regarding travel destinations, the length of trips and other factors such as the availability of environment-friendly modes of transport and environmentally responsible service providers.

In the past, for example, the idea of 'cultural' tourism was seen as a predominantly educational activity and researchers demonstrated that these 'cultural tourists'

tended to be better educated than the average visitor. Although this may still hold true, these educated visitors seem to favour locations that also offer entertainment and relaxation. Visitors are increasingly interested in experiences that are more active and creative than cultural. They are not content simply to view heritage sites or museum collections in a static way, and therefore welcome dynamic interpretation. They may want to participate in festivals and carnivals, rather than watching from the sidelines. They can learn to cook dishes and make wine as well as consuming them.

Tourism is evolving, partly as a result of changes in society and lifestyles. As was suggested earlier, consideration of the reasons why people travel, the travel and tourism industry is very dynamic and changes in the types of tourism activity that people prefer have encouraged operators to offer specialised packages catering for specific requirements. These focus on interests and activities which appeal to a particular sector of the tourist market. This has given rise to a variety of **specialised markets** based on the particular reasons or motivations for travel as illustrated in Figure 1.24.

 KEY CONCEPTS

Customer focus

Developing specialised markets is fundamental to the principle of being customer focused.

To help you understand about the relationship between a tourist's special interests and niche market products attempt the following exercises:

* Write a definition of each of the terms included in Figure 1.25.
* Give an example of each activity.

Polarisation of demand for budget and luxury products

Given the changes in distribution of wealth, and because of changing lifestyles, there is polarization in the demand for products and services in travel and tourism. At one end wealthy visitors are seeking comfort/luxury travel products, whilst at the other end people are looking for no frills/budget travel offers. This has very much changed the way in which travel and tourism products and services are marketed. As well as being polarised, there are now also moves to assimilate the two extremes.

31

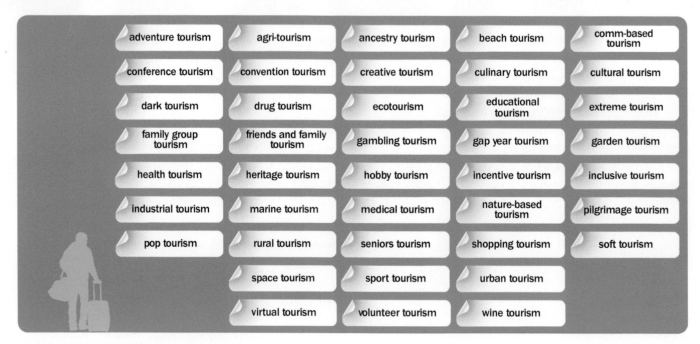

adventure tourism	agri-tourism	ancestry tourism	beach tourism	comm-based tourism
conference tourism	convention tourism	creative tourism	culinary tourism	cultural tourism
dark tourism	drug tourism	ecotourism	educational tourism	extreme tourism
family group tourism	friends and family tourism	gambling tourism	gap year tourism	garden tourism
health tourism	heritage tourism	hobby tourism	incentive tourism	inclusive tourism
industrial tourism	marine tourism	medical tourism	nature-based tourism	pilgrimage tourism
pop tourism	rural tourism	seniors tourism	shopping tourism	soft tourism
	space tourism	sport tourism	urban tourism	
	virtual tourism	volunteer tourism	wine tourism	

Figure 1.25 Main tourism specialised markets

Specialised packages

This is a way in which many travel and tourism organisations try to overcome criticisms about the industry being market driven. A specialised package is tailor made to a customer's individual requirements, which means travellers can customise their own itineraries to include elements of the holiday they wish and can omit those aspects that do not appeal. The benefits to customers are obvious; they can use specialist providers, who are expert in their field, and may save money on elements of the holiday they would not use. There are also benefits to the provider: increased customer satisfaction may lead to repeat business and word of mouth recommendations.

Sustainable and responsible tourism

KEY TERMS

Sustainable tourism: tourism that takes full account of its current and future economic, social and environmental impacts, addressing the needs of visitors, the industry, the environment and host communities.

Responsible tourism: tourism that creates better places for people to live in, and better places to visit. The major difference between the two is that in responsible tourism, individuals, organisations and businesses are asked to take responsibility for their actions and the impacts of their actions.

As more regions and countries develop their tourism industry, it produces significant impacts on natural resources, consumption patterns, pollution and social systems. The need for sustainable/responsible planning and management is imperative for the industry to survive as a whole. A sustainable tourism business must also be financially sustainable; in order for tourism to thrive, it has to be profitable for business owners.

Examples of sustainable tourism practices include conserving water and energy, supporting community conservation projects, recycling and treating wastes, hiring staff from the local community, paying them fair wages and providing training and sourcing locally-produced products for restaurants and gift shops. Sustainable tourism businesses take concrete actions to enhance the well-being of local communities and make positive contributions to the conservation of natural and cultural heritage. In doing so, they cut down on their own costs and preserve their operations for the long term.

Responsible tourism recognises that the impacts of tourism are very different in different places, and that some impacts are always more important than others. For example, in Sub-Saharan Africa, water conservation is a big issue, while in Wales it is not. Switzerland does not need to concern itself with poverty reduction as a priority, whereas Peru does. The issues are different everywhere, and the solutions must be too. Responsible tourism is not another form of specialised tourism; responsible tourism is about the legacy and the consequences of tourism, for the environment, for local people and for local economies.

Sustainability and responsibility

This section gives specific examples of how tourism providers have become more aware of the need to act sustainably and responsibly.

Product differentiation

Most organisations recognise the importance of product development, although rarely does this involve entirely new products or entirely new markets, rather a process of individualising mass market products by means of product differentiation, product line extension by branding policies or by changing the cost/quality ratio of the product. All firms try to simultaneously lower costs and at the same time achieve product uniqueness, for example through choice of destination, hotels or other packaging changes.

KEY TERMS

Product differentiation: marketing of generally similar products with minor variations that are used by consumers when making a choice.

A differentiated holiday product will give tourists a choice of flight options, for example, or a choice of three star or four star accommodation or a choice of a full board or half board meal plan.

Product line extension

A product line extension is the use of an established product brand name for a new item in the same product category. Product line extensions occurs when a company introduces additional items in the same product category under the same brand name such as a hotel chain opening new branches in different destinations.

Changing the cost/quality ratio of the product

This is closely linked with the actual costs of providing the product and the customer's perception of value for money. The price charged should be deemed to represent good value based on the quality of the product and services offered, in order to achieve customer satisfaction. However in an attempt to make cost savings and to boost an organisation's profitability, sometimes the quality of the product is stripped back or the price is increased beyond the true value of the product.

1.4 The structure of the travel and tourism industry

Travel and tourism is a global industry. The industry has experienced tremendous growth in the last 50 years and is now considered to be one of the most important industries in the world. However, what exactly are we talking about when we say 'the travel and tourism industry'? To put it simply, it is that whole mix of businesses and agencies that works together to serve the needs of people who travel.

Business ownership
Commercial organisations (for profit)

The majority of travel and tourism organisations operate in the **private sector**, for example most accommodation providers, airlines, travel agencies, tour operators, visitor attractions, car hire firms.

Some are very big companies, but most are small and medium sized enterprises (SMEs), employing up to 250 people, or even smaller 'micro-businesses' with fewer than ten employees.

The private sector is made up of **commercial** organisations that are in business to make money and generate a profit. All of their activities, whether it is to do with selling products and services, marketing, employing staff or investing in new equipment, are focused on realising this primary aim. Income from the sale of products and services is expected to be greater than the costs of operating the business so as to leave a surplus. This can either be taken as profit or re-invested in the business in order to create future success for the owners, directors, employees and any shareholders who may have bought a financial interest in the business.

Non-commercial organisations (not for profit)

The term public sector refers to services provided for the population that are financed from public money. Examples of these public services include education services, the police, public libraries, refuse collection and various leisure and tourism facilities. Public sector travel and tourism organisations play an important role in helping to promote destinations and they often provide a range of services to encourage tourism development, such as grants to start new businesses and advice on

Private sector: Virgin Atlantic

Virgin Atlantic was developed as an offshoot of Richard Branson's Virgin Group, which was better known at the time as a leading light in the world of pop and rock music. On 22 June 1984 Virgin's inaugural flight to Newark took place, a flight filled with friends, celebrities and the media. The airline's aim was simple: 'To provide the highest quality innovative service at excellent value for money for all classes of air travellers'.

Figure 1.26 A Virgin Atlantic aircraft

Virgin Atlantic is 51% owned by the Virgin Group and 49% owned by Singapore Airlines. On 20 December 1999 Richard Branson signed an agreement to sell a 49% stake of Virgin Atlantic to Singapore Airlines to form a unique global partnership. The cost of the transaction to Singapore Airlines was £600.25 million, which included a capital injection of £49 million and valued Virgin Atlantic at a minimum of £1.225 billion. The deal was finalised in early 2000.

Over the course of a year the airline carries over 5 million passengers, turns over in excess of US$3.5 billion and generates profits of around US$100 million. In 2015, Virgin Atlantic carried more than 5.94 million passengers, making it the eighth largest UK airline based on passenger numbers Figure 1.26 shows the well known Virgin Atlantic livery.

Mission statement:

'To grow a profitable airline... Where people love to fly... And where people love to work.'

To help you find out more about Virgin Atlantic, the airline has produced a student information pack available online.

Public sector: The Mauritius Tourism Promotion Authority (MTPA)

The Mauritius Tourism Promotion Authority (MTPA), established in 1996 by the MTPA Act, is administered by a board of directors and operates under the aegis of the Ministry of Tourism and Leisure. It has a very symbolic logo, shown in Figure 1.27 below.

Figure 1.27 The MTPA Logo

The MTPA has very clear objectives which include the following:
- to promote Mauritius abroad as a tourist destination by conducting advertising campaigns and participating in tourism fairs; it is responsible for organising, in collaboration with the local tourism industry, promotional campaigns and activities in Mauritius and abroad
- to provide information to tourists on the facilities, infrastructures and services available to them in Mauritius
- to initiate such action as may be necessary to promote cooperation with other tourism agencies
- to conduct research into market trends and market opportunities and disseminate such information and other relevant statistical data on Mauritius
- to advise the Ministry on all matters relating to the promotion of tourism.

The MTPA had a key role to play in helping the Mauritius tourism industry overcome the decline in international visitor arrivals caused by the 2008 global financial crisis. The 2009 increase in bookings was a direct result of the efforts of the MTPA. The government body charged with keeping Mauritius as a leading brand in tourism started a multi-faceted programme to boost visitor numbers. The central theme of the strategy was that Mauritius started to actively approach new markets. With the help of Air Mauritius, Emirates and other dominant airlines on the island, advertising campaigns were started in Russia, Asia, India and parts of Africa. Each campaign was different, offering Mauritius to South Africans as an activity-based destination where you could go diving or parasailing; to Indians it was marketed as the holiday of a lifetime, a chance to fulfil an aspiration. Even Reunion, only a few hundred kilometres south-west of Mauritius, was targeted with the 'So close, so different' tagline.

The message was that Mauritius has a great deal more to offer than the traditional image of sea, sun and sand. For a small island, it provides a remarkable array of options for the holidaymaker. As the country sets about its target of doubling the industry to 2 million tourists per year, at a rate of about 10% growth per annum, it is anticipated that these new areas of tourism will be able to absorb some of the extra visitors.

marketing/promotion. Unlike the private sector, public sector bodies are not primarily concerned with making a profit. They tend to have much wider social and economic aims, such as creating jobs through tourism and improving tourist facilities for visitors and local people.

There are also not for profit organisations that are not directly controlled by the state. Such organisations are diverse and include different types of clubs, societies and charities. They tend to be funded by their members through membership subscriptions, donations, grants, fund-raising activities and through revenues generated from the sale of goods and services.

They are sometimes described as operating in the voluntary sector. Such organisations within travel and tourism tend to have a variety of different aims and objectives and these may include aspects such as:

- to provide facilities that are not otherwise available to the community in a particular location
- to observe a non-profit making goal by returning all surplus income to the organisation's stated policy objectives
- to bring to the public's attention a major issue in society, such as conservation or protection of the environment.

Organisations influencing international travel and tourism

World Tourism Organisation

The World Tourism Organisation (UNWTO) is a specialised agency of the United Nations and the leading international organisation in the field of tourism. Their logo is shown in Figure 1.28. It serves as a global forum for tourism policy issues and a practical source of tourism know-how. Its membership includes 157 countries, 6 Associate Members and over 480 Affiliate Members, representing the private sector, educational institutions, tourism associations and local tourism authorities. UNWTO compiles the World Tourism rankings and thus it is a significant global body, concerned with the collection and collation of statistical information on international tourism. This organisation represents public sector tourism bodies, from most countries in the world and the publication of its data makes possible comparisons of the flow and growth of tourism on a global scale.

Figure 1.28 UNWTO logo

The UNWTO is committed to the United Nations Millennium Development Goals, geared towards reducing poverty and fostering sustainable development. The organisation encourages the implementation of the Global Code of Ethics for Tourism, with a view to ensuring that member countries, tourist destinations and businesses maximise the positive economic, social and cultural effects of tourism and fully reap its benefits, while minimising its negative social and environmental impacts.

National tourism organisations (NTOs)

National tourism organisations (NTOs) are an important part of a nation's tourism industry. They are responsible for the formulation and implementation of national tourist policy within a country and for coordinating the different activities involved in tourism development. They are closely linked with the government and in many countries are governed at ministry level.

There are two areas in which national and local governments can exercise a very specific influence over the development of the country's tourism industry. In terms of **planning**, this generally involves the designation of regions or areas to be targeted for tourism development. In terms of **regulation**, this is setting policy and guidelines about the way in which tourism should be operated.

The objectives of a NTO are to ensure that the maximum possible value from international tourism is gained for the country for its economic and social benefit. The following are generally accepted functions of a NTO:

- research
- information and promotion within the country
- setting and monitoring standards of lodging and restaurants
- publicity overseas
- international relations
- development of areas of national heritage
- overall tourism policy and promotion.

Among other activities, promotion of the country's tourism assets to both domestic visitors and to international markets is an important function of an NTO. This includes advertising, publicity of all kinds, public relations, the provision of information and the distribution of printed sales material. Planned publicity and promotion is carried out via the NTO website, attending trade fairs such as ITB Berlin or the London World Travel Market, or running campaigns using print and broadcast media.

To help illustrate the significance of the role of an NTO we can now look at a case study of what has happened in Dubai.

Regional and local tourism organisations (RTOs)

Regional tourism organisations (RTOs) establish and promote quality tourism experiences, implementing strategies to ensure their region maximises its tourism potential. A region may be a large geographical area, covering a number of countries, as in the case of The Pacific Asia Travel Association, an organisation which acts on behalf of the responsible development of the Asia Pacific travel and tourism industry. Or regional tourism

may cover a smaller geographic area within a country – a state, province or smaller area of territory. Figure 1.29 shows the many RTOs for New Zealand.

The role and functions of RTOs are similar to those of NTOs, but with direct responsibility for their own geographical area. RTOs and NTOs work closely together in their efforts to promote tourism.

Consular service providers

It is important that you have an understanding of the ways in which individual countries look after the interests of their citizens who are away from home and travelling overseas. Consular assistance is help and advice provided by the diplomatic agents of a country to citizens of that country who are living or travelling overseas. Such assistance may take the form of provision of replacement travel documents, advice and support in the case of an accident, serious illness or death and the repatriation of person under such circumstances.

 KEY TERMS

Repatriation: the process of returning a person to their place of origin or citizenship.

In the United States, the Bureau of Consular Affairs is part of the Department of State. Its mission is:

'Safety. Security. Service. Our highest priority is to protect the lives and interests of U.S. citizens overseas. We do this through routine and emergency services to Americans at our embassies and consulates around the world. We serve our fellow citizens during their most important moments – births, deaths, disasters, arrests, and medical emergencies.'

An estimated 8.7 million U.S. citizens live overseas and U.S. citizens take more than 80 million trips abroad every year.

In the United Kingdom, consular services are provided by the Foreign and Commonwealth Office (FCO). The FCO website provides detailed travel advice, including the 'Know Before You Go' ongoing campaign to help British citizens stay safe and healthy when they are travelling abroad.

ACTIVITY 5

Find out which organisation provides consular services for people from your country when travelling abroad.

Figure 1.29 Map showing the regional tourism organisations of New Zealand

CASE STUDY 6

The role of DTCM in Dubai

Figure 1.30 Tourism in Dubai

Dubai has developed rapidly over recent years and it is quite appropriate to look at this destination to examine closely the role and function of the Government of Dubai Department of Tourism and Commerce Marketing (DTCM). Dubai's tourism potential was clearly identified during the 1980s. For some time, Dubai had already evolved into the Gulf region's leading port, trading centre and exhibition venue. The city therefore already had a good basic infrastructure for leisure tourism development. The government made the strategic decision to maximise business and leisure tourism receipts and created in 1989 the Dubai Commerce and Tourism Promotion Board (DCTPB). Most countries promote tourism separately from trade and investment. However, in Dubai's case, it seemed quite logical to combine both of these aspects. The worldwide promotional activities of the DCTPB and its 1997 successor the DTCM are widely credited with being one of the key elements in Dubai's tourism boom. The government agency has won international awards and recognition as the leading

exponent of destination marketing in the Middle East and it has become a model to be emulated by other destinations.

The DTCM plans and implements an integrated programme of international promotions and publicity activities. This includes exhibition participation, product shows, marketing visits, presentations and road shows, VIP and executive missions, familiarisation and assisted visits, advertising, brochure production and distribution, media relations and enquiry and information services.

Within Dubai, the DTCM is responsible for the licensing of hotels, hotel apartments, tour operators, travel trade companies and travel agents. Its supervisory role also covers all touristic, archaeological and heritage sites, tourism conferences and exhibitions, the operation of tourist information services and the organisation and licensing of tour guides. As part of the development of Dubai's tourism facilities, the DTCM created a 3300 square metre Dubai Cruise Terminal in 2001. The move was designed to establish the emirate as the 'Middle East Hub' of the international cruising industry. In 2002, DTCM formed the Dubai Convention Bureau (DCB) to conduct all international bids on behalf of the emirate for attracting major events to Dubai. The DCB also carries out comprehensive promotional activities that relate to Dubai as a meetings and conventions destination and organises and participates in trade shows, workshops and road shows and prepares all collateral to promote Dubai as a leading business tourism destination.

Finally, one of the key strategies for both increasing visitor numbers to Dubai and providing quality experiences for visitors is specialist tourism industry training. Together with relevant tourism industry partners, the DTCM is committed to train and up-skill the workforce so that it becomes better qualified, competitive and challenged in a rapidly changing work environment.

Industry groups and trade associations

A wide variety of different industry groups and trade associations represent the interests of those working in the travel and tourism industry to provide products and services to customers. Some are global organisations, such as the International Air Transport Association (IATA), whose mission is to represent, lead and serve the airline industry, and Cruise Lines International Association (CLIA),

the world's largest cruise industry trade association, whose mission is to help its members succeed by advocating, educating and promoting for the common interests of the cruise community. Other organisations represent smaller sections of the industry and may be specific to one region, such as the Australian Federation of Travel Agents (AFTA), which involves itself in addressing major issues relating to the operation of all travel agencies in Australia.

ACTIVITY 6

Research at least three different industry groups or trade associations involved in the travel and tourism industry. Compare the roles and mission statements of each organisation. How many members does each organisation have? How important do you think these kind of organisations are?

Destination management companies (DMCs)

A Destination Management Company (DMC) is a professional services company, which has extensive local knowledge, expertise and resources, and which specialises in the design and implementation of events, activities, tours and transportation within a destination. DMC is a relatively new term that describes a company that specialises in the organisation and delivery of Foreign Independent Tours (FITs), group tours, meetings and events in a specific country, city or region. Their in-depth knowledge of the area, their proficient experience in organising visits and their creativity allow them to create customised programmes for customers. No matter what the event or occasion, the obligation of the DMC is to find a tailor-made solution. They are the local partners of outgoing tour operators, travel agents and conference planners. They are used extensively by conference organisers as they can arrange airport transfers, hotel accommodation, meal service, hospitality desks, sight-seeing and tours, themed events, room amenities and even gifts on behalf of their customers. The DMC may have special connections enabling them to negotiate special deals on customers' behalf. It is much easier to make arrangements from within the destination than trying to plan from a distance.

1.5 Subsectors of the travel and tourism industry

The various subsectors that go to make up the travel and tourism industry are shown in Figure 1.31.

Figure 1.31 Subsectors of the international travel and tourism industry

The characteristics of the tourism industry in any particular location will reflect the presence or absence of these subsectors. Indeed the attractiveness of any destination to various groups of tourists will reflect the scale and composition of the various subsectors. It must be remembered that a complex network of tour operators, travel agents, transport operators and accommodation providers work together to develop tourism in particular destinations. We can now examine some of the ways in which each of the component subsectors has contributed to the growth of travel and tourism industry in particular destinations.

Transport (including the products and services that each of the listed subsectors provide)

The methods of transport used by international and domestic travellers will vary according to the needs of the individual business or leisure tourist. Examples of these modes of transport are shown in the pictures below (Figures 1.32–1.35) which are all presented to show the particular mode of transport in a way which might appeal to a tourist. However, all travellers will be influenced by factors such as price, convenience, choice of departure points and timing of services when making their final travel arrangements for any given trip. There have been many transport developments over recent years and many destinations have become much more accessible to their markets in tourist generating areas as a result. We can now look at the characteristics associated with particular modes of travel.

Air transport

Air transport services are provided by the major national carriers (such as Air India, Air France, British Airways, Emirates and so on) as well as the low-cost, budget or 'no frills' airlines (such as flydubai, easyJet and Ryanair). A key feature of the service provided by both types of carrier is the operation of **scheduled flights**. These are flights that run to a published timetable and operate irrespective of whether there are enough passengers to make a profit. However, both types of carrier attract business and leisure customers because of their regular flights, the variety of routes that they operate and the standards of service that they provide.

Not all tourists flying to a given destination will travel on a scheduled flight, and **charter flights** are mainly used for package holidays. Tour operators contract charter airlines for a specific route for the peak holiday season. A feature of many charter airline services is that they mainly operate on routes, or to airports, where there are no scheduled

Figures 1.32–1.35 Modes of transportation

services. Many charter flights use small and medium sized airports and the survival of such airports often depends on the landing fees they receive from the charter airline companies. A chartered service is one whereby all of the seats for a particular flight have been pre-booked by a tour operator, for example, for use with package holiday customers to a specific destination. However, not all charter flights are associated with package holidays. It is possible for businesses or individuals to 'charter' a flight as well – this means to privately hire an aircraft for a specific purpose.

Nordwind Airlines is a charter airline with its head office in Moscow and its flight operations are from Terminal C at Sheremetyevo International Airport. The airline was founded as a result of cooperation between Pegas and Russian tour operators in September 2008. The airline began operations in December of the same year with an initial fleet of three Boeing 757–200 aircraft and has grown significantly.

Low cost/budget flights or 'no-frills' airline is one that offers generally low fares in exchange for eliminating many traditional passenger services. The concept originated in the US before spreading to Europe in the early 1990s and subsequently to much of the rest of the world. The term originated within the airline industry referring to airlines with a low – or lower – operating cost structure than their competitors. Through popular media the term has since come to define any carrier with low ticket prices and limited services regardless of their operating costs.

Key characteristics of such carriers include:

- a single passenger class
- a single type of airplane, commonly the Airbus A320 or Boeing 737 (reducing training and servicing costs)
- a simple fare scheme (typically fares increase as the plane fills up, which rewards early reservations)
- unreserved seating (encouraging passengers to board early and quickly)
- flying to cheaper, less congested secondary airports (avoiding air traffic delays and taking advantage of lower landing fees)

- short flights and fast turnaround times (allowing maximum utilisation of planes)
- simplified routes, emphasising point-to-point transit instead of transfers at hubs (again enhancing aircraft utilisation and eliminating disruption due to delayed passengers or luggage missing connecting flights)
- emphasis on direct sales of tickets, especially over the Internet (avoiding fees and commissions paid to travel agents and computer reservation systems)
- employees working in multiple roles, for instance flight attendants also cleaning the aircraft or working as gate agents (limiting personnel costs)
- free in-flight catering and other 'complimentary' services are eliminated, and replaced by optional paid-for in-flight food and drink (which represent an additional profit source for the airline)
- 'unbundling' of ancillary charges (showing airport fees, taxes as separate charges rather than as part of the advertised fare) to make the 'headline fare' appear lower
- low or lower operating costs relative to their competitors.

ACTIVITY 7

Choose a major international carrier serving your area and identify its route network.

Investigate frequency of service on these routes.

Provide details about what is available for First, Business and Economy class passengers on such routes.

Compare the chosen carrier with both a charter airline and a 'no frills' operator.

Suggest reasons for the various differences that you identify.

Sea transport

Up until the 1950s, most international travel was by sea. History is full of examples of famous vessels that sailed the oceans moving people and goods around the globe and many destinations such as New York and Buenos Aires grew because they were major seaports. There are far too many individual sea ports and ferry routes to list here. Figure 1.36 shows the world's major ports.

41

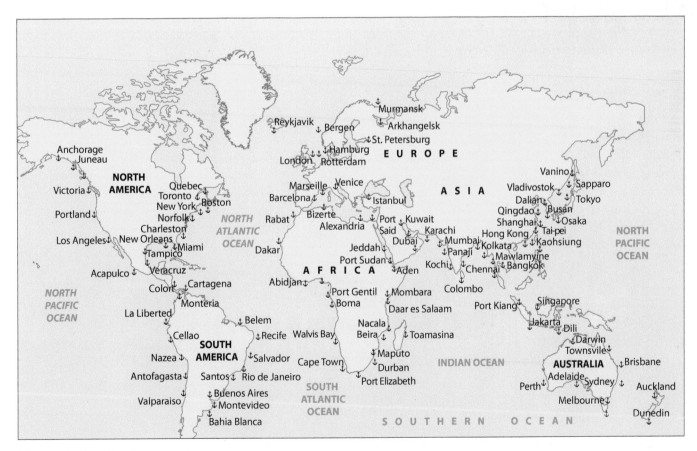

Figure 1.36 World major seaports

The main providers of water transport for international and domestic travel include ferry operators and cruise companies. The services provided by the ferry companies are particularly important because their services help to link otherwise remote destinations and thus increase levels of accessibility and connectivity. Important examples include the ferry services connecting groups of islands such as those found in Greece and services connecting island destinations to adjacent areas, such as the UK to mainland Europe across the English Channel.

Many countries in the world still rely on ferry crossings for everyday life such as in the Greek Islands, along the Adriatic Sea coastline, Hong Kong and in Singapore. A Star Ferry, in Hong Kong is shown in Figure 1.37. The cruise industry is now the fastest growing segment of the travel industry, having achieved more than 2100% growth since 1970. The cruise market is now worth US$35.5 billion and in 2015 cruise passenger numbers reached nearly 22.25 million. This growth is being supported by a range of increasingly innovative cruise ships being brought into service. Cruise Market Watch, a trade organisation representing the cruise industry, estimates that 45% of the population of the United States of America has taken a

cruise at some time in their life, thus showing the scale of popularity of this form of international leisure travel.

The cruise market is dominated by a number of major companies such as Carnival Cruise Lines, Celebrity Cruise Lines, Costa Cruises, Royal Caribbean, Holland America, Norwegian Cruise Line, Star Cruises and P&O Princess. Cruise ships belonging to these companies dominate sailings on the popular cruise circuits including the Mediterranean, the Caribbean, the Baltic, the Far East and Australasia.

In the past cruising was considered to be an expensive form of leisure travel and only the more affluent members of society, predominantly those of retirement age, were able to enjoy a cruise holiday. Over the years, however, cruise holidays have become popular and the cruise lines have attracted a much wider passenger base. The main reasons for this increase in popularity are that the cruise companies have expanded their itineraries to include more diverse ports of call, they have provided more convenient embarkation ports and new products such as fly-cruise options have been introduced. Furthermore, new cruise ships have also been introduced containing a much wider range of innovative onboard amenities and facilities. The

Figure 1.37 Star Ferry at Hong Kong Harbour

new generation of cruise ships now include technological advances with Wi-Fi zones, extensive leisure facilities, more luxurious accommodations and health and fitness facilities that easily rival luxury hotels. All of these innovations have opened up the market to customers of all ages and budgets and we can now look at a particular example of a recently introduced cruise ship in service with Costa Cruises.

The price paid by passengers will vary according to the length of cruise, the standard of cabin occupied and whether any promotional or seasonal discounts were offered at the time of booking.

Ferries form a part of the public transport systems of many waterside cities and islands, allowing direct transit between points at a capital cost much lower than bridges or tunnels. Hong Kong's Star Ferry carries passengers across Victoria Harbour and various other carriers can move travellers between Hong Kong Island and outlying islands like Cheung Chau, Lantau Island and Lamma Island. The Star Ferry in Hong Kong Harbour has been named as one of the top 50 places to visit by National Geographic Traveller, offering one of the world's best value-for-money sightseeing trips. Similarly, the Penang Ferry Service is the oldest ferry service in Malaysia. The Famous Ferry Service connects Sultan Abdul Halim Ferry Terminal in Butterworth on Peninsular Malaysia to Raja Tun Uda Ferry Terminal at Weld Quay in George Town on Penang Island. It has also become a famous tourist attraction among foreigners. Along the way, ferry commuters will get to see the Penang Bridge and also the skyline of George Town and Butterworth.

However, ship connections of much larger distances (such as over long distances in water bodies like the Mediterranean Sea) may also be called ferry services, especially if they carry vehicles. The busiest seaway in the world, the English Channel, connects Great Britain and mainland Europe. UK ferry services sail mainly to French ports, such as Calais, Boulogne, Dunkerque, Dieppe, Cherbourg-Octeville, Caen, St Malo and Le Havre. Ferries from Great Britain also sail to Belgium, Denmark, the Netherlands, Spain and Ireland. Some ferries carry mainly tourist traffic, but most also carry freight, and some are exclusively for the use of freight lorries. In Britain, car-carrying ferries are sometimes referred to as RORO (roll-on, roll-off) for the ease by which vehicles can board and leave.

Figure 1.38 shows the Brittany Ferries routes on which the vessel Pont-Aven is in service.

Carrying up to 2400 passengers and 650 cars, the Pont-Aven is Brittany Ferries' flagship, and the largest vessel within their fleet. Regularly serving on the Plymouth to Roscoff, Santander and Cork routes, Pont-Aven offers travellers very good crossing times to both France and northern Spain, reaching Santander from Plymouth in just 20½ hours. The ship itself boasts stunning features, including a pool and leisure area, a wrap-around promenade for deck strolls and a dramatic five deck high atrium with panoramic views from the lifts. Dining and associated facilities include an à la carte restaurant, cocktail piano bar and two-storey lounge bar and entertainment area. The Pont-Aven offers passengers a choice of 650 cabins – all of which are en-suite and air conditioned – plus a number of reserved lounge seats. There are also a number of cabins adapted for disabled passengers. Figure 1.39 shows a plan of the ship.

43

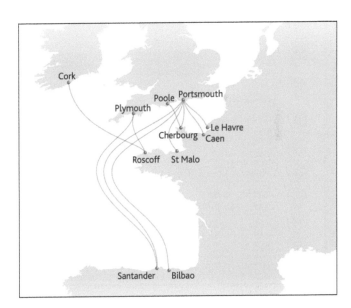

Figure 1.38 Brittany Ferries routes

ACTIVITY 8

Choose an example of an important international ferry route from the local area or elsewhere and also an example of an international cruise currently available for passengers living locally. For each:

- Identify the main service operators.
- Provide details of the vessels used.
- Describe and explain how the products and services available on-board meet passenger needs.

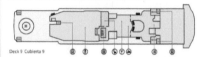
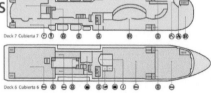
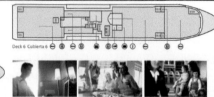

Guide to onboard services
Guía de servicios a bordo

Onboard services Servicios a bordo

Opening times are indicated at the entrance to the appropriate facility. Los horarios de apertura están indicados a la entrada de cada servicio.

 Information Información
Deck/Cubierta 6

Reception and information.Recepción e Información.

 Bureau de change Bureau de change
Deck/Cubierta 6

Change - Using credit/debit cards, travellers cheques or bank notes (we do not accept cheques or coins). Cambio - Usando tarjetas de crédito o débito, cheques de viaje o billetes de banco (no aceptamos cheques o monedas).

Cash withdrawals - Cash withdrawals may be made from the Bureau de Change on board using credit or debit cards. Cash will be provided in the card's native currency. Retirar dinero - Se puede retirar dinero en efectivo en la oficina de cambio a bordo usando tarjetas de credtio o debito. El dinero se facilitará en la misma divisa de la tarjeta.

 Baggage room Consigna   Deck/Cubierta 6

Children's playroom Sala de juegos Infantiles   Deck/Cubierta 7

Baby changing room Vestidor para bebés   Deck/Cubierta 7

'Games Planet' Sala de videojuegos   Deck/Cubierta 9

'Chance Planet' Sala de juegos (máquinas tragaperras)   Deck/Cubierta 8

Cinema Cine   Deck/Cubierta 6

Swimming pool Piscina   Deck/Cubierta 9

Disabled toilets Aseos para minusválidos   Deck/Cubierta 7, 8, 9

Kennels Jaulas   Deck/Cubierta 10

Lifts Ascensores

Sick Bay Enfermeria

Ask at Information Desk.Consulte en el Mostrador de Información.

Accommodation on board Acomodaciones

Your cabin or seat number is indicated on your ticket. The first digit indicates the deck number. En su billete se indica su número de camarote. El primer dígito indica la cubierta en que se encuentra situado.

 Cabins Camarotes   Deck/Cubierta 5, 6, 8

Reclining seats Asientos reclinables   Deck/Cubierta 9

 Commodore lounge Salón Commodor   Deck/Cubierta 8

Reserved for De-Luxe and Commodore Class cabins. Reservado para pasajeros en Camarotes de lujo y clase Commodore.

Eating and drinking Restauración

 Le Flora   Deck/Cubierta 7

A la carte menus, buffet selections and a selection of fine wines.Restaurante: menús a la carta, buffets selectos, carta de vinos.

La Belle Angèle   Deck/Cubierta 7

Self-service restaurant. Restaurante - self-service.

Le Café du Festival   Deck/Cubierta 7

Pastries, cakes and sandwichesSalón de té, snacks dulces y salados.

Le Grand Pavois   Deck/Cubierta 8, 9

Main lounge bar.Bar, animación musical.

Les Finistères   Deck/Cubierta 9

Pool bar. Piscina bar.

Le Fastnet   Deck/Cubierta 7

Piano bar. Piano-bar.

Shopping

 The Shop Monts et Merveilles   Deck/Cubierta 8

Spirits, tobacco, confectionery, toys, perfumes and cosmetics, leather goods, fashion wear, decoration, souvenirs, magazines, books.Alcohol, tobaco, textiles, juguetes, perfumes y cosmética, artículos de piel, moda, decoración, revista, prensa…

Paying for purchases Pagos a bordo

Purchases made on board may be paid for in Euros or Sterling. Payment can be made in cash, by credit or debit card. Prices are shown in both currencies and you can combine different payment methods.Las compras a bordo se pueden pagar en Euros o libras. El pago puede efectuarse en efectivo, con tarjetas de crédito o débito. Los precios se indican en ambas monedas y se pueden combinar distintas formas de pago.

Time La Hora

Time used on board is British time, which is normally one hour behind French time. Arrival and departure times shown on tickets are in local time. La hora oficial a bordo de todos nuestros barcos es la hora inglesa, es decir una hora menos que la española o francesa. Los horarios de salida y llegada que figuran en su billete, muestran siempre la hora local.

Wi-Fi

For information on Wi-Fi internet access please visit Information. Para acceso a Internet WI-FI, rogamos consulte en información.

Figure 1.39 Plan of Pont-Aven ship

44

Rail transport

Rail transport services are important for both international and domestic travel. **National** rail services are offered in many countries, and provide a scheduled and comfortable service. For example, the Shosholoza Meyl long-distance passenger trains in South Africa (shown below in Figure 1.40) are comfortable and cheap, long-distance passenger trains linking Johannesburg with Cape Town, Durban, Port Elizabeth and East London. They're perfectly safe, and one of South Africa's best-kept secrets, highly recommended by travellers. The Cape Town to Johannesburg train passes the same wonderful scenery as the much more expensive, luxury Blue Train, but costs only 690 Rand ($50) including a bed in a two-berth or four-berth sleeper. Durban to Johannesburg is even cheaper. Shosholoza Meyl's Tourist Class trains have modern sleeping-cars and a restaurant car.

Figure 1.40 The Shosholoza Meyl train service in South Africa

Rail travel has certain advantages over air travel for short haul journeys and many types of international traveller will now use the new generation of high-speed trains as a matter of choice. **International** rail services such as the Eurostar (shown in Figure 1.41) now carry more passengers between London and Paris than all of the airlines put together. The Eurostar route is shown in Figure 1.42. Rail travel is also popular with international business and leisure travellers because trains on major inter-city routes have many facilities, ranging from sleeping compartments to restaurant cars and laptop plug-in sockets. There are some very famous forms of rail transport such as The Orient Express.

Business and leisure travellers appreciate the following:

- Rail services run direct from city centre to city centre, resulting in reduced transfer times within the destination and thus more convenience for travellers.
- Major rail terminals are more accessible than airports located on the fringes of cities.
- Check-in and security procedures are much quicker, resulting in less time wasted than at an airport.
- Trains have fewer luggage restrictions, so passengers can more easily take the items they require for a particular trip.

Figure 1.41 Eurostar train stops at platform

The Blue Train travels 1600 km in South Africa between Pretoria and Cape Town and is one of the most luxurious train journeys in the world. It boasts butler service, two lounge cars, an observation car and carriages with gold-tinted picture windows, in soundproofed, fully carpeted compartments, each featuring its own en-suite (many of which are equipped with a full-sized bathtub).

The Maharajas' Express (shown in Figure 1.43) offers five itineraries: 'the Indian Panorama', 'Heritage of India', 'Indian Splendour', 'Treasures of India' and 'Gems of India'. Equipped with all modern amenities, the interiors of the train recreate the elegance and romance of the personal rail carriages used by maharajas of India. Each journey offered by Maharajas Express offers a glimpse into a different aspect of Indian heritage, culture and diversity. The attractions included in the itineraries are various World Heritage sites, tiger reserve, forts and palaces and the spectacular Taj Mahal in Agra. What sets this train apart from other luxury train journeys is a collection of unique insider experiences at several destinations.

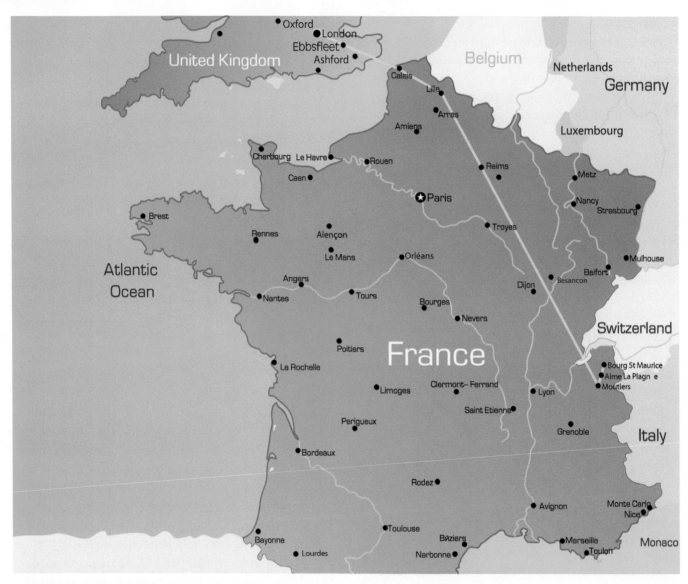

Figure 1.42 Eurostar route

46

Figure 1.43 Maharajas' Express

Road transport

Private motor vehicles can be hired independently through international chains such as Hertz, Thrifty and Avis or by making a reservation through travel agencies. Car hire is popular with independent travellers because it offers convenience and flexibility while away from home. Vehicles can be collected at an airport and returned to another office elsewhere if required. The advantages of hiring a car for leisure travel have made fly-drive holidays popular, particularly when visiting destinations such as Australia, New Zealand and the USA. In some destinations campervans are becoming increasingly popular such as New Zealand and the USA, where they are known as recreational vehicles (RVs). More than 25 million Americans now make use of an RV each year because it offers the advantage of flexibility and independence in providing both transport and accommodation.

International coach travel varies in scale and importance throughout the world. In many LEDC nations these services are very significant because they provide an economical form of transport to populations with a limited purchasing power. Furthermore, local infrastructures are not always well developed and so road transport is often all that is available.

Landlocked countries such as Rwanda in Africa shown in Figure 1.44 have no direct access to the sea and local transport networks are very much road based. Rwanda is linked by road with other countries in East Africa and the majority of the country's imports and exports are made by road.

There are several daily coach services from Rwanda to destinations in East Africa:

- **Jaguar Executive Coaches**, which connects Kigali to Kampala, the Ugandan capital, via Gatuna or via Kayonza and Kagitumba.
- **Regional Coach Services**, which runs services to Kampala (8 hours), Nairobi, Kenya (20 hours) and Dar es Salaam, Tanzania (36 hours), all via the Gatuna border crossing. These buses are usually air-conditioned.
- **Onatracom Express** – a Rwandan government service using quite basic buses, running between Kigali and Kampala.
- **Yahoo Car Express** – a minibus service running between Kigali and Bujumbura, Burundi. This service has been subject to ambush in the past by rebels in Burundi, although the new government claims to have sorted out this problem now.

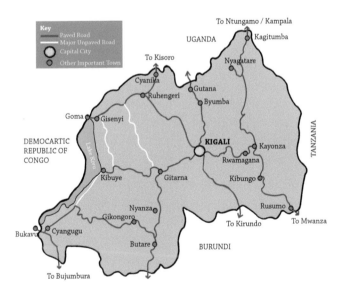

Figure 1.44 Map showing principal routes in Rwanda

In addition the national express share taxi services to Gisenyi and Cyangugu often cross the DRC border to carry passengers to Goma and Bukavu respectively.

Eurolines is a coach organisation, operating international bus routes within Europe and Morocco to over 500 destinations in over 25 countries. The Eurolines network therefore allows people to travel from Sicily to Helsinki and from Casablanca to Moscow. Rather than being a single company, Eurolines is a network of co-operating bus companies from all over Europe, offering integrated ticketing and extensive connections. Due to its decentralised approach, standards of service vary between countries. In the Baltic states, Lux Express, based in Poland and Estonia, travel to several European cities, including St Petersburg and Berlin, and Lasta Beograd, based in Serbia, travel in most of the Baltic region, including Bosnia, Herzegovina and Montenegro. Eurolines is a major method of travel between neighbouring countries. In other parts of Europe, international rail and air travel are more common and Eurolines coaches occupy a niche market of mainly overnight links.

Passes for unlimited travel between 45 main European cities for either 15 or 30 days are available under the name Eurolines Pass. Sea crossings, travel taxes and road tolls are all included in the price. Furthermore, most Eurolines services bring passengers directly to the city centres, so there is no need to pay for expensive transfers.

For all its members, the Eurolines organisation developed common quality standards, meaning that all passengers, wherever they are on the network, are assured the same level of quality and assistance. The Eurolines members use modern coaches with reclining seats, large picture windows, toilet facilities and comfortable legroom. All services are non-smoking.

Eurolines offers those on a budget, such as student backpackers, a good way to get to virtually anywhere in Europe. A Eurolines coach is shown in Figure 1.45. A 40 kg luggage allowance means that backpacks are easily carried. Eurolines allows such passengers to make hostel bookings in Paris through a partnership link with Hostelworld. This makes arranging accommodation easy and convenient. There is a choice of departures and returns to major destinations each day, and some of the best aspects of the service are the ability to book online and the cheap fares that make it affordable for travellers on a limited budget.

Figure 1.45 Luxury coach services

Coach transport takes place in a variety of contexts and travellers may use any of the following, depending on their individual circumstances:

- express coach services for both domestic and international travel
- private hire services
- tours and excursions
- transfers.

Another important coach company is Greyhound, which is the largest provider of intercity bus transportation, serving more than 3800 destinations across North America with a modern, environmentally friendly fleet. It has become a famous American brand, providing safe, enjoyable and affordable long-distance travel to nearly 18 million passengers each year in the United States and Canada. The company also offers a coach chartering service, which provides the convenience of a door-to-door service for group passengers.

Accommodation and catering

All tourists need somewhere to stay while they are away on holiday and most destinations will have a variety of accommodation types to suit a range of visitors. The more popular destinations will have many possibilities ranging from luxury five star hotels which provide guests with many facilities and services (such as restaurants and bars, 24 hour room service, leisure facilities and so on) to camp sites where the visitor is given access to a patch of ground on which to pitch a tent.

Hotels

We have already seen the broad range of hotels and the range of facilities offered according to their star rating earlier in this chapter. Most of the hotels used by international travellers have rooms with en-suite bathrooms and other features usually include a telephone, an alarm clock, a television and broadband internet connectivity. Food and drink may be supplied by a mini-bar (which often includes a small refrigerator) containing snacks and drinks (to be paid for on departure) and tea- and coffee-making facilities. The cost and quality of hotels are usually indicative of the range and type of services available. Due to the enormous increase in tourist demand standards have improved considerably. Let's now look at the range of accommodation available in one destination.

For example, Cape Town in South Africa has many **guest houses** and **lodges** that are an ideal alternative to staying at the more expensive hotels in the area. Meals besides breakfast are often available (dinner and/or lunch) usually on request. Many of the services offered at hotels can be expected, such as airport transfers, wake up calls and laundry service. **Bed and Breakfast** (B&B) establishments are usually less expensive than hotels and often offer the same standard of accommodation. Staying at a B&B gives visitors the opportunity to live as a local and enjoy the advice of their hosts, as these establishments are usually owner-managed. Cape Town also has a large number of **hostels**, which offer backpackers budget accommodation as a clean, comfortable, stylish place to stay for a great price.

Other accommodation options include camp sites. In Cape Town the notion of glamorous camping ('Glamping') has taken off and AfriCamps offer a range of boutique camp sites allowing guests to be close to nature, enjoying the outdoors with family and friends, whilst escaping technology and city life. Each AfriCamps site comprises five luxury tents, accommodating five people each. While the tents are strategically positioned to assure complete privacy for each unit, there are also communal gathering areas. This makes the camp sites ideal for large gatherings of friends and family.

Families often prefer the flexibility offered by **self-catering** accommodation, so that they are not bound by restaurant meal times, and have more space than hotel rooms offer. Self-catering accommodation provides a home-from-home experience. Cape Town also provides a range of self-catering accommodation, including cottages, villas and apartments. As the name suggests, guests must cater for themselves, as no meals are provided, but there will be a kitchen and all of the necessary equipment for cooking.

Jatinga Country Lodge and Restaurant, South Africa

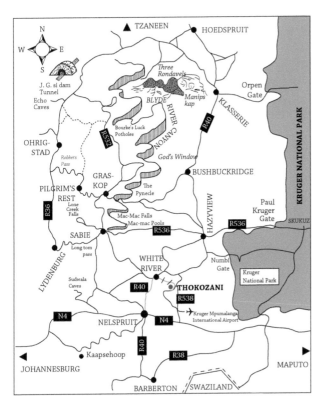

Figure 1.46 Location of Jatinga Country Lodge and Restaurant

Figure 1.46 shows the location of Jatinga Country Lodge and Restaurant. It is an easy 3½-hour drive from Johannesburg and only 4.5 km from Kruger Mpumalanga International Airport, making it easily accessible to both road and air travellers. Daily scheduled flights into KMI Airport are available. Originally established and operated as a hunting lodge, Jatinga's main building dates back to the 1920s. While extensive renovations were undertaken in 2001, when new owners bought the Lodge, the style and ambience of the original homestead has been retained.

The property offers guests the choice of 13 superior rooms and four luxury suites (one being their romantic honeymoon suite), all of which have been tastefully furnished in different styles – Colonial, Victorian, Provençal, French Country, African Colonial and English Country – and provide guests with luxurious comfort and secluded privacy. The six orchard and forest rooms form a little village on their own and, as their names suggest, some have a view over a citrus orchard while the others look into the pine forest. While different rooms offer guests different experiences, like outdoor showers, open fireplaces or half tonne concrete baths, each offers

the same standard of luxurious comfort and space. Private patios are part of the experience with the luxury suites offering a separate lounge. All rooms have:

- a mini bar available on request
- tea and coffee making facilities with fresh home baked biscuits
- limited room service menu
- air conditioner
- satellite TV
- telephone
- laundry service
- hair dryer
- bath robes
- complimentary amenities.

Figure 1.47 indicates that the Lodge is a very popular venue for weddings. Jatinga is undoubtedly one of the most romantic venues in the Lowveld for weddings and couples are offered a tailor-made wedding package service that will meet all their needs. The Lodge's management and banqueting team are available to couples throughout the planning stages and will set up appointments to meet with the individual suppliers and obtain relevant quotes for: flowers, hairdresser and beauty treatments, photographer, wedding cakes, music and the like. Jatinga's honeymoon suite provides a completely open-plan experience; an impressive four-poster bed has pride of place in the suite that has the most romantic of furnishings and fabrics. A private garden with a splash pool and outdoor shower ensures complete and total privacy for newlyweds. Furthermore, couples that book their wedding at Jatinga are offered this suite with the management's compliments.

Figure 1.47 Wedding facilities at the Lodge

49

Many of the Lodge's facilities can be used for business functions as well as for weddings. The restaurant can be used for private functions and there is a conference room within the grounds. This has fold-away doors along one wall opening onto a private garden with a view of a pecan orchard in the distance. The location and setting of the room creates a quiet and calm atmosphere that lends itself to serious business meetings. Depending on the seating configuration required, the room can comfortably seat up to 75 delegates.

The area's temperate climate often means that business and leisure guests may want to organise an outdoor function making use of Jatinga's gardens or the open air flagstone area. An elegant marquee can be set up in the gardens or, depending on numbers and the weather, on the elevated wooden deck, overlooking the White River. This offers a venue with a difference for a smaller, more intimate function. The elevated deck is a stunning setting for guests to enjoy pre-reception drinks and canapes.

There are many different activities that can be arranged both at the Lodge and off site. Not-too-strenuous river walks along the White River can be enjoyed at the Lodge. For guests seeking adventure activities there are plenty available in the surrounding area, ranging from bungee jumping to river rafting, quad biking, horse riding and other extreme sports. Big 5 game viewing trips into the Kruger National Park are also available see Figure 1.48.

Figure 1.48 View of Kruger National Park scenery

Food and beverage outlets

The availability of food and beverage facilities should not simply be regarded as being a basic tourist need. Although catering facilities are important, in some destinations they can be classified as tourist attractions in themselves. For example, in many cities, there are cafés and wine bars which are particularly attractive to tourists because of their historical value, menu and special atmosphere. Many visitors can be described as being 'culinary or food' tourists as they want to experience the food of the country, region or area.

According to a recent survey released by the Travel Industry Association of America and the National Restaurant Association, food is central to deciding vacation destinations for at least 25% of leisure travellers. The survey found that 58% of American leisure travellers are somewhat/very interested in taking a trip to engage in culinary or wine-related activities. The International Culinary Tourism Association points out that culinary tourism is about how to best develop and market a new kind of visitor attraction – unique and memorable food and drink experiences.

Tourists in most destinations can choose between fast food and street food outlets or can visit a themed restaurant, an ethnic restaurant or a fine dining restaurant, depending on their taste, budget and need for convenience. **Fast food** is cooked in bulk in readiness of a customer's order. It is not cooked to order. The main characteristic of this type of food and beverage outlet as the name suggests is the speed in which customers are served. Examples include KFC, McDonalds and Burger King. **Street food** tends to be cheap and is sold from a kiosk, stall, food truck or a push cart. A **themed restaurant** is usually based around a specific concept and the food is almost secondary to the décor and general ambience. Hard Rock Café is an example of a themed restaurant. **Ethnic restaurants** serve food that reflects a particular culture. The staff often wear uniforms that reflect this culture too. Examples may include Thai, Indian and Mexican restaurants. A **fine dining restaurant** is often found in a luxury hotel and is grand and stylish. The service at such a restaurant is likely to be silver service and there may be a formal menu. Prices here tend to be high. There will also be coffee shops and cafés where customers can buy refreshments in a destination.

Tour operations and travel agencies

Tour operators and holiday representatives

The chain of distribution indicates that tour operators can be regarded as product builders. Operators can produce a new product by combining or packaging the basic products or components offered by primary suppliers. The most common example of a tour operator's product would be a flight on a charter airline, a transfer from the airport to a hotel for a certain length of time and the services of a local representative, all for the one inclusive price. Tour operators negotiate with the providers and buy in bulk. For example they will book a certain number of rooms for the whole season in a hotel and will purchase in bulk a number of seats on a charter flight one day a week from the same airport flying to the destination where the hotel is located. The tour operator will then 'break bulk' by packaging these components and selling as a complete holiday package. Many tourists find buying a package holiday a very convenient, economical and secure way to travel because the components have been brought together at a lower price than if they were bought separately.

In order for tour operators to be able to stay in business and remain profitable it is important that they are able to identify and then meet consumers' needs, requests and expectations. To help them boost sales, operators promote their various products using leaflets, maps, brochures, video and CDs. New technologies such as Computerised Reservation Systems/Global Distribution Systems (CRS/GDS) are utilised to maximise distribution effectiveness.

The package holiday market is dominated by a comparatively small number of international tour operators such as Tui, Thomas Cook and more recent arrivals such as Emirates Holidays. The main trends in the industry are economies of scale, horizontal and vertical

integration. Through these strategies, tour operators can achieve considerable buying power and control over their suppliers, as well as the distribution of their products.

Horizontal integration refers to the situation where two or more companies join together with the intention of removing competition, increasing profitability through economies of scale or to increase the organisation's overall purchasing power. Horizontal integration thus involves mergers at the same level in the tourism distribution or supply chain such as the merger of different tour operating companies.

Vertical integration implies the take-over or formation of businesses at different levels of the supply or distribution chain. In terms of tour operators, this may involve:

- backward integration involving investing in suppliers of accommodation and transport
- forward integration involving investment in, for example, travel agents.

The main advantages to tour operators of doing this are having more control over supplies in terms of quality, availability, access and price and having an increased ability to reach consumers. Vertical integration has drastically increased in recent years and the largest tour operators all own charter airlines, accommodation, ground-handlers and travel agents.

There are many different types of tour operator around the world. Many operators specialise in specific destinations or in particular activities such as skiing. Other tour operators target specific segments of the market such as by age, appealing to seniors or young people, or by lifestyle such as ecotourism packages for the responsible tourist. Figure 1.49 shows Kuoni Travel, a UK-base travel and tour operator specialising in luxury travel.

Figure 1.49 Kuoni travel and tour operator

51

- Inbound tour operators: produce packages aimed specifically at overseas visitors coming into a destination.
- Outbound tour operators: are based in the tourist's home country and offer package holidays to destinations overseas.
- Domestic tour operators: specialise in putting packages together for the home market so they appeal to people living in that country. Figure 1.50 shows a typical image used in brochures for the UK domestic market.
- Specialist tour operators: tend to limit their products by destination, by activity, by theme, by transport, or by age group.

Tour operators employ representatives who work in the destination to welcome customers and help them transfer from the airport to their accommodation. The resort representative will offer advice and recommend activities and excursions within the destination. Some representatives will be employed specifically to look after children and to put on a range of activities for families.

Figure 1.50 Catering in a hotel with a lovely view

ACTIVITY 9

To help you appreciate the variety of tour operator products currently being offered to international leisure travellers, compare three types of holiday product that are available from your local area. Research an example of each of the following:

- a typical short haul family package holiday
- a long haul all-inclusive holiday
- an independent long haul trip including return flight, accommodation for ten nights in two locations and car hire.

Provide named details of what each will involve, the relative costs and come to a conclusion as to which offers the best value for money. Furthermore you can also try and explain how your chosen holiday products are meeting the needs of particular types of traveller, as indicated in Table 1.8.

Remember that travel will be from your local area to destinations of your choice for each of the three categories.

Customer type	Needs and expectations
younger child	Seaside or inland resort with facilities for young children. Entirely dependent on parent or guardian for choice.
teenager	Resort-based holidays with entertainment, nightlife and activities are usual requirements but still dependent on parent(s). If part of a group, will want semi-independent activity holidays.
young adult	Taking holidays dependent on time and resources, ranging from 'sunlust' to activity-based. High on adventure, backpacking and experiences.
younger couples	Busy lifestyles mean time is barrier to travel so shorter breaks popular to fit in with dual careers.
family groups	Seek family-centred holidays during school holidays. Will often engage in additional VFR trips at other times of year.
mature couples – 'empty nesters'	Wide ranging but higher disposable income to take more expensive 'explorer' holidays and second breaks.
retired – 'grey market'	One person or one partner retired; income fixed but more time available. As age increases seeking more passive holidays.

Table 1.8

Travel agencies

Travel agencies act as intermediaries providing information about destinations, tour packages and various ancillary travel services. They enable clients to access this information and make travel arrangements on behalf of their customers. Figure 1.51 shows the position of travel agencies within the chain of distribution.

Travel agencies act as agents for a variety of principals who are the suppliers of travel products. The travel agencies therefore sell on behalf of airlines, rail companies, hotels, tour operators, car-hire companies and currency suppliers. There are also specialised business travel agents who provide services for the business traveller in terms of timely and flexible travel arrangements with scheduled airlines and accommodation bookings with large international hotel chains.

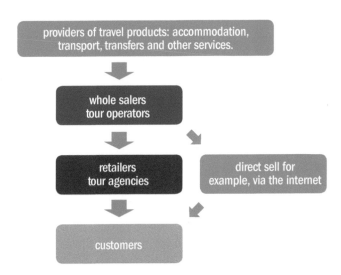

Figure 1.51 Chain of distribution

Figure 1.52 An independent travel agent in Phuket, Thailand

Travel agencies vary in their size and scale of operation. 'Multiples' are agencies that have branches throughout a country and, as in the case of an international travel agency chain, often in countries overseas. It is also possible to find smaller independent travel agents, called 'miniples', which are not part of a national chain, as shown in Figure 1.52. These are smaller scale operations, usually having only one retail outlet.

The role of travel agencies within the chain of distribution is under threat as many consumers now make their own arrangements using the internet. Online reservations systems allow customers to by-pass traditional intermediaries and deal directly with primary suppliers to obtain information and make reservations.

Visitor attractions

Most leisure travellers are motivated to visit a destination because there are certain attractions that appeal to their individual preferences and these may include opportunities for relaxation, amusement, entertainment and education. These visitor attractions are an extremely important part of the tourism industry and are the driving force behind much of the development that has taken place in a variety of destinations. Without attractions there would be no need for many other tourism services.

Tourist attractions can be classified according to whether they are **natural attractions** or **built attractions**. Natural attractions include national parks, coral reefs, wildlife reserves, mountains, forests, coastline, lakes/waterways and particular landscape features such as caves, waterfalls and volcanoes. Built attractions are considerably more varied and include zoos, aquariums, theme parks, museums, heritage centres, sports facilities, family entertainment centres, cinemas, cultural attractions, historic sites such as castles and shopping centres.

Most popular tourist destinations contain a range of visitor attractions. Every attraction, regardless of its size and scale of operation, will attempt to appeal to as many visitors as possible in order to maximise profits and to generate funding to support further its development. In this way, attractions will over time introduce new facilities in an attempt to remain profitably in business.

In 2011 over 130 million people visited theme parks and the world's most popular was Disney World Magic Kingdom in Florida with 16 972 000 visitors. In terms of natural attractions, Niagara Falls attracted over 22 million visitors in 2011 and is the world's most popular landscape feature. The world's top ten heritage attractions in 2011 are shown in Table 1.9.

Heritage visitor attraction	Visitors in 2011
Union Station in Washington DC, USA	37 000 000
Grand Central Terminal, New York, USA	21 600 000
Notre Dame Cathedral, Paris, France	13 650 000
Forbidden City, Beijing, China	12 830 000
Sacré Coeur Basilica, Paris, France	10 500 000
Great Wall of China	9 000 000
Musée Du Louvre, Paris	8 500 000
Sydney Opera House, Sydney, Australia	7 400 000
Eiffel Tower, Paris, France	6 700 000
Lincoln Memorial, Washington DC, USA	6 042 315

Table 1.9 World's top ten heritage attractions (2011)

Larger heritage attractions usually meet the needs of overseas visitors in a variety of ways. The visitor can obtain information in advance by visiting the attraction's website and can often pre-book their visit to avoid delays. On arrival, leaflets and books are usually available, some in foreign languages. Figure 1.53 would be of interest to a tourist who is researching in advance.

Similarly, guided tours will often have a multi-lingual guide and/or audio technology which offers a commentary in a choice of languages for the convenience of overseas visitors. Some attractions have a visitor centre with interactive displays which have a choice of languages and this is clearly a very appropriate way to provide services to foreign visitors.

ACTIVITY 10

To help you understand the appeal of visitor attractions to both international and domestic tourists you can undertake some personal investigative research in your local area or a destination of your choice. Using information obtained from the local tourist board, identify the main visitor attractions that the area has to offer. Put them into categories such as:

- museums
- art galleries
- sporting venues
- theatres and places of entertainment
- religious buildings.

You can then research visitor numbers for a selection of the attractions that you have identified and placed in particular categories. Data for a number of years may be available from published reports on the internet and this will allow you to assess the relative importance of key attractions found in your chosen destination.

Ancillary service providers

Ancillary services are the 'extras' you might need for your holiday, not already included in a holiday package, such as:

- travel insurance
- park/event tickets
- car hire
- airport parking
- foreign exchange
- tour guide.

These types of services can be provided by a number of different travel and tourism organisations as an additional service. Travel agents, hotels and airlines may offer some or all of these services for an additional fee. It is a way for the organisations to generate additional income.

Currency exchange

This allows customers to exchange one currency for another. There are specific businesses, called Bureaux de Change, which specialise only in offering this service, or tourists may exchange their money via the travel agent before they travel or at the hotel once they arrive. Those offering currency exchange profit from its services either through adjusting the exchange rate or taking a commission. Traditionally people were encouraged to use travellers' cheques as the most secure form of exchanging money abroad. However nowadays, people do not always need to use exchange services as it is possible to withdraw money in the foreign currency from ATMs in the destination using a debit or credit card. Many people will also pay directly with a credit card; even many taxi businesses will accept payment this way.

Car hire

We have talked briefly about car hire already in this chapter under road transport. Reserving a hire car can be done via the travel agent, via some hotels or online. Many tourists like to make sure they have booked their hire car before travelling for speed and convenience on arrival in the destination. This guarantees that the car will be waiting at their chosen pick up point and that the visitor can choose the size of vehicle before they pick it up. Families may also wish to hire child car seats for convenience, as these can be very bulky to travel with.

5 NIAGARA FALLS

22,500,000
ANNUAL VISITORS

PEAK SEASON
JUN-AUG

Covering its passengers in the dense mist of the falls, the maid of the Mist ferry service has been running since 1846. you will face larger crowds in the peak season but will be greeted by warmer weather.

4 UNION STATION, WASHINGTON D.C.

32,850,000
ANNUAL VISITORS

PEAK SEASON
MAR-JUN
SEPT-NOV

After basking in the wonder of the architecture, why not partake in one of the many city tours based at the station?

2 TIMES SQUARE, NEW YORK CITY

39,200,000
ANNUAL VISITORS

PEAK SEASON
JAN-MAR
JUN-AUG

A treasure-trove of LED lighting and attractions. Go on a walking tour first, or do some research at home, so that you can choose between the abundance of theatre, music and comedy shows.

3 CENTRAL PARK, NEW YORK CITY

37,500,000
ANNUAL VISITORS

PEAK SEASON
JAN-MAR
JUN-AUG

Attend a concert or play in the summer, or don your blades in the winter for a spot of ice skating on either the wollman or Laser rinks.

1 LAS VEGAS STRIP

39,668,221
ANNUAL VISITORS

PEAK SEASON
US HOLIDAYS

A treasure-trove of LED lighting and attractions. Go on a walking tour first, or do some research at home, so that you can choose between the abundance of theatre, music and comedy shows.

Figure 1.53 The 50 most popular visitor attractions in the world in 2014

Tourist information and guiding services

There are now many different sources of tourist information; tour operators and travel agents will provide some basic information about the main attractions and activities on offer within the destination, in order to help customers make an appropriate choice of where to travel. The internet also provides a broad range of additional information sources. However, many tourists still rely on a destination's Tourist Information Centre as an important source of information.

Figure 1.54 A tourist information centre in Japan

Tourist Information Centres (TICs), like the one shown in Figure 1.54, provide a range of services to meet theV needs of visitors. They offer visiting tourists a wide range of information about the local area and can provide copies of promotional leaflets, brochures, guide books and other material relating to the destination. TICs are usually found at locations where visiting tourists can easily find them,

such as airports, railway stations or at central locations within major tourist areas. Many visitors will use a TIC to help them find and book suitable accommodation. TICs are also used as an outlet for the booking of local sightseeing tours and they can also provide information about local guides. Larger TICs sell souvenirs and merchandise relating to the local area.

Many tourists visiting destinations for the first time may wish to employ the services of a **tour guide** for some of their time in the destination. A tour guide is an expert on the history of the location and will offer their tour groups interesting or enlightening information about points of interest at nature attractions, historic sites, museums, scenic locations and other attractions. Guides may give walking tours, bus tours or even lead river tours on a boat. In addition, guides answer visitors' questions and keep the tour organised, efficient and safe. Using guiding services will offer visitors peace of mind, especially in destinations with a strong cultural identity that differs from the visitors' own or in places where there is an element of danger, for example, a nature reserve where it would be easy for the unfamiliar tourist to get lost. Guiding services can be booked via the tour operator or travel agent at the time of booking the holiday, or may be booked independently online. Tourist Information Centres will be able to recommend a local guide once in the destination.

ACTIVITY 11

Visit your local Tourist Information Centre and investigate the variety of products and services that are offered to tourists.

Summary

We have seen how all aspects of the travel and tourism industry overlap and interrelate in creating the overall visitor experience. The component subsectors all depend on each other. All component subsectors will have some form of relationship with most of the other destination features. For example, the development of a new tourist attraction at a destination will have an effect on transport, the demand for accommodation and catering facilities, tour operators may want to organise tours to the new attraction and the local or regional tourism board will help to promote it.

For this section, you should be able to:

- give relevant examples of the current structure of the industry
- explain key organisations that make up the structure and their products, services, values and objectives
- analyse information and data relating to the structure of travel and tourism
- make appropriate judgements about the relationships between organisations within the industry.

Exam-style questions

Question 1

a   Explain, using examples, the difference between mass tourism and specialised tourism. **[4 marks]**

b   Analyse the relationship between the reasons why people travel and the types of destinations they visit. **[6 marks]**

c   Evaluate why LEDCs often find it difficult to attract tourists. **[9 marks]**

Question 2

The Seychelles islands are becoming an increasingly popular tourist destination after a 15% increase in arrivals was recorded between January and April 2015, when compared with the same period the previous year.

During 2014, the number of visitors who came to the Indian Ocean archipelago of 115 islands were almost the same compared with 2013, recording only a 1% increase. However, 2015 seems likely to have been a good year for the Seychelles tourism industry.

According to the National Bureau of Statistics (NBS), the months of March and April of 2015 recorded the highest number of visitors since January 2009 with 25 129 and 25 038 visitor arrivals respectively; a very promising figure for the small island state with a population of 90 000.

Tourism is the main pillar of the Seychelles economy. The island nation, which is situated in the Indian Ocean, east of the African Coast and northeast of Madagascar, is known for its white-sand beaches, turquoise sea water and its unique, well-preserved environment.

http://www.seychellesnewsagency.com

Refer to the information about tourism in the Seychelles.

a   Describe **two** reasons for the appeal of the Seychelles as a destination. **[4 marks]**

b   Analyse the data relating to tourist arrivals for the Seychelles and explain why these figures are important for the destination. **[6 marks]**

c   Discuss how ecological factors such as climate change might affect the future of tourism for an island destination such as the Seychelles. **[9 marks]**

Question 3

Zimbabwe can potentially generate $5 billion annually in tourism revenue if it can revamp its tourism infrastructure and regain its image as a prime tourism destination. Zimbabwe's Tourism and Hospitality Industry Minister has identified tourism infrastructure development as key to plans to revitalise the country's economy.

The government has embarked on upgrading the country's major roads and recognises that Zimbabwe needs an open policy on the country's skies and borders so as to attract more tourists. Experts have projected the growth of low-cost airlines in the country could help spur the growth of the tourism sector as connectivity improves and the cost of travelling becomes more affordable.

Some low-cost airlines are already operating in the country, such as Fly Africa and Fastjet, while authorities have also relaxed the visa requirements for visitors from emerging economies in a bid to increase arrivals.

The expansion of the Victoria Falls International Airport is also envisaged to improve the airport's handling capacity. It includes the expansion of the existing runway as well as construction of a new runway, construction of a new terminal building and improvements to car parking and the road network.

Zimbabwe has many natural and cultural heritage attractions and a wide range of accommodation options.

Adapted from an article on Mail & Guardian Africa http://mgafrica.com

a   Describe **three** ways Zimbabwe is making itself a more accessible destination. **[6 marks]**

b   Explain **two** reasons why governments encourage tourism development within a country. **[6 marks]**

c   Discuss the contribution that different subsectors of the travel and tourism industry make to the overall tourism experience. **[9 marks]**

Chapter 2
Principles of customer service

In this section of the syllabus you will learn about:

- the principles of customer service
- external and internal customers and their needs
- the impacts of quality customer service.

Introduction

The travel and tourism industry is highly competitive because a large number of organisations provide very similar products and services. It is often the quality of customer service that distinguishes one organisation from another. Customers expect the highest standards of customer service and this is why it is essential for staff to be aware of the part they play in satisfying this important customer need. Excellent customer service means consistently exceeding expectations of customers rather than just meeting them.

Furthermore, it needs to be recognised that the provision of excellent customer service is everyone's responsibility within an organisation. By its very nature, any organisation which deals with customers, offering products and services, adopts a customer focus.

KEY CONCEPTS

Customer focus

Travel and tourism organisations are unique because they do not really sell tangible products; instead they are selling an experience. Adopting a customer focus, i.e. putting the customer at the centre of everything you do, is essential for travel and tourism providers as this is what contributes to the overall customer experience and is what differentiates one provider from another.

KEY TERM

Customer service: the assistance and advice provided by an organisation to those people who buy or use its products or services.

The term **customer service** is now applied to any aspect of an organisation's dealings with its various customers.

In travel and tourism, there can be many complex relationships taking place under the umbrella of a single purchase and to illustrate this point we can examine what happens when an individual consumer pays for a holiday.

A holiday in Dubai, for example, involves the following:

- initial contact with a travel agent when planning or booking the trip
- dealing with airport staff and flight cabin crew during the journey
- using the services of the hotel staff and its facilities of the hotel staff during the stay
- seeking the help and advice of the resort representative.

A poor standard of service by any of these various employees would lower the value and satisfaction of the holiday product in the mind of the consumer.

Travel and tourism is very much a 'people' business and when a service or product is purchased, it invariably involves dealing with people. In the consumer's eyes, the quality of the customer service provision will be measured by the attitude of staff, such as the airport check-in employees, cabin crew, hotel receptionist, waiting staff and room attendants. Figure 2.1 shows the reception and lobby of Burj Al Arab hotel, Dubai. An enthusiastic team of workers will add enjoyment to the holiday experience while an irate or miserable member of staff may spoil the whole thing and prompt a series of customer complaints. It is of little surprise, therefore, that providing high quality customer service has become so important to the industry. This has become particularly so when products and prices are similar, making customer service one of the factors that will differentiate a good experience from a not so good or even a bad experience.

Figure 2.1 Reception and lobby of Burj Al Arab hotel, Dubai

2.1 Customers and their needs

When it comes to service, what customers want and expect are often different. In fact extensive research into this topic has been conducted and the following key dimensions of service have been identified:

- reliability: the ability to perform the promised service dependably and accurately
- responsiveness: the willingness to help customers and provide prompt service
- assurance: the knowledge and courtesy of employees and their ability to convey trust and confidence in dealing with a request
- empathy: the caring, individualised attention provided to the customer.

KEY TERMS

Customer: anyone who has the right to ask or expect an employee to provide a service as part of their job role. For most employees within travel, tourism and hospitality organisations, this means that they will have to deal with two types of customers at work: **external** and **internal customers**.

External customers are an organisation's visitors or users. They can be classified or segmented in many ways, such as:

- individuals
- groups, including different age or cultural groups, educational groups and special interest groups
- families
- foreign visitors with language and cultural differences
- people with specific needs: for example people with mobility and access difficulties, people with sensory disabilities; visitors with special dietary requirements.

External customers generally contact or visit an organisation because it can provide something they need. Some businesses have a wide variety of customers because most people need or use their goods or services, such as a public transport terminal, an airport or an entertainment complex. Others provide products or services which are of interest only to certain types of people. A conference centre concentrates on business delegates, whereas a farmhouse bed and breakfast focuses more on the needs of the independent leisure traveller. Some companies also supply to specific groups: for example, Saga only provides its travel, insurance and other services to people over the age of 50 whereas Club 18–30 targets a different group. In this situation it is easier to focus on the needs of the customer because they are more clearly defined.

2.2 Meeting external customer needs

While not initially developed with tourism in mind, Maslow's hierarchy of needs is used extensively in tourism literature to describe the needs and experiences of travellers and their host communities. Developed in 1954 to describe post World War II culture, Maslow purported that there was a particular range of personal needs that had to be met in order for people to live and prosper. He presented this as a hierarchical pyramid, as shown in Figure 2.2, maintaining that the lower level needs had to be met before a person (or society) could 'progress' to the higher levels.

Figure 2.2 Maslow's hierarchy of human needs

At its base are the basic physiological needs such as food, water, air and shelter, followed by the safety and security needs of protection, order and stability on the next level. Once these two levels are met, people need to fill certain social needs that include affection, friendship and belonging. Maslow identified two 'higher order' needs, namely ego needs that include the desire for prestige, success and self-respect, while at the apex of the pyramid are those seeking self-actualisation or self-fulfilment.

In the 1950s, it may have been considered frivolous to apply Maslow's hierarchy to tourism, yet it can relate not only to the ways that certain people travel, but can also provide some insight into their motivations and behaviour in undertaking a particular trip. For example, travelling often entails the traveller not having his/her primary needs of shelter and safety immediately met. By arriving at a destination with nowhere to stay and little understanding of safety structures, a traveller may feel anxious and upset, requiring those needs to be satisfied immediately. Once accommodation, food and safety are met, the traveller can now consider socialising and ultimately move through to the other levels. Some have criticised the model, claiming that not all of one level needs to be met for a person to reach another level; that is, each level is not mutually exclusive. However, when considered in terms of travel and tourism, such a hierarchy does explain, to some extent, the continued success and appeal of guided tours and all-inclusive travel such as cruises.

We can now consider some other travel and tourism applications of Maslow's ideas. Table 2.1 shows some of the ways in which Maslow's various levels relate to tourist needs and expectations.

Many organisations attempt to segment their external customers by age. This is quite understandable because there are significant differences between the generations and some of the key variations are shown next.

KEY TERMS

Segmentation: to divide the marketplace into parts, or segments, which are definable, accessible, actionable and profitable and have a growth potential. (See also section 3.5.) It is the process of dividing a broad target market into smaller subsets of customers, or tourist generating markets that have, or are perceived to have, common needs, interests and spending power, and then designing and implementing strategies to target them.

Figure 2.3 Retail outlets inside an airport

Maslow level	Tourist needs
physiological	• tour packages offering frequent rest stops • easy access to food outlets in theme parks • accommodation strategically located.
safety and security	• reservation service at government-approved agencies or locations • cruise ships providing doctors and medical facilities • tour guide services in exotic or unfamiliar locations.
docial/belonging	• group tours with people having similar interests and/or backgrounds • group recognition gained by membership in frequent-user programmes provided by organisations such as airlines and hotels • trips to explore one's ancestral roots.
esteem	• elite status (gold card or similar) in frequent-user programmes provided by organisations such as airlines • incentive travel awards for superior company performance • flowers, champagne and other rewards provided to guests in recognition.
self-actualisation	• educational tours and cruises • theme parks providing educational opportunities and glimpses of other cultures • learning the language and studying the culture of another country prior to travel.

Table 2.1 Maslow's hierarchy of human needs related to tourist needs

Figure 2.4 Entertainment complexes have a wide variety of customers

Baby boomers (born 1944–1960): 'getting older, thinking younger':

- like being treated as individuals, not as a group as most prefer personalised treatment
- emphasis on health and fitness
- affluent, brand loyal, more comfortable with traditional purchasing methods
- need good lighting, large clear text on written materials
- need ease of movement around the building.

Generation Xs (born 1960–1980): this group are technologically competent, independent and flexible:

- like efficiency and directness
- often require answers to a barrage of questions
- This group tends to be sceptical of the overselling of tourism products.

Generation Ys (born 1980–2000): this group is sociable, goal-orientated and highly familiar with digital media:

- this group likes quick solutions – not long explanations
- dislikes being talked down to – they may be young but they know what they want.

Research has confirmed that tourist requirements tend to vary according to the different stages of the family lifecycle. Table 2.2 indicates the characteristics associated with each stage.

However, each individual, regardless of their lifecycle stage, can have particular needs, requirements and related expectations. Let us now have a look at how some of these can be met by particular travel, tourism and hospitality organisations.

Many tourism-related businesses have specific methods for quickly identifying external customer needs. Restaurants display a menu at the door or window so that passers-by can see what is on offer and whether it will meet their particular needs. Many tour operators issue brochures and employ staff with detailed product knowledge to answer queries. Shops rely on large signs and distinctive product displays so that customers can find items easily. Floor staff can answer basic queries and specific customer service staff are employed to deal with more complicated issues. Learning how to establish and confirm a customer's needs quickly and accurately is important and is far more likely to result in a satisfied customer.

Lifecycle stage	Characteristics	Tourist behaviour
Early childhood	Entirely dependent on parent or guardian. Traditional sea and sand holidays.	Seeking seaside or inland resorts with facilities for young children.
Early teenage	More influence on decision-making but still dependent on parent(s).	Resort-based holidays with entertainment, nightlife and activities. Some use of youth hostels and semi-independent activity holidays. Group-based holidays.
Young person	Young, single and often not living at home.	Taking holidays dependent on time and resources. Many options available, ranging from 'sunlust' to activity-based. High on adventure, backpacking and experiences.
Partnership stage	Couples living together with busy lifestyles. Time is a major barrier to travel.	Wide ranging with more short breaks to fit it with dual careers.
Family stage – early	Financial and school constraints are important factors. The trend is to seek family-centred holidays. Includes single parents and separated partners.	Key interest in a main holiday and for visiting friends and relatives at other times.
Family stage – late	Still major restraints regarding education (cost and term dates). Holiday-taking patterns start to break up.	Mix of holidays and children seeking semi-independence.
Empty nest	Children leave home and parent(s) have increased freedom and spending power.	Wide ranging but higher disposable income to take more expensive 'explorer' holidays and second breaks.
Retired	One person or one partner retired; income fixed but more time available.	Continued search for quality. As age increases seeking more passive holidays. Old age no longer a barrier to travel.

Table 2.2 Tourist family lifecycle

Most international travellers will visit a Tourist Information Centre (TIC) at some stage during a holiday trip to a particular destination. Generally, good customer service for these visitors will involve being helpful, friendly and beneficial in some way. Thus, the delivery of appropriate customer service requires listening carefully to what visitors want and then responding appropriately to their needs and interests.

KEY CONCEPTS

Customer focus:

Staff at a Tourist Information Centre are totally customer focused. Their role is to use effective questioning techniques to establish the specific information needs of each visitor and to them use appropriate information sources to fulfil these needs.

ACTIVITY 1

What information would you need if visiting an unfamiliar area and how you would like to be treated? Think about how you would approach the attending to visitors if you were in charge of a Tourist Information Centre.

Would you:

- greet people as they enter?
- introduce yourself?
- be polite, friendly and professional at all times?
- treat all visitors with respect and courtesy?
- listen closely to what visitors are saying?

These are all key aspects of good customer service that help to create a positive first impression of you, the centre and the local destination.

Visitors are a diverse group of individuals with a wide range of interests and preferences. Clearly, anticipating and meeting their needs is not always going to be easy. Reflecting on the people who are likely to come into a TIC, they will tend to be a mixture of:

- families, singles and couples, some with particular disabilities
- older, middle-aged and young
- backpackers, campers, or five star hotel clients

- from local areas or overseas destinations
- those interested in nature, nightlife, shopping or cultural experiences.

The chances are that you would meet all of these types of customers, and possibly even all on the same day. Essentially, the only way to ensure you meet every visitor's needs is to ask direct questions about their preferences, listen closely to their responses, then provide them with a range of relevant tourism options from which to choose.

The needs of external customers are likely to include:

- travel and tourism products and services that meet specific needs of customers, for example a low cost flight between Amritsar and Delhi; a hotel that offers family rooms in Thailand.
- ancillary products and services, for example car hire upon arrival in Tenerife; theme park tickets for a full day's excursion during a four day stay in Singapore.
- information and advice, such as information about obtaining a business visa for a visit to Sri Lanka; advice for booking a tour guide in Florida.
- assistance, including help with making a Mediterranean cruise booking; meet and greet arrangements at Harare International Airport
- resolving customer problems and complaints, for example, the bedside light does not work in the customer's hotel room; the food served to the customer is not properly cooked.

Many sources of complaints can be avoided. For example, when hotel reservations are being made, there should be an easy and efficient booking service that includes the following:

- Prospective clients are told clearly what is included in the prices quoted for accommodation, meals and refreshments, including service charge, taxes and other surcharges.
- Other information which may impact on the guests' stay, for example the hotel's smoking policy, refurbishment work in progress, planned functions/events and so on, should also be provided.
- Where operational policy dictates that certain facilities need to be pre-booked, for example spa treatments, dinner and so on, these should also be mentioned at the time of booking.

- Advance warning should be given if the restaurant is to be closed or likely to become fully booked.
- Full details of the hotel's cancellation policy if there is one. This especially includes information about charging credit cards for cancellation or changes to the booking.
- Information about deposits if required, including details of how the deposit is taken and whether or not it is refundable upon cancellation.
- Clear explanation of charges for additional services or available facilities including cancellation terms.
- Information about any unacceptable types of payment, for example credit cards.
- Information and full details about any fees charged for the acceptance of credit cards.

KEY TERMS

Internal customers: members of staff within an organisation or an organisation's suppliers who contribute towards the service provided to external customers. Internal customers include:

- immediate colleagues and those in other departments
- management and supervisors
- employees of other organisations, for example, retail outlets at an airport are internal customers of the airport.

Internal customers have needs as well as external customers. If you are a manager and you are happy with your staff's effort, you should tell them; if you are not happy, you should tell them that as well. After all, it is far better that you and your staff identify and resolve any issues and/or gaps in service provision before your customers do.

Successful service organisations understand well the importance of carefully monitoring and managing customer satisfaction. The service encounter or 'moment of truth', in particular, can play a prominent role in determining a customer's satisfaction with the business. In recent years the concept of internal customers in service organisations has been highlighted and the general consensus is that the satisfaction of these internal customers (that is, employees) is also important to the success of the company. As with external customers, an internal customer's satisfaction with the organisation can be significantly influenced by service encounters experienced with internal service providers.

ACTIVITY 2

To help you appreciate the different types of staff role within one organisation, and to determine how they deliver quality service, you could undertake the following exercise based on the results of your personal research and/or an investigative study visit. Figure 2.5 illustrates a range of job roles and functions.

Prepare and make a presentation to your class on the career opportunities available within your chosen organisation. You should make the presentation as if you were the personnel manager and you should include information on all the training employees are likely to receive. Use appropriate images to illustrate your presentation.

Sources of information to inform your presentation might include:

- interviewing members of staff
- training course information
- your own observations and notes from the investigative visit
- careers information
- advertisements and job descriptions.

The likely needs of internal customers will include:

- A safe working environment. For example, employees expect their employers to provide them with an area to work where there are no risks or dangers to health and well-being. This includes providing any protective clothing or uniforms for the job role being undertaken, and also includes providing working conditions in accordance with local employment law.
- Training appropriate to their job role. For example, many job roles in the hospitality, travel and tourism industry require good product knowledge or specialist skills, therefore employees must be properly trained in order to be able to carry out their duties to the best of their ability. Employers should provide any such training and pay employees at their normal rate of pay while they undertake the training.
- Knowledge of procedures, routines and performance standards for carrying out specific duties. For example, staff should be familiar with the organisation's policies and other job requirements that will affect the way in which the employee carries out their day to day duties. Many organisations use industry specific performance standards, including a code of conduct to help staff recognise what is expected of them when performing their job.
- Job satisfaction. For example, how content an individual feels in their job role and the extent to which they feel motivated to perform all aspects of their duties effectively.

❶ Carrying Customer's bag

❷ Working in the reception desk

❸ Cleaning hotel rooms

❹ Talking to customers

❺ Interviewing other staff

Listening to a supervisor

❼ Working in the linen room

❽ Attending department meetings

❾ Reading health and safety documents

❿ Observing fellow staff

Figure 2.5 Dealing with internal and external customers at work

Please refer to the following scenario about job satisfaction.

To illustrate the concept of an internal service encounter, consider the following scenario.

A front office representative for a large hotel has had new software installed on their work computer while they were away on vacation. On returning, the representative experiences a problem when using the new menu to gather information in response to an external customer inquiry. So, the representative calls the computer support department which installed the software. Although no one answers the telephone, the representative is able to leave a voice mail asking a 'how to do it' question.

Fifteen minutes later a computer technician arrives at the front office and an internal service encounter or 'moment of truth' begins. There is an interaction between an internal customer (front office representative) and an internal service provider (the computer technician). The computer technician is very friendly, explains the new menu screen, tells the representative about other

software also now on their computer and answers some additional questions about using the computer that have nothing to do with the installation process or the new menu. Overall, the front office representative is very satisfied with this internal service encounter, which, in turn, allows them to respond in a timely fashion to the external customer inquiry.

The scenario indicates that the front office representative was able to provide a good level of service to the external customer partly because of the good internal customer service that they were able to receive. This illustrates a very important fact that employee satisfaction has a direct bearing on external customer satisfaction. Researchers have measured the relationship between employee satisfaction, customer satisfaction and organisation profit levels over time. These studies show that, although the effects of employee satisfaction and customer satisfaction on business profit at a given point in time might not be detectable, they become visible and prominent over time. Specifically, the researchers found:

- a positive relationship between change in customer satisfaction and change in profit/sales
- a positive relationship between change in employee satisfaction and change in business profit
- a strong relationship between employee satisfaction and customer satisfaction at any point in time.

There are several explanations as to why employee satisfaction affects customer satisfaction:

- Employees who interact with customers are in a position to develop awareness of and respond to customer needs.
- Satisfied employees are motivated employees; that is, they have the motivational resources to deliver adequate effort and care.
- Satisfied employees are empowered employees; in other words, they have the resources, training, and responsibilities to understand and serve customer needs and demands effectively.
- Satisfied employees have high energy and willingness to give good service: at a very minimum, they can deliver a more positive perception of the service/product provided.
- Satisfied employees can provide customers with adequate explanations for undesirable outcomes and therefore satisfied employees have enough emotional resources to show empathy, understanding, respect, and concern to the external customers with which they have direct contact.

This brings us to the idea of employee motivation and the positive steps that organisations can take to increase job satisfaction levels. It has been suggested that Maslow's theory can be applied to conditions in the workplace and Table 2.3 indicates some of the ways in which it might apply.

Maslow level	What is possible for an organisation to offer
self-actualisation	allocating more challenging and stimulating responsibilities.
esteem	feedback via appraisal system – generally praising and rewarding staff efforts
social/belonging	work-based social events
safety and security	safe working conditions
physiological	competitive salary/wage rates

Table 2.3 Application of Maslow's hierarchy of human needs to the workplace

Employees can be motivated to work to the best of their ability if offered some form of personal gain. This may often take the form of a bonus: a one-off payment to a travel agent for achieving or exceeding sales targets.

Examples of how TIC managers in some destinations might reward their staff include:

- organising familiarisation trips to other regions
- implementing staff exchange programmes with other TICs
- sending thank you cards, flowers and/or balloons
- organising morning teas/coffees to thank staff
- paying for attendance at industry conferences and workshops
- passing on complimentary tickets received from local businesses
- distributing 'staff member of the month' awards (this really only works well in centres with large numbers of staff).

There is considerable scope for rewarding staff, but generally the more enjoyable and interesting the reward, the more it is likely to be appreciated.

Gaining praise or recognition in the work place through an 'employee of the month' scheme, for example, helps boost morale and motivation.

ACTIVITY 3

If you were a manager of a TIC why do you think the following ten point guide would be of use?

Management checklist:

1. Greet your staff in a friendly, pleasant manner.
2. If you need to discipline staff, do it in private. Remain calm, explain exactly why you are upset and give them an opportunity to respond.
3. Be willing to deal with difficult customers – do not leave it up to your staff.
4. Support your staff's decisions whenever possible.
5. Admit when you do not know the answer.
6. Listen to your staff and do not interrupt while they are speaking.
7. Take time to socialise and celebrate major events such as birthdays.
8. Demonstrate good telephone etiquette.
9. Thank your staff on a regular basis (see next section).
10. Do not be afraid to tell staff when things are not going quite as well as expected – honesty is always the best policy.

Figure 2.6 An airport departure desk

All employees in travel and tourism organisations have to deal with a variety of customers and colleagues. Using the photograph as a guide, consider how the member of staff might be able to meet the needs of different types of internal and external customer.

Staff thrive on praise and public recognition of a job well done. As managers and supervisors it is important that you regularly reward staff for their efforts. This does not need to be formal or expensive; in fact, studies show that informal rewards such as praise are equally, if not more effective, than formal rewards. For maximum impact, praise should be given as soon as possible after the event and delivered in a sincere and heartfelt manner.

2.3 The impacts of quality customer service

The attitudes, service provision and commitment of staff often reflect those of management. Good customer service involves everyone in the organisation, not just front-line staff. If you are positive, enthusiastic and interested in your job, your staff are highly likely to follow suit. The aim should be for open and frank communication amongst staff. There should be total commitment from top down and bottom up if an organisation is serious about delivering excellent customer service.

Quality customer service will impact on all those involved with the organisation – the customer, the employee and the organisation itself. Consider the following activity.

ACTIVITY 5

To help you understand how important these key dimensions are in terms of employee/ customer interactions try the following activity with the help of friends, family or a group of fellow students. Ask each person to recall an experience they had as a consumer where an employee provided extremely poor service.

First, provide a statement describing the service failure. Was it:

- a faulty product?
- late or untimely service?
- a dispute over pricing?

Second, discuss what did the person providing the service do that was so offensive.

Was it:

- their attitude?
- their words or phrases?
- the tone of their voice or their non-verbal communication?

You might then consider the effect these experiences had on you as consumers with regards to the following points:

- would you use the organisation again?
- would you tell others of your experiences?
- what sort of customer service would you expect to receive?

Impacts of quality customer service for customers

The quality of customer service received will leave customers feeling either satisfied or dissatisfied. Customers will perceive their experience as being either positive or negative based on how well their needs are being met and whether they feel they have gained value for money or not. A perception of the quality of the customer service received may be based on only one tiny aspect of the overall experience.

Impacts of quality customer service for employees

If the employee is able to offer high quality customer service and receives positive feedback as a result, this will lead to a high level of job satisfaction. On the other hand, if the employee is unable to answer questions or lacks the appropriate training to know how to carry out aspects of their job role correctly, this is likely to lead to dissatisfaction with the job. Organisations that are willing to invest time and money in the training of their staff to enhance skill development greatly benefit the employee as their own level of employability will increase as a direct result of the training they receive. Organisations that encourage efficient team working practices will also contribute to the job satisfaction of their employees.

Impacts of quality customer service for the organisation

Investing time and money in developing staff pays off for any organisation as this results in a more efficient workforce. Staff will understand their job role within the specific context of the organisation and can make a positive contribution, which in turn helps build the reputation of the organisation. Staff who are comfortable and competent in carrying out their job roles will increase the satisfaction of customers. This in turn will lead to repeat business and customer loyalty. If an organisation can satisfy customers by meeting their needs and exceeding their expectations, then the satisfied customer is likely to return again in the future. This in turn creates excellent opportunities for the organisation to increase their earnings. The more customers they have, the greater the opportunity to generate revenue and income, which in turn allows an organisation to create profit.

KEY CONCEPTS

Change and development

Providing quality customer service means that an organisation will constantly adapt its products and services to better meet the needs of its internal and external customers. This is essential in the travel and tourism industry, where change is the only constant, because of the dynamic nature of what customers want and need from the tourism experience.

Clearly, there will be consequences for any organisation failing to provide acceptable levels of customer service.

The main implications of poor customer service delivery are likely to include things such as:

- customers not getting information they need
- loss of income to the organisation because of cancellations or customers not returning
- increased costs to an organisation if they have to attract repeat business or new customers through marketing
- high staff turnover because employees do not feel valued
- inefficient and unhappy workforce
- not meeting customers' needs or expectations, therefore fewer customers visiting the organisation
- lack of customer loyalty – no incentives to return, or products becoming outdated, as well as changing trends or the organisation is not keeping up to date with these
- poor public image –the effect of negative publicity on the organisation.

2.4 Assessing the quality of customer service in travel and tourism organisations

Most international travel, tourism and hospitality organisations have a range of informal and formal quality assurance systems to support meeting the needs of customers and to evaluate the effectiveness of their customer service provision. Commonly used strategies include monitoring customer feedback and maintaining staffing levels, together with training programmes and the monitoring of individual performances. Each organisation will have its own set of operational systems.

Most organisations have a customer service policy and this will state their strategy for looking after their various customers. Such policies will give emphasis to the ways in which the organisation will deal with their different types of customers. For example, the growth and expansion of Raffles Hotels and Resorts provides an appropriate overview of a customer service philosophy in action.

KEY CONCEPTS

Global and growing

Raffles Hotels and Resorts epitomises the principles of globalisation and growth which underpin the business objectives for most travel and tourism organisations. Offering the Raffles brand within a broader range of countries highlights the organisation's global expansion in an industry which has great potential for such growth.

Figure 2.7 Raffles Hotels and Resorts

Since 1887, Raffles has gone out of its way to give you the warmest welcome, the richest experiences and the fondest of memories. And today the legend continues all around the world. From the classic colonial splendour of Raffles Singapore, where it all began, to Dubai, the Seychelles, Cambodia, Paris, Beijing, Hainan, Makati and Makkah, the Raffles name is synonymous with luxury, glamour and extraordinary adventure. Each hotel is an oasis of calm and charm at the crossroads of a civilisation. Each is a carefully chosen destination in its own right. Each is uniquely, indefinably, sublimely Raffles.

Now, as we grow and reach new, and sometimes surprising, destinations, our guests can rest assured that wherever in the world we travel, we will remain distinctly Raffles – infused with the same spirit of adventure, luxury and sublime service. Exciting and enchanting, refreshing and reinvigorating, Raffles is loved by those with an adventurous spirit and a taste for the very best.

The main aim of all customer service policies will be to make an organisation's customers feel satisfied and valued so that they will want to return again. Staff working in any travel and tourism organisation need to be made aware of the company's customer service policy, as this will help them to understand the benefits of good customer service both for themselves and for the company. Most companies now organise specialist training courses in order to ensure that staff provide the best possible service to the organisation's external and internal customers.

Levels of customer service within the global travel and tourism industry tend to follow a normal distribution as shown on Figure 2.8.

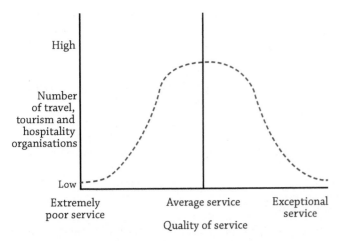

Figure 2.8 Global distribution of customer service

Take a moment to consider the normal distribution curve measuring the quality of service delivery in general terms. It shows that most service falls into the central zone of the curve, this is 'average service'. If an organisation supplies this level of service the customer will be satisfied. However, the curve can also be viewed from a slightly different perspective. Some researchers have concentrated on the existence of four zones running along the length of the curve, each approximating to a different type of customer experience. These zones are described in Table 2.4.

Zone	Customer experience
zone of outrage	The customer is upset by the very poor level of customer service provided by the organisation.
zone of dissatisfaction	The customer is unhappy with the level of customer service provided by the organisation.
zone of satisfaction	The customer is either satisfied or happy with the level of service provided by the organisation.
zone of delight	The customer is very happy with the level of customer service provided by the organisation because their expectations have been exceeded.

Table 2.4 Zones of customer experience

The implications for travel, tourism and hospitality organisations are quite clear. Customers experiencing a feeling of 'outrage' are clearly unlikely to return in the future. Many individuals in the two middle zones may or may not become repeat customers, depending on their perceptions of past experiences. In effect, these large middle groups will have no particularly strong feelings for or against particular organisations and will tend to be

ambivalent as regards using them in the future. It is thus only in the 'delight' zone that customers start to become loyal and regularly undertake repeat visits.

Every time a customer interacts with a travel and tourism organisation and experiences any of its operational procedures can be regarded as a **'moment of truth'**. Three such moments of truth are shown in Figure 2.9 and have been labelled A, B and C, in which A is the reception desk area, B is the restaurant and C is a guest room. Any service encounter between a customer and an employee is referred to as being a 'moment of truth'. It is at this moment that three sets of factors, listed in Table 2.5, come into play and their combined effect is to determine the quality of the customer's experience. To help illustrate the concept of the moment of truth we can now look at what is likely to be happening in the three service environments (A, B and C) illustrated in Figure 2.9. Table 2.5 lists key aspects of the three service encounters.

Figure 2.9 Moments of truth

Customer satisfaction is affected by customer expectations about the service they will receive. If the customer service they receive is different from what they expected, there is always a danger that customer satisfaction will be lower than expected. Therefore many organisations try to deliver the same customer service, time after time, so that the service customers receive matches their customer expectations and this gives customer satisfaction.

KEY CONCEPTS

Customer focus

Customer satisfaction can only be achieved where customers feel that their needs, wants and expectations have been fully met or even exceeded by travel and tourism providers. For this to happen, the customer must feel that they are valued and important to the organisation.

Factors	A	B	C
The nature of the service task being performed and what it involves	A couple have arrived at the reception desk to check-in to the hotel and the receptionist is following all the established checking-in procedures.	A member of the waiting staff is serving food ordered by the guests. Food is collected from kitchen and then served at table.	A member of the hotel's housekeeping staff is servicing a guest's room following an established check list of actions to complete within a specified time.
The service standards expected, both by the customer and the provider	The couple expect to be welcomed and checked-in in a timely manner. The hotel expects the receptionist to follow standard operating procedures.	The guests expect to have their food cooked to order and served in a timely manner. Staff are expected to follow standard service procedures to enhance the dining experience. Figure 2.10 shows a typical scenario.	The guest expects the room to be serviced when left unoccupied and all in-room items cleaned and replaced as appropriate. The hotel expects all standard housekeeping procedures to be followed.
The service delivery system for the task at hand	The receptionist has to use the computerised reservation system and access the guests' booking details.	Orders are cooked so that all dishes for a particular course are ready to be collected by waiting staff and then served at the same time.	The room is to be fully serviced during the room attendant's shift, making use of all material supplies made available for the task.

Table 2.5 Three aspects of service encounter

Figure 2.10 Hotel staff serving breakfast

2.5 Setting organisational, functional area and individual customer service standards

KEY CONCEPTS

Sustainability and responsibility

Employers in the travel and tourism industry have a responsibility to developing sustainable and responsible working practices. When setting organisational customer service standards, customers might nowadays expect to see corporate social responsibility as one such set of standards. This is because travel and tourism businesses have become increasingly aware of the positive and negative impacts that tourism brings to a destination.

ACTIVITY 6

Customer expectations generally increase as prices rise. Individually or in groups, identify how your expectations would change for five products and services of your choice, between the cheapest option and the most expensive. To start, think about spending a night in a bed and breakfast establishment as against a luxury five star hotel or flying on a budget 'no frills' airline as opposed to business class on a full fare, scheduled carrier.

Customer service procedures are the routines and detailed steps an organisation uses to deliver its customer service. Some organisations have formal procedures in writing and use those to train staff and to monitor service. These make up the service standards towards which employees must work.

A key ingredient in the provision of excellent customer service by an organisation's employees is the need for standards. **Organisational customer service standards** tend to specify what is to be done or said within any given scenario. For example, the receptionist in Scenario A might

Stage	Method	Standard	Reason	Understanding
Welcoming the guest	Acknowledge the guest and say: 'Welcome to ....' How may I help you?' If it is a repeat guest known to you then say: 'Good evening Mr/Mrs/Ms ...' 'Welcome back, it is nice to see you again.'	• eye contact • smile • greet the guest • use name.	So that the guest knows that you have noticed him or her. To make the guest feel welcome and recognised in the hotel.	Creating a positive first impression in the guest's mind.

Table 2.6 Hotel reception staff standards

have to wear a name badge as well as being told to smile and make eye contact with guests as they approach the desk and use their names whenever possible.

Functional area customer service standards are designed to describe the action an individual employee needs to follow to perform a task competently. These standards specify how a particular service task should be done. We can now briefly look at one example of how such standards might apply to hotel reception staff in Table 2.6.

Some organisations use a checklist to set the organisational standard for employees, such as these ones.

- Is your uniform clean, smart and tidy and do you look your best?
- Do you know what is on the menu and if there are any alternatives available if you are asked?
- Have you got a service cloth, a tray and an order pad and pen if required?
- Introduce yourself when guests arrive and tell them you will be looking after them.
- Serve all food from the left and all drinks from the right.
- Used plates should be cleared from the right.
- If some guests order a cold main course and some a hot, always serve the cold dishes first.
- Avoid a long wait between the service of the meat and the vegetables by working with a partner on the service of the main course.

Waiting staff will perform their functions in accordance with all agreed procedures. For example, when serving and clearing food and drinks:

- Collect food and beverage selections promptly from the kitchen or bar, check for accuracy and presentation, and convey them to customers safely.
- Serve food and beverage courteously and to the correct person, according to enterprise standards and hygiene requirements.

- Promptly recognise and follow up any delays or deficiencies in service.
- Advise and reassure customers about any delays or problems.
- Check customer satisfaction at the appropriate time.
- Remove used items in a timely manner and safely transfer them to the appropriate location for cleaning.
- Dispose of leftover food and disposables, according to hygiene regulations and enterprise practice.
- Dispose of recyclable items according to local regulations and enterprise practice.
- Thank and farewell customers courteously.

However, the earlier service checklists illustrate a more general point about the delivery of customer service. All employees not only represent the organisation but are in fact part of the team responsible for attracting sales and hence income. It is very important, therefore, that all staff present a positive image of the organisation. It is important that customers are not offended in any way by an employee's appearance. The mode of dress and the physical appearance of the individual should match the nature of the work done.

Front line members of staff, such as the waiting staff, must have interpersonal skills, sometimes also referred to as **communication skills**, **people skills** and/or **soft skills**. These are the skills that we all use to interact or deal with others, and how we do this can greatly influence our professional and personal lives. Improving these skills builds confidence and enhances our relationships with others. People with good interpersonal skills have learnt to identify the best ways of interacting with others in different situations.

Many organisations will encourage employees to deliver high standards of customer service by setting organisational, functional area and individual customer service standards. These posters and leaflets are often displayed in the staff room area to remind staff of the organisational standards expected. See following Figure 2.11.

WHAT WE EXPECT IS:

☺ – Friendly and enthusiastic staff

☺ – Smart looking staff

☺ – Staff who know about the establishment and its service

☺ – Staff who are willing to offer help without having to be asked

☺ – Prompt efficient service

☺ – Not to be hurried along by staff

☺ – An apology if kept waiting

☺ – An apology if things go wrong

☺ – Staff to put things right

☺ – To be treated as individual

Quality is remembered long after price is forgotten

Posture	– be alert and ready to help
Look and Listen	– show interest and concern
Expression	– friendly, natural smile!
Appearance	– smart, clean, correct uniform
Speech	– show courtesy and friendliness
Eagerness	– help others, show enthusiasm, enjoy your work

Figure 2.11

All major hotel chains issue quite extensive codes of conduct for their employees. The staff act as representatives of the company and so they are expected to take pride in their personal appearance, dress and general grooming. For front line staff who have direct contact with external customers, cleanliness and personal hygiene will be significant job requirements. The management issue grooming standards to act as general guidelines but individual units or departments may have more specific standards based on their particular operational requirements. The standards expected in a fine dining restaurant will be quite different from those expected in an al fresco setting.

Hotel receptionist

Figure 2.13 on the right shows the reception area of a major international resort hotel. The staff on duty at the reception desk are likely to be the first people who greet guests on their arrival at the hotel. Reception staffs are therefore particularly well placed to create a good first impression by welcoming all guests in an appropriate manner. The business-like appearance of visible front line staff and the appearance of the reception area itself all help to create a positive impression of the hotel. Some of the staff on duty in reception should have the ability to speak a foreign language, particularly at large resort hotels dealing with many types of international guest. It is also important that reception staff working on the front desk have good administrative skills, including having

full familiarity with the hotel's computer systems, so that they are able to deal with reservations accurately and efficiently. It is also important that they can communicate in a clear, concise and friendly manner, always making sure that none of the sensitive personal details provided by the guest are mislaid or left in public view. All of these aspects of the job of front line staff will be subject to customer service standards imposed by the organisation and by the functional area in which they work.

Figure 2.12 Reception desk

2.6 Delivery of customer service

All hotel customer service situations clearly illustrate the need for appropriately trained staff to be employed in such front of house environments. A key consideration

75

when arranging training for these members of staff will be the need for front line employees to meet and exceed customer expectations.

Figure 2.13 Professionalism and skill in service encounter

Customer service training will frequently focus on the following aspects:

- professionalism and skill in the service encounter, as in Figure 2.13, above.
- staff attitude and behaviour
- customers being able to access staff and feeling that they are flexible and able to respond to particular needs
- reliability and trustworthiness of staff
- recovery of a situation when things go wrong
- ensuring that the organisation's brand image has a reputation and credibility.

Individual customer service performance standards

Performance standards should form the heart of any job description as they describe the 'what', 'how-to' and 'how-well' of a particular job role.

Each performance standard states three things about each aspect of the job:

- what the employee is to do
- how it is to be done
- to what extent it is to be done (how much, how well, how soon).

Traditionally, job descriptions have simply listed the duties and responsibilities (what the employee is to do) for each job. Although this approach is better than no approach, a job description using performance standards is much

more useful. Here is an example of a performance standard for one aspect of the waiter or waitress job at a certain restaurant:

'The server will take food and beverage orders for up to five tables with 100% accuracy, using standard house procedures.'

Figure 2.14 breaks this standard down to give you the structure of a performance standard. The 'what' of the standard is the work aspect under consideration. The tasks become the 'hows' that make up the standard procedure. When you add a performance goal for each aspect, you set a performance standard: how much, how many, how good, how fast, how soon, how accurate – whatever it is that is important for establishing how well that aspect of work should be done in the restaurant's operation. Supporting materials explaining or illustrating the specifics of the standard house procedures are necessary to complete each performance standard.

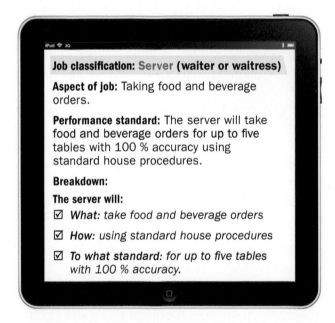

Figure 2.14 Anatomy of a restaurant performance standard

Performance standards can improve individual employee performance. When people are not given explicit instructions but are left to work out their own ways of getting their work done, they usually choose the easiest methods they can find. People also begin to find certain parts of their job more to their liking than other parts and will slack off on the parts they like least. The procedures and standards put all these things into the right perspective.

Sustainability and responsibility

Given the increased awareness of the need to minimise the impacts of tourism and to become more sustainable in our approach, some organisations now include an element of social responsibility within individual service standards they set for their employees. This may include encouraging customers to become more eco-friendly by checking if paper copies of invoices are required, before printing them out.

Once employees know what to do and how to do it, they can concentrate on improving their skills. Improved skills and knowledge, coupled with goals to be met, encourage people to work more independently. If a reward system is related to achievement – as it should be – people will respond with better and better work. Better and better work means better productivity, better customer service, more sales, and higher profits for the organisation.

Morale greatly benefits as a result. People feel secure when they know what to do and how to do it, and when their work is judged on the basis of job content and job performance. If they have participated in developing the objectives, they have a sense of pride and a commitment to seeing that the objectives work. Participation also contributes to their sense of belonging and their loyalty to the company. A performance standard system can reduce conflict and misunderstanding. Everybody knows who is responsible for what. They know what parts of the job are most important. They know the level of performance the boss expects in each job. This reduces the likelihood that one person is doing less than another who is being paid the same wage: often a cause for discontent and conflict.

Organisations also use performance management and appraisal procedures, similar to the example shown in Figure 2.15, in assessing the quality of their customer service provision.

In the example of the hotel receptionist's job, a supervisor or line manager will observe the receptionist performing their day to day duties and will feedback to the employee on aspects of the job that they are carrying out well and areas for improvement.

Performance management is also sometimes known as appraisal. Performance management is an ongoing management process that allows communication between a supervisor and an employee as well as providing feedback, accountability and documentation against performance outcomes or 'targets' for the employee.

Figure 2.15 Servers follow performance standards

Performance management enables an employee and his or her line manager to review past performance, to assess current achievements and any specific training needs, as well as analysing the employee's potential for development or promotion. A meeting is often held between the employee and the supervisor to set performance targets for the coming year based on the findings from the observations and other discussions carried out.

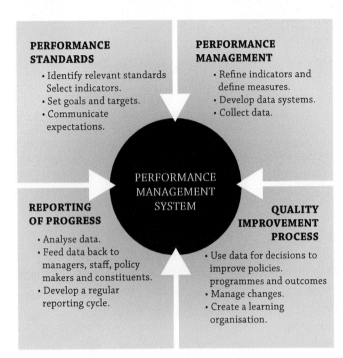

Figure 2.16 The typical performance management process

Benchmarking

Benchmarking is the process of identifying best practice in relation to customer service delivery. The search for best practice can take place both inside a particular organisation, and also in other types of service provider. For example, are there lessons to be learned from studying the practices used in rival organisations? The objective of benchmarking is to understand and evaluate the current position of a business or organisation in relation to best practice and to identify areas and means of performance improvement.

The benchmarking process involves looking outward (outside a particular business, organisation, industry, region or country) to examine how others achieve their performance levels and to understand the processes they use. In this way benchmarking helps explain the processes behind excellent performance. When the lessons learnt from a benchmarking exercise are applied appropriately, they facilitate improved performance in critical functions within an organisation or in key areas of the business environment.

The application of benchmarking involves four key steps:

* understanding in detail all existing customer service processes within the organisation
* analysing the customer service processes of others
* comparing own customer service performance with that of others analysed
* implementing the steps necessary to close the performance gap.

Figure 2.17 Jebel Ali Golf Resort

2.7 General customer feedback

Jebel Ali International Hotels, one of which is shown in Figure 2.17, the Dubai-based company with over 30 years of hospitality experience, recently undertook a strategic rebranding process. Their new identity ensures a consistent and engaging brand that will boost the group's reputation overseas as they look to expand into international markets. The company employs over 1500 people in Dubai and opened a property in the Seychelles in 2013.

The new brand, based on over a year's research into the qualities that the company presently possesses, retains existing traditions of hospitality and excellence but now also allows them to embrace the future. The company now believes that this has been achieved in JA Resorts & Hotels and their new mission statement is:

'To take real pleasure in welcoming you in to our space, where we capture the generous spirit of heartfelt hospitality, a space where we take pride in the grandest of gestures and the smallest of details. This is a place where everything is taken care of, and where you can truly feel that you have arrived.

But while a new name and logo have come into play, the promise of heartfelt hospitality at the group's properties remains the guiding principle.'

(Source: http://www.jaresortshotels.com/Home.aspx)

Benchmarking should not be considered a one-off exercise. To be effective, it must become an ongoing, integral part of an ongoing improvement process with the goal of keeping abreast of ever-improving best practice.

Many organisations actively seek customer feedback through a variety of methods including:

- response ratings on social media
- suggestion boxes
- customer comment cards, situated around the buildings used by visitors
- use of a feedback facility on their websites
- evaluation forms given out after specific programmes and events
- responding to assessments by external bodies and special interest groups such as disability groups and tourist organisations.

 KEY CONCEPTS

Customer focus

Organisations which actively seek customer feedback can be described as having a strong customer focus, because the opinions of customers are clearly valued. Responding to feedback is an important part of this process, allowing customers to feel more satisfied that their views are being taken seriously by the travel and tourism business.

We will now have a look at some of the major feedback techniques frequently used by international travel, tourism and hospitality organisations.

Informal feedback

Informal customer feedback refers to asking customers questions in a non-threatening, informal manner. Informal feedback could be gathered over a dinner or in a casual conversation, where the customer may feel freer to express his opinion. Such encounters will usually involve simple questions requiring little more than a standard yes or no answer. However, even such simple responses can lead to significant developments within particular organisations. Simple questioning of guests is common in restaurants and the head waiter will ask diners whether the meal was good, if everything is satisfactory or whether anything else is required.

Such questions invite guest feedback and provide an ideal opportunity for guests to comment on the standard of service and to identify anything that could be improved. The head waiter will note the customer's observations and these may inform future discussions between restaurant staff, kitchen staff, bar staff and management. Such informal feedback is important in highlighting trends or issues at an early stage before they can develop into serious operational problems. Furthermore, such

feedback sessions have no cost to the organisation and can produce significant benefits.

Other informal feedback can come from members of staff. Colleagues working together may identify a problem or an area of operation that could be improved. Some organisations offer rewards for staff who suggest a positive development that is then taken up within an area of service operations. It could be something as simple as the order in which a buffet is laid out or a physical change to the working area that improves the service given to customers.

Suppliers may also be asked for feedback on the organisation's systems or procedures. They can also be advised of any extra demand, such as when the organisation is aware of a probable increased demand for a product because of a special promotion. The suppliers will need to know so that they can ensure stocks are available. For example, exhibitors at a trade fair (Figure 2.18) will require sufficient copies of brochures and promotional leaflets but may warn suppliers that extra materials will be required if demand exceeds the initially anticipated.

Social media

Nowadays, most travel and tourism organisations recognise the huge value of social media in communicating with existing and potential customers. Many organisations therefore have created social media pages, such as Facebook, Twitter and YouTube (Figure 2.19). These allow customers to see regular updates of events and activities held by the organisation and allow customers to interact, gathering their opinions via the Like or Favourite buttons. Customers are encouraged to share information with other social media 'friends' to attract a wider customer base.

Suggestion box

The first recorded suggestion programme was implemented in 1770 by the British Navy. They realised the need for a process for listening to every individual in the organisation, without fear of reprisal. At that time, the mere mention of an idea that contradicted a captain's or admiral's opinion was likely to be punished by hanging.

The first physical box to collect ideas appeared at William Denny and Brothers shipyard in Scotland in 1880. It was intended to collect ideas from all employees and to pay a 'fair' reward for each implementable idea. This approach of the suggestion scheme, as it is still known in the United Kingdom today, spread rapidly through the country following government reports on the project's success.

Figure 2.18 Exhibitors at a trade fair

Figure 2.19 Examples of social media used to gather informal feedback

Suggestion boxes became popular in the manufacturing sector in World War II and the post-war years. They became part of the total quality movement and an integral part of cost, safety and quality improvement initiatives over the following 50 years. They are still the mainstay of corporate suggestion programmes, be they physical boxes or virtual boxes on company intranet websites.

Most people have some experience of suggestion boxes, from customer-centric boxes in retail outlets to the classic employee suggestion box. The boxes provide some benefit in their ability to capture ideas from anyone in the organisation. However, there are many issues: individuals must be

standing next to the box, they need some incentive to make a contribution and they want to be safe in the knowledge that both they – and their ideas – will be treated fairly.

Suggestion boxes are often quick to implement as they require relatively little infrastructure and pre-planning. Web-based suggestion programmes, typically a web-based form to collect ideas, can be created for as little as US$5000 for a very basic system, although most companies expect to pay from US$75 000 to US$300 000 for a working system.

More traditional suggestion boxes allow a wide range of employees to make their contributions, especially if they do not have access to computers. Boxes can be placed in production facilities and in retail outlets, providing a cost-effective means of collecting paper based suggestions. Unfortunately the benefits are often outweighed by the disadvantages. The boxes may not be emptied for long periods of time, and the initial novelty of the box can wane leading to disuse of the system. A research study found that the majority of programmes failed to meet initial expectations, and recommended that programmes should be closed down for a period of time in order to re-invigorate the system and workforce.

Customer comment cards

Please refer to the following Case Study 1, which gives an example of a customer comments card.

Bateaux Dubai survey

Figure 2.20 shows Bateaux Dubai's customer comment card used to survey the opinions of guests who have just experienced a dinner cruise along Dubai Creek.

Dear Guest,

As a valued patron, your opinion is important to us. We would be grateful if you could take a few minutes to assist us with our efforts to meet and exceed your expectations.

Thank you for your time and we look forward to welcoming you on board Bateaux Dubai once again.

Yours sincerely,
Your Hosts

Figure 2.20 Bateaux Dubai dinner cruise

How many times have you been on Bateaux Dubai?

How did you hear about Bateaux Dubai?

☐ Recommendation   ☐ Radio

☐ Magazine   ☐
Newspaper

☐ Other (please specify)

Please rate the following aspects of our Bateaux Dubai Experience

The Service

How friendly was your initial greeting from our reservations line?

☐ Excellent   ☐ Good
☐ Fair   ☐ Poor

Handling of your dining cruise reservation

☐ Excellent   ☐ Good
☐ Fair   ☐ Poor

Reception when boarding Bateaux Dubai

☐ Excellent   ☐ Good
☐ Fair   ☐ Poor

Handling of your menu and beverage order

☐ Excellent   ☐ Good
☐ Fair   ☐ Poor

Product knowledge of our service staff

☐ Excellent   ☐ Good
☐ Fair   ☐ Poor

The attentiveness of our service staff during the cruise

☐ Excellent   ☐ Good
☐ Fair   ☐ Poor

The speed of service

☐ Excellent   ☐ Good
☐ Fair   ☐ Poor

The overall courtesy of the Bateaux Dubai staff

☐ Excellent   ☐ Good
☐ Fair   ☐ Poor

Comments

_____
_____

The Dining Experience

Selection of beverages

☐ Excellent   ☐ Good   ☐
Fair   ☐ Poor

Presentation and quality of beverages

☐ Excellent   ☐ Good
☐ Fair   ☐ Poor

Menu selection

☐ Excellent   ☐ Good
☐ Fair   ☐ Poor

Quality of food

☐ Excellent   ☐ Good
☐ Fair   ☐ Poor

Comments

_____
_____

The Cruise Experience

Suitability of music to the ambience of Bateaux Dubai

☐ Excellent   ☐ Good
☐ Fair   ☐ Poor

Will you come back to Bateaux Dubai?

☐ Yes   ☐ No

If no, why?

_____
_____

Would you recommend Bateaux Dubai to a friend?

☐ Yes   ☐ No

If no, why?

_____
_____

Would you like to receive information regarding our promotions and special events?

☐ Yes   ☐ No

Can we use your comments and feedback for our promotional purposes?

☐ Yes   ☐ No

Figure 2.21 Bateaux Dubai's customer comment card

Specific market research

We can now look at some of the key features of Figure 2.21 design and examine ways in which it will be useful to Bateaux Dubai's management. First of all, it is a very appropriate instrument for undertaking market research because it meets the following criteria as proposed by the Market Research Society:

'the planned process of collecting, recording, analysing and evaluating data about customers and the market itself.'

The questions allow for the generation of both **qualitative** and **quantitative** data. Qualitative data refers to the information collected about customers' opinions and attitudes towards products and services, whereas quantitative data tends to be numeric or statistical by nature – frequency of visits, cost and number of users and so on. Quantitative data allows patterns and trends in the market to be displayed visually in chart or graph forms; qualitative data on the other hand is more difficult to represent graphically. Particular questions asked serve a variety of functions and Table 2.7 indicates the ways in which this survey information is likely to be used by Bateaux Dubai's management.

Once surveys have been undertaken the findings have to be properly analysed and evaluated. Table 2.8 shows the results of a customer survey conducted by a restaurant during one particular service session. Using the data, assess customer satisfaction levels and identify areas of improvement for the restaurant in order to exceed customer expectations.

Question	Purpose/Usefulness
How many times have you been on Bateaux Dubai?	Identifies repeat guests and identifies customer loyalty
How did you hear about Bateaux Dubai?	Assessment of marketing and promotion methods' effectiveness
Please rate the following aspects: The service... The dining experience... The cruise experience...	Extent to which Bateaux Dubai is meeting guests' expectations and identifies areas/aspects needing improvement
Would you like to receive information regarding our promotions and special events?	More efficient, targeted marketing and extended database
Can we use your comments and feedback for our promotional purposes?	Endorsements and on printed marketing materials

Table 2.7 Purpose of the survey

Service feature	Excellent	Good	Satisfactory	Poor	Very Poor
welcome/arrival	21	25	9	1	0
value for money	8	31	8	3	0
reception on arrival	12	32	10	0	1
menu offered	10	22	13	1	0
food quality	13	19	13	3	0
wine selection	10	22	12	1	1
speed of service	15	20	13	2	0
friendliness	14	27	11	1	0
overall dining experience	12	25	9	1	0
cleanliness	20	26	9	0	1

Table 2.8 Restaurant customer survey results

You might care to try a simple customer service survey yourself, such as the following exercise. During your visit to a chosen organisation, select three or four members of staff at different locations to answer questions such as the following:

- Where can I buy a drink?
- What special events are on today?
- Where is the nearest public toilet?

You can then evaluate the quality of customer service the staff were able to provide using the following assessment grid.

Staff member	Location				
	Poor		Average		Excellent
Clarity of speech	1	2	3	4	5
Accuracy of information	1	2	3	4	5
Body language	1	2	3	4	5
Overall helpfulness	1	2	3	4	5

Table 2.9 Customer service assessment grid

In many cases, information and comments gathered are fed through to the organisation's customer service department, often a small team of staff who ensure standards are met and action is taken to sort out problems across the whole organisation.

Surveys

In order to achieve customer satisfaction, organisations must in some way meet the needs and wants of their customers. However, it is not always easy to identify exactly what these needs and wants are, especially for intangible products and services being offered by the travel and tourism industry. The most common method used by any business, to determine not only the customers' needs and wants, but also to establish who the customers are, is to carry out market research. Market research can be carried out in a number of different ways. Some larger organisations may decide to conduct the research themselves, using appropriately trained professionals from the marketing department. Other organisations choose to pay for a market research project via a market research agency or a market research consultancy service.

Primary market research requires organisations to go out into the marketplace to find out about customers' experiences and expectations. There are many commercial organisations which will carry out primary research on behalf of other organisations, but this is particularly costly. Primary research could be done by conducting a survey at the airport or within the reception area of a number of hotels. Primary research methods include self-completion questionnaires, which are a series of open-ended, closed or multiple choice questions given directly to the customer or potential customer to fill in. Telephone surveys and internet surveys are also common forms of primary research in which existing or potential customers are contacted either by telephone or by email or are randomly targeted when visiting a website on the internet and asked questions relating to travel and tourism products and services.

Customers acting as mystery shoppers

The mystery shopper is a tool used externally by market research companies or internally by companies themselves to measure quality of service. The mystery shopper's specific identity is generally not known by the organisation being evaluated. Mystery shoppers perform specific tasks such as purchasing a product, asking questions, registering complaints or behaving in a certain way, and then provide detailed reports or feedback about their experiences.

Mystery shoppers are often given instructions or procedures to make the transaction atypical to make the test of the knowledge and service skills of the employees more stringent or specific to a particular service issue. For instance, mystery shoppers at a restaurant may pretend they are vegetarian or wheat-intolerant. While gathering information, mystery shoppers usually blend in to the service environment being evaluated as regular customers. After the visit the mystery shopper submits the data collected for review and analysis. This allows for a comparison on how particular outlets are doing against previously defined criteria.

Change and development

An organisation which analyses the market research data it gathers, in order to bring about specific changes in its customer service provision, is responding to the dynamic nature of the travel and tourism industry, in which nothing is constant.

The details and information that mystery shoppers take note of typically include:

- the number of employees in the service area on entering
- how long it takes before the mystery shopper is greeted
- the name of the employee(s)
- whether or not the greeting is friendly, ideally according to objective measures
- the questions asked by the shopper to find a suitable product/service
- the types of products/services offered
- the information provided by the employee
- whether the employee invited the shopper to come back to the service outlet
- the cleanliness of service outlet
- the speed of service
- the degree of compliance with company standards relating to service, the overall appearance of the service environment and also personal presentation/grooming.

Focus groups

Focus groups are an example of qualitative research where the subjective opinions and perceptions of a small targeted group of consumers on a certain topic are elicited. Focus groups can be used to gather information on the acceptability and usability of new or re-launched products or services, reactions to new advertising campaigns or specific advertisements or consumer perceptions of a whole product class. They are generally used to elicit depth data such as that related to motivation, branding and complex attitudinal structures (in comparison to the more shallow but broad data elicited by traditional surveys) and sometimes to assist in developing a more structured survey.

For the purposes of market research, focus groups are usually made up of six to eight targeted consumers (though this may vary), a moderator whose role is to ask the required questions, draw out answers and encourage discussion, an observation area usually behind one way mirrors and video and/or audio taping facilities. Usually focus groups run for an hour, the time determined by the concentration limits of participants. Participants are screened according to often fairly rigorous selection and recruitment qualifications, related to demographics, usage and past consumer behaviour related to the product or service being tested. They are paid a cash or gift incentive for their attendance and participation in the event.

Observations of interactions between customer service staff and customers

Performance management in the travel and tourism industry often provides many circumstances in which observation is part of normal workplace routines. However, observation is also an opportunity to collect feedback about an organisation's customer service procedures. The activities of the personnel performing their usual duties can be observed and a note made of any particular aspects that need further consideration and development. The observation may be undertaken by an internal colleague or a member of management or it could be someone from another outlet or department. Such observation is likely to include all aspects of customer service from the performance of routine functions to aspects of personal presentation and grooming. Such observation may form part of an employee's performance management and their annual review process by a line manager.

Summary

Nearly all travel, tourism and hospitality organisations undertake some form of customer care analysis and many use a variety of techniques in order to obtain an accurate reflection of what is happening in their business operations. The reports and findings need to be studied carefully in order to identify areas for development, either in operational procedures and practices or staff training requirements. It is essential to ensure that staff are maintaining the values and attitudes of the organisation as expressed in the mission statement and that they are acting as good representatives of the organisation.

Exam-style questions

Question 1

a **i** List three external customer types likely to use a scheduled airline. **[3 marks]**

ii Give one example of how an airline might meet the specific needs of each of the customer types in (a) (i). **[3 marks]**

b Analyse two likely impacts of quality customer service for an airline. **[6 marks]**

c Evaluate the reasons why training appropriate to the job role is important for the airline's internal customers. **[9 marks]**

Question 2

a **i** Give two examples of a hotel's internal customers. **[2 marks]**

ii Describe how a hotel might create a safe working environment for these internal customers. **[2 marks]**

b Suggest three ways a hotel might meet the needs of foreign visitors. You should use examples to support your answer. **[6 marks]**

c Evaluate the likely impacts of a customer sensing that they are not gaining value for money from their hotel stay. **[9 marks]**

Question 3

Guidance for handling verbal complaints

- Remain calm and respectful throughout the conversation.
- Listen – allow the person to talk about the complaint in their own words.
- Do not debate the facts in the first instance, especially if the person is angry.
- Show an interest in what is being said.
- Obtain details about the complaint before any personal details.
- Ask for clarification wherever necessary.
- Show that you have understood the complaint by reflecting back what you have noted down.

a **i** Give two examples of complaints that a visitor to a tourist attraction might make. **[2 marks]**

ii Describe two ways the complaint might be made. **[2 marks]**

b Refer to the guidelines for handling verbal complaints. Assess the importance of following these guidelines when dealing with a complaint from an angry customer. **[6 marks]**

c Discuss the reasons why customer loyalty is important in travel and tourism. **[9 marks]**

Chapter 3

Destination marketing

In this section of the syllabus you will learn:

- how market research and analysis define the tourism market
- how establishing a destination identity builds the destination brand
- how implementing the destination brand is achieved through communicating brand messages and by overcoming challenges that branding destinations poses
- how to monitor the effectiveness of destination brands using a range of methods and through key performance indicators (KPIs).

Introduction

The places that tourists choose to visit impacts on the overall tourism experience for that tourist. Tourism also plays an important role in developing the economies of **tourist receiving countries**, with significant financial contributions being made to a country's gross domestic product (GDP) through visitor expenditure on tourist accommodation, transport and tourism activities. Tourism represents one of the main sources of income for many developing countries. According to the United Nations World Tourism Organisation (UNWTO), tourism has 'become one of the fastest growing economic sectors in the world'. This growth goes hand in hand with an increasing diversification and competition among destinations.

> **KEY TERM**
>
> **Tourist receiving countries:** countries which attract the highest number of international visitors each year, and tend to be the destinations with good tourism infrastructure. Typical examples of tourist receiving countries are France, the USA, Spain, China, Italy and the UK.

Competition amongst destinations results in more choice for visitors. This, in turn, means that tourism providers in destinations around the world are having to work hard to appeal to visitors in order to gain customers. One means of attracting potential customers is through marketing, but it is often not feasible for each individual tourism organisation to market and promote itself on a global scale. Given the significant economic benefits of a country, or destination, being able to attract more visitors, the task of marketing the broad range of tourist attractions and providers in that destination often falls to the tourism

Figure 3.1 The White Temple in Chiang Rai, Thailand

authorities within the country, as these have both the status and the financial resources with which to make their presence felt on a global scale. Tourism authorities often use aspects of the country's cultural heritage in marketing destinations, such as the beautiful temples in Thailand. See Figure 3.1.

3.1 Defining the tourism market

Before a destination can be marketed or promoted, it is important that the tourism authorities, and providers of visitor products and services within that destination, understand the market in which the destination operates. For well-established destinations in popular tourist receiving countries, the market environment may be very different from that for a less well-known destination within a developing country.

In order to understand the tourism market, there is a need to carry out an assessment of all aspects of the market environment, using a broad range of market research techniques and market analysis tools.

Market research and analysis

> **KEY TERM**
>
> **Market research:** the systematic, objective collection and analysis of data about a particular target market, competition and/or environment (according to Market Research World **www.marketresearchworld.net**). It always incorporates some form of data collection. More simply, it can be defined as the act of gathering information about customers' needs and preferences.

There are many reasons why market research and analysis are carried out by those responsible for marketing a particular destination.

The main purpose of market research and market analysis for a destination is to identify specific features of the tourism market in terms of who will visit, what will visitor expectations be when they visit and which other destinations are appealing to the same visitors.

3.2 The aims of market research and analysis

The market

There are a variety of ways in which a tourism market can be determined. Traditionally, tourism is classified by purpose of visit, i.e. for business, for leisure or for visiting friends and relatives. (For more information of these classifications, please see Chapter 1.) The tourism market may be made up of both international and domestic visitors. Research data may give us an indication of market size, that is, the total number of visitors to a destination within a specific time frame, or it may reveal information about market share, such as the percentage of visitors to the destination compared to the total number of visitors to the region.

It is also possible to define the tourism market in terms of a destination's maturity linked to the stages of the Butler 'Destination Lifecycle' model. This is discussed in Chapter 4. Market research and analysis enables us to classify destinations by their place in the market, relative to the extent of development within the destination.

For example, Papua New Guinea is a newly emerging destination country, confirmed by its number one position in the Top Emerging Destination category of the *Wanderlust* Magazine's 2015 Travel Awards.

Top emerging destinations

1   Papua New Guinea
2   Mongolia
3   Montengero
4   Iran
5   Bolivia.

London, on the other hand, is a well-established city destination, with a long history of winning awards, which makes it a popular choice.

Customer needs and wants

KEY CONCEPTS

Customer focus

The purpose of market research is to establish the needs and wants of customers. This is a key concept in the travel and tourism industry as it will allow a destination's tourism authorities and tourism providers to really understand their customers and assess what they must do to meet their needs.

A key element of marketing for any business is to understand exactly what it is that customers are looking for from the products and services they purchase. This is certainly no different from the perspective of a tourism destination.

KEY TERM

Customer needs: according to Abraham Maslow and his theory, the hierarchy of needs (1943), a need is a basic human requirement. People require food, clothing, shelter, safety, a sense of belonging and self esteem. These needs are not created by marketing professionals: they exist in the human condition.

Customer wants are described as being specific satisfiers of need. These are not actual requirements, rather a person's preference for how a need might be fulfilled.

KEY TERM

Customer demands: those wants backed by the customer's willingness and ability to purchase particular products and services.

Therefore, a key element in market research is not only finding out exactly what customers need and want from a destination, but also identifying how many tourists would be willing and able to visit a specific destination.

KEY CONCEPTS

Global and growing

Competition arises because of the continuing growth of tourism as an important economic factor for many countries. The growth in technology has intensified this competition, with destinations vying for visitors to choose them over the competition through the use of social media and websites.

The competition

Competition between tourist destinations continues to grow with the greater choice in transportation and through advances in technology, which has brought even the remotest of destinations to customer's attention via computer screens and smart phones. One of the aims of market research is therefore to identify the specific destinations that pose the most competitive threat, by appealing to the same customers, and by offering a similar tourist experience.

Destinations will often carry out an analysis of the competition as part of their process in defining the tourism market in which they operate. For example, a small island destination such as Trinidad will use market research to identify other small island destinations which offer a similar range of products and services to visitors and determine its own level of popularity. According to *The Travel and Tourism Competitiveness Report 2015*, published by the World Economic Forum, Trinidad and Tobago are ranked 69th of all destinations. This puts these islands ahead of most of their Caribbean counterparts in the rankings, as destinations such as the Bahamas, Antigua and St. Lucia did not make it onto the list at all because of insufficient tourism data. The Travel and Tourism Competitiveness Index (TTCI) suggests that most Caribbean countries rely extensively on their beaches but do not seem to promote their cultural resources sufficiently. This type of information enables destinations such as Trinidad to stand out from its competitors by publicising a major cultural attraction – the annual Trinidad and Tobago Carnival (Figure 3.2), held on the Monday and Tuesday before Ash Wednesday, which is well known for colourful costumes and lively celebrations.

Figure 3.2 Trinidad and Tobago Carnival

Travel trends

The term **travel trend** refers to the ways in which patterns of travel have developed over a period of time. Travel trends can be used to predict future changes.

KEY TERM

Travel trend: the general direction in which something is developing or changing.

Many tourism authorities collect, collate and analyse data relating to the number of visitors to specific destinations, and the results are used to predict travel patterns in the future. Trends are measured over a period of time, usually not less than a 5-year period, so that a more meaningful comparison of sets of data can be made.

Let's have a look at some of the research data that is available.

World travel trends

Extract from ITB World Travel Trends Report 2014/2015:

'In the last five years people around the world have been increasingly travelling abroad on holiday, although different trends regarding the types of holiday can be seen, according to the World Travel Monitor®. Sun and beach holidays have grown by 18% over the last five years and remain the most important category with 28% of all holiday trips. However, touring holidays have grown by 32%, thanks in particular to more tours by Asians. In contrast, countryside holidays have declined by 17% over the last five years and now only represent 11% of all holidays.

The boom market segment, however, has been city trips which have soared over the five years to reach a 20% market share. This dynamic growth has been supported by the increase in low-cost flights and the expansion of budget accommodation. According to World Travel Monitor® figures, Paris is the world's top city destination with 18.8 million international arrivals in 2013, followed by New York, London, Bangkok, Barcelona and Singapore.'

Pos	City	Arrivals (millions)
1 Paris 18.8		
2 New York 18.5		
3 London 16.1		
4 Bangkok 14.6		
5 Barcelona 12.4		
6 Singapore 10.6.		

Table 3.1 Destination areas trips

ACTIVITY 1

1. Identify **two** types of destination that have continued to grow in popularity over the last five years.
2. If you were a tour operator specialising in offering touring holidays, explain how you might use the information from this research data.
3. Explain **two** reasons why European city destinations might have gained in popularity over recent years.

Customer behaviours

Customer behaviour is generally defined as being concerned with all activities directly involved in obtaining, consuming and disposing of products and services, including the decision processes that precede and follow these actions. In terms of 'tourist behaviour' or 'travel behaviour', there have been many studies of different types of 'tourists' based on their travel motivations, their stage on the lifecycle model, their preferences, which may or may not be helpful in understanding the concept of customer behaviour.

Classification of tourists

Erik Cohen's classification of tourists is based on the theory that tourism combines the curiosity to seek out new experiences with the need for the security of familiar reminders of home. Most tourists prefer to explore the destinations from a familiar base. The degree of familiarity of this base underlies Cohen's typology in which he identifies four tourist roles.

Stanley Plog proposes a theory that associates the popularity of a destination to the inherent personalities of travellers. Plog suggests that travellers can be classified into the following types based on their different personalities: allocentric, psychocentric and mid-centric.

Allocentric type

This is a person who seeks new experiences and adventure in a variety of activities and is outgoing and self-confident. An allocentric person prefers to fly and to explore new and unusual areas before others do so, and enjoy meeting people from foreign or different cultures. They prefer good hotels and food, but not necessarily modern or chain-type hotels. For a tour package, an allocentric would like to have the basics such as transportation and hotels, but not be committed to a structured itinerary. They prefer the freedom to explore an area, make their own arrangements and choose a variety of activities and tourist attractions.

Psychocentric type

Psychocentrics are more conservatively oriented and tend to be inhibited and non-adventuresome. They prefer to revisit familiar destinations where they can relax and know what types of food and activity to expect. Psychocentrics prefer to drive to destinations, stay in typical tourist accommodations and eat at family-type restaurants. When arranging a package tour, psychocentrics would prefer a heavily structured itinerary so that they know what to expect. Safety and security are very important to this group.

Role	Category	Classification
Organised mass tourists	Institutionalised tourism	The least adventurous type of tourist. They spend most of their time surrounded by a similar living environment to home while abroad. Typically take a guided tour in an air-conditioned bus. The itinerary is decided in advance and all the attractions and stopping points are well fixed and guided. Tourists have almost no decisions on their trip.
Individual mass tourists		Similar to the organised mass tourist, except that the tour is not entirely fixed. The tourist has a certain amount of control over the time and itinerary, and is not bound to a group. However, all the major arrangements are still made through a tour agency. They are still confined by their 'environmental bubble'.
Explorer	Non-institutionalised tourism	They arrange their trips alone. They try to go somewhere unusual, but still look for comfortable sleeping places and reliable means of transportation. They retain some of the basic routines and comforts of their native way of life. They try to mix with the people they visit and also try to speak their language. The explorers dare to leave their 'environmental bubble' more readily but they are still careful about their ventures.
Drifter		This type of tourists goes further away from the 'environmental bubble' and from the accustomed ways of life in their home countries. They keep away from any kind of connection with the tourism establishment, such as hotels and tour coaches. The drifters have no fixed itinerary or timetable. They tend to make their trips wholly on their own, and often live with the local people. They try to live the way the locals live, and to share their houses, food and habits.

Cohen Erik, 'Toward a Sociology of International Tourism', *Social Research*, vol. 39, no. 1, 1972

Table 3.2 Cohen's classification of tourists

Mid-centric type

A large number of people fall between the allocentric and the psychocentric types of tourists. This type, called mid-centrics, are not particularly adventurous, but they are receptive to new experience.

All theories agree that there are three stages to the way in which customers take action, namely pre-visit, on-site and post-visit. The following simplified model attempts to show the influences that affect what we shall call 'tourist behaviour'.

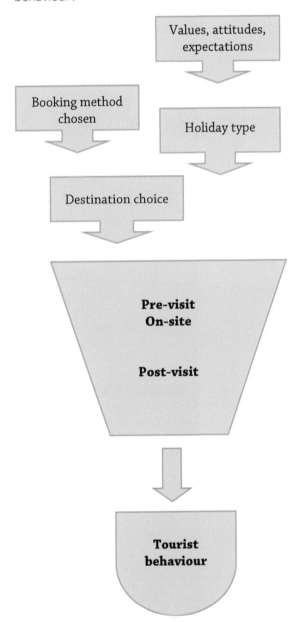

Figure 3.3 Chart depicting some of the influences on tourist behaviour

The choice of destination is crucial to the decision-making process within tourist behaviour and as such, tourist authorities aim to influence the tourist's choice through marketing activities. In order to do so, it is important that 'customer behaviour' is researched and understood.

Customer preferences for destinations

The type of destination that a tourist chooses is clearly influenced by a number of different factors, many of which have been detailed in the earlier section on 'customer behaviours'. Preference implies an element of personal taste, based on our own inherent set of values, attitudes and expectations.

For example, people will choose different destinations for a honeymoon holiday based on their own preferences. For many, the word 'honeymoon' conjures an association with pristine, white sand beaches, palm trees, relaxation and romance, such as on the beach in Figure 3.4.

Figure 3.4 Bora Bora – a traditional 'romantic' honeymoon destination

> **KEY CONCEPTS**
>
> ### Change and development
>
> The dynamic nature of the travel and tourism industry enables it to respond to the changing needs of customers. Tourism providers in destinations around the world seek to update their product portfolios to offer exciting new products and services and to attract a growing number of customers by offering unique tourism experiences.

But many couples are now looking for a unique experience for their honeymoon, so choose destinations where they can take part in more adventurous activities, or stay in unusual accommodation, as in Figure 3.5. Research enables destinations to discover the preferences customers have.

Figure 3.5 A more 'adventurous' honeymoon experience

Popularity of destinations

There are many different measures of popularity through industry-based tourism awards, customer opinion polls, total number of visitors or trips, and so on. We have already seen examples of some of these measures earlier in the chapter (in Table 3.1, and Papua New Guinea). What is important is the fact that tourism authorities in destinations have access to some of the data that indicates which destinations are popular, and which are losing their popularity. This helps inform marketing decisions for destinations aiming to increase or maintain their popularity.

Competition amongst destinations

We have already examined the reasons why market research might identify a destination's competition in the market. Competition, in marketing terms, is considered healthy, as it encourages tourism authorities to look more closely at their product offerings and to find ways of becoming more attractive. It is every destination's aim to gain competitive advantage over similar destinations and to increase market share, because of the economic advantages that this brings. Researching what your competitors are offering is an important stage in ensuring you can offer something better, at a lower price.

Stages in the Butler 'Destination Lifecycle' model

The concept of tourist destinations having a life cycle was first proposed by R.W. Butler in 1980. He suggested that destinations would follow the series of evolutionary stages that he described in his Tourism Area Life Cycle (TALC) model. This is now commonly referred to as the Butler 'Destination Lifecycle' model.

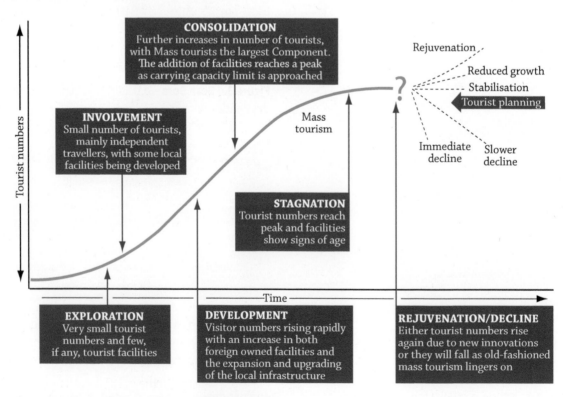

Figure 3.6 The Butler 'Destination Lifecycle' model

As with all life cycles, the final stage is death and if a tourist destination is to survive it must re-invent itself in some way and continue to develop – a process known as 'rejuvenation'. Butler's ideas fit many destinations very well and we can see clear evidence, both in the MEDC and LEDC nations, of locations that fit into one of the six stages of development that he proposed.

1 **Exploration stage:** Small number of tourists that have usually made their own travel arrangements. There are only a few visitors coming to the destination, maybe backpackers or some other type of independent traveller. There are no charter flights or tourist services and the cost to the traveller, both in time and money, can be high. No investment in tourist infrastructure has been made at this stage. However, the economic, social, cultural and environmental impacts caused by tourism will be minimal.

2 **Involvement:** Some local residents begin to provide facilities exclusively for the use of visitors. Visitor numbers increase, local businesses start providing services. The local population has accepted the arrival of visitors and the destination starts to grow, with locals actually becoming involved with promotional activities.

3 **Development:** Local suppliers and providers of tourism products and services become increasingly involved in the development process. The area becomes established as a tourist destination with a defined market. As the visitors keep coming, more businesses enter the market, which is now becoming profitable. Package holidays begin and the destination sees marked expansion with the arrival of foreign operators and investors. As the country becomes more popular and the infrastructure begins to take shape, more tour operators become interested and organise package tours to the country. A range of brochures become available at travel agents, advertisements appear in the media. Competition between businesses grows, so prices start to fall and so do profit margins. With increased competition resulting in falling prices, different type of customers will now be able to visit the destination. This reflects a well-defined tourist destination shaped by heavy marketing in tourist generating regions.

4 **Consolidation:** Tourism now starts to dominate the economic base of the area and begins to have an adverse effect on the traditional economy and lifestyle. Local agricultural land is given over to resort development but there is not a proportional increase in local wealth, per capita income or job creation. The rate of increase in numbers of visitors will have started to decline, although total numbers will still increase.

5 **Stagnation:** Peak numbers of visitors will have been reached. There is a growing awareness of negative environmental, social, cultural and economic tourism impacts. Sales go down as the country goes out of fashion and there is evidence that the original cultural and natural attractiveness of the destination has been lost. Profits are low and businesses may leave the market or diversify to other types of product. Furthermore, because there may be fewer businesses in the local tourism marketplace, prices can be increased, thus accelerating the decline.

6 **Decline versus rejuvenation:** Butler's model of destination development and evolution ends with a series of options that all resorts will have to face at some time. Figure 3.6 shows the following:

   • Immediate decline: Visitor numbers fall quite rapidly and the tourism base severely contracts, resulting in a local economic depression.
   • Decline: The destination will face a declining market and will be unable to compete with newer destinations or destinations that better meet the needs of the modern tourist.
   • Stabilisation: The destination is able to maintain its market share but there is little, if any, continued growth and development.
   • Reduced growth: The effects of competition mean that even with new development plans, the destination is never able to return to the levels of previous growth and development.
   • Rejuvenation: If major changes are made, such as improving the environment and tourism infrastructure, better marketing or the addition of more attractions, for example, then the destination may experience a period of rejuvenation, with further growth and development brought about by innovation and renewed diversification. In effect, the destination re-invents itself and extends its appeal to different market segments.

It is important to remember that the Butler model is a generalisation, and so not all destinations will follow this process exactly. However, many destinations will use the general principles of the model to identify the stage which best describes their stage of development.

Myanmar: A case study of destination development

Myanmar (formerly known as, and still sometimes referred to as Burma) is strategically located in Southeast Asia, and is currently experiencing rapid growth in international tourist arrivals and tourism receipts. It has become an emerging tourist destination for international travellers keen to experience Myanmar's abundant wealth of cultural and natural heritage, hospitality and spiritual values.

Taking this opportunity, the Ministry of Hotels and Tourism of the Republic of the Union of Myanmar has placed considerable emphasis on developing and managing tourism in sustainable and responsible ways in line with the Government's reform strategies and economic plans. This has led to the development of the Myanmar Tourism Master Plan 2013 to 2020. The goal of this Master Plan is to maximise tourism's contribution to national employment and income generation while ensuring the social and economic benefits of tourism are distributed equitably. The Government set a high target of 3.01 million international visitors in 2015 and 7.48 million by 2020.

News article

Things are changing in Myanmar. For the past four years the country has been experiencing greater political transparency. This is also having an impact on the tourism sector, which has seen the number of visitors to the country more than double: in 2010 tourists numbered around 800,000, whereas in 2014 Myanmar welcomed two million visitors.

Myanmar is one of the world's poorest countries, so tourism represents an important source of income. Many new hotels are currently being built in Myanmar, and with this development comes tourism development advice from around the world. That may start with the simplest things, such as cutting down on waste by getting hotels to use laundry bags made of linen rather than plastic and fitting refillable soap dispensers.

The hospitality industry provides jobs for many people. Beyond this, however, the tourism sector also offers enormous potential for economic development in the country. There is also advice to business start-ups on how to gain a foothold in the tourism sector.

From hotel bakery suppliers to cycle hire shops – the potential for business concepts is huge. With its Buddhist temples, deserted beaches and majestic Himalayan landscape, Myanmar has much to offer tourists. There is potential here to develop a wide range of travel opportunities, and to do this in a way that benefits all involved – both tourists and local people.

Myanmar ranks high among emerging Southeast Asia destinations. Myanmar ranks top in several surveys.

United States Tour Operation Association (USTOA) members ranked Myanmar as 2015's top emerging destination – ahead of Cuba, Croatia, Iceland, India, Peru, Sir Lanka, Vietnam, Cambodia and Panama. This was the third straight year that Myanmar took top spot in these rankings.The following predictions are based on the analysis of Skyscanner flight search data from the last three years, combined with qualitative research carried out by a market research agency, Trendhunter, to provide additional insight on destination trends and influences.

Skyscanners' list of top 10 destinations for 2015:

1	Myanmar	2	Mykonos, Greece
3	Iceland	4	Brazil
5	Panama	6	New Caledonia
7	Seoul, South Korea	8	Colombo, Sri Lanka
9	Nicaragua	10	Okinawa, Japan.

The results of a recent visitor satisfaction survey carried out in Myanmar are given below. Figures in brackets refer to the percentage of people who rated various aspects of the visitor experience in Myanmar in terms of satisfaction.

Most Satisfied

Choice of different activities/things to do (76)
Overall service (tour guides) (76)
Availability of local/traditional cuisine (75)
Value for money (local food and beverage) (75)
Ease of access to cultural/historic attractions (74)
Overall service (tour operators) (72)

Least Satisfied

Value for money (accommodations) (34)
Cleaniliness of transport options (25)
Availability of information on destinations (22)
Choice pf transport options to destinations (21)
Value for money (tours/travel) (18)
Overall service (hotels) (15)

Use the information from case study 2 to consider how well tourism authorities in Myanmar have met their research aims in trying to define the current tourism market for the destination.

Consider how the research identifies:

• the market
• customer needs and wants
• the competition
• competition among destinations
• travel trends and customer behaviours
• customer preferences for destinations
• popularity of destinations
• stage in the Butler 'Destination Lifecycle' model.

3.3 Market research: advantages and disadvantages of each research method

To conduct market research, tourism organisations may decide to undertake the project themselves, using their marketing department to carry out this task, or they might choose to commission it via a professional market research agency or consultancy firm.

Collecting data is central to the market research process. There are a number of research methods available to capture the data required by undertaking market research on any scale. There are also limitless sources of appropriate data that can be accessed. The next section of the chapter will look at these methodologies and techniques in detail, to identify the advantages and disadvantages of using each.

Primary research methods

Primary research is often called 'field research', as it is obtained first hand from customers in the market. This type of research can be carried out by asking customers questions or by observing consumer behaviour. There are many commercial market research companies that will carry out primary research on behalf of tourism authorities but this is very costly. Questionnaires and surveys are the main methods used in primary research, although in-depth interviews, focus groups and participant observations may also be used.

Questionnaires

Questionnaires must be carefully designed to ensure that **respondents** can easily understand what they are being asked.

Respondent: a person filling in a questionnaire or taking part in a survey (the person responding to the questions).

The language being used in a questionnaire needs to be simple and should avoid the use of jargon. Closed questions (those with a yes/no response) or multiple-choice questions are used to guide respondents towards a uniform answer. The advantage of this is that it is quicker for respondents to answer and it also makes data analysis more straightforward because of the uniformity of the answers.

Scaled-response questions, as in Figure 3.7 are also useful in gauging customers' opinions (for example, 'Rate the service you received on a scale of one to ten, one being poor, ten being exceptional.').

Open questions where respondents are left to answer in any way they choose make analysis more difficult and are also off-putting to those completing the questionnaire.

Questions should begin by being quite general and gradually become more specific. The number of questions included is also very important – too few and the research may not gather sufficient data to be considered valid; too many questions may leave respondents frustrated at the time it takes to complete. Between 10 and 15 questions is recommended for most questionnaires.

Here is an example of a destination questionnaire used by tourism authorities in Slovenia.

Tourist destination questionnaire

Dear Sir or Madam!

Good morning/afternoon and welcome to our tourist destination. We are pleased that you decided to stay here. If you have spent at least one night at our destination we kindly ask you to participate in a survey which will help us make your future stay here even more pleasant. The interview will take about 10–15 minutes and is conducted anonymously.

1   How did you arrive to Slovenia? (mark the appropriate answer)

    1   By car

    2   By bus

    3   With low-cost airline

    4   With major airline

    5   By train

    6   Other, what: _____

2   Where did you hear about this tourist destination? (mark the appropriate answer, more answers possible)

    1   I already knew of it

    2   The Internet

    3   Friends and relatives

    4   Media

    5   Books and guides

    6   Travel agency

    7   Fairs and/or exhibitions

    8   It was part of the travel package

    9   Other, what: _____

3   Is this your first visit to this tourist destination? (mark the appropriate answer)

    1   No. How many times have you visited this tourist destination in the past? _____

    2   Yes. How many nights are you planning to stay at this tourist destination: _____

4   What are the main reasons for your visit to this tourist destination? (mark the appropriate answer)

    1   Rest and relaxation

    2   Visiting relatives and friends

    3   Business reasons

    4   Attending a conference, congress, seminar, and other forms of educations

    5   Culture

    6   Fun

    7   Sports and recreation

    8   Health

    9   Religious reasons

    10   Other, what: _____

7-8. Below are listed some elements that you might consider when you chose a tourist destination. We ask you to evaluate them twice. First, please indicate HOW IMPORTANT is each of these elements to you when you chose any tourist destination (in general) (rate them on a scale »1« - completely unimportant to »5« - very important). Then we ask you to indicate on a scale 1 – 5 to what extent do you agree with the statement that these elements are EXCEPTIONAL or are at the EXCEPTIONALLY HIGH LEVEL at this tourist destination (where »1« means – I completely disagree, »5« - I completely agree).

ELEMENTS OF TOURIST DESTINATION	»HOW IMPORTANT IS THIS ELEMENT?«						»AT THIS DESTINATION, THIS ELEMENT IS EXCEPTIONAL/AT EXCEPTIONALLY HIGH					
	Completely unimportant				Very important	I don't know	I completely disagree				I completely agree	I don't know
1. Personal safety and security.	**1**	**2**	**3**	**4**	**5**		**1**	**2**	**3**	**4**	**5**	
2. The destination can be easily reached.	1	2	3	4	5		1	2	3	4	5	
3. Overall cleanliness of the destination.	1	2	3	4	5		1	2	3	4	5	
4. Unspoiled nature.	1	2	3	4	5		1	2	3	4	5	
5. Climate conditions.	1	2	3	4	5		1	2	3	4	5	
6. Diversity of cultural/historical attractions (architecture, tradition and customs…)	1	2	3	4	5		1	2	3	4	5	
7. The quality of the accommodation (hotel, motel, apartment…)	1	2	3	4	5		1	2	3	4	5	
8. Friendliness of the local people.	1	2	3	4	5		1	2	3	4	5	
9. Organization of the local transportation services.	1	2	3	4	5		1	2	3	4	5	
10. The offer of local cuisine.	1	2	3	4	5		1	2	3	4	5	
11. Possibilities for shopping.	1	2	3	4	5		1	2	3	4	5	
12. Night life and entertainment.	1	2	3	4	5		1	2	3	4	5	
13. Opportunity for rest.	1	2	3	4	5		1	2	3	4	5	
14. Availability of sport facilities and recreational activities.	1	2	3	4	5		1	2	3	4	5	
15. Offer of cultural and other events.	1	2	3	4	5		1	2	3	4	5	
16. Thermal spa offer.	1	2	3	4	5		1	2	3	4	5	
17. Wellness offer.	1	2	3	4	5		1	2	3	4	5	
18. Casino and gambling offer.	1	2	3	4	5		1	2	3	4	5	
19. Conference offer.	1	2	3	4	5		1	2	3	4	5	

Figure 3.7 An example of scaled-response questions.

Surveys

A survey is often referred to as a contact method for market research. There are various types of market research surveys including:

- Exit surveys: often used by tourist attractions and hotels. Tourist destinations also often carry these out in airport departure lounges. Users are invited to provide customer feedback on the level of service they have received during their visit. These often use a scale of response in order to assess levels of customer satisfaction.
- Postal surveys: take place when a respondent is sent a copy of the questionnaire and a reply-paid return envelope. This method was commonly used in the past, but its major disadvantage was a generally poor response rate. To try to overcome this, many organisations link responses to an entry into a free prize draw but even with this encouragement, the average response rate for postal surveys is less than 10%.
- Telephone surveys: allow an organisation to input responses as the respondent speaks, thus saving administration time and costs. However, many people resent the unsolicited call and often refuse to take part. These tend to be used by organisations selling time-share holidays.
- Online surveys: commonly used by tour operators and transport companies who have access to customers' email addresses. An invitation to take part in the survey is sent via email together with a hyperlink to the survey page. Response rates here are variable, depending on the nature of the questions and how quickly the survey pages load.

- In-depth interviews: usually conducted face-to-face while the customer is in the destination. They allow for detailed opinions and attitudes to be sought but are expensive and time-consuming to organise. Respondents are usually offered a reward for taking part; this could be a 20% discount coupon against a future visit.
- Focus groups: usually comprise 8–12 respondents, led by a moderator, who discuss in detail a product design or similar issue. Discussions are usually recorded and observed to allow the organisation to analyse respondents' reactions and behaviour during the discussion. These are costly to set up and time-consuming to carry out. They take a long time to plan and put into place as a venue is needed as well as recording equipment (see Figure 3.8).
- Participant observation: is particularly difficult to manage. If respondents know they are being filmed or secretly watched, their behaviour may be unnatural. This type of research is rarely used in isolation in travel and tourism, although some travel agents monitor how long a customer spends browsing the brochure display using this method, before offering assistance.

98

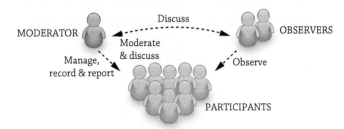

Figure 3.8 How a focus group works

ACTIVITY 3

Imagine you work for the tourism authority of a popular holiday destination. Visitor numbers have started to decline this year for the first time in a 10-year period. You have been asked to conduct primary research to find out the reasons behind the decline in visitor numbers.

Explain what method of primary research you would select. Give reasons for your answer. Describe the advantages and disadvantages of the methods you rejected.

Advantages of primary research methods include:

- Data is relevant and specific to the organisation.
- Research is up-to-date, thus primary data is more accurate.

Disadvantages of primary research methods include:

- Costly: the organisation has to be involved throughout and has to design everything.
- Time consuming: it is a lengthy process making contact with respondents and carrying out a survey.
- High risk of bias: the interviewer or moderator may influence the results of the feedback received.

Secondary research methods

This is also known as 'desk research' as it involves researching information that has already been collected for another purpose. As much of this is in printed or electronic format, the researcher can sit at a desk to carry out the research. An incredible amount of data already exists in a variety of government or trade reports (though these are not always readily accessible by the general public). Travel and tourism organisations also have a considerable amount of internal data from their own sales records with existing customers. External secondary data sources may include:

- the United Nations World Tourism Organisation (UNWTO) online statistics service
- government publications, such as international passenger survey results
- intelligence-gathering agencies and market reports, for example Euromonitor, World Travel and Tourism Council reports
- the trade press, such as *Travel Trade Weekly*
- academic journals like the *International Journal of Tourism Research*
- trade bodies, for example The Tourism Society.

Advantages of secondary research methods include:

- Ease of access: there is an abundance of information available because of the internet.
- Much of the data is free of charge: most sources are available at little or no cost.
- Data may already have been collated, presented and analysed, which is hugely beneficial.

Disadvantages of secondary research methods include:

- Relevance: when conducting secondary research, it is important to remember that much of the available data may not be relevant to your specific research objectives or purpose.
- Validity: data sources should be checked for authenticity and validity, especially when using the internet as a research tool. Much of the data on the internet is out of date.
- Bias: secondary data sources should also be checked for author bias. This occurs when the writer expresses a personal perspective rather than objective facts.

ACTIVITY 4

Research the internet and other sources of information to find data about visitor numbers to your country.

Evaluate the range of secondary research data you found, in terms of their relevance, validity and reliability.

Qualitative research

Qualitative research provides an understanding of how or why things are as they are. This involves the study of attitudes or motivation. It relates specifically to consumer preferences and opinions and generates data through the use of open-ended questions. Unlike quantitative research there is no fixed set of questions to use in qualitative research. Much of this type of research is carried out in the belief that a customer engaged in a tourism activity is best placed to comment on their experience and that this experience is best communicated using the customer's own words. Research of this sort is mostly done face-to-face, through interviews, or focus group discussions.

Advantages of qualitative research include:

- Depth and detail: it looks deeper than analysing ranks and counts by recording attitudes, feelings and behaviours.
- Creates openness: encouraging people to expand on their responses can open up new issues not initially considered as a research objective.
- Reflects people's individual experiences: a detailed picture can be built up about why people act in certain ways and their feelings about these actions.
- Attempts to avoid pre-judgements: if used alongside quantitative data collection, it can explain why a particular response was given.

Disadvantages of qualitative research include:

- Usually fewer people are surveyed: collection of qualitative data is generally more time consuming than quantitative data collection and therefore unless time, staff and budget allows, it is generally necessary to include a smaller survey sample size.
- Less easy to generalise: because fewer people are generally surveyed, it is not possible to generalise results to that of the whole population. Usually exact numbers are reported rather than percentages. Cannot always display using charts and graphs.

- Difficult to make systematic comparisons: for example, if people give widely differing responses that are highly personalised.
- Dependent on skills of the researcher: particularly in the case of conducting interviews, focus groups and observations.

Quantitative research

Quantitative research is numerically oriented, focuses on the measurement of market data and involves statistical analysis. For example, an airline might ask its customers to rate its overall service as either excellent, good, poor or very poor. This will provide quantitative information that can be analysed statistically. The main rule with quantitative research is that every respondent is asked the same series of questions. The approach is very structured and normally involves large numbers of interviews/questionnaires. Surveys are the most common form of quantitative research carried out.

Advantages of quantitative research include:

- Allows for a broader study: involving a greater number of respondents, and enhancing the generalisation of the results.
- Can allow for greater objectivity and accuracy of results: generally, quantitative methods are designed to provide summaries of data that support generalisations about the issue being researched.
- Standardised: the research can be repeated and then analysed and compared with similar studies over time
- Personal bias: can be avoided by researchers keeping a 'distance' from respondents.
- Easy to present in graphs, tables and charts: makes interpretation and analysis more straightforward.

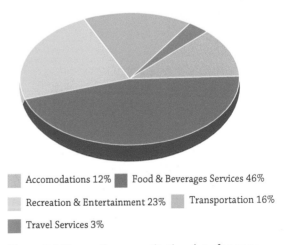

Accomodations 12% Food & Beverages Services 46%
Recreation & Entertainment 23% Transportation 16%
Travel Services 3%

Figure 3.9 Presenting quantitative data for easy interpretation

ACTIVITY 5

Better Stay Hotels is a small hotel chain located in Eastern Europe. This chain consists of five hotels located in several Eastern European countries.

Their target market is the weekend break market. This is because couples regularly choose a weekend break in Europe for their holidays. In line with this location strategy, the hotel group promotes itself with the slogan 'a perfect place for a break.' The individual hotels in the Better Stay group vary a little in quality, but all have either a three- or a four star rating. This means that they are either medium (three star) or good (four star) quality in terms of facilities and general standard of accommodation and service. Each hotel has approximately 40 rooms and a range of facilities including a heated swimming pool, room service, a restaurant and a small gym; some of the hotels also have a tennis court and a gift shop.

Table 3.3 shows how the hotels vary their pricing throughout the year. Pricing is generally used to overcome the issue of seasonality.

The table also shows the results of a customer satisfaction survey for Better Stay Hotels. On average, 80% of customers indicated that they were satisfied with their stay and 10% were delighted with their stay. However, 10% indicated they were dissatisfied. These figures vary by season, whether the customer was a first-time customer and by the quality of the individual hotel. Additionally, the table includes information on average room rates (per night) and occupancy levels. (Note: the term occupancy level means the percentage of rooms occupied per night.)

	Average	Low season	High season	First time customers	Repeat customers	Three star locations	Four star locations
Delighted customers	10%	20%	5%	25%	5%	10%	20%
Satisfied customers	80%	70%	75%	60%	90%	70%	70%
Dissatisfied customers	10%	10%	20%	15%	5%	20%	10%
Average room price	€120	€75	€160	€140	€100	€100	€140
Occupancy level	80%	50%	100%	N/A	N/A	85%	75%

Table 3.3

Questions

1 Review the customer satisfaction information. Does it make sense? Why/why not?

2 Given these research results and the other information in the case study, what advice would you give to Better Stay Hotels?

3 Which of the data did you find helpful? Which did you basically ignore?

4 What other information would have been helpful?

Disadvantages of quantitative research include:

- Generally collects a much narrower: sometimes superficial dataset.
- Results are limited: they provide numerical descriptions rather than detailed narrative.
- Preset answers will not necessarily reflect how people really feel about an issue: in some cases it might just be the closest match. This can lead to 'structural' bias and false representation, where the data actually reflects the view of those designing the questions rather than the respondents themselves.

3.4 Market analysis tools and techniques

There are a number of important marketing tools and techniques which are essential in helping tourism authorities define the market in which destinations operate. Many of these tools and techniques are covered in general marketing textbooks. The following section attempts to provide an applied context to these tools and techniques by showing how these can be used within a specific tourism destination context.

Statistical analysis of data

We have already seen that research data often provides us with numeric data about travel trends, customer behaviours, customer preferences for destinations and the popularity of destinations. Surveys which measure the number of visitors to a destination by travel motivation, for example, will produce a set of figures.

It is important that these figures can be collated and presented appropriately, in order for their meaning to be derived. This means the figures can be interpreted and analysed, so that tourism organisations understand their significance in marketing terms.

ACTIVITY 6

Study the following chart.

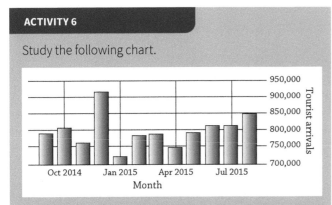

Figure 3.10 Indonesia tourist arrivals

1   Explain the pattern in tourist arrivals in Indonesia between September 2014 and August 2015.

2   Analyse how useful this data is in defining the tourism market in Indonesia. Suggest other data that might be needed to make a better analysis.

Analysis of strengths, weaknesses, opportunities and threats (SWOT analysis)

A SWOT analysis is a marketing tool used in many business contexts. SWOT is an acronym for:

Strengths

Weaknesses

Opportunities

Threats

These are assessed in relation to the market position of a product, an organisation or, in this case, a destination. Strengths and weaknesses are internal factors (meaning within the control of the organisation or tourism authorities) and opportunities and threats are external factors (beyond the control of the organisation or tourism authorities.)

 KEY CONCEPTS

Change and development

A SWOT analysis allows a destination to review the internal and external influences on its operating environment, which are always subject to change. Where opportunities are identified, tourism providers will seek to develop new products and services to advance tourism development.

A SWOT analysis is often conducted as the initial stage of a full situation analysis to determine the market environment in which an organisation or destination operates. A SWOT analysis looks at the current market situation and tourism development relies heavily on the outcome of such analyses – tour operators may decide not to promote certain destinations if the weaknesses and threats from the SWOT analysis outweigh the strengths and opportunities.

A strength of a destination may be the well-established cultural traditions practised by the local population, whilst a weakness could be the lack of trained tourism staff to work at local attractions and hotels. An opportunity may present itself in the government's plans to extend the local airport, in order to attract more international carriers, whilst a threat may come in the form of competition from a neighbouring destination.

 KEY CONCEPTS

Global and growing

The external business environment in which all destinations operate can be seen as one global market, which is affected by changes in political and economic circumstances. A PEST analysis allows a destination the opportunity to determine the extent to which global tourism growth may benefit tourism in that country.

Analysis of political, economic, social and technological external influences (PEST analysis)

PEST analysis is another marketing tool that forms part of a full situation analysis. It is used to assess the external influences on the market environment and is known by its acronym:

Political

Economic

Social

Technological influences

101

As the travel and tourism industry is always changing, there are many forces affecting market trends which in turn affect the popularity of specific tourist products and destinations. These forces include the political arena: civil unrest, military coups and acts of international terrorism are detrimental to tourism development. High levels of government support within a destination, on the other hand, can positively influence tourism practices.

Economic conditions can have both positive and negative impacts on tourism provision; foreign exchange rate fluctuations, for example, make the dollar, the euro or the pound stronger or weaker, offering better or worse value for money for a tourist. Government subsidies may be offered to tourism business start-ups in a destination, or increased taxation may make increased demands on small businesses within the destination.

The social and cultural environment is also an important market force for travellers and tourists. Experiencing a different culture can in itself be the motivator for visiting a specific destination.

Modern technology plays a vital role in marketing travel and tourism products and services. The Internet has opened up a world of opportunities for destinations to gain recognition around the world, with virtual tours, direct marketing and 24-hour access to customers. There are, however, many destinations where technological development is still limited, which may impede the number of visitors attracted to the destination.

A PEST analysis allows an organisation to assess how great a threat is posed by the various external influences upon the market. Although the influences identified through PEST analysis remain outside the control of the organisation, it does not mean that their impacts cannot be minimised.

> ### ACTIVITY 7
>
> Use all of the information from the case study to analyse the internal and the external influences on tourism in Florida, USA.
>
> Suggest how the information gathered from a SWOT and a PEST analysis can be used by destinations in Florida to gain more visitors.

Competition amongst destinations

Another important analytical tool used by destinations is known as a competitor analysis. As its name suggests, this tool is used within a competitive market to identify which destinations pose the biggest threat and also to estimate the probable extent of competition that each rival destination poses. Competitors may be divided into direct competition and indirect competition.

Direct competition exists between destinations which offer an identical or similar experience to customers, resulting in tourists having a choice. Thus a city destination such as London would consider another European city such as Paris as a direct competitor. Indirect competition exists in the form of substitute products and services, so in the case

CASE STUDY 3

A situation analysis of tourism in Florida, USA

Like many states, Florida was negatively affected by the economic downturn in 2008. However, recent increases in tourism marketing have increased Florida's total visitor numbers and moved Florida toward its 100 million annual visitor goal. Moreover, since the beginning of 2013, more than 75 000 jobs have been created in Florida as a direct result of the state's investment in tourism. This increase also translates into an increased usage of the state's roads, airports, cruise terminals, attractions and other resources. Ensuring that the state has enough capacity to welcome additional visitors is key to retaining Florida's position as a competitive, world-class tourism destination.

Strengths	Weaknesses
• the weather – known as the Sunshine State and has a mild climate all year round • diverse range of activities – beaches, golf, theme parks, the Everglades • accessibility – can drive or fly or arrive by cruise ship.	• the product offering is not 'new' – Florida has an image of being old and familiar.
Opportunities	**Threats**
• can target different market segments – minority visitors.	• competition from Hawaii and the Caribbean in terms of weather; from California and New York in terms of product offerings • risk of hurricanes.

Table 3.4 An analysis of the tourism situation in Florida, USA

of a destination such as London, an indirect competitor may be any other type of destination, a resort or a country.

Recognising who your competitors are and being aware of their marketing activities allows you to seek competitive advantage over them.

Stages in the Butler 'Destination Lifecycle' model

Please see the section on this market analysis tool earlier in the chapter. Butler saw destinations as fragile and that they need to be carefully managed so that they are not allowed to exceed their **carrying capacity**. After all, who wants to stay at a resort that feels overcrowded and over-commercialised?

> **KEY TERM**
>
> **Carrying capacity:** the number of people that a region can support without causing harm to the environment.

The lifecycle model is based on the following proposition:

Visitors will come to an area in small numbers initially, restricted by lack of access, facilities and local knowledge. As facilities are provided and awareness grows, visitor numbers will increase. With marketing, information dissemination and further facility provision, the area's popularity will grow rapidly. Eventually, however, the rate of increase in visitor numbers will decline as levels of carrying capacity are reached. These may be identified in terms of environmental factors (land scarcity, water quality, air quality), of physical plant (transport, accommodation, other services) or of social factors (crowding, resentment by the local population). As the attractiveness of the area declines relative to other areas, because of overuse and the impacts of visitors, the actual number of visitors may also eventually decline.

> **KEY CONCEPTS**
>
> **Sustainability and responsibility**
>
> One benefit of destination marketing is the conscious decision by the tourism authorities to manage the development within the destination. Managing environmental factors through the various stages of the Butler model allows tourism providers to promote and practise the principles of sustainability and responsibility in managing the development.

Being able to identify a destination's place within the model allows decisions to be made about further development of tourism provision and in this respect, the Butler 'Destination Lifecycle' model becomes another useful market analysis tool.

The Ansoff Matrix

The Ansoff Matrix is also commonly used in business to analyse a product's position in the market, and is also therefore used to determine a destination's position in the market. It is based upon a fourfold classification, (often using a quadrant diagram such as the one in Table 3.5), according to whether the destination is an emerging destination or an existing one being marketed to new or existing target markets.

> **KEY CONCEPTS**
>
> **Change and development**
>
> Using the Ansoff Matrix in tourism destinations helps promote the principles of development and change. Adapting products in response to market changes is crucial for survival in a competitive market.

Market penetration	Product development
An existing product in an existing market for example, the Maldives as a honeymoon destination	A new product in an existing market for example, trekking in Patagonia as a honeymoon destination
Market development	Diversification
An existing product in a new market for example, the Maldives as a family holiday destination	A new product in a new market for example, the Poseidon Mystery Island underwater resort currently under construction in Fiji as a unique underwater holiday destination

Table 3.5 Characteristics of the Ansoff Matrix, applied to destination examples

> **ACTIVITY 8**
>
> Explain the advantages and disadvantages of using the Ansoff Matrix to analyse the market position of a destination. Which category of destination would be most difficult to market? Explain the reasons for your answer.

The Boston Matrix

The Boston Matrix approach is named after the Boston Consulting Group, which devised this market analysis tool to assess market growth rates and relative market share. This tool is commonly used by businesses to assess their product portfolio, in order to identify which products are most successful and which are not performing well in the market. It is possible for destinations to adapt the model to assess how well they are performing compared with other destinations. It is also possible to use the Boston Matrix to analyse how well a destination is performing with different categories of visitors. The results are then used to suggest different marketing strategies to use for different destinations or with different customer groups. An example of the Boston Matrix is given in Table 3.6.

Category	Characteristics	Relative market share	Market growth
star (Dubai)	market leader fast growing high profitability	high	high
cash cow (Paris)	profitable generates more cash than is needed to maintain market share operates in a mature market	high	low
problem child (Luxor, Egypt)	rapid growth poor profit margins needs huge input of cash	low	high
dog (Aleppo, Syria)	high failure rate no market growth	low	low

Table 3.6 An example of the Boston Matrix

Kenya

The threat of terrorism, coupled with Ebola in West Africa, resulted in travel warnings being issued in tourist source markets in Europe and America; consequently, the number of tourist arrivals in 2014 continued to be heavily affected. Despite these challenges, growth in tourism value for most travel categories, such as airlines, car rental, lodging and intermediaries, continued to record an increase in 2014. This can be attributed to increasing collaborative efforts by travel and tourism organisations, innovative marketing campaigns, incentive packages for tourists, and a single visa for East African visitors.

The increasing availability of internet access, coupled with improving infrastructure and the introduction of simpler electronic payment methods, is boosting online travel bookings in Kenya. Additionally, the government continues to play a significant role by partnering with travel service providers to improve customer experiences, as part of achieving the country's Vision 2030. Many tourism organisations continue to invest in online and mobile platforms (Figure 3.11) to reach a wider audience including social media, to market their products and services to travellers.

Kenya's airline market continues to be dominated by scheduled flights; however, the entry of low cost carriers, such as Jambojet and Fly540.com, is making the market more competitive. Domestic business and leisure travellers are increasingly using low-cost carrier

www.MagicalKenya.com

Figure 3.11 Magical Kenya logo

airlines to travel around the country. These airlines appeal to travellers as they are cheaper, with prices at less than KES6 000 for return flights from cities such as Nairobi to Eldoret. Airlines, travel agencies and hotels in Kenya have formed strategic partnerships to bolster tourism. Key stakeholders, such as the Kenya Tourism Board (KTB), also continued to engage with officials from source markets to reassure tourists of Kenya's safety. Kenyan Airways partnered with the global travel agency Amadeus, while the Kenyan Tourism Board has partnered with Jovago to integrate bookings between the board's destination website, Magical Kenya, and increase the visibility of different lodging brands among travellers. These alliances are expected to continue playing a significant role in reviving the country's tourism industry.

ACTIVITY 9

With reference to the case study materials provided, use a range of market analysis tools and techniques to draw conclusions about Kenya as a destination.

Which tools were the most appropriate and useful? Which tools did not help you draw any meaningful conclusions about Kenya as a tourist destination? Why?

If you worked for the Kenya Tourism Board, suggest how you could use the information from your analyses to help drive the tourism market for the country.

KEY CONCEPTS

Customer focus

Market segmentation ensures that the customer is firmly at the centre of everything that an organisation does. In terms of destination marketing, this means selecting target customers for whom the destination will be appealing; the destination must then ensure it provides the products, services and facilities that these customers require.

3.5 Market segmentation (target customers)

In order to establish an effective marketing strategy for a destination, it is important to first choose the correct **target market**. This is done through a process known as market segmentation. This means that customers are classified according to pre-set characteristics. The total market is then divided into a series of subsections or 'segments' based on these characteristics.

KEY TERM

Target market: a group of customers towards which an organisation has decided to aim its marketing efforts and ultimately its products and services.

There are four main types of segmentation used in travel and tourism to 'target' customers, although many organisations create several smaller sub-categories of these segments. Market segmentation allows an organisation to focus its marketing efforts only on those people who are most likely to buy or use its products or services. It is also beneficial to customers as they only receive marketing information for products or destinations that are likely to be of interest to them.

Segmentation by travel motivation

The reason a tourist is making a trip automatically segments customers (e.g. business travellers, leisure travellers, VFR tourists, sports tourists, religious tourists and so on).

Many destinations rely extensively on travel motivations for their specific target markets. For example, consider Lourdes in France or Mecca in Saudi Arabia (Figure 3.12). Both of these destinations attract millions of visitors each year who make a pilgrimage as part of their faith. Destinations such as Costa Rica and India have developed travel packages targeted specifically at medical tourists (Figure 3.13), who seek specialist treatments in these countries at reduced costs.

Figure 3.12 Example of religious tourism

Figure 3.13 Example of medical tourism

Demographic segmentation

This means that data relating to customers age, gender, ethnicity or **level of disposable income** may be used to segment customers. Let us consider each of these categories in turn.

KEY TERM

Level of disposable income: refers to the amount of money that households have available for spending and saving after income taxes have been accounted for.

Age: Some destinations may try to target customers by age as a means of overcoming issues of seasonality. Destinations such as Malta and Cyprus will target the 'grey market' (retirees) as a means of attracting customers at times of the year when other visitors tend not to travel. Some destinations will target the 18–30 market with their 'party destination' image. Destinations such as Universal Studios, Singapore or Disneyland Paris target the very young by offering 'Free Benefits for Kids under 7'.

Gender: Research has been conducted into gender differences in choosing tourism destinations. It is believed that women consider choice of destination far more important than men do. One of the reasons why men and women may want different things from a tourism experience is that they are 'getting away from' different things in the home environment. An example, based on the conventional division of labour, and male/female stereotypes, is that a self-catering camping holiday may be experienced differently by males, for whom it represents a change, and by females, for whom it may be a variation on a familiar theme. It is not suggested that tourist destination marketers should try to appeal to either males or females; that is, to promote single-sex destinations, but rather that, in order to appeal to both males and females, it may be advisable to emphasise certain characteristics important to each gender. The emphasis may vary depending on whether the primary purchase decision-maker is likely to be a male or a female. Research also suggests that women are often the primary planners and decision-makers of their trips.

Ethnicity: Destinations will appeal to people based on race and ethnicity, depending on the cultural norms and customs practised. People from some ethnic backgrounds will have to choose their destination carefully because of the need for certain food types and food preparation requirements.

Level of disposable income: This is closely linked to age and position in the family lifecycle. For example, a young single person will have reasonable levels of disposable income, whereas a young couple with a baby will have decreasing levels of disposable income. This will influence choice of destination, in terms of travel costs, as well as general cost of living once in the destination.

Table 3.7 offers an overview of the relationship between levels of disposable income and stage on the family lifecycle. These are clearly generalisations as not everyone's income falls into this same pattern.

Stage in family lifecycle	Level of disposable income	Destination choice
young single	reasonable	short haul, party destination
young couple	high	exotic, romantic
full nest one (young couple with baby)	decreasing	domestic or short haul destination, with wide choice of self-catering accommodation
full nest two (couple with young children)	low	domestic or short haul destination, somewhere that offers all inclusive packages
full nest three (couple with older children)	low	destinations which offer wide range of activities and all inclusive packages
empty nest one (couple whose children have left home)	increasing	cultural destinations, overseas
empty nest two (older couple, main income earner retired)	restricted	destinations offering low season packages
solitary survivor one (single or widowed, still working)	restricted	destinations offering low season packages
solitary survivor two (retired single or widowed person)	low	destinations offering low season packages

Table 3.7 Destination choice relative to disposable income and position in the family lifecycle.

Psychographic segmentation

The term psychographic means 'by type of lifestyle'. Psychographic segmentation involves dividing a market into segments based upon different personality traits, values, attitudes, interests and lifestyles of consumers. This is an important classification within the tourism industry, as many organisations will use specialist markets or niche markets to target customers. This means that some destinations will try to attract one 'specialist' type of customer based on their lifestyle choices, for example spa tourism will appeal to those visitors who have an interest in health and wellbeing. Similarly adventure tourists will look for destinations with a broad offering of a variety of adventurous activities.

Geographic segmentation

As its name suggests, this type of segmentation requires targeting customers based on where they live. Many tourist authorities will use geographic segmentation to target specific markets, such as the domestic market, or visitors from specific geographic locations.

For example, Australia has developed a strong geographic segmentation strategy for visitors from India, as shown in the Case study 5.

ACTIVITY 10

Look at Case study 5 and answer the questions.

1   Explain how market segmentation has benefitted tourism authorities in Australia.

2   Analyse the forms of market segmentation used by Australia in selecting their target customers.

3   Tourism Australia has created a **'customer profile'** for a typical visitor from India. Evaluate the value of customer profiling in this way.

KEY TERM

Customer profile: this is created when an organisation uses the analysis of market segmentation to build an understanding of the target market, based on the characteristics of a 'typical' customer.

3.6 Visitor profiling

This form of market analysis builds further on the concept of a customer profile, using specific criteria to establish the type of people who visit a destination. Much of the data regarding visitor profiling is determined from databases of existing and past customers, that is, from users of the products, services and facilities in the destination. This data is used to build a clearer picture of a 'typical' visitor, so that the destination can learn what appeals to these customers or can attempt to target a different customer group by doing things differently.

The criteria used in visitor profiling includes the following categories.

Length of stay

Being able to research the average number of nights that visitors spend in a location provides a useful insight into how attractive the destination is. If the average length of stay is one or two nights, it would imply that visitors find the tourist offering limited. The aim of tourist authorities is to entice visitors to spend as long as possible in a destination. The longer the stay, the more money will be injected into the local economy, creating more jobs for the local population.

2020 summary of Tourism Australia's India Strategic Plan

The India 2020 Strategic Plan has been developed to help Tourism Australia and the Australian tourism industry maximise the potential of India.

The current India market

Australia welcomed 215 000 Indian tourists in the year ending March 2015. This is a 25% increase over the same period in the 2013–14 year. India is now the eighth largest inbound market for tourist arrivals in Australia.

It is expected that visitor numbers from India could reach 300 000 by 2020, with an overnight visitor spending of AU$1.9 billion.

Tourism Australia will implement a tightly focused geographic strategy, based on an economic and demographic forecast of the top 50 cities in India by 2020.

In the short term the focus will be on Delhi and Mumbai. Four other cities in India have also been identified with future potential.

The target customer

The target customer to drive the future growth of travel from India to Australia has been identified as:

- Affluent, mid-life travellers who are:
- self employed or entrepreneurs
- highly qualified professionals
- senior executives at multinational companies.

They will travel as:

- couples (including honeymoon), often with their children
- increasingly as independent travellers
- usually first time visitors to Australia.

The following two sets of data (Andalucia and Romania) are indicative of the different sources available for the purpose of visitor profiling analysis.

International tourists in andalucia – spend and stay

Table 3.8 below shows the average length of stay of the international tourist in Andalucia, the average spend per day and per holiday and the total monetary value to Andalucia of the international tourist in the 10-year period from 2004 to 2014.

Year	Average stay	Average spend per day–euro	Average spend per holiday–euro	Total value in euro
2004	11	84	942	6813
2005	11	83	924	6775
2006	11	82	947	7082
2007	12	82	965	8134
2008	12	84	986	7863
2009	12	82	993	7416
2010	12	90	1052	7820
2011	11	92	1014	7912
2012	11	92	1022	7749
2013	11	97	1067	8398
2014	11	94	1038 est.	9100 est.

Table 3.8 The average length of stay of the international tourist in Andalucia from 2004–2014

Statistics: Tourist arrivals in Romania up 3.5% in 2013

Arrivals in tourist accommodation in Romania amounted to 7.9 million in 2013, up 3.5% year-on-year, according to the data provided by the National Statistics Institute (INS).

The arrivals of Romanian tourists represented 78.3% of the total, while foreign tourists' arrivals were 21.7%.

Most of the foreign tourists arriving in tourist accommodation in Romania were from Europe, according to the INS. The overnight stays amounted to 19.3 million in 2013, up 1.1% compared to the previous year. The average length of a stay was 2.6 days for Romanian tourists and 2 days for foreigners.

The arrivals of foreign tourists to Romania, registered at the customs, amounted to some 8 million in 2013, slightly up compared to the previous year. Most of the foreigners came from European countries, namely 93.9%.

Accommodation preference

The type of accommodation that visitors choose also helps build up a clearer picture of the target market for a destination. If the majority of visitors are hoping to book self-catering accommodation, and the destination boosts a large number of five star hotels, then customers are likely to be disappointed, and the occupancy rates of the hotels are likely to remain low.

Occupancy rates across the range of accommodation types within a destination will help establish customer preferences and this information can be used by tourism authorities in developing the appropriate accommodation stock matched to customers' wants and needs.

KEY TERM

Occupancy rate: this is the percentage number of rooms sold calculated against the total number of rooms available (excluding complimentary rooms, rooms occupied by hotel staff and out-of-order rooms).

For more information about the different types of accommodation offered in different destinations, please see the section on accommodation and catering.

Spending power

This refers to the extent to which people have money to buy products and services. This will be affected by levels of disposable income, covered previously in this chapter, and also by fluctuations in exchange rates.

The following news report from June 2014 highlights the impact of exchange rates on the spending power of British tourists.

The current strength of the pound is making holidaying abroad an attractive option, particularly when buying US dollars. Price-conscious tourists are also being advised that, because the US dollar is often used as a marker currency, several other destinations have also become far cheaper. What British holidaymakers may not have considered is that there are other currencies promising great exchange rates due to their relationship with the dollar. The spending power of British holidaymakers and travellers has increased in the countries where the currency is linked to the US dollar. In fact, their travel money will go 10% further than this time last year.

In destination terms, many tourism organisations are particularly interested in the concept of secondary spend, that is, the additional purchases made by visitors on top of the income already made from accommodation, transport and meal plans. This contributes to the multiplier effect in the destination, whereby money spent in the area by tourists circulates, is used to pay local employees, and is then re-spent by the local residents, thus augmenting the total spend, or making it 'multiply'.

Choices of products and activities

Many destinations are keen to learn more about the exact nature of tourism products and services that appeal to customers as well as the type of activities that visitors engage in during their stay. This type of information is very valuable in ensuring that the destination's product offering meets the needs of its existing and potential customers.

Many destinations do not only offer standard, resort-based products, but also try to develop authentic tourism experiences which tourists cannot find at home. These experiences are often emphasised through marketing activities.

 KEY CONCEPTS

Sustainability and responsibility

Using local people and products supports the general principles of sustainability. This means maximising the positive impacts of tourism on local communities and developing long-term strategies so that visitors make responsible travel choices.

Destinations will also involve local people and use local products as this strengthens the perceived authenticity of the product/service offering. Tourism organisations try to be flexible by offering tailor-made products/services, or offering different types of components with different types of activities and accommodation that customers can combine to create their own, unique travel itinerary. This is more likely to appeal to a wider customer base. Looking back over sales records will allow organisations to gain a good insight into the types of products and services that are most popular with different types of customers.

Media type

Many people are travelling and making their travel decisions on their own, with little or no help from travel agents or tour planners. Instead, to make these decisions, they use information from multiple sources of media, which include TV, radio, newspapers, books, magazines, films and the internet.

The range of media available to us has evolved over time. In 1900, there was no radio, television or internet. Newspapers were the only means of communicating with markets. However, during the last century, mass media came into being. It started with the first radio broadcast taking place about 100 years ago. Then came the first television broadcast approximately 75 years ago; the internet was born about 50 years ago; first generation cellular networks became popular about 30 years ago; search engines came into the picture about 25 years ago. The result is that media today has evolved into a series of powerful forces that have become an integral part of our life, influencing almost everything we do. Media is no longer a one-way communication system. Using available technology, and social media in particular, we can now communicate and interact with one another at the click of a button anywhere in the world. Images, videos and stories can be shared around the world, using limited resources and at little cost.

Destinations use a combination of traditional print and broadcast advertising together with modern technology in the form of social media such as Facebook, Flickr, You Tube, Twitter, mobile blogs and RSS feeds (Figure 3.14), in order to raise awareness with customers.

As part of the visitor profiling process, it is important that tourism authorities can research and analyse the types of media that reach the target market most effectively. Thus there is often a question included on visitor questionnaires about 'Where did you hear about us?'

By collecting and processing the answers to this question, tourism organisations can make more effective marketing decisions in the future. For example if television reaches more of the audience than full-colour magazine advertisements, future advertising may be redirected to additional TV timeslots.

Figure 3.14 Social media concept

Booking method

Customers have greater choice nowadays in how they can book or make reservations for their visit to a destination. Traditionally this was always done in person through a travel agency, by physically visiting the branch. There is now, however, a clear trend towards online sources for first identifying a holiday destination, and then planning, booking and subsequently sharing holiday experiences.

For visits to Egypt, many tourists, both domestic and foreign, are heading for online booking sites and the service is witnessing rapid growth in sales. Internet services are improving dramatically in Egypt, with about 40 million users already having internet access through different media. Many intermediaries and airlines are currently exploiting the high potential of this to their advantage, especially online booking sites such as Expedia and Booking.com. Nowadays, mobile booking is also becoming more popular due to the user-friendly apps launched by travel intermediaries that allow tourists access to all travel bookings such as airlines, hotels and tourist activities.

Figures show that seven in ten people who took a holiday in the last year booked entirely online. Fewer than one in ten customers now believe that travel agents are better informed about holiday destinations than professional bloggers or review websites, such as TripAdvisor, according to a study of booking methods by research analysts Mintel in 2015.

Furthermore, over half (52%) of consumers believe that holidays are better value for money when booked online and 40% enjoy being able to put together their own holiday on the internet. Many basic trips are easy and quick to research online and with price comparison sites making this even more efficient for consumers, the rise of not only researching but also booking online is set to continue. For more complicated itineraries it is still beneficial to speak to a specialist agent in person in a shop or on the phone due to the advice they can give in booking complicated trips.

Even once at the destination, mobile apps allow visitors to book excursions online rather than always using the booking services of a tour operator or tour rep in the country.

3.7 Product positioning

Product positioning is a market analysis tool which enhances the attractiveness of a destination. The objective of positioning is to create a distinctive place in the minds of potential visitors; a position which evokes images of the destination and which sets the destination apart from other destinations. Positioning is the natural follow through from market segmentation and visitor profiling.

Visitor perception of destination through image and reputation

Positioning of a destination is a reflection not necessarily of the reality of the destination, but more of how a customer perceives that destination to be, based on the messages communicated, images shared and the experiences of others, all of which contribute to the reputation of the destination. Different customers may well perceive the destination in different ways based on their own experiences with it. Market research and analysis of the results of the research will help tourism authorities in destinations understand how the destination is perceived by both existing customers and by potential visitors.

Relationship of destination to competitors through differentiation strategies

Market analysis enables the tourism authorities within a destination to identify the strengths and weaknesses of customers' perceptions of themselves measured against other similar destinations. This also contributes towards 'positioning' the destination within the scope of the competition. In selecting an effective position, tourist authorities are likely to consider differentiation strategies.

This means choosing a marketing campaign which will make the destination stand out from its competitors. Destinations will try to find a way to ensure they appear different to the alternatives. Implementing a differentiation strategy involves finding a way in which the destination can gain competitive advantage, that is, by making itself 'better' than other similar destinations. Market research enables the tourism authorities in a destination to pursue effective differentiation strategies by understanding what customers are being offered by rival destinations.

The importance of the unique selling point (USP)

By pursuing differentiation strategies, destinations automatically seek to find a unique selling point (USP) – something that only they can offer; something that customers cannot experience anywhere else.

Some destinations are blunt and to the point in the message they give about their USP, as can be seen from Figure 3.15.

Figure 3.15 A concise brand message for Jordan

Other destinations are more subtle in conveying their message. South Africa's tourism providers are advised to use the following to create a USP for the country.

Use the top ten reasons to visit South Africa as your unique selling points. Briefly, these key points are:

*   affordability
*   wildlife
*   beaches
*   scenic beauty
*   friendliness
*   weather
*   adventure activities
*   history
*   excellent tourist infrastructure
*   responsible tourism.

Market research and analysis will show tourist authorities how other destinations have created their own USPs, in order to avoid duplicating the same message.

Communication and presentation of clear and attractive image/position

Destinations strive to make themselves attractive to as broad a customer base as possible. This means that any marketing messages they use must be appealing to many different visitor types. Tourism providers need to build a positive association in the minds of customers, 'positioning' a destination firmly in the consciousness of potential visitors. We will look at the ways in which the image and position of destinations are communicated further on in this chapter. Market research provides the opportunity to assess the effectiveness of this aim.

ACTIVITY 12

Study Figures 3.16 and 3.17. Evaluate the product positioning of the destinations based on your personal perceptions of each destination.

Figure 3.16 Tanzania

Figure 3.17 Caymen Islands

3.8 Review the marketing mix

Marketing mix: the term used to describe the emphasis that an organisation or destination places on the four main factors that influence a customer's purchasing decision. Often referred to as 'the 4 Ps', the marketing mix comprises product, price, place and promotion.

This section will examine each of the four elements of the marketing mix in detail – product, price, place and promotion – and explain how each contributes to customer choice. Organisations and destinations will undertake a review of their marketing mix, as part of their market analysis, in order to try to improve their marketability to existing and new customers.

Product (what the destination offers)

It is always interesting to click on the website of a National Tourist Board, such as the Italia one shown in Figure 3.18, and to view the menu of attractions, features and activities being promoted. These are all the products of a destination.

In marketing terms, a product is 'anything that can be offered to a market for attention, acquisition, use or consumption that might satisfy a need. It includes physical objects and services' (*Oxford Dictionary of Business*). This definition provides an overview of what a product might cover, but does not help distinguish between products, services or brands, which are all essential to the product element of the marketing mix.

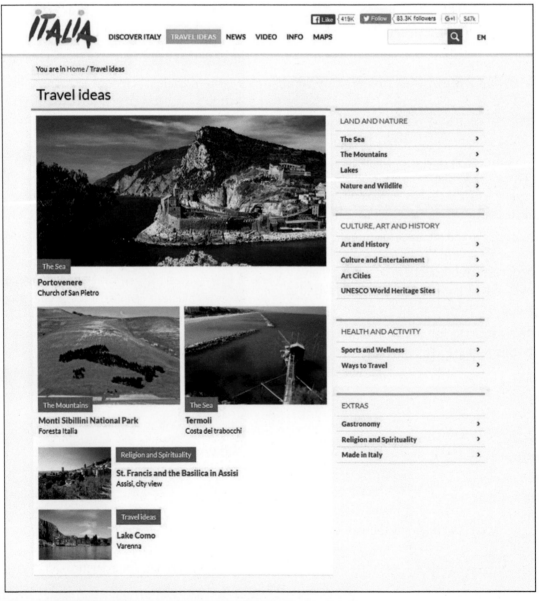

Figure 3.18 An approaches to presenting the destination's products

The tourism product is especially difficult to define because:

'the product covers the complete experience, from the time the tourist leaves home to the time he returns to it.'

(Medlik and Middleton, 1973, page 85)

Defining the products and services of a destination is challenging, as it is often impossible to separate out any of the components. For example, staying in a hotel in the destination will bring the tourist into contact with a broad range of products and services, from the check-in facility, through to housekeeping services and use of the pool and gym. Each aspect can be categorised as a distinct product or service, but in staying in a hotel, the tourist expects to receive the whole visitor experience, not just the features of one product or service. It is the way in which all of the individual elements come together that determines the overall 'hotel product' for which a guest is paying. This can be described as the 'augmented product', which means the level of customer experience needed to achieve customer satisfaction on top of the 'core product', that which constitutes the primary benefit of what is being purchased.

When reviewing their marketing mix, destinations must consider the full range of products and services that are available to visitors; their analysis should focus on the complete product offering which visitors can access while in the destination. In so doing, tourism authorities should consider all subsectors of the travel and tourism industry, which were covered in Chapter 1. Therefore the products and services of a destination will include:

- transport
- accommodation
- catering services
- tour operations, including holiday representatives
- travel agents
- visitor attractions – natural and built
- ancillary service provision.

In reviewing the product element of the marketing mix, it is possible to focus more on one aspect of a destination's product offering, as part of the differentiation strategy or to create a USP. This can be seen from the way in which Sweden, in Figure 3.19, uses its natural attractions as a product focus to attract international tourists, especially the family market.

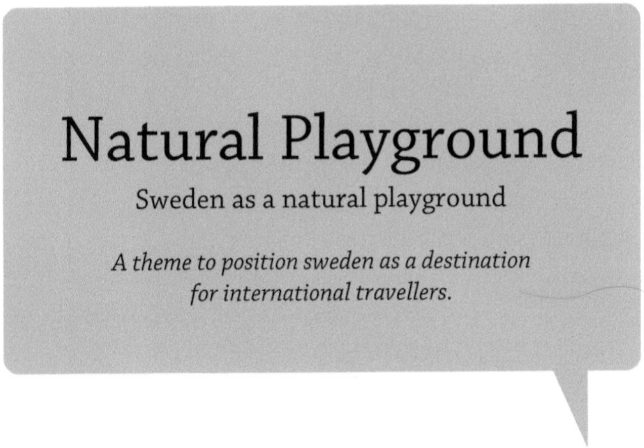

Natural Playground
Sweden as a natural playground

A theme to position sweden as a destination for international travellers.

Figure 3.19 Sweden using its natural attractions as a USP

Price (approaches and strategies used to charge customers for using the products and services of the destination)

There are a great many factors that affect the price of a travel and tourism product or service. Obviously providers need to ensure they recover the actual cost incurred in providing the product, as well as generating additional income for their survival in the market. The business orientation of the provider will also determine the strategy used in setting a price for the products and services offered. Profit-seeking organisations adopt a very different approach to pricing compared with organisations which are financed through public funding.

Other influences that tourism providers will consider under a review of the price element of the marketing mix include:

- The price-quality relationship and customer expectations: this is tied into the concept of a customer's perception of value for money. Certain destinations are considered to offer good value for money, while others are considered to be over-priced. For example, Honduras in Central America offers the same 'white sand-and-palm beaches' experience as Belize and Costa Rica, but at a fraction of the cost. Switzerland has traditionally been described as an expensive destination to visit, with two Swiss cities (Geneva and Zurich) being voted in the top three most expensive destinations in 2015.
- The uniqueness of the product and the level of competition in the market: this ties in with the concept of product positioning. Where there are few substitute destinations offering a similar experience, a higher price may be set than for a product offering with a large number of competitors in the market. This is a simple version of the principles of supply and demand. The

113

greater the supply and the lower the demand, then a low price must be considered to entice visitors to a destination. This also links specifically to the issues of seasonality, whereby high prices can be charged to visit popular destinations during peak season.

- The positioning of the destination and its products in the market: places such as Paris and London will always attract large numbers of visitors and gain a large share of the tourism market, therefore can set a high price for the experience visitors will receive. Destinations with limited tourism development tend to set lower prices to entice more visitors.

- Government influence: levels of taxation and subsidies will impact on the pricing strategies adopted in different parts of the world. Greece made the travel trade headlines early in 2015 when it was announced that the country was to hit holidaymakers with 18% tax on the use of hotels and restaurants. Tax on restaurants was raised from 13% to 18%, whilst hotel tax almost tripled, raising fears that tourists would go elsewhere.

KEY CONCEPTS

Global and growing

One of the key aims of UNWTO is to use tourism as a means to alleviate poverty across the globe. Tourism activity brings wealth and prosperity to a destination, enabling the growth of local economy.

General economic factors: destinations will review the general levels of prosperity, standards of living and interest rates affecting the local economy. These can affect the approach to pricing for tourism products and services within the destination.

The tourism market is known for being price sensitive. This means that people's spending on tourism products and services is dependent on prevailing economic conditions. In times of recession, such as the global economic downturn in 2008, people had decreased levels of disposable income, which resulted in fewer people being able to afford to travel for pleasure. This impacted on the prices tourism providers could charge in fdestinations around the world. Even countries where the local economy remained buoyant at the time had to carefully consider the price element of their marketing mix when the rest of the global tourism market was experiencing the financial 'squeeze'.

Tourism organisations in destinations must make conscious marketing decisions about the pricing strategies they will adopt. The following provides a brief

outline of the most common pricing strategies used in travel and tourism.

Market skimming

This is commonly used to break into the market, for products which have little competition. A high price is charged initially for customers who do not mind paying for the privilege of being amongst the first to try the product. These customers are often called innovators. Once the product has been adopted by a number of customers, the market is said to have been 'skimmed' and the price is gradually decreased as more people experience the product. This strategy could be adopted in an emerging destination hoping to sell its unique appeal to a limited number of visitors.

Penetration pricing

When launching into a highly competitive market, artificially low prices are set to entice visitors. The intention behind this strategy is to gain a large market share and earn increased revenue from a high number of sales. Customer loyalty is sought, even where the price later increases. Penetration pricing may result in price wars between providers or destinations.

The going rate

Where there is a high degree of similarity in the product offering of rival destinations, a policy of **price-matching** may be used. This is also commonly known as **competitor-based pricing**.

Promotional pricing

Figure 3.20 A Mozambique promotion

Examples of promotional pricing include special offers, discount prices, Buy-One-Get-One-Free (BOGOF), money-off coupons and so on (Figure 3.22). These are all commonly used in travel and tourism, when sales are slow or when the product is close to its expiry, such as heavily discounted standby tickets sold hours before departure or heavily discounted room rates to increase hotel occupancy rates for a particular night.

Prestige pricing

This strategy is sometimes also known as premium pricing. Where products are of high quality or have an exclusive appeal, high prices can be set, on the assumption that people associate high prices with high quality. Resort destinations in the Caribbean (Figure 3.21) are able to charge a premium price for their products because of the exceptional quality of the experience they offer.

Figure 3.21 An example of a prestige location

Variable pricing

Also known as **price discrimination**, this strategy is based on the principle that demand for product varies. Examples are peak-time and off-peak travel. Lower prices are set in off-peak seasons to stimulate demand and encourage higher sales during less busy times. This type of pricing strategy is used by resorts in destinations such as Mauritius. Hotel rates are the lowest in Mauritius during June and July. During these months, it is possible to find very attractive deals offered by most of the hotel chains and by the smaller hotels on the island. Prices can also vary according to the customer type. It is common practice for organisations to use a price tariff which varies for adults, children, students and the elderly.

CASE STUDY 6

Singapore

The hotel industry in Singapore continues to enjoy healthy demand despite rising room rates and strong competition, as the destination's appeal draws more regional tourists. Singapore attracts nearly 4 million international visitors each year, the majority of whom stay in hotel accommodation in the country.

	2014	2013	2012
Number of hotels	392	373	338
Number of rooms	57,172	55,018	51,579

Table 3.9 Singapore hotel data

ACTIVITY 13

A new hotel chain wishes to expand its operation to open up three new hotels at key locations in Singapore.

Use your understanding of the price element of the marketing mix. Carry out a review of the approaches and strategies that the hotel chain might use when setting the price it will charge visitors to its hotels in Singapore.

115

Place (the distribution channels used in making the destination accessible to customers)

Place is used to describe two aspects of the marketing mix in relation to tourism products and services – the physical location of destinations and their facilities, and the chain of distribution used by tourism providers to ensure customers can purchase their products and services.

 KEY TERM

Chain of distribution: also known as channels of distribution. Both terms refer to the process of moving products and services from the provider to the customer. This process may be direct, or may also involve other organisations, agencies or intermediaries.

Physical location

The term 'destination' describes a broad spectrum of physical places. It may refer to a whole country, such as Spain, or to a specific region or city within that country, such as Andalucia or Seville. Many of these destinations occur naturally. However, it is also possible to 'create' destinations with purpose-built resorts – Resorts World Genting in Malaysia is an example of this.

The features of an area will determine the suitability of a location for the purposes of becoming a tourism destination. Cost and suitability of the land for tourism is a major consideration in locating new facilities or attractions within a destination. The character of the local area will also contribute – tourists will not feel safe in areas with a high crime rate or comfortable in a destination where the cost of living is high.

Natural features within the locality are clearly essential to a location being developed as a tourist destination – beaches, mountains, and countryside play an important part as a 'pull' factor for visitors.

Transport and access links are also crucial – a destination must have the necessary transport infrastructure, for example in Figure 3.22, to manage tourist arrivals/departures as well as providing appropriate local transport services for visitors while they are in the destination.

Figure 3.22 Kuala Lumpur Sentral – an example of an advanced integrated transport hub

There must also be local people to work in the tourism industry within a destination. Other tourist facilities must also be nearby, in order to cater for the broad needs of customers within the destination – this means there should be restaurants, banks, shops, accommodation and leisure facilities within easy reach.

Whilst many of the features of the physical location of a destination cannot be changed, a review of this aspect of the place element of the marketing mix can still be undertaken at regular intervals. Transport links can be improved, other tourism facilities developed and so on, in order to enhance the appeal to customers.

Choice of distribution channels

There are two main ways in which tourism providers can make their products and services available to customers, directly or indirectly. Traditionally this has involved intermediaries such as travel agents but with the increased use of technology, the focus has now become direct links between providers and customers using web-based channels, including mobile apps.

The choice of channel is strongly influenced by two main factors:

- Cost: the use of intermediaries brings increased costs by way of the commission that is paid to the middleman. Direct selling has its own cost consideration, as this type of channel requires high capital investment in marketing and promotion
- Control of the product: using intermediaries can dilute the control a provider has over the product. This means that travel agents may exert personal bias on a customer's perceptions of a product or destination.

Tourism distribution channels

Direct - channels can be online or offline
direct online booking and sales mainly via the booking engine of the provider's website direct offline bookings and sales via email, telephone or face to face
indirect – channels are through the travel trade, via intermediaries such as travel agents, and can be online or offline
tour operators, travel agents, destination management companies (DMCs) – online via organisation's website or offline by email, telephone or face to face third party websites – comparison sites such as Orbitz and Expedia, or using global distribution systems (GDS)

Table 3.10

E-ticketing is nowadays used widely across the travel industry. Customers make online bookings using computer reservation systems (CRS), which allow real time checks on availability. The inter-connectivity of these computerised systems has led to the creation of global distribution systems, which facilitates the booking of multiple products from different providers in one destination. Once the reservations have been completed and payment has been made online, the provider will issue an e-ticket (electronic ticket) to the customer. This is a paperless document, which holds all of the booking details in a database. When the customer cites the ticket reference, the corresponding booking is retrieved allowing the customer to check in for flights, or at the hotel. Mobile apps now allow customers to use QR scan codes (Figure 3.23) via their smart phones or tablets, in place of boarding cards or e-tickets.

The use of direct and indirect distribution channels can be reviewed and destinations can encourage more widespread use of e-ticketing and mobile app bookings as part of the review of the place aspect of the marketing mix.

Figure 3.23 QR Code, a machine-readable code consisting of an array of black and white squares, typically used for storing URLs or other information for reading by the camera on a smart phone

Promotion (using a range of promotional methods to raise awareness of the destination with customers)

KEY TERM

Promotion: any activity that arouses the interest of a customer or a potential customer.

Promotion is the publicising of a product, an organisation or a destination to increase the number of sales, customers or visitors by raising public awareness. A destination has many different ways in which it can use promotion due to the very broad range of promotional methods available. Promotion is also often known as marketing communication, because of its primary purpose of communicating marketing information to customers.

When reviewing a destination's marketing mix, the promotion aspect is often the element that may be most obvious to visitors. If the destination uses promotional methods effectively the destination will be visible to both existing customers and to new customers. Choosing which promotional methods to employ is central to any review

of a destination's marketing mix and will depend on a number of other factors, which will be explored in more detail later. Next is a brief overview of the main types of promotion that a destination may use.

Advertising

This is one of the most expensive forms of promotion, especially if the services of an advertising agency are sought. Advertising can be done using a broad range of media: **broadcas**t, which includes television, cinema and radio advertisements; **print**, which includes newspapers, magazines and information leaflets and **display**, which includes billboards, point of sale displays, touch screen information boards and so on.

The impact that advertising has on potential customers to a destination is difficult to measure. National tourist organisations will often survey customers to find out what influenced a decision to visit the destination. This is to help ascertain whether costly advertising campaigns achieve the desired outcomes.

KEY CONCEPTS

Customer focus

Direct marketing allows a destination and its tourism providers to communicate directly with customers who have shown an interest in visiting. The marketing materials are often personalised to make customers feel special and to uphold the impression that the destination and its stakeholders are focused on the customer experience.

Direct marketing

Advances in digital technology have significantly changed the way in which travel and tourism organisations can use direct marketing. In the past, this form of promotion relied on a company using information from a customer database to send out mail shots by post to those previous customers. However, with the advent of social media and mobile technology, travel and tourism organisations make effective use of their followers and subscribers on platforms such as Facebook, Twitter and YouTube, in order to post marketing information which is directly targeted towards customers who have a clear interest in the products and services offered by the organisation.

Public relations (PR)

Public relations refers to the way in which a positive image is professionally upheld by an organisation. According to the Chartered Institute of Public Relations 'Public Relations is about reputation - the result of what you do, what you say and what others say about you.'

Public relations are particularly important in travel and tourism as this enables organisations or destinations to project themselves in a favourable light to the public. Examples of public relations activities include: press releases, features on television, in newspapers, magazines and so on, attendance at trade fairs, hosting familiarisation trips and holding press conferences.

Sales promotion

This is one of the most important promotional methods used in the travel and tourism industry. This form of promotion can be targeted specifically at customers or at trade partners. Discount coupons such as those shown in Figure 3.24, special offers and loyalty incentives are commonly used by travel and tourism organisations to entice customers. Trade promotions include incentives such as commission or bonuses paid to travel agents or tour operators for endorsement of a destination's products, or for its inclusion in a package tour.

A review of the marketing mix will allow organisations to update the promotional methods it uses, to keep the image of the destination 'fresh' in the minds of customers. Changing promotional methods or adopting new pricing strategies are easier for a destination to manage than making radical changes to the product and services offered or to the infrastructure of the destination.

118

Figure 3.24 Examples of discount coupons available from the Gyeonggi Tourism Organisation promoted on the VisitKorea website

Connecticut Holiday Package

The following is a description of a domestic holiday package to Delamar Greenwich Harbor in Connecticut in the USA.

Title: Connecticut Still Revolutionary Culture Seekers

Date(s): Saturday, November 1, 2014 – Friday, May 27, 2016

Contact Info: (203) 661-9800, or toll-free (866) 335-2627

Description: Located under an hour from Grand Central Station. Delamar Greenwich Harbor is the ideal getaway from New York City. With shopping, beaches, amazing restaurants and museums all within walking (or biking) distance from the hotel, there is plenty to keep you occupied for the weekend. Leave the car at home and take advantage of this package.

This overnight offer includes complimentary entrance to the Bruce Museum, a special discounted rate at the hotel, and other area discounts including a 10% discount at the Bruce Museum store.

Package includes:

- Two round-trip rail tickets on the New Haven Line to Greenwich Station.
- Deluxe accommodation for two.
- A welcome drink on arrival.
- Manager's Wine & Cheese Reception in our Lobby on Friday and Saturday evenings.
- In-room split bottle of champagne.
- Complimentary continental breakfast for two in our Lobby.
- Two one-day passes to the Bruce Museum, a member of the Connecticut Art Trail.
- 10% discount on purchases in the Bruce Museum Gift Store.
- Complimentary transportation within a 3 mile radius.

Rates From: $269.00 per night.

Use your knowledge and understanding of the marketing mix to identify each component of this package.

Explain how the tour operator could make changes to improve this marketing mix, in order to attract more visitors.

3.9 Building a destination brand

Branding destinations is an extension of this concept, because a destination is clearly made up of a range of products and services offered by a large number of different travel and tourism organisations, each of which may already have their own specific brand identity. For example, in the Cayman Islands each island has resorts and hotels owned by international chains including Marriott, Holiday Inn, Ritz-Carlton and Wyndham. Each of these chains has its own distinct brand image, but they are also used in contributing to the islands' overall destination brand.

 KEY TERM

Branding: is the business process involved in creating a unique name and image for a product in the customer's mind.

This, coupled with the fact that many destinations are, in fact, quite similar, makes it much harder to build an effective destination brand. The next section will examine ways in which a destination brand might be established.

Establishing the destination identity

A destination that wishes to increase its economic well-being and protect and sustain the environment in which its population lives, will endeavour to attract more visitors. Establishing a specific destination brand identity is important in appealing to visitors but this can only be achieved if those in charge of marketing the destination understand the process of establishing a specific brand identity. Some of the key considerations will include:

- what they want the destination to be known for
- how they can make the destination appear unique, in order to make its mark in a very competitive market
- what thoughts and images do people already associate with the destination name
- how can existing resources be better utilised in promoting sustainable tourism practices.

These factors will influence the brand identity that a destination establishes for itself, amongst other things. Let's now look at the whole process of establishing an effective brand identity.

Reasons for branding a destination

There are many reasons why destinations wish to brand themselves, including the need to enhance their competitiveness in the global marketplace. A holiday or business trip to a specific destination is an **intangible** purchase; therefore the image and reputation of the destination play a crucial part in making someone want to visit.

KEY TERM

Intangible: 'unable to be touched; not having physical presence.' So although the destination itself does have a physical presence, a holiday experience does not. It is instead made up of a series of different components, many of which are dependent on the quality of service given, which is again intangible.

Change the perception of unfavourable stereotypes of a destination

Certain destinations have evolved over time and established well-known reputations. The Spanish Costas (Costa Brava, Costa del Sol, Costa Blanca) have long since been known as traditional 'sun, sea and sand' beach holiday destinations. Ayia Napa in Cyprus, Playa de la Américas in Tenerife and San Antonio in Ibiza have also

established a reputation for their party atmospheres and 18–30 appeal. Ask anyone you know, and the chances are that they will describe Paris as being the most romantic city in the world. All of these are examples of stereotypes of destinations. Some of these stereotypes appear to be entirely favourable – why is having a reputation for being a romantic destination in any way negative?

But such a reputation can affect a destination's ability to attract a broader target market. The Costas began only to appeal to families. Only couples are attracted to Paris, thus narrowing the appeal of the destination to other visitor types.

Re-branding the destination – changing the brand association – can help overcome any negative stereotypes and can increase the destination's appeal to different target markets. For example, the tour operator Thomsons, part of TUI UK, is working hard to re-establish Ayia Napa in Cyprus as a tranquil beach destination (see Figure 3.25), despite it being a stone's throw from the Centre of Ayia Napa itself. This is to try and rid the destination of its negative image of being overrun with young people seeking the party nightlife and therefore allowing the place to appeal to a much broader customer base.

Figure 3.25 Nissi beach, Ayia Napa

Create a common vision for the future of the community and its potential as a tourist destination

 KEY CONCEPTS

Sustainability and responsibility

Recognising the potential of a destination to generate income through tourism, and involving the local population in tourism provision contributes to the sustainability of tourism activity. The whole concept of creating a common vision for the future embraces the principles of sustainable practice.

It is important for the whole host population to understand and accept the reasons for creating a brand identity. This means the local people, as well as travel and tourism providers and representatives from tourism authorities. If people within the local community do not agree with the image of the destination that is being presented, then the destination brand is not likely to succeed. Locals must be able to identify with the brand identity and must also understand the likely costs and benefits associated with destination brand development.

This involves regular communication between the tourism providers and local authorities within the destination, the host population and the visitors themselves, so that key brand identity messages are conveyed and upheld, and the local people can recognise the part they play in implementing tourism development strategies in their area.

Provide a consistent representation of the destination

A consistency in representation is important for a destination. There are many different tourism providers in all destinations and it would be very confusing for visitors and potential visitors if the destination tried to market itself with lots of different brand messages. If certain parts of the destination use a 'luxury, tropical paradise' brand message, but other parts tried to create a '18–30 party atmosphere' brand image, it could result in a decrease in visitor numbers, as neither market segment would want to visit.

Consistency in representation is also of major importance for a destination wanting to attract repeat customers; those who have previously visited and wish to repeat a positive experience will look for the same brand representation on their return to the destination.

New visitors will use the brand representation from marketing materials to make their decision to visit. If this is not consistent with the destination brand they actually experience when visiting, they are likely to be disappointed.

Therefore consistency in representation is important to ensure customers are attracted to a destination and are satisfied when they are there.

 KEY CONCEPTS

Global and growing

Raising awareness of a destination is key to its development and success. Destination marketing is a means for a destination to create a global presence and to contribute to its economic growth.

Enhance local, regional, national and/or global awareness of a destination

In these times of intense competition, a destination has to continually add to its value in order to be successful. One way of adding value is by raising awareness of the destination among as many people as possible. It is therefore important that a destination considers as many different target audiences as possible and establishes its name and reputation across all of these markets.

Creating awareness globally is the ideal for every destination; however, this is often very difficult for emerging destinations, given that it takes a lot of investment and a long time for a new destination brand identity to embed itself with customers around the world, especially when other destinations, offering a similar experience, are already well established.

It is therefore sometimes more advisable to start by enhancing awareness of a destination at a more manageable scale – rolling out the destination brand launch at a national level will raise awareness within the host country, for example.

The more a destination targets specific markets with its destination brand marketing messages, the more likely it is to enhance its image. Raising awareness with local, regional and national markets is especially important, as these are the source of domestic tourism for a destination.

Excitement as Grenada launches a new destination brand

PURE GRENADA

Figure 3.26 The 'Pure Grenada' brand logo

Grenada, a country in the Caribbean, recently unveiled a new destination brand (Figure 3.26), in a significant move aimed at repositioning the country as a major tourist destination.

More than 100 invited guests from the island's tourism, diplomatic, corporate and media circles gathered to witness the unveiling of the island's new brand identity at a reception hosted on the patio balcony of the Ministry of Tourism's offices. The event was also attended by members of the foreign press. Highlights of the evening included live cultural performances by local dancers and musicians.

In an innovative move, the Minister of Tourism has partnered with the private sector Grenada Hotel and Tourism Association to re-position the island's brand.

The new brand will be the signature calling card of the destination going forward, and will be implemented in a phased-rollout across the island and in local and overseas markets.

According to Eurostat data from 2013, almost half of all Europeans (47.3%) made at least one domestic tourism trip with at least one overnight stay in 2013, while only 30% made at least one trip abroad. Countries with the highest participation rates in domestic tourism were Finland (83.2%), Norway (68.9%), France (68.3%) and the Czech Republic (66.5%). Similarly statistics from New Zealand show the important contribution of domestic tourism in that country. Domestic tourism has been increasing steadily in New Zealand over a considerable period of time. Today it is worth almost NZ$14 billion annually to the tourism industry and makes up 59% of total tourism earnings. Domestic visitors spend NZ$39 million per day, benefiting cities, towns and communities throughout New Zealand.

Make the destination more appealing

This ties in with all of the other reasons for branding a destination. If customers do not find a place appealing, they will not choose to visit. In marketing terms, the process of branding and rebranding has been described as 'changing the wrapping' on a product. It is essentially the same thing, when branding a destination, because the tourism authorities are trying to change our perceptions of that destination by attaching a new brand identity to make it seem more appealing, in much the same way as a chocolate company try to make a chocolate bar seem more appealing by putting it in different packaging.

3.10 Characteristics of an effective destination brand

So the all-important question remains: what makes a successful destination brand? There has been much research into this question and many journal articles and textbooks have been written in trying to provide the answers. Much of this research evidence focuses on a series of complex concepts and processes. But the bottom line is, a successful destination brand often actually relies on hard-working people, with limited resources and a modicum of marketing expertise. The secret to their success in creating an effective destination brand is that they utilise the resources they do have to their full potential, and remain customer-focused, strategic, open-minded and imaginative in creating a brand which will invoke positive feelings, respect and loyalty from the destination's stakeholders and from its customers.

The following characteristics act as a kind of checklist in creating the 'perfect' destination brand identity:

- memorable
- attractive
- matched to destination attributes
- consistent with destination's positioning
- easily understood by customers
- integrated into promotional activities at a local, national and global level
- sustained over a significant period of time
- reflective of customers' actual experiences

- targeted at both existing customers and at prospective visitors
- accepted by stakeholders
- credible.

Memorable

An effective destination brand is one that sticks in your mind and is easy to recall. There needs to be something unique, quirky or significant about the brand to make it stand out and to ensure that customers and potential customers remember it.

Let's compare a few recent destination brands:

We have already considered the most memorable of destination brands, one that needs little explanation:

Figure 3.27 I LOVE NY logo

Figure 3.28 shows the brand image for the city of Amsterdam in the Netherlands; does this strike you as effective?

Attractive

An effective destination brand will also be attractive; this means that the logo, slogan and associated brand identity must be visually appealing and must evoke a positive feeling in order to work in the way that a good brand should. This relates to the actual words chosen as the tagline – do these conjure up an attractive image in the potential visitor's mind? Attractiveness also relates to the font chosen to represent the words. Some written texts are more visually appealing than others. The same applies to the colour schemes chosen. Lastly, it is also important to consider the attractiveness of the images used in communicating the brand.

Matched to the destination's attributes

This is an important characteristic. A brand must reflect the authentic experience a visitor can expect to receive. The 'Land of Origins' brand communicated in Ethiopia's coffee plant image, See Figure 3.29, is a good match – Ethiopia, as well as being the birthplace of coffee, is an ancient country known for its unique cultural heritage and impresive history. The longest river in the worls – the Nile– originates there and its remarkable biodiversity includes species of mammals and birds not found anywhere else in the world.

In the same way, the brand for Hong Kong is truly reflective of the destination – Hong Kong is known for being a cosmopolitan, lively city destination, and one of the finest in Asia's. This is represented simply in its current brand.

123

Figure 3.28 The Amsterdam brand image

Figure 3.29 Ethiopia logo – 'Land of Origins'

It is essential that tourism authorities use a destination's most noticeable features within the brand they create in order to ensure the brand is matched to a destination's attributes.

Consistent with a destination's positioning

It is also important that a destination correctly represents itself in terms of its brand positioning. Using phrases like 'the number one destination' only actually works if the destination is ranked highly around the world. If every destination uses the word 'best' in its tagline, this becomes meaningless.

Here is a realistic example of a brand which is consistent with the destination's positioning.

Figure 3.30 The use of 'go your own way' in the Albania brand logo and slogan help convey the potential of this destination

Albania, a country in the Balkans, is an emerging tourism destination with one of the top ten fastest-growing tourism markets globally. The country was ranked third among 15 best destinations tourism for 2015 according to *L'Express Magazine* and listed as fourth in the *New York Times'* '52 places to go in 2014.' The logo and tagline of 'Go your own way' aim to emphasise the country's huge and varied potential for tourism and investment.

Easily understood by customers

This characteristic sounds obvious. However, sometimes the creators of a tourism brand become so creative in wanting to design a brand that is truly unique, that the message gets lost.

Integrated into promotional activities at a local, national and global level

We have already concluded that a brand must be consistently represented within local, regional, national and global markets. In order for this to happen, the brand must be used in all communications about the destination. Many tourism authorities assume the responsibility for promotional activity, with national tourism websites such as VisitDubai, DiscoverTunisia, VisitMozambique and so on.

Most of these websites target specific markets. For example, Discover Tunisia has a website run by the Tunisian National Tourism Office in the UK. However, to ensure the consistent integration of the destination brand at all levels, many tourism authorities issue strong brand guidelines about the use of tourism logos and associated brandings.

ACTIVITY 14

Visit a national tourism website such as VisitDubai

http://www.visitdubai.com or VisitEngland https://www.visitengland.com and search for the guidelines on the use of the destination brand. Dubai has a section on terms of use, whilst England has a media centre with permission-free images that can be used.

Explain how these tourism authorities approach the characteristic of integrating their tourism brand into all promotional activities at various levels.

Sustained over a significant period of time

Many destinations create a brand image and expect instant results. In order to be effective, a brand takes time to establish itself, especially on a global level. Admittedly the successful 'I ♥ NY' gained almost immediate recognition, but on the whole, it takes prolonged exposure to ensure the success of a brand identity. The Incredible India campaign is a good example – this was conceptualised in 2002 and is still running in 2015. Similarly the Malaysia, truly Asia identity was first used in 1999 and is still incorporated within some of the destination's brand messaging today.

However, not all destination brands enjoy the same longevity as these. Some brands are short-lived because of the adverse reactions they provoke. An Australian brand campaign was cut short because of the offence its language caused in certain markets; a video campaign by the Singapore Tourism Board was deleted within days of it being uploaded to the tourism board's social media platforms in 2014 following global criticism; Denmark also experienced a similar media outcry for its YouTube tourism campaign in 2009 which appeared to promote promiscuity. While these latter two examples do not relate specifically to the overall destination brand, but rather a single advertisement used to promote the brand, it is clear that poorly thought out advertising can damage a destination brand and curtail its effectiveness.

Reflective of customers' actual experiences

This ties in with many of the other characteristics already mentioned, such as being matched to the destination's attributes and being consistent with a destination's positioning. If the brand does not reflect the actual experiences of visitors, then this is likely to lead to disappointment on the customer's part. This in turn will cause bad 'word of mouth' reputation for the destination and will adversely affect the number of repeat visits and of recommendations to visit. Therefore it is essential that there is no gap between a destination's promise and its reality.

> **KEY CONCEPTS**
>
> **Customer focus**
>
> Many of these characteristics have the customer as a focus. A destination brand must be meaningful to the people who experience it – whether because they have already visited or whether they are planning to visit. Tourism providers therefore ensure that the brand characteristics are closely associated with the characteristics of particular customer groups.

Targeted at both existing customers and at prospective visitors

This is perhaps one of the most difficult characteristics for a destination to uphold. Appealing to people who have

already visited a destination through a brand identity is more tricky then enticing a first-time visitor with promises of what the destination offers. To do both using only one destination brand is a real challenge for tourism authorities around the world.

> **ACTIVITY 15**
>
> To which market segment do you think the following brands are targeted? Why?
>
>
>
> Figure 3.31 Canada keep exploring brand logo
>
>
>
> Figure 3.32 Amazing Thailand brand logo

Accepted by stakeholders

This is an important characteristic, but again difficult to always achieve. Consider the large number of different stakeholders for any given destination: the national tourist organisations (NTOs); other public sector agencies of tourism, such as museums and galleries, tourist information centres and regional tourism development agencies; private sector organisations such as tour operators, travel agents, entertainment providers, hotel chains and restaurant owners or private sector investment companies; voluntary sector organisations such as Tourism Concern, or wildlife conservation charities; the host population; and tourists from different market segments.

> **KEY TERM**
>
> **Stakeholder:** a person, group or organisation that has interest or concern in a business, or in this case, in a destination.

125

The list is extensive. The brand identity chosen must communicate a message that rings positively with people with a broad range of different interests in the destination. Therefore to be able to create a destination brand that is acceptable to all of these different stakeholders is again no mean feat!

Credible

There are varying definitions of what credible means, but the following best describes the characteristic of an effective destination brand: 'able to be believed'; 'convincing'; 'capable of persuading people that something will happen or be successful'.

In order for a tourism brand to be credible, it needs to harness many of the other characteristics already mentioned here. It needs to be realistic, based on what the destination boasts, and related to what customers have experienced on previous visits. It needs to present a consistent message, and one that is accepted by everyone involved in its delivery.

So it is clear to see that creating an effective destination brand is not a simple process; yet it is something that most visitors take for granted when they first click on a tourism website or watch an advertisement on television.

3.11 Creating a brand identity

Many of the destination brands we have already looked at have used a number of different 'tools' in creating their **brand identity**.

> **KEY TERM**
>
> **Brand identity:** how a business (or in the case of destination branding tourism authorities) wants to be perceived by consumers. The components of the brand (its name, logo, tagline, typeface) are created by the organisation to reflect the value that it is trying to bring to the market and to appeal to its customers.

We shall now examine some of these components or tools in more detail, to see how a brand identity can be designed and established.

Brand name

We have already seen several destination brands which use a brand name as part of their initial brand identity. VisitEngland, DiscoverTunisia, and Your Singapore are all brand names that have been adopted by destinations to gain attention. They create an instant association with the country they are representing, which is crucial in the case of destination branding.

Slogan/Tagline

A tagline has been described as the spirit of the destination or a destination's promise. An effective tagline should sum up the essence of the destination, and could come in the form of a tease, a short description or an invitation. Some say a tagline should comprise no more than five words to be effective. A tagline is not compulsory; many destinations do not actually have them. Destination taglines are designed to become an integral part of the brand identity and are usually incorporated into the logo.

Slogans in destination branding are used slightly differently. A slogan tends to form part of an advertising campaign and can therefore have a more limited lifespan than a tagline. As mentioned previously, it is important that key words are not over-used in establishing a brand identity as they then lose their effectiveness. Market research has shown that so many destinations are 'the best-kept secret' or 'have it all', that visitors now take little notice of such promises.

> **KEY TERM**
>
> **Slogan:** a simple and catchy phrase accompanying a logo or brand that encapsulates a product's (here, a destination's) appeal and makes it more memorable. When used consistently over a long period of time, the slogan becomes an important component of the destination's identity or image. A slogan is also called catch line, strap line, or tagline.

> **ACTIVITY 16**
>
> Use the internet to look for some more examples of taglines. Which ones do you personally find most appealing and why?

Logo

> **KEY TERM**
>
> **Logo:** a symbol or other small design adopted by an organisation to identify its products, uniform, vehicles and so on. They are often defined as the trade mark of a company. In the case of a destination, the logo is adopted by major stakeholders and is used in all marketing communications.

Logos create an instant brand association with no language barriers because they are a visual representation. Over time, logos act as a trigger to help recall the positive attributes for which a place is known. However, it can be argued that a logo alone is not sufficient in creating a brand identity strong enough to attract a visitor without them having been exposed to other compelling components about the destination brand.

Simple logos work best. The wide use of mobile technology means logos have to be compressed to use on small screens via apps. Complicated designs are difficult to reproduce and to maintain. A logo is not intended to represent every attribute or feature of a destination; instead it is supposed to represent a major theme of the destination. Logos are rarely used in isolation in destination branding.

USP (unique selling point)

Many destinations attempt to create a USP as part of their brand identity. Being unique means to be the only one of its kind. For a destination, this is both very true – no two cities are 100% the same; no two islands are identical – and also very difficult to prove. The characteristics of a place which are important to visitors tend to be quite similar from destination to destination. What actually differentiates one place from another is the mix of all of these characteristics. All destinations have some form of cultural heritage or local cuisine; they all have some aspect of a natural environment and have built attractions. But the amalgamation of each of these elements is what sets each destination apart and it is this 'mix' which a brand identity must attempt to convey. In so doing, most destinations tend to home in on one particular set of characteristics in order to establish a so-called USP, for example Egypt is known for its pyramids, although in actual fact pyramids are not unique to Egypt; there are more than 1000 pyramids in Central America, more than 300 pyramids in China and 8 clearly man-made pyramids in Greece.

ACTIVITY 17

Choose one city destination, one island destination, one winter resort and one summer sun resort. For each destination, try and work out what the USP is.

How easy a task is it to determine the USP? How might this affect the target markets for such destinations?

Use of colour

Figure 3.33 Logo for Spain

Colour is used to create brand association too. The above logo for Spain is easy to recognise because of its use of colour, representing the colours of the Spanish flag. This is a common tool for using colour within destination branding.

When designing brands, tourism authorities need to be aware of the strong emotional associations people have with colours too. Black and red are both considered to be powerful colours; brown is associated with earth and tradition; green is a fresh colour often linked with nature; blues are thought to be restful and are often associated with water whilst yellows and oranges are fun colours often linked to sunshine and summer seasons. White is meant to represent calmness and truthfulness, which is why most brands use a white background.

Price in association with image

According to UNWTO, the World Tourism Organisation, a destination's appeal is shaped by a number of different factors, including:

- accessibility
- accommodation
- attractions
- amenities
- affordability.

Thus, there is a clear link between the image of a destination and the prices it charges. This contributes to a destination's overall brand identity. For example, destinations are often ranked in terms of the average cost of a hotel night or by the average spending by visitors within the destination. Island destinations often feature

127

in rankings for most luxurious destinations and as such appeal widely to the honeymoon market, based on the association of high price equalling high quality.

Distinctive packaging

In tourism marketing the word packaging takes on a new meaning. Tourism packaging doesn't involve a physical package surrounding a product as it does in general marketing terms. Instead, packaging is the process of putting together, or bundling, the core tourist product (a holiday) with additional services desired by tourists. The package is then promoted to tourists, who can then easily purchase their desired travel experience. When a destination brands itself, it will often offer a complete package via inbound tour operators. Packages offer tourists convenience by reducing the amount of time they need to spend researching what the destination has to offer. Tourists also find packages attractive because with a single purchase everything they need for their visit is provided, including lodging and attractions. An example is a fly-drive package whereby the tour operator books flights and arranges car-hire on behalf of the tourist and produces an itinerary based on both elements of the package.

Tourism packaging has become more dynamic nowadays; consumers prefer to create their own packages, rather than purchase pre-packaged tours. Therefore destinations use dynamic packaging to help create brand identity, whereby their websites offer the facility for individual consumer search requests. This allows a potential visitor to combine several different travel components (typically air, car and hotel) in real time. It also allows services to be purchased from different sources, known as dynamic sourcing, but purchased as a single, dynamically priced package. Dynamic pricing means hiding the pricing of individual components. Destinations which offer such a package create a distinct identity for themselves.

Corporate identity

The number of **resort destinations** is growing. Each resort destination creates a strong brand identity, incorporating many of the components already discussed in this section. They do, however, also benefit from the ability to create a corporate identity. This means that staff working within the resort wear uniforms which help to create a corporate identity, making them easily recognisable. Furnishings in rooms around the resort are also branded to create a uniformity or standardisation in the product offering.

> **KEY TERM**
>
> **Resort destination:** a location that draws its customers based on its all-inclusive product offering, with high quality amenities, an attractive physical setting and an extensive range of on-site activities, as opposed to its convenient location in close proximity to other sites or attractions. The implication is that the resort is a destination in itself, not merely a place to stay when visiting a specific geographical area.

Some resort destinations are purpose built, for example Disneyland Paris, whilst others may be island destinations dominated by one private tourism provider, as is the case with the atolls of Bora Bora in the South Pacific Ocean.

CASE STUDY 9

Hilton Head Island, South Carolina, USA

In Shelter Cove Harbour, overlooking Broad Creek on Hilton Head Island, you will find two neighbouring Marriott Vacation Club resorts, Marriott's Harbour Point and Marriott's Sunset Pointe. The central location makes it easy to get to everything you want to do on the island. From both resorts, you can challenge your skills on some of the country's best golf courses and tennis courts. At Shelter Cove Marina, you can take advantage of everything from fine dining to deep-sea fishing charters. Beach lovers will find sands perfect for jogging, bicycling or lounging. In between adventures, these resorts provide plenty of opportunities for on-site recreation. With its charm, hospitality and natural beauty, Hilton Head Island is an ideal family getaway year after year.

Resort Amenities:

- The Marketplace Express: A quick stop for an assortment of essential snacks and sundry items
- Heated outdoor pools and whirlpool spa
- Tennis courts, fitness centre, shuffleboard court, bocce court, basketball court
- Golf practice tee
- Kids activity centre and games room
- Daily activities programme for all ages
- Set sail with a number of Hilton Head charter companies
- Stroll Savannah's historic district
- Enjoy summer fireworks at HarbourFest
- Take a day trip to Daufuskie Island
- Explore Harbour Town
- Discover the nature of the Coastal Discovery Museum.

Use the information from the case study to explain how the resort destination at Hilton Head Island can create a corporate identity. Give as many examples as you can to support your answer.

3.12 Marketing activities for launching the brand

Once the various stakeholders within a destination have carried out their market research and, often working in conjunction with a specialist marketing agency, decided upon the brand characteristics and the components of the brand identity, the next stage within the branding process is to determine which marketing activities will be used in launching the destination brand. This process is sometimes known as brand activation or more commonly as the marketing plan. This can be summarised as planning when, how and where the brand will be launched.

KEY TERM

Marketing plan: a business document written for the purpose of describing the current market position of a business and its marketing strategy for the period covered by the marketing plan. Marketing plans usually cover a period of one to five years. It will include details of the market research, the marketing budget, an analysis of the competition, an identification of the potential customers as well as the four elements of the marketing mix.

Agree timing for action

From the initial outline proposals to brand a destination to the point at which a destination will be ready to launch the brand takes time. The brand activation plan or marketing strategy should show the timing of each stage of the plan, preferably in the form of a chart. Each of the stakeholders

involved in the brand launch must be consulted about the proposed timescale for the various stages in the process.

Gantt charts are often used to record the proposed time schedule. A Gantt chart, shown in figure 3.34 is commonly used in project management, is one of the most popular and useful ways of showing activities (tasks or events) displayed against time. On the left of the chart is a list of the activities and along the top is a suitable timescale. Each activity is represented by a bar; the position and length of the bar reflects the start date, duration and end date of the activity. This allows you to see at a glance:

* what the various activities are
* when each activity begins and ends
* how long each activity is scheduled to last
* where activities overlap with other activities, and by how much
* the start and end date of the whole project.

Agree costs and resources

Any planned marketing activities within a brand activation programme for a destination will have to be carefully resourced. This can include physical resources, in terms of deciding which type of media to use; it will also include deciding the human resource implications, that is, allocating specific tasks to various different personnel involved in the brand activation process. Lastly, and perhaps most significantly, the stakeholders must allocate financial resources to the process. This means determining the available funds for the proposed plan of activities and fixing the budget for how much money should be spent on each individual stage in the brand activation process.

Decide upon 'guardians of the brand' and level of involvement of key personnel

This ties in with the allocation of human resources, mentioned in the previous section. Human resources is the term for the manpower required to accomplish a task.

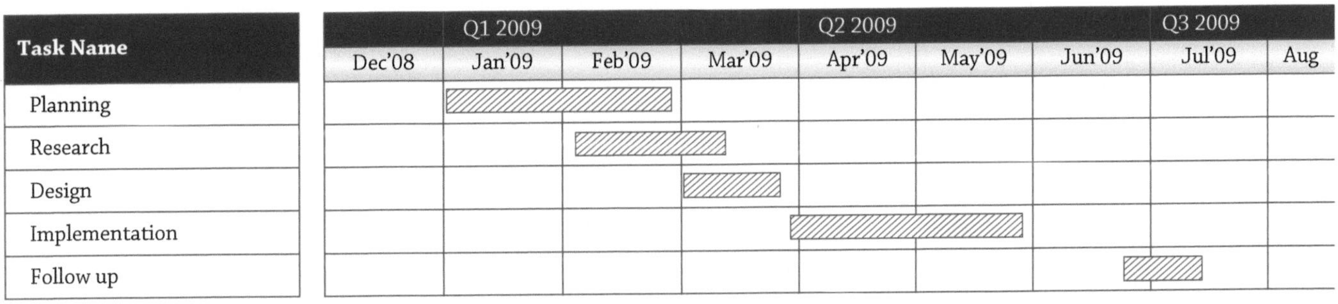

Task Name	Q1 2009				Q2 2009			Q3 2009	
	Dec'08	Jan'09	Feb'09	Mar'09	Apr'09	May'09	Jun'09	Jul'09	Aug
Planning		▨▨	▨						
Research			▨						
Design				▨					
Implementation					▨▨	▨			
Follow up								▨	

Figure 3.34 An example of a Gantt chart

We know there are many different stakeholders involved in creating and upholding the brand identity within a destination. This stage in the process determines exactly who will be involved and to what extent. Each person will be allocated a specific role within the brand activation 'team'.

> **KEY TERM**
>
> **Guardians of the brand:** a term used to describe the key personnel involved in the branding process. These personnel are sometimes also known as the Brand Champions, the Chief Branding Officers or the Directors of Brand Advocacy.

Guardians of the brand are the people in a leadership position, usually at the executive level, who embody the brand promise, champion the brand promise internally and externally and ensure that the brand identity of the destination is protected against negative criticism.

In simplest terms, the guardians of the brand have a variety of critical responsibilities. Most of their responsibilities are intangible, in working to change customers' perception of the brand identity of the destination.

Set objectives

A marketing plan provides direction for marketing activities. The marketing plan details what the destination is aiming to accomplish by establishing a brand, and helps to determine the objectives that will ensure the branding process is successful.

As with any strategic initiative a marketing plan should start with objectives. An objective is a goal that tourism authorities in a destination will work towards on creating the brand. The marketing objectives will guide the entire brand activation process and will be used for evaluation purposes. Without objectives it is easy to get off track, and it will then become difficult to achieve the goal of creating an effective destination brand.

In setting objectives for marketing activities, it is important to use the SMART GOAL principles.

SMART is an acronym:

- S for SPECIFIC – be specific, by targeting a specific target market with the brand.
- M for MEASURABLE – be measurable in quantitative terms, such as number of visitors, volume of sales and so on.
- A for ATTAINABLE – ensure the goals set are achievable.

CASE STUDY 10

Creating a brand activation strategy for Tourism Tasmania

Table 3.11 is an extract from Tourism Tasmania's priorities for 2013–16.

GOALS	OBJECTIVES	STRATEGIES
Drive demand for Tasmania	Make Tasmania a preferred travel destination in key and emerging markets	• Incorporate the brand into activities and programmes • Develop new content to support brand position • Develop new content that reflects brand • Implement two domestic PR campaigns • Implement two major domestic integrated marketing campaigns per year • Deliver and implement a five-year marketing and communications strategy embracing domestic and international markets • Implement a social media plan • Implement two social media campaigns • Enhance and develop the Discover Tasmania website www.discovertasmania.com
	Create and maintain effective marketing and promotional partnerships	• Implement Tourism Tasmania's international strategy • Focus on attracting business events and conferences • Work with brand partners to extend the reach of the Tasmanian brand message • Work with Business Events Tasmania (BET) to ensure the alignment of Tourism • Tasmania's and BET's tourism marketing strategies

Table 3.11 Tourism Tasmania's priorities, 2013–2016

- R for REALISTIC – set ambitious goals but not unrealistic ones that are bound to fail.
- T for TIME-FRAMED – set goals within a specified timescale, so that it is possible to monitor progress towards the goal at regular intervals, and adjust the marketing plan as necessary.

ACTIVITY 19

Use information from the case study materials to choose three key brand strategies for Tourism Tasmania. Use the SMART GOAL principle to change these strategies into SMART objectives. For example: 'Implement two social media campaigns' would become:

'Use Tourism Tasmania's Facebook platform to promote the new Tourism Tasmania brand between January and June 2016, with a target of 250 000 likes and 100 000 new followers from the overseas leisure market.'

Decide on communication methods and events

In preparing to launch the destination brand, it is important to decide how information about the brand will be communicated to the target audience. This will be examined in more detail later on, reflecting on the broad range of communication methods available to a destination in communicating brand messages, but for now it is enough to know that the brand activation key personnel must select from a range of options, including public relations activities, traditional and digital advertising media and sales promotion. The available budget will largely determine the choices made; some forms of promotion are much cheaper than others. A formal brand launch event is often planned, such as the one seen earlier in the chapter launching the Pure Grenada brand. A brand launch event offers an opportunity to raise awareness of the destination brand across a broader customer base, because of the involvement of other media partners.

Design promotional materials

These will be needed to support the marketing activities planned as part of the brand activation process. Most destinations will employ the services of a marketing brand agency to help champion all of these stages of the process, so the task of designing the promotional materials will usually fall to the brand agency, who use professional designers to create the materials to a

131

CASE STUDY 11

Southern Laos launches tourism destination brand

The new brand 'southern Laos, charming by nature' has been officially launched to promote the four southern provinces of Saravan, Xekong, Attapeu and Champassak as one tourism destination.

The event took place in December 2015 in Champassak province and was attended by high level public and private sector representatives from all four provinces, as well as the Ministry of Information, Culture and Tourism. In his opening speech, Deputy Governor of Champassak, Buasone Vongsongkhone said 'Like the anniversary of our country, today's brand launch event is about our identity, about who we are, about what we stand for. The brand reminds us about what we need to treasure and what kind of tourism we want to promote such as a sustainable tourism which is respectful to our culture, to our environment and which helps to share economic benefits amongst all members of the society in southern Laos'. The brand was developed in a participatory process over a period of ten months, facilitated by Swisscontact and supported by international branding expertise from the marketing agency QUO, based in Bangkok. According to Tim Gamper, country manager of Swisscontact in Laos, the most important element of the branding process for southern Laos was not its output of a logo and a tagline, but the fact that it brought tourism stakeholders together from the public and private sector, across provincial borders and across business interests.

CEO of QUO, David Keen, underlined that the brand launch event was just the start of a journey which is likely to contribute significantly to the economic success of the four southern provinces of Laos. But he stressed the importance for local stakeholders to take ownership of the brand and to live it in their day-to-day operations. The event was supported by cultural performances from southern Laos and brought to life by large picture banners, giving a glimpse of the charming nature of the destination.

A big list of media tools was also launched for stakeholders to incorporate with their own material. Part of the media package is a new website (www.southern-laos.com) filled with highlights of things to do or see, as well as an area for tourism trade professionals.

specific brief, agreed upon by the key personnel of the brand activation team.

Agree the overall campaign

These key personnel will work in close partnership with representatives from all major stakeholder groups within the destination to agree the brand activation campaign. Tourism authorities will take advice from the brand agency about the best way forward. The campaign will not only target actions for the proposed destination brand launch, but will also usually include key milestones for after the launch, to ensure delivery of the brand promise is being upheld and maintained over a prolonged period of time. This is to ensure that the brand remains current and fresh, and does not quickly lose its appeal.

ACTIVITY 20

1 Use information from the case study to identify the guardians of the southern Laos destination brand.
2 Assess how effective the tagline for this brand identity is likely to be. Give reasons for your answer.
3 Identify two communication methods used to raise awareness of the brand. Explain why these methods may have been chosen.

3.13 Implementing the destination brand

The planning stage has now drawn to a close and the destination is ready to launch its new brand identity. This section examines the ways in which a destination can communicate the brand to raise awareness among targeted audiences.

Communicating the destination brand

According to Baker (2012), the next stage in the brand activation process is to 'make the brand come to life' (Bill Baker, 2012, *Destination Branding for Small Cities – Second Edition*). This means using a variety of communication methods and other brand activities to make potential visitors aware of the destination brand. Baker suggests that this requires careful synchronising of all advertising, public relations, web marketing and other communications to present an integrated marketing message, which will be most effective in eliciting the desired response from customers.

This section will examine all aspects of implementing and communicating the destination brand, those likely to be involved in the process and factors that will impact on the communication methods selected.

Interdependent stakeholders in the destination branding process and the role each plays

We have already briefly mentioned the different stakeholders that are engaged in the destination branding process. This section aims to examine these stakeholder groups in more detail, and will explain how their roles in the process are interdependent.

National tourism organisations (NTOs)

Tourism authorities within a destination play a central role within the branding process. Tourism authorities are known by different names in different countries – National Tourist Boards, Ministries of Tourism, National Tourism Agencies and Departments of Tourism. NTOs in most countries are public sector organisations, established by the government of that country. They have the responsibility to encourage, promote, and develop tourism as a major socio-economic activity, to generate foreign currency and employment, and to spread the benefits of tourism to both the private and public sectors. NTOs are major instigators of tourism development within destinations and are customarily the main guardian of the destination brand, taking the lead in the branding process.

Some examples of NTOs include: the Belarus National Tourism Agency; the Ministry of Tourism, the Ghana Tourist Board and the Ghana Tourism Federation in Ghana; the Marshall Islands Visitors Authority (MIVA) and China National Tourist Office.

Regional tourism organisations

While NTOs look after tourism development and promotion of whole countries, regional tourism organisations are created to focus on specific tourism regions. A region is a geographical area that has been designated as having common cultural or environmental characteristics. These regions are often named after historical or current administrative and geographical regions. Examples include the Pacific Asia Travel Association, the Australian Regional Tourism Network, the Regional Tourism Organisation of Southern Africa and the Northern Tourism Alliance in North East England.

Regional tourism authorities also usually operate in the public sector, but may have private sector members. Their main role is to support the tourism industry to improve the visitor experience in a cost effective and sustainable manner by representing, advocating and championing tourism in a particular geographic region and to be a voice for the tourism industry in that area. They are important in representing regional interests within destination branding decisions.

Local tourism organisations

A local tourism organisation is one which operates at a local level, within a smaller defined locality. It is likely to be at province, state or county level and will be involved in the development and promotion of tourism within a town, city or local authority boundary. Local tourism organisations will represent the interests of private sector tourism businesses that operate within the destination as well as the local population.

Examples of local tourism organisations include: tourism departments within the local government; municipal, town and borough councils. Local governments tend to have the most direct involvement in tourism, through funding and operating tourism activities, events and attractions (for example, museums and art galleries, parks and trails) at a local level. They are the ones responsible for maintaining and cleaning publicly owned visitor attraction sites and may operate local accommodation grading schemes and issue licences for tour guides and so on. Therefore it is reasonable to expect local tourism organisations to play a major role in how a destination in their locality is branded.

Commercial travel and tourism organisations (for profit)

These are the privately owned tourism businesses that operate within a destination, which in reality make up the significant majority of travel and tourism providers within the industry. These include accommodation providers ranging from the multi-national hotel chains such as Holiday Inn or Hilton through to a small, family-owned and run guest house. Other examples of commercial organisations include restaurants, coffee shops and other food and beverage outlets. Tour operators, travel agents, entertainment facility owners, and transport operators are also all usually commercial organisations.

While many commercial organisations operate under their own brand identity, such as the TUI travel group or the Universal Studios Theme Park group, these organisations are encouraged to contribute to the destination branding process. They often invest heavily in a destination's infrastructure that supports tourism and therefore have a keen interest in tourism development and the branding process. Many visitors are attracted to a destination because of the commercial tourism providers that operate there.

Non-commercial travel and tourism organisations (not for profit)

Technically, this category of stakeholders includes all the public sector organisations including national, regional and local tourism organisations. However, as these have already been covered, this section will focus on other types of non-commercial tourism providers.

There will be non-commercial providers who operate within the destination for the benefit of all, not just for visitors – these might include the local police force, public libraries, refuse collection services and so on, from which visitors as well as the local population will benefit. There will also be other organisations, including associations, clubs and charities with connections within the destination. These may provide amenities that would otherwise not be available within the locality, or may have a strong community focus. Many non-commercial organisations work towards sustainable tourism practices, in order to conserve and protect local environments and their populations for future generations.

KEY CONCEPTS

Sustainability and responsibility

Many of these non-commercial organisations play a key role in promoting sustainability, through involving the local population as well as visitors in conservation and preservation activities.

Examples of non-commercial tourism organisations include the Community Empowerment Network, which supports community-based tourism programmes; the Pachamama Alliance, which encourages sustainable tourism practices; and Blue Ventures, a non-commercial company which helps to sustain marine conservation in places where the ocean is vital to local cultures and economies.

The local community

Local communities form a fundamental part of tourism as they are the focal point for the supply of accommodation, catering, information, transport services and other facilities. The local natural environment, their buildings and institutions, their people, culture and history, all form core purposes of what visitors come to see. The representation of interests of the local community in a destination's brand activation is crucial to the long term success of the branded destination. Yet, the exact role that the local community plays and how its views may be incorporated in the whole planning and development process is often unclear.

Having identified a broad spectrum of different stakeholders that are likely to be present in a tourism destination, it is clear that each stakeholder group will bring a different set of values to the branding process. None of these stakeholder groups should be viewed in isolation; all will be involved to a greater or to a lesser degree in contributing to the destination branding process and will share responsibility in determining the success of the destination brand. A shared understanding of the brand goals and close partnership working is most likely to ensure the successful implementation of the destination brand. The fact that representatives from each stakeholder group are required to work together leads to a greater sense of interdependency of these stakeholders, which in turn leads to a greater sense of shared responsibility for the brand activation and its outcomes.

Tourism in Nova Scotia, Canada: A case for branding?

In the past 10 years, visits to Nova Scotia have declined by 9%, while global travel continues to grow. Visits to Canada are down 18% over the same period. However, Nova Scotia is also faced with a number of barriers to industry growth, including a lack of clarity around roles and responsibilities, widely dispersed spending with little focus, aging product, outdated technology, and an uncoordinated approach to major events. Results from the 2010 Visitor Exit Survey show only 19% of visitors to Nova Scotia are visiting for the first time. Research shows once they visit, they tend to return, offering an opportunity to focus on the first-time visitor.

The Nova Scotia tourism industry is made up of a diverse group of private businesses and public organisations of varying size, including regional tourism industry associations, the Tourism Industry Association of Nova Scotia (TIANS), community groups, specialised tourism associations, and municipalities. By building strategic partnerships and encouraging investments, Nova Scotia is building a strong tourism industry that will allow it to become more competitive and innovative in key tourism markets.

NOVA SCOTIA.COM
CANADA

Figure 3.35 Tourism Nova Scotia

ACTIVITY 21

Use the information from the case study to answer the following questions:

1 Identify three different stakeholder groups of the Nova Scotia tourism industry.

2 Explain how each of the stakeholder groups may contribute to development of the Tourism Nova Scotia brand.

3 The brand identity of Tourism Nova Scotia is currently not successful. Explain three improvements that could be made to increase the brand effectiveness of this region as a destination.

3.14 Communication methods used to raise awareness of the destination's brand identity

Brand communication is essential in order to let people know what is on offer within a destination, especially within such a competitive market. We have already briefly looked at the broad range of marketing communication methods used by tourism providers to raise awareness of products and services, such as advertising and public relations. We will revisit some of these methods here.

Many destinations feel that they need a huge advertising budget in order to produce great marketing communication materials. However, research evidence shows that today's customers actually place low trust in advertising messages and that many tourists do not take much notice of the aggressive attempts to interrupt their television watching, radio listening whilst driving or newspaper/magazine reading habits by advertisers.

Tourists today have become accustomed to bypassing things that have little interest to them, hence it is much more difficult for travel and tourism providers to send subliminal marketing messages to potential customers. Digital competencies means you can fast forward and skip the adverts or disable pop ups on your computer screen. Therefore advertising has had to become much more creative in order to gain a customer's attention. This has given rise to a number of new communication methods to raise awareness of a destination's brand.

Websites, especially that of the NTO

Now that a significant proportion of the population is computer savvy and has continuous access to the internet, an increasing number of tourists choose to make their own travel and holiday arrangements. Once the decision has been made about the type of destination a customer might like to visit, the next part of the process is a visit online to search the websites of providers in those countries that offer the type of tourism experience being sought.

Therefore the websites of national tourism organisations (NTOs) play a very important role in communicating a destination's brand identity to potential visitors. These should be the central hub for visitors, media, and trade partners and should provide easy access to information, enquiries and feedback from others' experiences within the destination. The NTO website is the most cost effective and vital tool in reaching customers and in representing the destination brand. The website should include a search engine and provide hyperlinks to key, associated webpages. It should contain links to social media platforms, include electronic brochures and provide public relations (PR) information via a newsroom of press releases and other related PR activity.

Publicity materials

In destination branding, **publicity** materials can relate to any type of promotional materials issued to raise the attention of potential customers. It can include printed brochures, press releases, sales literature and other publications. Despite the advances in online communications, publicity materials continue to play a part in communicating brand messages to customers.

KEY TERM

Publicity: generally refers to notice or attention that is given to something by the media. In marketing terms this has broadened to encompass any form of giving out information about a product, person, or company for advertising or promotional purposes.

Use of social media

People have online connectivity through an ever-broadening range of digital platforms, with large numbers of the population owning smartphones, tablets and laptops. This provides them with broadband connectivity virtually everywhere they go. As a result of this increased mobile technology it is hardly surprising that tourism providers have recognised the power and potential of social media in communicating with customers. Therefore many tourism authorities have their own social media accounts so that they can reinforce destination brand messages using this communication method. Facebook, Twitter, YouTube and Instagram are common social media tools used to engage with potential customers.

Social media also plays a crucial part in the digital 'word of mouth' process. This aspect will be covered later on in this section.

Email marketing

This is a powerful communication tool if used appropriately by travel and tourism organisations. Once someone subscribes to newsletters or email marketing, they become a captive audience. Destinations can take advantage of this by contributing regular press releases to online travel news agencies, such as eturbonews or Travelmole. This ensures that subscribers to such channels will receive updated brand messages.

When customers sign up to an organisation's email marketing facility, it provides the organisation with an opportunity to make use of subject lines, the email content itself, special offers, editorial voice, personalisation, and so on. These are some of the many tools that an organisation can utilise to coerce the recipient to open up an email and engage with it in order to gain awareness of a destination brand.

Public relations (PR)

Public relations (PR) play a really important role in brand development and enhancing the reputation of a destination by building relationships to advance, promote and benefit the destination. It can lead to strong community and business partnerships and may even bring financial benefits for the destination and its marketing campaign. Customers nowadays are more likely to trust a first-hand account of a destination by a trusted source than they do paid advertising, because of the implied sense of marketing bias that advertising carries with it. PR includes press releases, media visits, a press toolkit, media briefings, bids, speeches and sponsorship. These are all designed to improve the goodwill of the public towards the destination and are particularly important in brand activation activities.

PR can be cost effective as it can increase a destination's visibility and exposure to potential customers. It will generate interest and cost a fraction of the price for paid advertising.

CASE STUDY 13

So Miami

In July 2014 visitors to Times Square in New York found an unexpected lime green life-size vending machine placed by Greater Miami Convention and Visitors Bureau. By pushing the giant #SoMiami button, users were awarded destination branded t-shirts, sunglasses, flip-flops or a trip to Miami. Video sharing of the promotion was also encouraged by using the hashtag SoMiami for an additional opportunity to win a trip for two.

ACTIVITY 22

Explain how the #So Miami brand has adopted an integrated approach to communicating its brand identity.

Search the internet for other examples of innovative destination brand public relations activities. How successful do you think these types of activities will be in raising brand awareness?

Advertising

There are many different forms of advertising that a travel and tourism organisation can use in order to promote a destination. But advertising has lost some of its impact, given how much exposure a customer has to different adverts during a typical day. Advertising itself comes in many different forms; print advertisements are still used in newspapers and magazines; broadcast advertisements are still to be found interrupting our television viewing and online advertisements pop up when we least want them to. However annoying we may find advertisements, and however mistrustful of them we have become, advertising is still considered to be one of the most important communication methods that a destination can use in raising awareness of its brand.

Sales promotion

KEY TERM

Sales promotion: can be defined as the process of persuading a potential customer to buy the product. Sales promotion is designed to be used as a short-term tactic to boost sales – it is rarely suitable as a method for building long-term customer loyalty. Some sales promotions are aimed at consumers. Others are targeted at intermediaries and travel trade partners, such as incentives or bonuses.

When trying to entice tourists to visit a newly branded destination, **sales promotions** are sometimes used. If targeted at customers, there may be a discount coupon offered or a loyalty reward scheme introduced. A prize draw or a competition may be set up as a way of luring customers to subscribe to online newsletters and similar devices, thus giving tourism providers access to customer's details. An offer to book for ten nights and get two nights free is another example of a sales promotion technique that providers in the destination might use to attract customers.

Travel trade partners, namely travel agents, may be offered similar incentives for helping to promote the destination brand, with the promise of a free gift, a prize draw or a familiarisation trip as a means of enlisting their support in 'selling' the destination.

Word of mouth

Word of mouth recommendation has always been a powerful communication method for the travel and tourism industry. Given the intangible nature of the tourism experience and the high cost of the holiday product, many customers like to seek the recommendations of others in helping make a decision over which destination to visit. Traditionally, advice and recommendations were sought from a travel agent as the professional with expert product knowledge. However, with the decline in number of customers using the face to face services of a travel agent and the increase in interactive digital media, word of mouth recommendations have taken on a new lease of life. More and more people now use customer comments, reviews and feedback online ('digital word of mouth') as a key source of information in determining their travel plans.

Websites such as TripAdvisor, trippy.com and travelpost. com have become powerful tools in raising customer awareness of tourism products and services. Similarly social media such as Facebook, Twitter and Instagram encourage customers to post comments on their experience – both positive and negative feedback is easily accessible to any potential visitor to a destination. This can pose a significant challenge to tourism authorities, as they have limited control over this form of word of mouth promotion.

Signage

We have already seen Amsterdam's answer to using signage to communicate its destination brand identity with its 'I amsterdam' statue. There are many other examples such as the Las Vegas signage shown in Figure 3.36.

Figure 3.36 Welcome to Las Vegas branding

Signage allows a destination to reinforce its brand messages, using taglines, logos and specific colour schemes to attract the attention of visitors.

Destination environment

A destination's sense of place and how it functions as a tourism environment is also important in creating awareness. A destination's appearance sends clear messages to visitors to the place. It provides a glimpse of what visitors will experience within the destination and will influence their perceptions of the destination brand. It is a good idea to ensure that all key guardians of the brand spend time in public spaces within the destination, checking out the facilities and amenities that visitors will experience within the destination environment. Hopefully this will create a favourable and lasting impression and a positive sense of welcome.

We are Dublin Town

Dublin Town is a Business Improvement District in the Dublin City Centre area. It is a not for profit organisation charged with creating a welcoming and economically viable city environment in Dublin.

Dublintown.ie was established in 2012, but it quickly became a go-to site showcasing what's on and what's in Dublin city centre. An app was also created so users can find out what events are happening around town or to find a particular kind of business, whether it is a restaurant, service, shop or accommodation while they are on the go.

Despite Dublin Town's successful website Dublintown.ie and high-profile activities, such as Dublin Fashion, Dine In Dublin and Dublin at Christmas, there remains a lack of brand awareness with regard to Dublin's City Centre. Could the visual links between the organisation, the Dublin Town website and the events be strengthened to bring a more cohesive visual structure to the brand? Would this brand awareness help entice the visitors into choosing Dublin City over other destinations?

In creating a brand identity, a stamp for We Are Dublin Town was developed (Figure 3.37) that could be used on all the service providers' merchandise. The We Are Dublin Town badge gave the stakeholders a real sense of community and pride. The brand has become very visible throughout the city centre, and is seen on local businesses signage and is used in all publicity materials.

Figure 3.37 We are Dublin Town branding

ACTIVITY 23

Analyse the communication methods used to raise awareness of the We are Dublin Town destination brand.

3.15 Considerations for selection of communication methods

When a destination wishes to communicate its brand identity to customers, tourism authorities and other guardians of the brand must decide which of the many different communication methods to employ. A number of different factors must be taken into consideration before the final decision can be made. The next section will examine these factors in more detail.

Costs

Like most other things, the actual costs of each communication method need to be taken into account. In the ideal world, every destination would utilise all or most of the communication methods to ensure widespread coverage of the brand message. However, bearing in mind that many destinations are very small and exist in a fiercely competitive environment, this is clearly not feasible. Most NTOs are public sector organisations and therefore are funded by the government. Although they often have the support of private sector organisations, they do not always benefit from huge budgets with which to finance brand activation and raise awareness of the destination. We have already concluded that advertising costs are very high; some public relations activities may be secured at relatively low cost. The guardians of the brand and those responsible for the brand launch must adhere carefully to the available 'marketing' budget, consider who and where their target market is, and then put together a strategy which utilises the best resources to communicate the brand message as effectively as possible to target customers, without exceeding the proposed budget.

KEY CONCEPTS

Global and growing

Designing marketing materials with a wide global reach has become increasingly important ... and increasingly easy, with the extensive use of social media platforms as a marketing tool. Such technological advances have removed the traditional barriers of language and time zones and have opened the way for global customers within a global market.

Global reach

Another very important consideration is the global reach of the chosen communication methods. Global reach means how wide the message will spread among potential visitors from around the world. The benefit of digital technology is that internet promotion can reach customers around the globe 24 hours a day, via websites and social media. There are fewer time zone issues, although online chat with a travel advisor may not be available around the clock, but access to information and online booking systems certainly will be. Email marketing also has a low cost, high global reach, provided that the customer signs up with a valid email address.

Advertising tends to have regional boundaries, especially broadcast advertising. A destination would need to identify key potential source markets and provide language specific advertisements for those key markets. There is more uncertainty about whether the intended audience actually accesses the brand messages through broadcast media and given this is such an expensive form of communication media, the destination would want to have some assurances that they had not wasted their budget in this way. Print advertising also has a more limited global reach, with newspaper and magazine circulation tending to be local, regional or national, but rarely international.

Publicity materials can be shared online, but hard copies of sales literature, brochures and leaflets are often bulky and expensive to mail overseas for distribution.

24 hour marketing

This is another important consideration. Traditional communication methods using travel agents or other booking agencies are bound by the working hours in the source market, which may be different to those in the destination due to world time zones. This has caused much frustration and loss of interest in destinations by customers who cannot access the information when they first require it. As already mentioned, digital technology has overcome many of these associated issues and allows customers to have access to marketing information about a destination 24 hours a day. Some tour operators will even ensure they have advisors on hand to answer queries live 24 hours a day by employing people in different time zones to 'man' their website, or feeds on Facebook and Twitter. The timing of other forms of marketing communication may be more difficult for a destination to control, for example, cost and competition may require a destination to accept unfavourable timeslots for television advertising, when few potential visitors are likely to be watching television.

Lead times

Preparing materials with which to communicate the destination brand message varies from method to method. A simple press release can be written in a relatively short time span, whereas the lead time for a television advertisement may take months or possibly even more than a year from initial idea conception to broadcast. A destination will have to take into careful consideration the lead time for each chosen communication method within their brand activation plan. These lead times should be accounted for within the Gantt chart of the planning phase, allowing sufficient time to ensure all materials are ready in time for the destination brand launch.

Options for personalisation

Research evidence suggests that customers are more likely to engage with a brand message which has been customised or personalised with them in mind than the influence of generic marketing communications.

Email marketing and other forms of direct marketing will, in theory, therefore be more effective than pop up advertisements or an advertisement in the daily newspaper, which cannot be personalised in the same way.

This factor will also be considered when selecting which communication methods to use.

Ability to track success/conversion rates

A destination will be keen to monitor the effectiveness of their destination brand and its brand awareness campaign, as we will see in section 3.4 of this chapter. One method used is to track numbers of users, for example, of the website, or the number of people 'liking' a Facebook post. Some communication methods are easier to monitor in this way than others: TV viewing figures can be monitored, but the number of people who leave the room while the advertisements are showing cannot. The number of copies of a magazine sold can be measured, but whether readers took notice of a specific feature cannot be monitored so easily.

Figure 3.38 is an example of how the impact of a destination brand might be measured by the number of Facebook 'likes'.

A conversion rate refers to the number of sales made as a direct response to a customer having received a brand message from one of these marketing communication methods. This is crucial data in determining which communication methods to use but is not always easy to ascertain. The use of specific sales promotion discount codes or coupons is one means of gathering such specific data.

Figure 3.38 Facebook 'likes'

3.16 Different media used to communicate the destination's brand identity

The traditional categorisations of print media (published sources such as newspaper articles, leaflets and so on), broadcast media (television, radio and cinema advertisement), display media (billboards, telextext or touchscreen, bus and taxi advertising) still hold as do the categorisations of **'above the line'** and **'below the line'**.

 KEY TERMS

Above the line media: the five major media of the press, television, radio, cinema and outdoor marketing. These are all usually commissioned through an advertising agency, with costs directly related to a promotional campaign.

Below the line media: not 'mass media' marketing communications; they include direct mail, point of purchase displays, sales promotion and sponsorship. The costs of these forms of media do not generally fall under the categorisation of advertising costs but rather more generically are attributed to the supplementary marketing budget.

Nowadays the traditional categorisations of media types have been augmented with several new categories, each of which will be covered in the following section. These relate specifically to how the media is used.

Owned media

Owned media is the content that the destination brand guardians create and includes media, content and assets that the destination brand guardians control, like websites, blogs, newsletters and brand social media accounts. Destination brands are increasingly behaving like publishers with editorial staff managing content creation. 'Content Marketing' is a new media concept which can facilitate brand information discovery through search facilities and social channels. 'Content' engages customers by serving broad and niche audiences, which can provide long-term benefits without significantly increasing costs.

Paid for media

Media you pay for is often thought of as 'traditional' online advertising through display advertisements, pay per click search advertisements and sponsorships. The advantages of paid for media are the ability to work 'on-demand' and the ability to have some degree of control. The use of keywords and content need to address the problems or solutions your potential customer is looking for. The growing popularity of social advertising on sites like Facebook, Twitter, LinkedIn and YouTube adds more options for destinations to gain brand presence in channels where visitors and potential visitors are spending their time. The appearance of brand messages and content within paid for media can work together with social sharing and generic search facilities.

Earned media

This is where the customer becomes the channel. Big influencers here are word of mouth (WOM), reviews and ratings, press releases or any buzz or content that goes viral. This describes the results of public and media relations efforts to gain coverage in publications, both on and offline. In other words, brand presence within media without having to advertise.

Shared media

Brand social web participation and interaction with customers on content on sites like Facebook, Twitter and YouTube that results in content is 'shared media' since it is a result of a shared interaction. This is largely influenced by social media activity. Even if the destination only has 400 people following its page, those 400 people also have followers and so on. So the network could potentially reach thousands of people that can choose to click on or download information about the destination brand.

Paid and owned media can inspire shared media as illustrated in Figure 3.39. Shared media can inspire earned media. The key message is that whichever forms of media a destination brand uses online, those responsible for uploading information should always take time to monitor and engage with customers on social media sites. Owned media in particular needs to be constantly updated in order to maintain relevance within search engines.

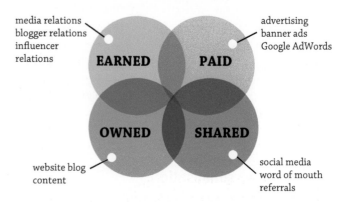

Figure 3.39 The relationship between different media in communicating the brand identity

> **ACTIVITY 24**
>
> Explain how the brand identity for this destination could be communicated to potential visitors and make recommendations for the communication methods and media to be used.

3.17 Difficulties in implementing the destination brand

The branding of consumer goods has long been accepted, but the concept of places adopting a brand identity only really emerged in the 1990s. Even now, there are still numerous reasons why destination branding causes some difficulties, in a way that branding goods does not. The next section will examine some of the challenges faced in branding places.

3.18 Challenges in branding destinations

A destination is made up of composite products, not just one product

Places are certainly not homogenous. There is a broad range of products and services that contribute to the destination's appeal. Many of these work hand in hand

Shrewsbury, England

In 2012, a British town tries to reinvent itself for tourists, via branding.

It's not that Shrewsbury, a small medieval town between Liverpool and Birmingham, is boring. *'A lot of cities would envy Shrewsbury's community feel, that its high street isn't a cookie-cutter row of the same shops, and that it's a modern town with a lot of history mixed in,'* explains designer Dan Bernstein, of London agency &Smith.

But Shrewsbury doesn't have one single, overriding thing it's known for – like a music festival, or a market, for example. And that's made it difficult to market the bustling historic British village to potential home owners and tourists. So, earlier this year, the town council appealed to &Smith and fellow Londonites We All Need Words for help. In response, the team devised an unusual visual identity that goes beyond the typical boilerplate logo-and-colour-scheme branding package. *'Shrewsbury didn't need a vision in a PowerPoint presentation'*, explains Rob Mitchell, who runs We All Need Words with partner Molly Mackey. *'It needed good ideas and practical things that everyone in the town could use.'*

They came up with the concept of a customisable logo that every local business, from bike mechanics to bread bakers, could use. After slinging around ideas, they chose a slogan ('A Shrewsbury One-Off Since…' that focuses on authenticity – something Shrewsbury has in excess. The logo, printed on rubber stamps and stickers, gives shop owners the latitude to personalise the slogan to fit their wares. 'Since 5.15 a.m.' for a pastry chef, or 'Since 1552', for the town's castle visitor centre.

The rest of the identity fell into place fairly easily. The designers picked out timber patterns on the town's Tudor-style buildings and made them into typographical elements that mix with the Dalton Maag typeface Efra. In print ads, the bespoke typeface is overlaid on images of centuries-old vandalism on the town gates ('Graffiti') or a shot of a bike shop ('Chainstore').

The point? London it ain't, and that's the way we like it. 'The key thing is not to try to compete with cities', explains Bernstein, who adds that 'it's a beautiful old place, but it's also got a busy theatre, an art gallery and museum opening in an old music hall next year and great little shops. This is a place where people live and work, so the pattern had to be confident and modern too'.

The team is excited to see if the 'One-Off' idea will catch on amongst the town's shop keepers. 'If Shrewsbury's businesses make more of their one-offs and we can encourage new one-offs too', adds Mitchell, 'that's when we'll know this brand's really working'.

Figure 3.40 The 'One off…' destination brand image for Shrewsbury

and cannot not separated from one another. A resort destination comprises the accommodation, the catering, the entertainment and the activities. No single element alone would offer a visitor the full destination experience; all of these elements build together to give the destination its brand identity. A destination brand has to encapsulate all of these things.

Intangibility of the tourism offering

A destination comprises a mix of different elements – some are the tangible features of the destination, such as the natural and built environment the destination boasts – beaches, lakes, forests, museums, temples, castles; but many of the elements of a place are intangible – the warmth of the welcome that the host population extends visitors, for example. Or consider the sights, sounds and pungent aromas of the Jemaa el Fna main square in Marrakech, with its authentic Moroccan food stalls, street entertainers and travelling barbers, tattooists and craftspeople.

A destination brand has to communicate these intangible elements as well as the tangible ones (Figure 3.41).

Figure 3.41 Jemaa el Fna in Morocco; overcoming the intangibility of a destination

The destination's reputation and image are not created by the destination management organisations in charge of its marketing and promotion

The guardians of the destination brand will assume some responsibility for the brand activation and marketing activities. However in reality, many destinations buy in the professional services of a brand agency to take charge of the marketing and promotion of the destination brand. The reputation and image that visitors have of a destination are built up over a long period of time and are based on a set of associations within people's minds. Reputation and image are based largely on the interactions visitors have with the local population, not on the image a brand designer tries to sell to us. That said, however, destination management organisations and tourism authorities within the destination must use marketing and promotion of the destination to make the perceptions of visitors shift.

Diverse range of organisations and partners involved in crafting and delivering the brand

There are also many different providers that 'represent' the destination to external customers. We have already explored a range of these providers under the stakeholder heading in interdependent stakeholders in the destination branding process and the role each plays. As we have already mentioned, a majority of these organisations are also operating their own brand identity. Therefore it may be challenging for them to additionally incorporate and uphold the destination's brand into all of their own marketing communications with customers.

There will be the expectation that all involved stakeholders – public sector bodies such as the local government, or the airport authority; private sector companies, such as hotel groups, restaurants and taxi firms; and voluntary sector organisations such as Tourism Concern – all work together in delivering a unified representation of the destination brand. However, the more people that are involved, the greater the potential for the brand message being diluted, distorted or confused. This will be due to the subjective interpretation and understanding of the brand message by individuals, rather than a deliberate attempt to complicate or 'sabotage' the branding process.

ACTIVITY 25

Study the following two destination brand images. Which one appeals to you most? Describe your reaction to each brand image.

Figure 3.42 Visit Seychelles brand logo

Figure 3.43 Visit Maldives brand logo

Lack of funding for marketing efforts

We have previously considered the cost implications associated with communicating the brand message. Any form of marketing communication requires finance, and emerging destinations may not have access to huge reserves of capital with which to fund expensive advertising campaigns. A destination will seek funding from the local, regional or national government and from private sector stakeholders in support of the branding process, but the allocated budget is unlikely to be high, making it difficult to run an effective destination brand campaign or to launch the brand extensively because of the limited funds available.

Difficult to create a unique identity in the face of stiff competition

Although we know that no two destinations are actually identical, from a visitor's perspective one island destination, such as the Seychelles, is pretty much the same as another island destination, such as the Maldives. Both destinations are made up of a group of tropical islands, located in the Indian Ocean. They both offer unspoilt, and often private, white sand beaches, with over water bungalow accommodation. There are cultural activities and local crafts to experience, and extensive menus of seafood to sample.

So how can each destination create a totally unique brand identity when there is little to differentiate these destintations?

Coming up with unique logos, unique taglines and unique brand names requires a high degree of creative thinking as well as a good understanding of the destination's features and of the competition.

Destination image is affected by natural disasters, political unrest, acts of terrorism and other social, economic and political factors

One of the biggest challenges that a destination brand faces is that which comes from external sources and is therefore largely beyond the control of the travel and tourism providers within the destination.

A destination's image and reputation can be positively enhanced by media coverage of community spirit and cultural exchange, but these instances are rare as they are not really newsworthy. Instead, destinations find much of their media coverage focuses on negative events, and in current times there have been many such instances.

Consider the terrorist attacks in 2015 in destinations including Egypt, Thailand, Tunisia and Paris and how these affected the image and reputations of these destinations. What about the effects of the earthquake in Nepal, the intense heatwave in Pakistan and India and the outbreak of Ebola in West Africa? How do such situations affect how visitors feel towards these destinations?

ACTIVITY 26

Research **three** different social, economic, environmental or political situations which have adversely affected tourism destinations. How did media coverage of these events affect the destinations' image and reputation? Explain the likely short term and longer term impacts this has had on these destinations.

Monitoring the effectiveness of the destination brand

Although activating a destination brand takes months/ years to plan and implement, tourism providers in destinations cannot sit back and sigh with relief once the brand has been launched. The brand launch is just the beginning of a lengthy and ongoing process. Maintaining the brand is important in order to stay relevant and competitive. Effective brand management strategies are required to keep the brand 'alive' and to ensure that the destination delivers on its brand promises. Setting up a strategy to closely monitor and evaluate the performance of the brand is essential and will allow adjustments to be made as necessary.

A variety of methods can be used to monitor the brand performance, which will be considered in this next section.

3.19 Methods used to monitor costs and marketing activities

These are the so-called 'brand health metrics' – measures of the effectiveness of the destination brand that can be used at regular intervals by the guardians of the brand. Specialist staff are often employed to gather and analyse data using a range of the following techniques.

Resources invested

This requires a regular check on the broad range of resources used to implement the destination brand: a check on the physical resources of signage within the destination, the availability of brand merchandise and publicity materials stocked at key visitor locations; a check on the human resources involved in delivering on-brand messages and a check on financial resources – how much of the delegated advertising budget has been spent to date, for example.

Marketing activities

Given the focus on marketing communications in establishing the brand and in raising awareness of the destination with potential customers, it is important that the effectiveness of such marketing activities is monitored. This can be achieved by ascertaining how many brochures have been distributed to inbound tour operators, for example, or by checking the number of views that a video uploaded to YouTube has had. This type of monitoring exercise is important as it allows the marketing team to amend brand activities to be amended in line with the success rates of previous marketing activities.

Visitor surveys

A common approach to monitoring the success of a destination brand is to conduct a survey with visitors or potential visitors. Market research staff are often employed to circulate airport departure lounges to use a questionnaire to find out how well a visitor's in-destination experiences matched the destination brand promise.

Provider surveys

Various organisations carry out surveys of tourism providers within the destination. The purpose of these surveys is to review how well local providers perceive the destination brand to be working and to monitor the impacts of the brand on sales and usage.

Website traffic

This is another way of monitoring the effectiveness of marketing communications in conveying the destination brand. At the bottom of many websites, a small 'counter' is displayed, to show how many people have navigated to the webpage in a given period of time. Invisible tracking is also available.

Some websites also monitor how many people are simultaneously browsing the site at that point in time. This allows analysis of the level of interest in a destination and allows comparative data before and after a brand launch.

Search engine optimisation

This is the process of affecting the visibility of a website or a web page in a search engine's results. This means whether the destination's website appears on page 1 of the search results or on page 10, for example. This can be used to increase popularity of the destination brand, because those destinations that appear 'higher' in the search results stand a better chance of being seen than those further down the search results hierarchy.

Social media response rates

We have already mentioned the importance of cultivating a social media presence for a destination brand. The number of followers on Facebook or Twitter, the number of 'likes' a picture receives on Instagram and the number of views or subscribers to a YouTube account are all key measures of brand effectiveness.

Attendance at trade fairs, take-up for familiarisation trips, incentive tours, numbers of sponsors

These are all measures of the power of public relations activities with which a destination may engage. The more fairs that a destination's marketing team attend, the more exposure the brand receives. The total number of visitors at a fair also indicates the reach of the destination brand. Similarly, if familiarisation trips or incentive tours offered to representatives from the travel and tourism trade are oversubscribed or have a small number of interested participants, this helps a destination gauge the popularity of the destination brand. If sponsors are difficult to obtain for the brand launch, the destination brand guardians will use this as an indicator of a failed destination brand.

3.20 Key performance indicators (KPIs)

Many of the methods used to monitor the effectiveness of the destination brand provide key performance indicators of the brand.

KEY TERMS

Key performance indicators: a business measure used to evaluate factors that are crucial to the success of an organisation.

The following are all KPIs used in evaluating the success of a destination brand.

Destination popularity ranking

An infinite number of different popularity rankings are available for tourist destinations, based on many different sets of parameters, depending on which organisation has collected the data. The UNWTO World Tourism Organisation World Tourism Barometer provides a retrospective and prospective evaluation of tourism performance, whilst the UNWTO Tourism Highlights offers the world's top tourism destinations based on visitor numbers, visitor send and so on. Travel trade publications often poll their readers in order to find the most popular destinations based on purpose of visit or value for money.

All of these can provide reassurance that a destination brand is working effectively, if the destination increases its position in the rankings.

KEY CONCEPTS

Change and development

Many of the key performance indicators are rooted in the concept of change – increased visitor numbers, increased tourism spend and so on being the overarching objective of a destination branding itself. With these changes, a destination is able to bring about further development.

Changes in arrival numbers

Visitor arrival statistics are one of the main KPIs used to measure a destination's performance. An increase in visitor numbers is an indicator of increased popularity, which implies that the destination brand is delivering the required results. A decrease in visitor numbers is a cause for concern, and may require more marketing efforts to raise the profile of the destination.

Changes in visitor spend

This is another important KPI for a destination as it shows the amount of revenue that visitors bring to the local economy. A change in visitor spend is not always a true reflection of increased popularity in the same way that increased arrival numbers are. Exchange rates and the cost of living in a destination fluctuate; sometimes it costs a visitor more to spend the same amount of time doing the same things in the destination than on a previous visit because of inflation.

However, this is still used to measure performance as it offers a broad indication of whether visitors are willing to part with their money in-destination, implying that customers find the products and services worth spending money on.

Changes in average length of stay

This is another useful KPI as the average number of nights a visitor spends in a destination is proof of how much the

destination has to offer. The higher the average, the greater the destination's popularity. Changes tend to be small – going from 3.4 nights to 3.5 nights – but destinations will be happy with any positive trend. If the number of nights starts to fall, then the marketing team will take action to try to increase interest, perhaps by offering a reduction on subsequent night's accommodation fees.

Changes in occupancy rates

Accommodation stock within a destination records occupancy as the number of beds used out of the total number of bed space available. An average of 75%–80% occupancy is deemed to be good. Where numbers fall significantly below this, accommodation providers will be encouraged to run promotions under the destination brand to entice more customers to come to stay. Looking for upward or downward trends in occupancy rates is another KPI used by destinations to analyse performance.

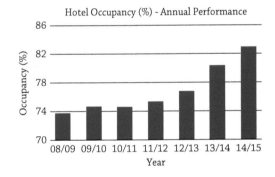

Figure 3.44 All three charts show monitoring of trends in occupancy rates in Glasgow. Source of all three charts glasgowtourismstrategy.com

Job creation within the tourism sector

Tourism contributes significantly to the local economy and one of the key measures of this contribution is the number of jobs that tourism supports within a destination both directly and indirectly. A destination with an effective tourism brand should see an increase in demand for its products and services, which in turn leads to an increase in the number of staff needed to work in the tourism industry.

Changes in market share

This is an interesting performance measure. It is hoped that a branding campaign may make a destination more competitive and therefore cause an increase in overall market share among rival destinations. But what can also sometimes happen is that a particular brand campaign targets one type of customer more than other customer types, so the internal market share balance between, for example, business and leisure tourists might also change as a direct result of a new destination brand.

Brand awareness

The results of visitor surveys and other methods used to collect data about the performance of the brand can be analysed to monitor the effectiveness of the destination brand. It is interesting to see how brand conscious visitors are – many surveys will ask the specific question about how the visitor learnt of the destination. This will help control the use of different communication methods based on their ability to raise brand awareness. Showing the visitor a range of different brand identities and asking them to select the one(s) with which they are familiar is an interesting exercise in assessing actual brand awareness, but requires some creativity in producing feasible alternatives.

Return on investments (ROIs)

KEY TERMS

Return on investments (ROIs): a business term and is the most common profitability ratio. There are several ways to determine **ROI**, but the most frequently used method is to divide net profit by total assets.

Within the destination brand context, return on investments is often used to estimate the economic impact of destination marketing on particular source markets. This requires some complex economic analysis, usually carried out by specialists in this field.

ROI estimates

net revenue generated:	$	3 401 951 199
total marketing expenses:	$	72 740 306
total budget, including start-up costs and overhead:	$	99 022 800
estimated marketing ROI:		47:1
total budget ROI:		34:1

For example, the data shown here relates to the ROI of Brand USA in 2013.

$3.4 billion was generated in tourism receipts, that is, spending by visitors. Investments totalled less than $100 million.

The $3.4 billion in additional international visitor spending produced by Brand USA marketing is estimated to have generated the following U.S. economic impacts:

- $7.4 billion in business sales (output)
- $3.8 billion in value added (GDP)
- $2.2 billion in personal income
- 53 181 jobs created, including 27 895 directly in industries serving visitors
- $512 million in federal taxes
- $460 million in state and local taxes.

This data shows the detailed breakdown of the economic impacts of the Brand USA ROI as at 2013.

It is not a requirement to understand the actual calculation of ROI; just that this economic data analysis act as a powerful KPI.

New/Repeat business

As part of the visitor survey data collection exercise, destinations will be able to identify whether customers are visiting the destination for the first time or making a return visit. This information acts as a KPI in terms of market segmentation and the type of communication method that might be best employed to convey the destination brand to these customer types.

ACTIVITY 27

Study the information about Bloom's Country Brand ranking for tourism destinations in Africa.

1. Identify and explain **two** performance indicators used by Bloom to calculate its country tourism ranking analysis.
2. Explain the likely impacts of these results for:
   i South Africa   ii Botswana
3. Suggest ways in which Mauritius might respond to its loss of position in the rankings.
4. Evaluate the importance of such destination brand rankings from a visitor's perspective.

Bloom's Country Brand Ranking, Tourism Edition 2014/2015

Bloom Consulting is a country branding consultancy company with more than a decade of research experience in ranking destination brands.

Present Ranking

Current measurement systems

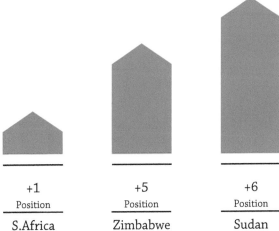

Transactional

? Perceptions   🔍 D2 ©
📈 Revenue   ☺ Happiness

These three objectives are transactional and can be measured more tangibly, using metrics such as D2 © and revenue as well as perceptions.

Non-transactional

? Perceptions   🔍 D2 ©
📈 Revenue   ☺ Happiness

These two objectives are non-transactional and can only be measured intangibly, using metrics such as perceptions D2 © and happiness.

2014/2015 Results - Africa

South Africa leaves Egypt behind

For the first time ever, South Africa tops the list in the African continent of Bloom Consulting's Country Brand Ranking © 2014 / 2015 Tourism Edition. Taking advantage of a debilitated Egypt, South Africa has steadily risen to the top slot in the region, and breaking into the global top 25. Morocco maintains its third place position in Africa.

Biggest improvements

South Africa takes the leadership in the region and is the most impressive change of this year's Country Brand ranking Tourism Edition in Africa. Zimbabwe and Sudan have experienced an extraordinary improvement in the ranking due mainly to their recent growth rate in tourism receipts.

Biggest drops

Egypt, due to its continuous political instability since 2011, has finally felt the effects of a lack of security on its tourism industry. The drop in tourism receipts, a relatively weak brand image and an unfavourable online presence have contributed to Egypt's drop to second position in the tourism-related Country Brand for Africa. The lack of growth in tourism receipts over the past few years is the main reason to explain the loss of position for Mauritius (-1) and Botswana (-4) along with better relative performances from their main competitors.

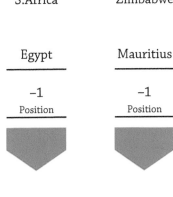

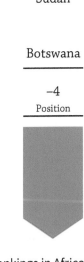

+1 Position	+5 Position	+6 Position
S.Africa	Zimbabwe	Sudan

Egypt	Mauritius	Botswana
−1 Position	−1 Position	−4 Position

Figure 3.45 Changes in destination rankings in Africa

Summary

Destination marketing is an important process in raising awareness with potential visitors. Adopting a destination brand has become integral to the destination marketing process and allows each destination to differentiate itself from its competitors. Choosing the right destination brand identity is essential and tourism authorities have to be mindful that once the brand has been launched, there is still much work to be done in upholding the brand image, in order to ensure that visitors continue to be attracted to the destination.

Exam-style questions

Question 1

Read the following extract and answer the questions that follow.

> *New Brand Bahrain on way*
> *March 2016*
>
> Brand Bahrain, an international campaign to promote the kingdom as a top tourist destination, will be launched next month.
>
> The campaign will focus on the kingdom's heritage, culture and business-friendly environment.
>
> It is being spearheaded by the Bahrain Tourism and Exhibitions Authority (BTEA), which will launch the project's logo and objectives in the coming months.
>
> It will have a distinctive visual identity that captivates audiences globally and strengthens Bahrain's position as a top tourist destination.
>
> The soft launch of the initiative will be held during the Bahrain Formula One to be held in April 2016.
>
> A huge influx of Chinese visitors is expected in the kingdom in 2016 as part of a plan approved by both countries. With visas on arrival already provided to Chinese nationals, officials are now urging the hospitality sector to gear up to welcome the increased number of visitors. Bahrain signed an agreement with Chinese authorities that will result in more approved tour operators from China sending large groups of travellers.
>
> Bahrain has announced year long celebrations marking its capital 'Manama Gulf Capital of Tourism 2016'. A Handicraft Festival in Bab Al Bahrain will be held from April 1 to April 8, an Annual Heritage Festival will take place on April 24 at Arad Fort and the Bahrain Light Festival in Manama will be held from May 5 to May 9.
>
> Last year, Saudis spent around $7billion in tourism abroad and tourism officials in Bahrain are keen to benefit by hosting these events, especially when 59% of the kingdom's visitors come from Saudi Arabia.

a   Explain **two** methods that BTEA will use to create a brand identity for Bahrain. **[4 marks]**

b   Analyse the marketing activities that are planned to launch Bahrain's new destination brand. **[9 marks]**

c   Evaluate the importance of market segmentation to Bahrain as a destination. **[12 marks]**

Question 2

Yucatán, one of the 32 federal entities in Mexico, is centre of the Mayan culture, offering a great diversity of attractions, a scenic cultural heritage and experiences that range from archaeological sites and sophisticated haciendas to internationally-awarded Mayan nouvelle cuisine. Yucatán is also recognised for how safe it is and its friendly and peaceful environment.

MBLM, a brand agency, was invited by the Tourism Board of the Yucatán government to develop a marketing strategy to create a spotlight on the area as an international and renowned destination. In addition to improving the perception of Yucatán and its strong and positive attributes, the project aimed to increase partnership working amongst stakeholders and to increase the number of visitors, the length of their stays and their day-to-day average spending.

MBLM first conducted an in-depth market research process through focus groups, online surveys, workshops, data mining and international benchmark analysis to understand the opportunity for differentiation and greater audience relevance. As a result, marketing of Yucatán was aimed at five key market segments: local residents, second-home residents (mostly retired foreigners), DINKYs (double income, no kids yet), honeymooners and families. All of them have been part of Yucatán's past and are essential to the destination in the future.

a   Describe **two** different market research methods that the brand agency MBLM used in researching the tourism market for Yucatán. **[4 marks]**

b   Discuss the aims of the market research and analysis process in destination marketing. **[9 marks]**

c   Evaluate the likely reasons for the Tourism Board of the Yucatán government wanting to brand the destination. **[12 marks]**

Question 3

CEBU, Philippines – The province of Cebuissetto unveils its brand to define the essence of Cebu, as it aims to become one of the favourite leisure and business destinations of travellers around the world.

Led by the Cebu Chamber of Commerce and Industry (CCCI) and the community organisation, MegaCebu, the Cebu brand team have finally come up with the right brand that will be used in all promotional activities about the province, both in tourism and for investment opportunities.

This unified approach is supported by Cebu provincial and city governments, as well as by the Department of Tourism. The ceremonial and formal unveiling of the Cebu brand is to be held in November 2015 at the Ayala Centre, Cebu.

The branding conceptualisation and process took more than five months, where all initiatives to craft the distinctive concept of Cebu and express it in a simple yet meaningful way was finally captured through the collaborative efforts of the branding team.

The CCCI Tourism Committee and MegaCebu invited Singaporean branding expert Jacqueline Thng to conduct a workshop on the branding framework, followed by the CCCI Tourism Forum and a series of interactive research-based meetings, where stakeholders and the public shared their branding slogans and taglines.

Branding goes beyond slogans and taglines which was the reason why the Cebu brand team researched long and hard to come up with the right brand for Cebu. From all these initiatives, the Cebu brand team pooled their expertise and finally came up with the Cebu Brand.

Tourism players in Cebu had been working to come up with an official, sustainable and integrated tourism brand for the entire province to enhance the attractiveness of Cebu as a tourism and investment destination.

a Describe **two** different market research methods that the brand agency MBLM used in researching the tourism market for Yucatán. **[4 marks]**

b **i** Identify two stakeholders involved in the branding process for Cebu. **[2 marks]**

    ii Describe the likely role of each of these stakeholder groups in the branding process. **[2 marks]**

c Other than slogans and taglines, assess the different methods available to the Cebu brand team in establishing the destination brand identity. **[9 marks]**

d Cebu aims to create a 'sustainable and integrated' tourism brand.

Evaluate the difficulties that the destination may face in implementing the tourism brand. **[12 marks]**

Chapter 4
Destination management

By the end of this chapter you should have covered:

- which organisations are involved in destination management, including their roles and priorities
- the objectives of tourism development and management
- destination management activities
- economic, socio-cultural and environmental impacts of tourism.

Figure 4.1 Elizabeth Tower (previously named 'Big Ben'), London.

Figure 4.2 Great Belt Bridge, Denmark

Figure 4.3 Arches National Park, USA

Introduction

This chapter focuses on how destinations are managed. The objectives of tourism management are many, but the overall aim is to minimise the negative impacts of tourism and to maximise the positive impacts.

Destinations are places where tourism has developed (see the three examples in Figures 4.1, 4.2 and 4.3). Social, cultural, environmental, economic and political conditions influence tourist destinations. The people who are responsible for destination management have to try and ensure that tourism development integrates with other social and economic activities of the particular area so that future development can be sustained. The perceived benefits of tourism will vary depending on the needs and expectations of those involved. Indeed, any anticipated benefits will vary from one destination to another and, as such, what works in one destination is not guaranteed to work in another. This may seem to complicate the management process, but ultimately the success of destination management relies upon sound objectives implemented by organisations with clear roles and priorities. These organisations may be national or local government departments, regional tourism organisations, international companies, NGOs and commercial organisations.

Tourism development occurs for many reasons and can boost the economy, particularly where regeneration is required as it may assist with rejuvenating areas that are in decline. Tourism development is carried out by a wide variety of commercial and non-commercial organisations which belong to the public, private and voluntary sectors. These organisations may work in partnership or may have conflicting objectives. For example, national and local tourist boards often work together with commercial providers to promote a destination to increase visitor numbers and income. However, an area of land in a prime tourism development site may be valuable to the landowner, particularly if a property development company wants to build a hotel on the land or if a community group wants the land for local community use.

The tourism industry is complex, incorporating a network of interrelated stakeholders and organisations, both in the public and private sector, working together. Sustainable tourism is tourism attempting to make a low impact on the environment and local culture, while helping to generate future employment for local people. The aim of sustainable tourism is to ensure that development brings a positive experience for local people, tourism companies and the tourists themselves. As a concept, the principles of sustainable destination management are becoming much better understood:

It is about managing the visitor impact on a local destination's economy, social fabric and physical environment in a way which benefits everybody – residents, businesses, landowners and visitors alike – both now and in the future.

These principles can be applied to all tourism destinations and to all sectors and forms of tourism, whether niche or mainstream, rural, coastal or urban.

> **KEY TERM**
>
> **Sustainable tourism:** is tourism attempting to make a low impact on the environment and local culture, while helping to generate future employment for local people.

4.1 Organisations involved in destination management, their roles and priorities

Government ministries and national tourism organisations (NTOs)

These organisations generally have responsibility for managing tourism within a budget. They will have key priorities such as research, development and funding in order to fulfil a successful and sustainable tourism strategy for their country or destination. These strategies will include protecting the environment while encouraging investment and developing the economic benefits of tourism. NTOs can protect and manage areas by passing laws and by-laws such as designating an area as a national park or an area of outstanding natural beauty. They may also encourage new businesses and innovations in order to expand tourism provision to both the mass and specialised (niche) markets.

Key marketing strategies are also employed to develop tourism and to gain positive images of an area. Developing a strong destination image is vital in order to be able to promote to as many tourists as possible. Retaining tourism numbers and encouraging repeat visitors are essential for successful destination management.

The following case study is of a national tourism organisation and a destination management company – Singapore Tourism Board – with their marketing brand, 'Your Singapore', launched in 2010.

CASE STUDY 1

Your Singapore

The Singapore Tourism Board (STB) is a statutory board under the Ministry of Trade and Industry of Singapore. It champions the development of Singapore's tourism sector, one of the country's key service sectors and economic pillars, and undertakes the marketing and promotion of Singapore as a tourism destination.

The tourism sector currently contributes 4% to Singapore's gross domestic product and supports some 160,000 jobs. Tourism plays an essential role in reinforcing Singapore's status as a vibrant global city that is a magnet for capital, businesses and talent. It also enhances the quality and diversity of leisure options for local residents and helps to create a living environment that Singaporeans can be proud to call home.

The Singapore Tourism Board not only markets Singapore as a compelling destination for visitors and investors, it also plays many other roles, including developing the tourism sector, enhancing industry competitiveness and capabilities, regulating key tourism industries, and placemaking, that is, establishing a destination as a place to visit (Figure 4.4).

In March 2010, STB launched an evolution of Singapore's destination brand – from 'Uniquely Singapore' to 'Your Singapore' – that underpins Singapore's unique strength in providing an experience that can be easily personalised. This is premised on our concentration of sights, sounds, tastes, culture and attractions, coupled with unparalleled user-friendliness.

Your Singapore helps ensure that Singapore remains relevant and compelling to today's travellers. It delivers on Singapore's promise to provide a concentration of multi-faceted and user-centric travel experiences as well as positions the destination as one that is future-facing and inspiring. Doing well in this area is critical as brand equity and brand recall have a tremendous impact on visitor arrivals and tourism receipts.

Figure 4.4 Singapore at night

Sustainability and responsibility

The previous section refers to strategic roles that governments and policy makers take in order to complete set priorities within a timeframe. They main focus is the ability to work with other interested parties.

KEY TERMS

Brand equity: the value of having a well-known brand name which can be used on products and services.

Brand recall: the ability of customers to memorise and recall brands and associated products.

ACTIVITY 1

Research other destination brands. Is there an obvious one for your country/destination? Does it work? If not, can you suggest one?

Local authorities, regional tourism organisations, destination management companies (DMCs)

Local authorities are government funded organisations that provide a service to both the local and visiting populations. They will engage in activities that will help boost the image of their local area and the services which they supply. They are equally concerned to see an increase in visitors, as many types of service have to generate additional revenues to operate efficiently.

A destination management company is one that uses its extensive local knowledge and resources to offer a professional service in organising and running of events, assisting with transport, activities, accommodation and so on. It can organise meetings and book accommodation and restaurants. By coordinating all planning elements and logistics for any service required, such as excursions, conferences or events, they can offer competitive fees due to their established contacts within the industry.

154

The Ministry of Tourism in Zimbabwe aims to develop and manage policy programmes and strategies to enhance the sustainable development and growth of the tourism and hospitality industry.

They wish to be the destination of choice and leader in the development of sustainable tourism in Africa by 2018. The following outlines their mission and values:

Mission

To facilitate the delivery of high quality, sustainable tourism products and services that contribute to the economic development of Zimbabwe.

Core Values

Professionalism:
Conforming to high standards of ethical and moral conduct in the execution of our Mandate.

Utilizing our skills, intelligence and effective communication to positively respond to our clients and offer them the highest quality of service.

Accountability:
Taking full responsibility for the outcomes and outputs of what has been entrusted to the Ministry:

Making an honest acknowledgement of our actions on issues whenever called upon to do so.

Team Work:
Understanding that the sum of the whole is greater than the sum of individual parts.

National Pride:
Driven to achieve common National Goals and Objectives and putting National interests ahead of personal interests.

Leadership:
To provide exemplary leadership and direction to the entire tourism sector

For further information visit - www.tourism.gov.zw

Destination management companies (DMCs) in Malta

Local destination management companies incorporate fresh ideas, designed to suit particular event requirements. They will ensure that guests get a taste of remarkable historic sites, unique venues and places of natural beauty, during their visit. This guarantees authentic cultural experiences which will help to develop the image of Malta through strong marketing and brand identity.

Destination management companies (DMC) quality scheme

The Quality Assured seal, is a voluntary scheme run by the Malta Tourism Authority that recognises destination management companies (DMCs) committed to high levels of quality, consistency and professionalism (see figure 4.5).

Figure 4.5 Malta Destination Management Company Logo

International development agencies, non-governmental organisations (NGO)

> **KEY TERM**
>
> **NGO:** non-governmental organisation

International development agencies and non-governmental organisations are mainly charitable ventures supporting a particular cause and rely on donations from their various supporters. They will also support activities that increase the profile of the local destination as they constantly seek additional support to fund their various activities. They will conduct research and gain expert knowledge of destinations and issues of interest to them. They are often consulted on proposed projects to give extra information to help partners, developers and destination management companies to deliver acceptable and sustainable products and services. They work to empower the local community whilst calling to account larger organisations who may exploit local people or the destination.

> **ACTIVITY 2**
>
> **Research an NGO**
>
> Research the work of the World Wildlife Fund for Nature. With a partner, choose one of their campaigns and present compelling evidence to gain support from the rest of the class.

155

Tourism Concern is a NGO charity registered in the UK

What do we do?

We expose tourism's worst human rights abuses and campaign against them.

Equally importantly, we promote tourism that benefits local people in tourist destinations.

We do this through our staff, our volunteers and our members.

Our Vision

Tourism which is ethical, fair and a positive experience for both travellers and the people and places they visit.

Our Mission

To ensure tourism always benefits local people by challenging bad practice and promoting better tourism.

Our Principles

- Independence: we are a non-industry based organisation and strongly believe that our independencev is vital to our role.
- Listening: we believe in listening to the opinions and perspectives of our partners in destination communities. Many campaigns have been sparked off by communities asking us for help.

- Shared values and vision: we believe in working with organisations that share our values and vision and we strive to work collaboratively towards common goals.
- Inclusivity: we believe that all people have the right to participate in all decision-making that affects them.
- Ethical practices: we believe in, and strive to adopt, low impact "green" policies and practices, purchasing and promoting fair trade products.

Our approach to tourism development

- Local communities must have the right to participate in the decision-making about tourism development where they live.

- Tourism industry operators and governments must be accountable to the people whose land and cultures are being utilised for the benefit of tourists and tourism businesses.
- Strategies must empower people to have a say in the development of their communities and country.
- Attention must be given to marginalised and vulnerable groups such as women, children, minorities, illegal workers and indigenous people working or affected by the tourism industry. http://tourismconcern.org.uk

---

ACTIVITY 3

Comments with regard to local authorities, regional organizations and DMCs

Research two contrasting destinations such as the English Lake District, UK and Dubai, UAE, and assess the role of public sector organisations in relation to economic strategies, marketing, and land use regulations. Are there any constraints for tourism development activities? What are the intended plans for the future?

- photography trips
- adventure – (soft and hard)
- eco tourism
- cultural tourism
- painting courses
- wilderness tours
- sports tours.

If there is a hobby or interest, you can almost be guaranteed that there will be an operator, agent or business that will accommodate your interest. All these elements make up an important aspect of destination management, as they are the providers and facilitators of the tourism industry, by bringing together products and services to the general public.

Commercial organisations

Commercial organisations are privately owned businesses and their main concern is with generating a profit to pay dividends to owner/shareholders. They will engage in all types of activity that will advertise and promote their brand, raise awareness amongst potential customers and lead to an increase in sales, which will boost revenues.

Commercial organisations include: tour operators, travel agents, accommodation providers, transport operators, attractions and guiding services. These organisations put together packages which they then market to the public and sell. Products and services vary according to the different companies. There are many different niche markets covered by commercial organisations such as:

KEY TERM

Inbound: tourists travelling into a destination. Outbound is where tourists travel outside their home country to an overseas destination.

KEY CONCEPTS

Change and development

The previous section reinforces the need for organisations to be resourceful in terms of providing the correct products and services to a variety of customers. Staying on trend and remaining dynamic is vital in a competitive environment.

Brunei developing its products: ecotourism and golf tourism

Brunei has a wealth of established cultural and natural attractions.

Figure 4.6 Kampong Ayer Museum is one of many historical and cultural attractions in Brunei

Figure 4.7 Food delicacies on market stall in Brunei's capital, Darussalam

At present Brunei has beautiful untouched forests where ecotourism can flourish. 2013 saw an increased number of **inbound** tourists who visited Brunei for ecotourism and golf tourism packages. Other niche markets are also being considered such as dive tourism and medical tourism. The national tourist board of Brunei see the adaptation of new tourism products and services as integral to its growth and development in the tourism sector.

Figure 4.8 'Dive' tourism in Brunei

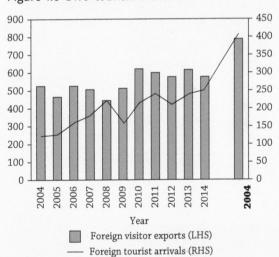

Figure 4.9 Graph showing visitor exports and international tourist arrivals Brunei 2013

The data from the World Travel and Tourism Council for 2013 shows that Brunei has a steady growth in overseas tourist arrivals. However, it must continue to develop its products and services along with strong marketing techniques in order to remain competitive and continue the upward trends.

157

Welcome to JacTravel

Established in 1975, JacTravel is one of the world's leading suppliers of hotel accommodation for the global travel industry and provider of specialist inbound travel services to the UK and Ireland. With headquarters in London, regional offices throughout the UK, Europe, Asia, the Middle-East and North America and worldwide representation, our team of over 500 travel professionals is well placed to serve over 20,000 clients globally. This is facilitated by a directly contracted inventory of more than 12,000 hotels and, an additional aggregated portfolio of over 100,000 properties and an extensive range of preferred group tour suppliers.

A business-to-business specialist, JacTravel operates a number of distinct but complementary divisions:

- Global wholesale accommodation solution available through a simple API connection
- Worldwide travel agent booking website through HYPERLINK "http://www.totalstay.com" Totalstay
- Specialist inbound group travel services to the UK, Ireland and key European destinations

JacTravel has received a number of awards, including the very prestigious Queen's Awards for Enterprise: International Trade 2016, UKinbound's Tour Operator of the Year in 2011, 2013 & 2015, identified in London Stock Exchange's '1000 Companies to Inspire Britain' and listings every year since 2012 in various Sunday Times surveys of high growth companies.

www.jactravel.co.uk

ACTIVITY 4

Research tour operators in your country. Find out:

- What products and services do they offer?
- How long have they have been in business?
- Who are their main competitors?

TUI Deutschland GmbH – Germany's leading tour operator

TUI Group is the world's number one tourism business. From now on, the broad portfolio gathered under the Group umbrella will consist of strong tour operators, 1800 travel agencies and leading online portals, six airlines more than 130 aircraft, over 300 hotels with 210 000 beds, 13 cruise liners and countless incoming agencies in all major holiday destinations around the globe. This integrated offering will enable us to provide our 30 million customers with an unmatched holiday experience in 180 regions. A key feature of our corporate culture is our global responsibility for economic, environmental and social sustainability. This is reflected in more than 20 years of commitment to sustainable tourism. In the 2013/14 financial year the TUI Group, with a headcount of 77 000, recorded turnover of €18.7 billion and an operating result of €869 million. The TUI Group's share is listed on the London Stock Exchange in the FTSE index and in the regulated market of the Frankfurt Stock Exchange.

www.tuigroup.com

Specialised tour operators can fulfil a growing need in the tourism industry by educating visitors with a variety of interesting destinations whilst allowing local communities to benefit from receiving tourists.

One of the most popular specialised markets is that of adventure tourism and today there are hundreds of commercial organisations offering activity-based holidays. In the African National Parks, there are many holidays and tours that include safaris. Whilst many tour operators are in the private sector, some specialist operators exist to entice visitors to not only enjoy the wildlife but to educate them in conservation too.

Figure 4.10 The endangered black rhino

The Earthwatch Institute is a voluntary sector organisation which offers opportunities to take a holiday in Nairobi in Kenya for up to 15 days with the specific role of helping to gather data on the distribution of wildlife and vegetation in the African Savannah. Their aim is to prevent black rhinos (Figure 4.10) from becoming extinct. Unfortunately there is now a massive trade in rhino horn and poaching is rife. The horns are particularly sought after in China, and the great demand secures high prices. At one time in 2011, rhino horn was more valuable than gold. Efforts to protect the animal (black rhino in Africa and the Javan rhino in Vietnam) are proving difficult. Some conservation economists believe that it is now time to have a legal trade in rhino horn because a total ban is seen to be ineffective. As the rhinos have decreased in number their horns become even more valuable. This means that there would be some trade allowed. Supporters of this view believe that it is important to make the rhino more valuable alive than it is dead. The message of conservation can be spread around the globe thanks to the work of voluntary sector organisations where research and education is as important as the holiday, ensuring that their conservation message stays prominent and in the public domain.

4.2 Objectives of tourism development and management

We saw in the previous chapter that the different types of travel and tourism organisations have an important role to play in the development of the tourism industry within any destination, regardless of the level of economic development: MEDC (More Economically Developed Country) or LEDC (Less Economically Developed Country). The aims and objectives of these sometimes very different organisations will vary.

It is commonly accepted that tourism development issues involve a triangular relationship between the following interest groups:

* the host population: the local people living in the destination
* the agents of tourism development: including national tourism organisations, destination management companies, NGOs that are present in the destination
* the tourists who come to visit the destination.

The aims and objectives of tourism development can vary amongst these groups. It is important to remember that each of the groups cannot be engaged in the same way and some people can be in more than one group; visitors can also be local residents; the industry is also part of the community.

However, broadly speaking, stakeholders in the tourism development process can be divided into **two** broad types:

* public sector, landowners, and industry: who must lead and set an example by taking co-ordinated action and facilitating the participation of the remaining stakeholders
* visitors, environmental interest groups and local residents: who should not necessarily be expected to initiate action of their own, but whose engagement and participation is essential for the success and sustainability of any development plan.

National governments play an important role in tourism development. This is because governments often seek to develop tourism in their countries for a variety of reasons. Government interest in the tourism industry can be explained by reference to the various policy aims shown in Table 4.1.

159

Policy aim	Related aspects of government interest
Economic	Tourism can boost employment creation, both direct and indirect. Tourism generates increased foreign currency earnings, which in turn contributes to GDP and overall balance of payments. Tourists who spend money locally will help contribute to the multiplier effect, as money will be recirculated into the economy and it will help to increase income for commercial operators thus boosting tax revenues. New tourism ventures boost economic development and regeneration and so help to develop the country's infrastructure and improve both the local area and conditions for local people.
Political	The fact that tourism can help to enhance the image of an area is particularly important to the government of LEDCs or of countries that may be perceived in a negative way due to war or natural disasters. Therefore tourism helps a destination to be seen as safe and secure. Governments can claim credit for helping to create a regional or national identity that boosts domestic morale and encourages increased visitor numbers.
Socio-cultural	Tourism can help to promote understanding between the cultures of visiting tourists and the local population. The development of tourism can improve the quality of life for the local population by providing facilities that can be used by both tourists and locals. Any revival of traditional activities, festivals and ceremonies help to celebrate local culture and this helps the local population to develop a sense of pride in their national and/or regional identity.
Environmental	Tourism can help with the regeneration and conservation of the built and natural environment. A concern for the environment can stimulate improvements for the benefit of local people as well as tourists.

Table 4.1 Government policy aims

KEY CONCEPTS

Customer focus

Triangular relationship is the relationship between the tourist, the local community and agents of tourism.

KEY TERMS

LEDC: Less Economically Developed Country
MEDC: More Economically Developed Country
GDP: gross domestic product

Economic objectives

We can now look at an example of the ways in which government development strategies can combine the above aims and objectives to produce 'National Tourism Policy Goals'.

The Caribbean is one of the most tourism-dependent regions in the world. The tourism sector in the Caribbean is a significant contributor to income, employment, foreign exchange and growth of the region. Trinidad and Tobago accounted for less than 2% of the 22.1 million international arrivals to the Caribbean in 2009. By contrast, the Dominican Republic accounted for almost one-fifth of international arrivals to the region with almost 4 million international visitors recorded in 2009. In 2009 the travel and tourism industry accounted for 14.7% of total employment in Trinidad and Tobago. This figure represented a total of 88 000 (**direct** and **indirect**) jobs in the sector. Direct industry employment was calculated to be 5.4% of total employment or 33 000 jobs. However, as shown in Figure 4.11, tourist arrivals were stagnating and showed clear signs of decline between 2007 and 2009.

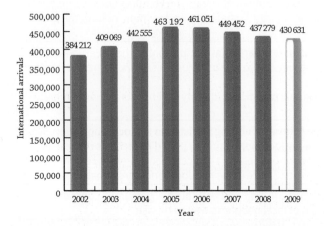

Figure 4.11 Tourist arrivals in Trinidad and Tobago

The feature provides an overview of the functions of Trinidad and Tobago's Ministry of Tourism. They have set in place strategic tourism guidelines to assist with research and monitoring of tourism. This includes evaluating the trends, encouraging partnership work and promoting the destination to create a strong industry presence.

The functions of the Ministry of Tourism include:

- conducting research on tourism-related issues
- formulating policies to guide the industry
- monitoring and evaluating tourism industry initiatives and development
- partnering with industry stakeholders
- developing and implementing tourism-related projects
- facilitating tourism investment and the general development of the industry
- building awareness of the tourism industry
- providing lifeguard services
- monitoring and guiding guiding the operations operations of the Tourism Development Company Limited (TDC)
- monitoring and guiding the operations of the Zoological Society of Trinidad and Tobago.

KEY TERMS

Direct tourism employment: working in the industry, such as a hotel, visitor attraction, cabin crew, where workers are dealing directly with tourists.

Indirect tourism employment: working for suppliers to the industry, for example catering supplies, manufacturing of aircraft.

Against this background Trinidad and Tobago launched its new National Tourism Policy in October 2010, and this has set clear targets for the medium term including:

- significantly increasing the contribution of tourism to GDP
- increasing visitor arrivals and tourist expenditure
- increasing both the quantity and the quality of jobs generated by the tourism industry
- increasing the multiplier effect of tourism throughout the economy and particularly the agriculture, culture and sports sectors

- monitoring the implementation of the National Tourism Policy, ensuring that development is consistent with the goals for responsible and sustainable tourism development in Trinidad and Tobago.

The new Tourism Policy has a series of economic goals that will help to make tourism a national priority and become the economic base that will sustain the social and economic transformation of Trinidad and Tobago. In this way, the country will be more likely to advance in accordance with the principles of the Rostow model as previously shown on Figure 1.17.

In order to achieve this, the Tourism Policy will help the country to:

- create employment and make a sustainable contribution to the well-being of all citizens
- significantly increase the potential of travel and tourism to generate both the quality and quantity of jobs needed in the industry
- aggressively promote the tourism industry as a generator of economic growth and foreign exchange
- significantly increase the number of visitor arrivals to the country
- develop mechanisms to encourage higher visitor expenditure and more activity-oriented visitors
- maximise the economic benefits of tourism by establishing linkages between tourism and other sectors of the economy, in particular agriculture, culture and sports
- encourage spin-off effects in the growth of the entertainment sector, marine industry, telecommunications, non-traditional manufacturing based on cultural traditions, clean energy research, festivals management and manufacturing industries that cater for the sector
- encourage and support local participation in the tourism industry
- develop and strengthen local communities to achieve a more diversified range of tourism products to promote economic development
- create opportunities for small and medium-sized businesses as well as emerging entrepreneurs and the informal sector
- make Trinidad and Tobago a more attractive cruise and yachting destination
- strengthen the linkages between the Trinidad and Tobago economy and the tourism sectors of other Caribbean countries
- encourage the further growth of the regional (Caribbean) tourism market.

Socio-cultural objectives

To go hand in hand with these is a series of **socio-cultural reasons** for the tourism industry. Tourism is planned to act as a vehicle for nation building and an improved quality of life for the citizens of Trinidad and Tobago through development of infrastructure, services, amenities, job creation, increased competitiveness and economic diversification.

The Tourism Policy in Trinidad and Tobago will help the country:

- to promote a domestic tourism programme that will have the social development of citizens as its primary objective
- to address issues of drug trafficking, crime and harassment of individuals and the incidence of HIV/AIDS that are critical to both the health of citizens and tourists alike
- to develop tourism with dignity by encouraging mutual respect for all cultures and eliminating all forms of discrimination on the basis of language, religion, culture, race, sex, age, wealth, ability, or other
- to promote pride in all of the cultural forms of the country
- to support the revival of dying traditions, art and culture and to expose and record endangered historical facts, particularly in music and art, for example in Figure 4.12, below.
- to utilise the cultural, historical and recreational assets of Trinidad and Tobago as anchors for the development of a highly differentiated and competitive tourism product
- to promote peace nationally, as well as regionally and internationally, and greater respect for human life
- to provide appropriate education, training and awareness programmes for tourism, as well as capacity-building for disadvantaged groups
- to promote human resource development, focusing on gender equality and career development, as well as the implementation of national labour standards
- to encourage the active participation of local communities at all levels of the tourism sector and in the development, management and implementation of tourism projects
- to encourage participation by all citizens of Trinidad and Tobago in the development of plans and policies for the tourism sector.

Figure 4.12 Children taking part in a traditional dance celebrating in Trinidad and Tobago

KEY CONCEPTS

Global and growing

The previous section introduces the issues of tourism development as a global force and one which may bring both positive and negative aspects. Governments are working consistently on management strategies and implementation of projects that will make them unique and bring economic benefits.

Environmental objectives

We saw earlier that sustainable tourism development was about attempting to make a low impact on the environment and local culture, while helping to generate future employment for local people. The Trinidad and Tobago Tourism Policy thus seeks to develop tourism in a sustainable and responsible manner and intends to develop the management and monitoring tools required to ensure the sustainable development of the sector.

Political objectives

The Tourism Policy shows the ways in which the government of Trinidad and Tobago is attempting to drive change within the country. In terms of political goals, the policy offers a framework for the sustainable development of the country. The government sees the policy as an opportunity to achieve its mission to promote a process of 'people-centred development'.

The government has recognised that building a viable tourism sector requires strong public/private sector partnerships and the support of the national community. Furthermore, the government clearly appreciates the potential of the tourism sector to create employment, alleviate poverty, earn foreign exchange, enhance the

The Trinidad and Tobago Tourism Policy has key environmental goals including:

- to continuously monitor the impacts on sensitive areas
- to require and ensure that environmental impact assessments are conducted for all tourism-related projects
- to evaluate and consider the impacts of proposed tourism projects on other sectors of the economy
- to work with the Environmental Management Authority (EMA) and other agencies to develop a co-ordinated, country-wide environmental strategy
- to consult with all land-use agencies to ensure the optimal allocation of land for tourism development
- to ensure that the tourism sector's physical structures are in accordance with the building codes and regulations of the country

- to work towards developing carrying capacity regulations that will ensure the protection of ecologically sensitive areas
- to encourage and promote the use of sustainable practices and strategies throughout the sector, including delivery of service, the design, construction and operation of visitor accommodation, sites and attractions and other tourism projects
- to encourage adherence to global environmental standards and related certification
- to develop initiatives fostering a more environmentally-conscious population
- to aspire towards the achievement of reducing carbon footprint for the local industry
- to encourage a more responsible tourism in all its various forms.

destination reputation and image and stimulate the creation of inter-industry linkages, particularly with the agriculture, construction, manufacturing, sports and other service industries.

For these reasons the government of Trinidad and Tobago is committed to the development of a responsible, sustainable and competitive tourism industry because it is viewed as a means for the social and economic transformation of the country and its people.

ACTIVITY 5

Research your country's most recent tourism development plans.
- What are the main aims and objectives?
- What new developments are planned?
- What evidence is there of co-operation between the government, NGOs and commercial organisations?

4.3 Destination management activities

Destination management activities can include the management and organisation of events, festivals, trips and tours. Activities are linked to marketing functions such as producing print and on-line information that is accessible for both the local community and the visitor. Many activities are done in partnership, for example, as a public/private enterprise with many stakeholders involved. At the heart of successful destination management activities is the principle of sustainability. The need for long-term, appropriate activities is vital in order to ensure sustained growth and development.

Sustainable tourism policies and practices

Principles of sustainability

The definition of sustainable tourism, according to the World Tourism Organisation, 2004 is:

Sustainable tourism development requires the informed participation of all relevant stakeholders, as well as strong political leadership to ensure wide participation and consensus building. Achieving sustainable tourism is a continuous process and it requires constant monitoring of impacts, introducing the necessary preventive and/or corrective measures whenever necessary.

Sustainable tourism should also maintain a high level of tourist satisfaction and ensure a meaningful experience to the tourists, raising their awareness about sustainability issues and promoting sustainable tourism practices amongst them.

 KEY TERM

Stakeholder: anyone who has an interest in an organisation or project.

'Sustainability' is very much a 'buzz' word at the present. Taking the earlier World Tourism Organisation definition, sustainable tourism therefore encompasses holidays that are good for local communities, the environment, holidaymakers and tourism businesses. With climate change and the depletion of the Earth's resources often in the forefront of our minds, sustainability has become an important and accepted practice that many industries believe in. Tourism is by no means an exception. Tourism development whether in the public, private or voluntary sectors is heavily influenced by sustainable practices.

This can be seen through the regeneration of derelict areas, new hotels and visitor attractions and staging of events, where planners try to minimise the negative impacts that large groups of people make on the landscape. New or rejuvenated places are often subject to strict building and planning regulations. This will prevent poor use of materials, safeguard a destination's image and enhance the built environment. Governments are able to influence development policies and issue guidelines to potential tourist developers.

At the heart of sustainable practice is the need to help businesses meet consumer demands whilst protecting the resource on which their future depends. In terms of adventure tourism, this is often a vital ingredient to the success of an activity where earth, water and air are all integral to the experience. Good sustainable practice should boost local economies and employment opportunities whilst improving quality for the holidaymaker.

Local community involvement is therefore integral to sustainability. Without the local community the major support networks may be lost and difficulties will arise due to poor communication and lack of understanding. This may be exacerbated where community and public facilities are involved. Facilities and infrastructure are important to the success and stability of a community and often can be improved with funds generated from tourist activities.

KEY CONCEPTS

Customer focus

The earlier section highlights the importance of both the community and the customer within destination management. Techniques must be developed to ensure that customer needs are integral to any development process. These should now be sustainable and realistic. Consumer demands change constantly and having up to date practices are essential for longevity.

It has long been known that tourism, although no panacea, certainly has the means to create new business opportunities and relieve poverty and assist with wealth distribution. Development of tourism can offer real possibilities for local people where diversification of the economy can benefit the community at all levels, such as enhancing the standard of living of local people whilst giving hope and renewed economic and social confidence for the future.

Carrying capacity

Earth provides enough to satisfy every man's need but not every man's greed.

Mahatma Gandhi

The definition of 'carrying capacity' is often referred to as 'The number of individuals who can be supported in a given area within natural resource limits, and without degrading the natural social, cultural and economic environment for present and future generations.'

The Travel Foundation

Founded in 2003, the Travel Foundation was set up to respond to concerns over the sustainability of travel and tourism. It is an independent UK charity which helps the travel industry understand, manage and take effective action on sustainable tourism.

It protects and enhances the environment and improves the well-being of destination communities, as well as the holiday experience for visitors. Originally set up in collaboration with UK government and leading travel companies, it is:

- a central point of contact for, and leading authority on, developing and promoting sustainable tourism in mainstream destinations worldwide

- an essential resource of tools, guidelines and training to help companies take effective action integrating sustainability into every aspect of their business
- a unique and expert resource helping to set priorities and establish best practice
- since conception, it has had a full programme of activities, with projects in sixteen overseas destinations, as well as support to help the travel industry and destination authorities take effective action on all things green.

Our approach

The Travel Foundation is great news for both visitors and the places we love to visit. We partner with UK travel companies to make tourism a force for good that minimises negative eects upon the environment, and uses income from tourism to protect and preserve both precious natural resources and local traditions and culture.

We encourage the tourism industry to buy goods and services from local producers and suppliers, decreasing transport emissions, boosting local economies and beneting communities with new opportunities and employment.

Businesses are better able to meet the needs of their customers, at the same time as protecting the resources on which their future depends.

Quality is improved for the holiday maker and a more enriching experience is delivered, hand in hand with the reassurance that today's favourite destinations will exist for future generations. Our work means local and national governments have evidence to develop eective tourism policies and support destination communities and environments.

Figure 4.13 The Travel Foundation; an NGO in the UK

Sustainable tourism helps to identify the maximum carrying capacity of a destination. If this capacity is exceeded then there is likely to be a change in the physical environment. This could lead to a decline in the quality of the consumer's experience. Tourists can be fickle and keeping them happy is a very important consideration, but not to the detriment of the landscape and the community. There is undoubtedly a limited number of restaurants, bars, hotels and so on that a destination requires. Should adventure tourism become so popular that an area tries to develop more and more facilities to cater for a greater number of visitors, this will naturally have an impact on the physical, visual and perceptual capacities. At what stage does an area reach saturation point? The physical capacity will suffer in the form of damage to the flora and fauna. Overcrowding and congestion would not enhance an adventurous activity – indeed, it would spoil the experience completely as it would have the opposite effect of reducing the remoteness and uniqueness of the activity.

4.4 Encouraging responsible tourist behaviour through education

Good behaviour travelling to, and whilst in, a destination is vital in order to protect and maintain our environment. Tourists who are educated and informed regarding cultural practices and good behaviour can bring positive messages to the areas they are visiting. Tour operators have the potential to ensure that good education exists through their advertising in brochures and via the internet. With the growth in new technologies information is easily sent around the world in the blink of an eye. Internet searches can bring new information to a tourist's phone, iPod, tablet or computer in seconds. Apps for devices can give up to date information on weather, crime, safety, security scares and other topics before a visit is made. In today's world there is no excuse not to be fully informed about best and most appropriate practices in given areas. Books and lectures at universities and schools also bring the opportunity to inform members of the public. Adventure tourism associations are often the best form of advice for good practice and often will respond to email queries and questions.

ACTIVITY 6

Draw up a ten-point code for good tourist conduct to your country. Consider issues of clothing, behaviour, drinking and eating customs.

Development of new products and services including specialised products

Today innovations in the travel industry have enabled us to move around the globe with incredible ease. The Airbus A380 and the Boeing Dreamliner have increased the capacity of airlines of up to 550 passengers per trip. There is virtually no place on earth left undiscovered. Tourists still seek to find new places and experience and organisations must develop new products and services in order to stay competitive and meet changing demands. Travellers move around the globe not just for leisure or business purposes. Today, medical and health tourism are important growing markets. However, there are many new specialised products emerging such as unusual tours like vampire tours in Romania, Dark tourism (visits relating to death and the macabre) and slum tourism – where voyeurism on the poor is seen as an acceptable pursuit.

165

CASE STUDY 3

Virgin Galactic's new space ship VSS Unity

It seems that there is only one place left to go and that is outer space! This idea might not be as fanciful as it first seems.

The Federal Aviation Administration (FAA) has already given its blessing to some commercial flights and the following article details Virgin Galactic's preparations. To date, there are over 500 astronauts wishing to join the trip at a cost of US$250 000 each. If you should wish to charter the space ship just for you and your friends, it would cost over US$1 million for you and five friends!

FAA Launch Permit Gives Virgin Galactic's Space Vehicles the Green Light for Powered Flight. SpaceShipTwo Set to Go for Heavy-Weight Glide Tests with Supersonic Flight Targeted for Year End Virgin Galactic, the world's first commercial spaceline, announced today that its vehicle developer, Scaled Composites (Scaled), has been granted an experimental launch permit from the Federal Aviation Administration (FAA) for its suborbital spacecraft, SpaceshipTwo, and the carrier aircraft, WhiteKnightTwo, shown in figure 4.14.

"This important milestone enables our team to progress to the rocket-powered phase of test flight, bringing us a major step closer to bringing our customers to space," said George Whitesides, president and CEO of Virgin Galactic. "We thank the FAA for their timely issuance of this permit, and for their responsible oversight of the test program."

Already, SpaceShipTwo and WhiteKnightTwo have made significant progress in their flight test program. With 80 test flights completed, WhiteKnightTwo is substantially through its test plan, while the more recently constructed SpaceShipTwo has safely completed 16 free flights, including three that tested the vehicle's unique 'feathering' re-entry system. Additionally, ten test firings of the full-scale SpaceShipTwo rocket motor, including full duration burns, have been safely and successfully completed.

Figure 4.14 Virgin Galactic WhiteKnightTwo

Frixion Adventures focuses on adrenaline and action-based activities in and around Cape Town. Running a number of canyoning, abseiling, river rafting and coasteering trips for both the local and the tourist, we offer adventure days, team building events and outcomes based programmes with something to suite everyone. Many of our trips can be tailored to accommodate and thrill all, from the extreme adventure enthusiast to the not so brave at heart.

Perhaps travel to outside of our world is not so unrealistic. However organisations must think 'outside of the box' in order to stay fresh and appealing. The importance of establishing new products or services alongside innovative branding is essential in a very competitive market. This helps to build trust and customer loyalty. Good brands create an emotional link with the customer, reinforcing a company's credibility and at the same time motivating the customer to stay with that brand and finally purchase the product.

Two more ANA planes will be decorated with Star Wars characters as part of an agreement with The Walt Disney Company.

Figure 4.15 Star Wars themed plane

BB-8, a brand new character from Star Wars: The Force Awakens, which was scheduled for theatrical release in December 2015, will be displayed on the livery of the BB-8 ANA Jet, a Boeing 777-300ER.

KEY CONCEPTS

Change and development

The earlier section highlights the importance of dynamic tourism activities in order to effect a successful commercial organisation appealing to both mass and specialised markets.

Heritage and cultural visits are still one of the most popular forms of tourism. Revamping or refurbishing of historic sites or retelling of stories in a modern way all help to develop products within the industry.

Visitor and traffic management and widening access to facilities

There are many types of visitor- and traffic-management systems used in the tourism industry. They are integral to good management practices and successful business development. Methods are often dependent upon the nature of the business, for example, whether it is in natural surroundings or in an urban environment. Issues of overcrowding and traffic congestion are common in popular tourist sites and may result in deterring future customers. Some of the most successful methods of visitor and traffic management used by policy makers include one or more of the following:

- creating park and ride schemes
- seasonal or temporal limitation of visitor numbers
- zoning of an area
- pedestrianisation of areas
- using interpretation boards and signage, maps, brochures and leaflets
- restricting the use by different groups – ages/genders/ height size
- steering visitor flows by using natural features, pathways, trails, roads and the like
- use of technology for issuing of e-tickets, fast passes and so on
- use of pricing mechanisms to encourage and discourage customer usage at different times, for instance seasonally or daily.

Restricting visitors to a certain time or place allows for a tourist destination to incorporate some planned maintenance or corrective maintenance on fragile ecosystems by addressing any potential health and safety issues that may arise, for example, a footpath that had become worn and dangerous and therefore required re-routing.

Visitor and traffic management must take into account all types of customers and this includes accessibility for those with specific needs. Access must be considered for not only those with specific physical needs, such as wheelchair users, but also those with illnesses, limited vision, impaired hearing or special educational needs. In the UK, the Disability Discrimination Act was brought into force in 2005. This requires all public facilities to make reasonable changes to their premises in order that any disabled person has safe access and is treated fairly.

A lack of investment can also be a barrier for customers where poor development creates inaccessible areas. Sensible planning is essential in such cases, however some destination developments have been too rapid and do not always allow for clear or strategic accessibility.

In order to provide for all types of customers, managers must consider pricing mechanisms, such as discounts for the young, students and the old. In this way, everyone is able to enjoy the benefits of all aspects of tourism.

KEY TERM

Fragile ecosystem (environment): easily destroyed or under threat.

167

Opportunities Attract & Disperse

Figure 4.16 Agatha Christie tourism in the English Riviera

"Non visitor research highlighted that the current English Riviera tourism product is perceived by many as lacking wow factor and is not considered compelling or modern enough to buy into…Product development needs to focus on developing opportunities that will attract year round, higher spending visitors to the Bay with a positive impact on the economy through increased employment, footfall and visitor spend".

Turning the tide for tourism in Torbay 2010 – 2015

Five **attack brands** were identified through the development of the Tourism Strategy as offering tourism businesses across the resort an exciting opportunity to attract more visitors all year round. The attack brands are:

- Agatha Christie
- Global Geopark
- Maritime Leisure
- Events and Festivals
- Business Tourism

4.5 Destination branding and marketing: mass and specialised markets

The following case study shows how important it is to have a strong brand. It enables potential visitors to have some knowledge of your destination and can act as a strong pull factor.

KEY TERM

Attack brand: a move to push a brand into the public domain.

ACTIVITY 7

Using your country or a destination with which you are familiar, decide what attack brands might work.

4.6 Partnerships of commercial and non-commercial organisations

Investment in long-term benefits for local community and tourism economy

A positive aspect of tourism that can have a long-lasting benefit to the local community is to invest the funds gained from tourists into projects that will benefit the community. Funds may be put towards improving infrastructure, building new community based facilities such as a youth club, recreational park or community centre. Destinations should manage their tourist activities alongside community representatives to ensure that benefits can be utilized to the best requirements of the local people. It may be that a doctor's surgery is more important to the community than a new football ground.

Planning control

Good controls on planning for tourism are essential in order to prevent inappropriate or dangerous buildings or resorts from being developed. The rapid growth of the Costas in Spain are well documented, where small fishing villages were soon dwarfed by large hotels and resulted in a change in the scenic value of the area along with a loss in community facilities.

Destinations that have shown rapid and clear strategic growth include the Middle East (Dubai) and Asia (Shanghai). A case study of the evolution and growth of Dubai is covered at the end of in this chapter.

Well planned infrastructure and benefits for the community are essential for any sustainable long-term plan. Many large sporting events such as the Olympic Games, Commonwealth Games and African Cup of Nations, may have to build new facilities for the duration of the games and often, as part of the requirement of funding received, will intend to leave a legacy of facilities behind for the local community. This is not always successful and in some instances large debts are left behind.

Elephant Welfare Project in Eastern Mahout Communities

Based in Thailand's Eastern province of Surin, this project works with the communities that have lived and worked with elephants for hundreds of years. Since the country's ban on logging and prevalence of machinery, work for elephants is limited. With few other opportunities, the people of these communities and their elephants often starve. The government has developed initiatives that aim to encourage communities to use elephants to help attract tourists to the area. This project works alongside these communities to encourage tourism development to be shaped by ethical and responsible eco-tourism approaches.

Currently under-represented by Western tourists, the region's tourism development focuses on entertainment shows, which see the elephants learn tricks and stay tied up for a lot of the day. Through volunteer participation on this project, we work with a selected group of committed Mahouts, their families and their elephants to develop eco-tourism approaches that provide the elephants a better standard of life.

Project location

The camp is situated approximately 50 km from the small city of Surin, which receives very few tourists. The area around the project is inhabited entirely by Mahouts and their families. You will have your own room onsite with an elephant (or two) living in the garden outside your door! Houses have electricity with fans and an outhouse with running water. Beds with mosquito nets are provided and volunteers eat together at the village's community centre.

Figure 4.17 Mahouts giving children a ride

This rural area has forested areas in which to go walking. Onsite, the elephant museum has a number of stalls selling snacks and gifts. At weekends, volunteers can take a public bus into the small city of Surin for a glimpse of authentic Thai rural life.

Rio 2016: Embracing sustainability

With a modern sustainability plan, Rio 2016 aims to be a catalyst for positive change, benefitting Brazil and its population.

In conjunction with various stakeholders, the organising committee is working so that the changes and improvements instigated for the Games become a lasting legacy for the city of Rio and across Brazil.

Any discussion on holding the Olympic and Paralympic Games in Rio de Janeiro involves huge numbers, considering that the planet's biggest sporting event will be staged over 45 days. Imagine the impact of this on the consumption of natural resources, like water and energy, on the consumption of food and raw materials, and on waste production.

Now imagine the challenge of transforming this impact into an opportunity to adopt and disseminate sustainable practices. Got the picture? The Rio 2016 Organising Committee has not only taken on this challenge, but is fully embracing the cause. Hence the Rio 2016 sustainability brand – Embrace.

Sustainability challenges for the Rio 2016 games, include:

- 17 000 tonnes of waste
- Consuming 23.5 million litres of fuel
- Consuming 29.5 GW of energy
- Consuming 6000 tonnes of food
- Estimated emissions of 3.6 million tonnes of CO2eq (carbon dioxide equivalents)
- Using 1500 buses to transport athletes, technical commissions and referees

4.7 Regular environmental impact auditing

Environmental Impact Assessment (EIA) is a useful tool that allows policy makers and managers to assess and predict the environmental impacts of any proposed development. An EIA may reveal positive or negative impacts. It is designed to assist decision makers on whether or not to embark on a project such as building a new resort, swimming pool or shopping centre. The EIA may propose adjustments to any plan in order that the project can go ahead. Properly applied, an EIA can reduce the loss of natural resources and environmental degradation or social disruption which may accompany tourism development. The EIA may be subject to public consultation in order to allay fears by local residents. Most EIAs are strongly linked to the carrying capacity of an area.

Monitoring and evaluation of how a destination is being managed.

Following assessment of an area the planned development can go ahead. However, once in place, it is essential that monitoring and evaluation of the destination takes place. Tourism is a dynamic industry and, as such, destinations and their management cannot stagnate. Keeping up to date with technology and being able to assess the needs and wants of customers is essential in order to remain viable. New solutions to problems must be considered and detailed discussions along with networking with relevant partners must be applied. Consideration should also be undertaken for possible new developments or refurbishing/regeneration of current projects. Monitoring systems may include the following issues:

- visitor numbers/return visits
- budget controls, assessment of income and expenditure
- ability to adhere to health, safety and security
- number of complaints and how issues are resolved
- staff turnover/staff motivation
- consultation with partners during regular meetings with interested parties
- introduction of new marketing techniques and the monitoring of the current ones by tracking of success
- public relations, checking on number of free editorials and stories in the media
- application of new methods, taking into consideration new technological advancements such as booking systems, web design and customer comments via social media.
- continual development of facilities for both staff and customers
- amount of training undertaken by staff
- regular maintenance undertaken, with full details of repair, damage and refurbishment.

Communication and liaison with visitors and providers

As we have seen, travel and tourism is a large service industry and, as such, communication methods for customers and providers continue to be essential to the success of

destination management activities. Communication takes place before, during and after any visit.

The most common forms of communication are:

- travel guide books
- hiking and road maps
- promotional leaflets and brochures (Figure 4.18)
- pre-departure literature from tour operators
- advertising boards
- airlines' seat pockets
- car-hire desks
- visitor centres
- literature available at entrances to protected areas
- interpretation boards
- hotel rooms and campsites
- sales desks
- retailers selling, for example, scuba, hiking, bicycling
- souvenir stands
- restaurants and cafes.

Figure 4.18 Information point in a city centre

Encouraging responsible tourist behavior

Increasingly, destinations and tourism operations are endorsing and following 'responsible tourism' as a pathway towards sustainable tourism. Responsible tourism and sustainable tourism have an identical goal, that of sustainable development.

Responsible tourism can be regarded as behaviour. It is more than a form of tourism as it represents an approach to engaging with tourism, be that as a tourist, a business, locals at a destination or any other tourism stakeholder. It emphasises that all stakeholders are responsible for the kind of tourism they develop or engage in. Whilst different groups will see responsibility in different ways, the shared understanding is that responsible tourism should entail an improvement in tourism. Tourism should become 'better' as a result of the responsible tourism approach. Within the notion of betterment resides the acknowledgement that conflicting interests need to be balanced. However, the objective is to create better places for people to live in and to visit.

Importantly, there is no blueprint for responsible tourism; what is deemed responsible may differ depending on places and cultures. Responsible tourism is an aspiration that can be realised in different ways in different originating markets and in the diverse destinations of the world.

Focusing in particular on businesses according to the Cape Town Declaration on Responsible Tourism, it will have the following characteristics:

- minimises negative economic, environmental and social impacts

- generates greater economic benefits for local people and enhances the well-being of host communities
- improves working conditions and access to the industry
- involves local people in decisions that affect their lives and life chances
- makes positive contributions to the conservation of natural and cultural heritage, to the maintenance of the world's diversity
- provides more enjoyable experiences for tourists through more meaningful connections with local people and a greater understanding of local cultural, social and environmental issues
- provides access for people with disabilities
- promotes cultural sensitivity, engendering respect between tourists and hosts and building local pride and confidence.

If such an approach was followed in all tourism destinations there would be far less danger of there being a rapid, unplanned development of tourism that can spoil what tourists originally travelled to see.

4.8 Community involvement, community projects, education training and employment of locals

Tourism brings a wealth of opportunities for staff training and development. From management to customer service skills, there are a large variety of areas where new skills can benefit both holidaymakers and employees. Adventure tourism most certainly will require the ability to deal face to face with customers. Good training benefits the organisation itself. This can increase revenue and enhance the public image of an organisation. Reputation is very important in the adventure tourism field and if staff can create good customer satisfaction and confidence then revenues will surely increase. Good training is essential for health and safety aspects of the industry. An accident may cause dreadful consequences not just for the parties involved but also through the media coverage and consequently by poor reputation. With traditional industries in decline, many LEDCs in particular look to tourism for the answer to create new job opportunities. Many governments have introduced sponsored training schemes to assist with improving good customer service and at the same time increase staff happiness and motivation.

ACTIVITY 8

Figure 4.19 The Mac Mac Falls

The Mac Mac Falls are classed as a South African national monument and are part of a cluster of scenic waterfalls in Mpumalanga's Sabie area. Visitors come to see the twin falls plunge dramatically 70 m into the gorge below. The Mac Mac falls are 13 km from the town of Sabie on the R532, and visitors can drive to the site as it is clearly signposted from the main road. Access to the falls from the car park is by a pathway down to a viewing deck.

How would you suggest that a small natural visitor attraction, such as the Mac Mac Falls be developed in a responsible and sustainable way?

4.9 Impacts of tourism development

Many people think of tourism in terms of its economic impacts, such as the number of jobs created, contribution to GDP and the generation of taxes. However, the range of impacts from tourism is broad.

Here, the impacts of tourism have been sorted into three general categories:

- economic impacts
- socio-cultural impacts
- environmental impacts.

Furthermore, each category includes both positive and negative impacts. Not all impacts are applicable to every destination because conditions and/or available resources differ. Local community and tourism managers must balance an array of impacts that may either improve or negatively affect destinations and their resident populations. Figure 4.20 shows how different relationships are at work within any given destination.

The idea behind the VICE (Visitor, Industry, Community and Environment) model of destination management is the need to achieve a balance between:

- a prosperous tourism industry which sustains jobs and the local economy
- the environmental and social pressures from increased numbers of visitors which could undermine the quality of life and the resources on which the industry itself depends.

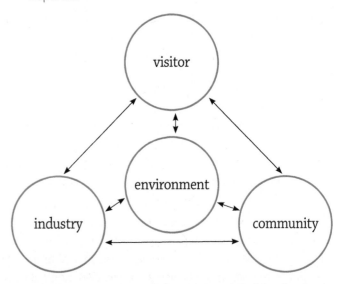

Figure 4.20 Components of the VICE model of destination management

Different groups are often concerned about different tourism impacts. In theory, the interests of each group could be completely separate. For example, the local tourism industry includes members of the business community and people who are in need of the jobs offered by tourism (see Figure 4.21). The local community includes residents who might feel displaced by an influx of visitors. Some visitors might be outdoor enthusiasts concerned about changes to the natural environment. In such a scenario, each group is likely to have a completely different outlook on the development of tourism within the destination. When group interests are divergent, the differing perspectives can make a consensus on tourism development difficult to achieve.

Economic impacts

Tourism makes a significant contribution to the economy of particular countries and facts and figures about a particularly country can be found from the World Travel and Tourism Council's website. So, for example, if you lived in South Africa you could find a variety of details contained in the report found at https://www.wttc.org

The report highlights the following:

- The direct contribution of travel and tourism to GDP in 2011 was ZAR79.5 billion (2.7% of GDP). This forecast is to rise by 5.7% to ZAR84.1 billion in 2012. This primarily reflects the economic activity generated by industries such as hotels, travel agents, airlines and other passenger transport services. It also includes, for example, the activities of the restaurant and leisure industries directly supported by tourists. The direct contribution of travel and tourism to GDP is expected to grow by 4.3% per annum to ZAR128.2 billion (2.8% of GDP) by 2022.
- The total contribution of travel and tourism to South African employment was 1 188 000 jobs in 2011 (9.0% of total employment). This is forecast to increase by 3.2% in 2012 to 1 226 000 jobs (9.2% of total employment). By 2022, travel and tourism is forecast to support 1 498 000 jobs (9.4% of total employment), an increase of 2% per annum over the period.

In recent years, tourism has been increasingly recognised for its economic potential to contribute to the reduction of poverty in Less Economically Developed Countries (LEDCs). The travel and tourism industry's geographical expansion and labour-intensive nature has supported the spread of employment and this can be particularly relevant to remote and rural areas, where 75% of the world's 2 billion people live under conditions of extreme poverty. Statistics show that tourism in LEDCs is still limited: in the first decade of the 21st century it amounted to 1.2% of the world market share in terms of international tourist arrivals and 0.8% in terms of international tourism receipts. However, the share is rising as the group of LEDCs are growing at a markedly faster pace. Between 2001 and 2010, international tourist arrivals in LEDCs increased by some 48%. This was in contrast to a growth rate of 17% worldwide.

In terms of economic development within a country, the opening of a new tourism-related activity has the potential to generate many benefits for the local economy in a particular destination. The multiplier effect is shown in Figure 4.22 and this illustrates the ways in which any new economic activity can lead to prosperity and increasing economic development within a destination which has some form of initial advantage. Once the new activity is established it will tend to draw in additional investment and labour from surrounding areas leading to further economic growth and expansion of the economy.

Once the new development becomes established it can lead to the concentration of related activities within the area. This can be thought of as a 'snowballing' process whereby more and more tourism-related activities cluster in a relatively small area.

Figure 4.21 Construction on Dubai skyscrapers due to tourism

Positive economic impacts of tourism

MEDC and LEDC countries welcome the various economic impacts that tourism developments are able to generate at the local, regional and national scales. The Gross Domestic Product (GDP) is readily increased by the multiplier effect, as illustrated in Figure 4.22, because tourism spending generates income to the host economy

173

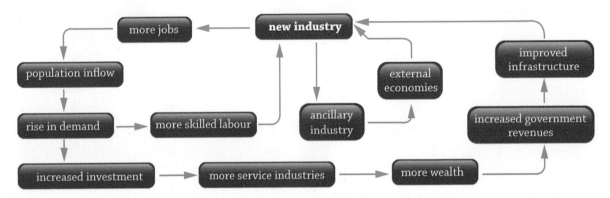

Figure 4.22 Myrdal's Model of Cumulative Economic Growth

and can stimulate the investment necessary to finance growth in other economic sectors. Some countries seek to accelerate this growth by requiring visitors to bring in a certain amount of foreign currency for each day of their stay. An important indicator of the role of international tourism is its generation of foreign exchange earnings. Tourism is one of the top five export categories for as many as 83% of countries and is a main source of foreign exchange earnings for at least 38% of countries.

The WTO estimates that travel and tourism's direct, indirect, and personal tax contribution worldwide in 2010 was over US$800 billion. The rapid expansion of international tourism has led to significant employment creation. Tourism can generate jobs **directly** through hotels, restaurants, nightclubs, taxis and souvenir sales, and **indirectly** through the supply of goods and services needed by tourism-related businesses. Tourism supports over 10% of the world's workers. One in every eleven people on the planet is employed in the tourism industry. Money is earned from tourism through **informal employment** (see figure 4.23) such as, street vendors, informal guides, rickshaw drivers). The positive side of employment is that the money is returned to the local economy, and has a great multiplier effect as it is spent over and over again. Furthermore, tourism revenues can then be used to fund new infrastructure and facilities which local people can also use.

Negative economic impacts of tourism

Tourism can have a number of unfavourable economic effects on the host destination and it is often richer countries that are better able to profit from tourism than the poorer ones. LEDCs usually view tourism development as a source of income and as a generator of employment to help raise standards of living. However, they are frequently unable to fully realise such benefits. Unfortunately, many job roles are still low skilled and low

paid and due to the seasonal nature of the industry will not supply economic benefits all year round. Tourism jobs are often seen as a panacea to economic struggles, however tourism development can replace the more traditional employment roles, leaving an area depleted of its original skills base. An important economic issue is the large-scale transfer of tourism revenues out of the host country and the exclusion of local businesses and products from many parts of the tourism marketplace.

The direct income for any tourist destination is the amount of tourist expenditure that remains locally after taxes, profits and wages are paid outside the area and after imports are purchased. Money lost from the destination is called **leakage**. On average, most all-inclusive package tours will only yield about 20% of travellers' expenditures going to local business within the destination. Approximately 80% will go to the airlines, hotels and other international companies. To give a further illustration of this point, it is estimated that only 30% of all money spent by tourists remains in Thailand and in certain parts of the Caribbean only 20% remains in the destination.

Leakages from the destination's economy can take place in a variety of ways. Import leakage occurs when tourists demand standards of equipment, food and other products that are not readily available in the host country. This is common in LEDCs, as food and drinks must often be imported because local products may not be up to the standard required by foreign guests staying at local hotels or the country simply does not have a supplying industry. Therefore, in such circumstances, much of the income from tourism leaves the country to pay for these imports. Export leakage takes place when foreign multi-national companies operate in LEDCs. An export leakage arises when overseas resorts and hotels take their profits back to their country of origin.

Figure 4.23 Street vendors; an example of informal employment generated through tourism.

 KEY TERM

Leakage: money lost from a destination through, for example, foreign labour, foreign ownerships and imports.

There are other negative economic impacts in destinations with many all-inclusive resorts and a large number of cruise ship arrivals. Both of these types of tourism can exert a clear restraining influence on local economies because local businesses cannot earn income from tourists when they remain for their entire stay at the same resort or follow a programme organised by the cruise line. Furthermore, major all-inclusive resorts also tend to import more and employ fewer local people and so a much smaller multiplier effect is felt within the local economy.

Tourism development can also cost the local government and local taxpayers a great deal of money. In order to secure a new tourism development the government may have to improve the airport, roads and other infrastructure. It may possibly even have to offer incentives to developers such as tax breaks and other financial advantages. Spending public resources on subsidised infrastructure or tax incentives will reduce government investment in other areas such as education and health.

The local population can suffer in other ways as increasing demand for basic services and goods from tourists will often cause price rises and lead to inflation. This has a significant negative effect on local residents whose incomes do not increase proportionately. In the same way, tourism development can increase the price of buildings and land as investors seek to capitalise on recent growth. This makes it more difficult for local people to live in tourist areas and can result in the displacement of the local population because they cannot afford the increasing costs of living.

The positive spread effects from tourism may be limited if the industry is spatially concentrated in just one or two highly favoured areas. This can result in there being increased regional inequalities in the country between the tourism areas and the less economically developed parts of the country that are well away from the tourist trail. The more remote areas turn into downward transition zones where labour and resources will be in short supply as development is concentrated in the tourism areas. These declining areas thus suffer from out-migration and lack of investment.

Many LEDCs have embraced tourism as a way to boost their economies, particularly if they have limited raw materials on which to base their economic development. However, there are dangers associated with an over-reliance on tourism. Countries which have a tourism-dependent economy are greatly at risk from an economic recession, the impacts of a natural disaster or from changing patterns of tourism demand. Any circumstance that causes the number of visiting tourists to decline will have a devastating effect on the destination. If the destination has a narrow economic base it stands the risk of going into serious economic decline.

Tourism and economic development

There is no doubt that many countries are keen to develop tourism because they are of the opinion that the potential benefits clearly outweigh the possible disadvantages.

To help illustrate this point we can look at the case study on the island of St Helena in the southern Atlantic Ocean.

KEY TERM

Multiplier effect: recirculation of money, for example, money spent by tourists will be re-spent in the area.

St Helena in the southern Atlantic Ocean

St Helena Island
Secret of the South Atlantic

Figure 4.24 St Helena Asta and Traveller ads brochure

St Helena is one of the remotest places on Earth. It is an Overseas Territory of the United Kingdom with a population of just over 4000 residents. Strategically important for trade for some 400 years, the island now suffers the problems of many small island economies with a lack of natural resources, net out-migration and a dependence on aid and remittances. The island's only link to the outside world was, until recently, by ship. Changes in UK Government strategy and policy with regard to the British Overseas Territories, following the change in UK Government in 2010, has placed a focus on providing an improved environment for economic and social development and promoting self-sufficiency. In line with many previous studies of St Helena, it is intended that is achieved through the provision of air access, utilising tourism as the key driver in economic development.

St Helena's remoteness, along with its remarkable history and environment, has always attracted some tourists, with visitors coming on the RMS St Helena shipping service. Yachts regularly call at the island, as do occasional cruise ships. However, the biggest barriers to tourism development (and, therefore, to economic growth) were the restrictions presented by sea access and the lack of serviced accommodation meeting international visitor expectations. On November 3, 2011 Island Governor Mark Capes announced that construction contracts had been signed and that an airport would be fully open by June 2016. This laid the foundation for the development of a St Helena tourist industry. St Helena has no significant natural resources, and no volume exports that currently can sustain or grow the island's population and economy.

Tourism utilises the resources – built and natural (Figure 4.26)– that are in place on the island, and consequently optimises visitors through their presence and, more importantly, their expenditure to directly input into the economy as well as expand and develop the economy. This can be done through extending the provision of tourism services as well as ensuring that tourism expenditure flows around the economy (the multiplier effect). These expansions will generate further business opportunities, not necessarily directly part of the tourism sector. This would include support services for the tourism sector – such as laundry, transport and similar services – but also businesses supporting the wider business sectors, such as accountants and marketing services, as well as food production and processing.

The Tourism Plan for St Helena anticipates growth in the following markets, particularly now that the airport is completed:

1   Independent travellers: The existing core group will extend to reach slightly younger age groups (probably still in work), where air access provides a better timescale for visits for this wider audience

2   Soft and hard adventure niche tour operators: Wanting to exploit potential opportunities that have been opened up with air access, particularly focussing on soft adventure including sport fishing, sub aqua, mountain biking, rock climbing, alongside extensions to existing product

3   Napoleon 200 anniversary: Individuals and tour operators interested in visiting the island during the Bi-centenary period (2016–2021)

4   Cruise operators: Larger scale operators where air access may provide fly-cruise opportunities

5   Mainstream tour operators: With 'far away' or specialist product offerings.

Figure 4.25 Information on the island

Figure 4.26 Volcanic terrain of St Helena Island

Tourism planners for St Helena calculate the following types of visitor spending:

- GBP 80 per day for 'pure' tourist visitor
- GBP 40 per day for yachting visitor staying visitor staying on yacht
- GBP 80 per day for expedition cruise visitor
- In addition, it is estimated that cruise ship day visitors spend approximately GBP 10 per person (excluding tours)
- An estimate of GBP 100 per day has been given for future air visitors.

In terms of economic benefits for the island, it is important to ensure that this visitor spend is circulated around the economy, rather than being lost through leakage. This multiplier effect is an important factor in all industries, but particularly in a service industry such as tourism, where there is a focus on further spends through wages and supplies.

In order to evaluate the impact on the economy of the increased tourism spending, one must calculate the multiplier effect. The multiplier effect estimates by how much injections of money from the tourism sector contribute to further rounds of spending, for example, hotels using the money spent by tourists on supplies, or tourism workers spending their wages in local shops. It has been estimated that the current tourism multiplier effect on St Helena is as little as 0.3. In more developed economies the multiplier is between 2.5 and 3 but St Helena's Tourism Plan works with a more conservative multiplier value of 1.5. However, this is very significant as the Tourism Plan's projected figures suggest that by 2020, a forecast visitor spend of GB£9 840 000 by 30 000 tourists will be worth GB£24 600 000 to the island's economy.

177

4.10 Socio-cultural impacts of tourism

Tourism developments can generate significant social and cultural impacts within particular destinations. Problems can arise when tourism brings changes in to the host population's value systems and traditional patterns of behaviour start to change. Over time this can result in an alteration of the local social and cultural identity. Furthermore, changes can occur in the structure of local communities and there may be altered family relationships, weakening of traditional lifestyles, the loss of traditional ceremonies and the acceptance of different moral standards. However, tourism can also generate positive socio-cultural impacts as it can act as a supportive force for peace, foster a sense of pride in local cultural traditions and help to minimise the imbalances caused by past rural to urban migrations by creating local job opportunities.

There are four important factors that influence the extent to which tourism creates particular types of socio-cultural impact within destinations and these can be summarised as follows.

1   The types and numbers of tourists: an important consideration. Low numbers of tourists, particularly independent travellers, result in low destination impacts whereas mass tourism will generate a much wider variety of impacts. However, this may not always be the case. It can be argued that independent travellers could exert a quite severe 'culture shock' on remote and isolated communities and that purpose-built resorts, catering for large numbers of visitors, limit overall levels of negative impact by keeping tourists within confined geographical areas.

2   The relative economic importance of the tourism industry: within a destination is also very important. The impacts of tourism are likely to be less in a mixed economy than on an economy reliant on tourism.

3   The size and stage of development of the tourism industry: will also have an effect on local socio-cultural conditions. As indicated in point one, larger host populations are better able to withstand the influence of tourists because contact with visitors is diluted. Similarly, established tourist resorts are likely to experience less change than newly emerging destinations.

4   The pace of tourism development: very significant because some destinations have experienced rapid growth which has been relatively uncontrolled and social impacts are likely to be much higher in these areas.

The positive socio-cultural impacts of tourism

There are many positive consequences of tourism that arise when tourism is practiced and developed in a sustainable and appropriate way. Depending on the destination, these positive impacts include:

- the preservation of customs and crafts
- the provision of community facilities and public services
- aiding of international understanding
- encouraging travel, mobility and social integration.

A good illustration of these aspects actually taking place is the example of Uluru (Ayres Rock) within Uluru-Kata Tjuta National Park in the Northern Territories of Australia. The Park's management has attempted to provide tourists with a rewarding experience, while protecting the natural environment and securing a sustainable future for the local aborigine population. The Park achieves these goals using a variety of strategies which have significant positive socio-cultural impacts. The public are requested to respect sacred aboriginal sites. A purpose-built Cultural Centre raises visitor awareness of issues and helps to counter the effects of commodification. Furthermore, sales of authentic souvenirs also help to preserve and revitalise traditional crafts, which otherwise might be replaced by cheap, mass-produced imitations. Finally, some members of the local Anangu tribe are also employed as Park Rangers and there are plans to establish a National Tourism Training Academy in the area so that eventually local people will form 50% of the workforce.

Tourism in many locations supports the creation of community facilities and services that otherwise might not have been developed and it can bring higher living standards to a destination. Other benefits can include upgraded infrastructure, health and transport improvements, new sport and recreational facilities, restaurants and public spaces, as well as the availability of new commodities and foodstuffs. Tourism can also boost the preservation and transmission of cultural and historical traditions, and a renaissance of indigenous cultures, cultural arts and crafts.

ACTIVITY 9

Consider Figures 4.27 and 4.28 from South Africa and assess the extent to which tourism is generating positive socio-cultural impacts on the host population.

Figure 4.27 Traditional dance performance

Figure 4.28 Sale of local traditional handicraft items

The negative socio-cultural impacts of tourism

Tourism allows people from different countries to meet and mingle. Many people from developing countries would not have the chance to meet westerners if tourism did not exist. However, in some destinations, the impacts of tourism on the local host population are not always positive. Negative socio-cultural impacts can include:

- conflicts with the host community
- crime
- loss of cultural identity
- the Demonstration Effect
- changes to family structure
- social problems, such as begging and prostitution.

The inflow of people (tourists, investors/entrepreneurs and jobseekers) into a previously undeveloped area increases congestion and overcrowding as more residential and commercial establishments are built. An area limited in size will struggle to support the ever-increasing number of people. The development of facilities aimed at wealthy tourists can leave sections of the host community feeling marginalised and excluded. Many tourists appear to be either negligent or ignorant about local customs and moral values. As such, tourists' behaviour, from the standpoint of the local community, is disrespectful and offensive, particularly in their mode of dressing, for example, or by overt displays of affection between partners in public places.

The demonstration effect considers the socio-cultural impacts tourism may have on the behaviour of the host population and is generally defined as behaviour that members of the host population copy from the tourists. The Demonstration Effect can thus lead to the erosion of traditional culture and values as the local population adopts visitor behaviour and this is often a major cause of tension within sections of local society. A good illustration of this would be the Middle East where western lifestyle is frequently at odds with Muslim tradition.

In addition to the demonstration effect, there is a range of negative sociocultural impacts that can result from the growth of international tourism and these are particular causes of concern in destinations with traditional societies. The main negative impacts are shown in Table 4.2.

Socio-cultural issues associated with slum tourism

'Slum tourism' is quite a recent development and researchers in many locations are starting to investigate the effects of the increasing commodification of the urban poor and their particular spaces within the city. In many cities the authorities have been eager to clean up central areas and to remove pavement dwellers, beggars, street children and other disadvantaged individuals. This has been done in order to present a more favourable image to visitors and potential investors. However, in other cities positive attempts are being made to draw attention to social issues such as marginalisation, poverty and social

Issue	Negative socio-cultural impacts
Conflicts with the host community	In some destinations there is a culture clash as tourists often fail to respect local customs and moral values. The attitude of local residents towards tourists can change through time. In the early stages of tourism development there will only be a few visitors who will be made to feel very welcome. However, with increasing visitor numbers, there is frequently a rise in both apathy and antagonism amongst particular sections of the local population.
Crime	This is associated with the presence of a large number of tourists. The visitors have a lot of money to spend, they often carry valuables such as cameras and jewellery and this increases the attraction of tourist areas for criminals. Crime also brings with it activities like robbery and drug dealing to the detriment of local residents. There may also be increased damage to artefacts and heritage sites where visitors steal items or simply want to touch them.
Loss of cultural identity	Commodification can take place in some destinations when local cultural events and activities are turned into commodities. For example religious rituals, traditional ethnic rites and festivals can be altered or reduced to conform to tourist needs and expectations. This can lead to staged authenticity, when cultural activities are turned into show performances for tourists as if they were real life. Similarly, tourist demands can result in changes to the ways in which traditional crafts and souvenirs are made. Globalisation can have an effect. Although tourists want to experience exotic locations and new facilities they also look for well-known hotels and familiar food brands. This can leave traditional features of a destination neglected.
Changes to family structure	Young people migrate to tourist areas in search of work. This leaves behind an ageing population in the surrounding areas and disrupts the traditional extended family structure.
Social problems	As with the growth in crime, tourist destinations can be associated with both begging and prostitution. The commercial sexual exploitation of children and young women has been associated with the growth of tourism in many parts of the world. Though tourism is not the cause of sexual exploitation, it provides easy access to it in a number of destinations.

Table 4.2 Negative socio-cultural issues

exclusion and to positively market former no-go slum areas with a history of gang violence, crime and drug problems as tourist destinations. Increasingly, tourists seem to be keen to visit these areas, but in a controlled and safe way. Examples of such activities can be found in many cities and 'slum tourism' is not confined to the shanty town squatter settlements of the less economically developed countries.

San Francisco's Tenderloin District is frequently described as being the worst neighbourhood in the city and it has a reputation for being home to drug dealers, addicts, prostitutes and mentally unstable street people. However, it is also one of the city's most exciting and diverse locations. The process of urban gentrification and the arrival of many Vietnamese families in the last two decades have been instrumental in helping to transform the area. However, visitor interest in the area has been helped by the fact that tour companies such as The Urban Safari include the Tenderloin district as part of their itinerary and tourists are encouraged to:

Enjoy the local flavours and see the local wildlife (residents) in their natural habitat (the neighbourhoods) as you travel through the jungles of San Francisco not explored by other tours.

It was the success and popularity of the film *Slumdog Millianaire* that boosted tourist interest in viewing the slum areas of Mumbai. Within Mumbai, Dharavi is regarded as being one of the largest slums in Asia. However, as tour companies such as Reality Tours and Travel point out to clients, there is much more to this historic area of Mumbai than poverty. Dharavi's industries have an annual turnover of approximately US$665 million. Visitors taking the company's tours listed on Figure 4.29 can experience a wide range of these activities: recycling, pottery-making, embroidery, bakery, soap factory, leather tanning, poppadom-making and many more.

To combat possible charges of voyeurism and exploitation of the poor, as suggested by the cartoon, Reality Tours does not allow its clients to bring cameras nor does it take groups of more than six people into Dharavi. It also pays all operating costs for the Reality Gives community centre and school. The company also puts 80% of its profits (after taxes and salaries) back into the community through this charity arm.

Tour	Price (in Rupees)	
	SHARED	**PRIVATE (for groups of 5 people)**
SLUM TOURS		
Dharavi Short Tour	600/650	3 000
Sights		
Recycling area Dharavi residential areas	Small-scale industries Community centre	
Modes of transport: Walking, Train		
Dharavi Long Tour	1 200	5 000
Sights		
Red light area Recycling area Dharavi residential areas Marine Drive	Dhobi Ghat Small-scale industries Community centre	
Modes of transport: Walking, Car		
Dharavi and Sightseeing Tour	N/A	7 500 lunch@300pp
Sights		
Red light area Recycling area Dharavi residential areas Marine Drive Banganga Tank Kamala Nehru Park Haji Ali Mosque Others	Dhobi Ghat Small-scale industries Community centre CST train station Jain Temple Mahalaxmi Temple Gandhi museum	
Modes of transport: Walking, Train		
CITY TOURS		
Street Food Tour	1 300	7 000
Sights		
Chowpatty Beach Bhendi Bazaar	Minara Masjid	
Modes of transport: Walking, Taxi		
Bicycle Tour	1 000	5 000
Sights		
CST Railway Station Cow Shelter Khao Galli (Food street) Marine Drive	Sassoon Dock Crawford Market Mumbadevi Temple	
Modes of transport: Bicycle		

Tour	Price (in Rupees)	
	SHARED	**PRIVATE (for groups of 5 people)**
Mumbai by Night Tour	950	4 750
Sights		
CST Railway Station Banganga Tank Kamala Nehru Park	Chowpatty Beach Jain Temple	
Modes of transport: Taxi		
Public Transport Tour	850	4 250
Sights		
CST Railway Station Chor Bazaar Dabbawallahs	Dadar Flower market Null Bazaar	
Modes of transport: Walking, Train, Taxi, Bus		
Market Tour	800	4 000
Sights		
Cow Shelter Mangaldas market Mumbadevi Temple	Crawford Market Flower Galli	
Modes of transport: Walking		
Sightseeing by Car	N/A	50 002
Sights		
CST Railway Station Banganga Tank Kamala Nehru Park Haji Ali Mosque Others	Marine Drive Jain Temple Mahalaxmi Temple Gandhi museum	
Modes of transport: Car		
VILLAGE TOURS		
1 Day Village Tour	2 750	10 000
Sights		
Food with local family Experience village life	Village School Partake in farming activities	
Modes of transport: Walking, Bus, Boat, Autorickshaw (tuk-tuk)		
2 Day Village Tour	N/A	15 000
Sights		
Food with local family Experience village life Village home Partake in farming activities	Village School Overnight stay in local	
Modes of transport: Walking, Bus, Boat, Autorickshaw (tuk-tuk)		

Figure 4.29 Summary of Dharavi slum tours

ACTIVITY 10

Carry out further research into slum tourism. Consider the positive and negative impacts that can result. What are your opinions? For example, do you agree with the following?

- It can be something very beneficial to the locals, because it brings some income to the population, but also, some ill-intentioned people could try to make money out of poverty.

- It's a good thing if it makes the tourists realise the true life of the inhabitants.

- Slum tours are just like a human zoo for the rich ogling poor people.

- Watching how people survive in tough conditions and then going back to easy life is somehow immoral. Asking how they built their house or what they eat is not kind. It can make people jealous, and they will feel even more miserable.

Dubai Desert Conservation Reserve (DDCR)

In 2003, the Government of Dubai decided to create a nationally significant conservation area, shown in Figure 4.30 and charged Emirates with its management and protection. Since then Emirates has invested over 10 million AED in support of wildlife conservation programmes, scientific research and protection of this 225 sq km area. The DDCR has come to be regarded in the same terms as some of the world's most treasured conservation areas, including such reserves as Yellowstone National Park in the US and the Great Barrier Reef in Australia.

Since the opening of the Al Maha resort complex, the successful re-introduction of the Arabian Oryx, Arabian Gazelle, Sand Gazelle and large-scale indigenous flora re-seeding programmes are just some of the major projects that have been delicately carried out in the DDCR. It is the only location within the UAE where visitors are able to experience completely free-roaming wildlife within their natural desert and dune surroundings. Confirmed by scientific research, the environment and habitat within the DDCR has greatly improved from what it was ten years ago. Quite apart from the wildlife which has been reintroduced, many species that had disappeared from the area are now returning on their own accord.

The DDCR is segregated into four utilization zones. In some areas, only researchers are allowed to enter on foot. In another zone a select number of safari operators – who worked closely with the reserve management to create a foremost example of sustainable desert tourism in the region – can conduct safaris for visitors, providing an experience of the desert and dunes, and its unique fauna and flora, and gaining a better understanding of Dubai's conservation efforts.

Much of the region's natural resources, habitats and wildlife are under pressure; however, sustainable developments such as Al Maha offer the biggest opportunities to develop the tourism economy while also protecting natural and historic heritage into the future.

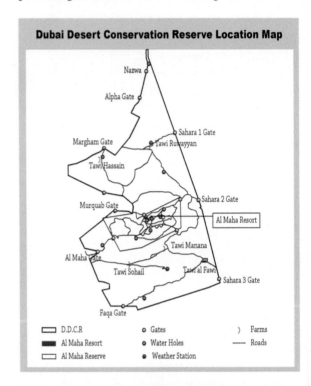

Figure 4.30 Location map of the reserve

4.11 Environmental impacts of tourism

The quality of a destination's environment, both natural and man-made, is an essential consideration when developing tourism in the area. However, tourism has a complex relationship with the environment because many popular tourist activities can create significant negative environmental impacts. Many of these negative effects can be linked to the construction of general infrastructure such as roads and airports as well as to specific tourism facilities like resorts, hotels, restaurants, shops, golf courses and marinas. This is a very significant problem because the negative impacts of tourism development can start to undermine and even destroy the environmental resources on which it depends. On the other hand, the development of a tourist industry has the potential to create positive environmental impacts by contributing to environmental protection and conservation.

Tourism can also help to raise awareness of environmental values and it can help generate funds to finance schemes to protect and conserve natural areas.

The positive environmental impacts of tourism

Tourism developments taking place in a planned and controlled manner can bring about a range of positive environmental impacts such as improved assets, landscaping, conservation, regeneration and compliance with building regulations. However, as tourism takes place in both natural and built environments, the relative significance of such improvements will depend on the nature and characteristics of the particular destination. The positive environmental impacts that may result from tourism development will thus vary with the type of destination. However, as we shall see in the following examples, tourism development can bring many environmental benefits to particular locations.

Tourism can significantly contribute to environmental protection, conservation, the restoration of biological diversity and to the sustainable use of natural resources. There are many examples of the ways in which tourism has had a positive effect on wildlife preservation and protection. The best-known examples are probably in Africa but there are also important wildlife reserves in South America, Asia, Australia, and the South Pacific. Environmental threats exist all over the world and numerous animal and plant species have already become extinct or may become extinct soon. Many countries have therefore established wildlife reserves and enacted strict laws protecting the animals that draw nature-loving tourists. Many tourists snorkel with dolphins in the Indian Ocean, Mauritius. Boat numbers are restricted and strict speed reductions are in place to protect both the coral reefs and marine life.

Figure 4.31 A beach in Mauritius

The built environment in many destinations has been improved by redevelopment schemes using tourism as a focus for urban regeneration. In particular, cities with waterfront areas have embarked on major schemes to upgrade local infrastructure and transform formerly declining urban areas into vibrant locations offering a range of improved facilities for visitors and local communities. To see how such transformations can improve the local built environment we can now look at an important example from the UK, the regeneration of Liverpool's Albert Dock complex.

183

The Albert Dock

The Albert Dock contains the UK's largest group of Grade 1 listed buildings outside London. It is also Liverpool's most important visitor attraction, according to the Merseyside visitor survey. The Dock was officially opened by Prince Albert on 30 July, 1846. It was of great significance then because it was the first enclosed non-combustible dock warehouse system in the world and the first structure in Britain to be made entirely of cast iron, brick and stone.

Although the Albert Dock was built to accommodate the most modern sailing ships of its day, it thrived for just half a century. By 1900, only 7% of ships using Liverpool were sailing ships and the Albert Dock was too small to accommodate the larger iron and steel steamships. There was virtually no commercial shipping activity in the Albert Dock after 1920 and, after decades of disuse, it finally closed in 1972. By 1981, the entire complex was a scene of utter abandonment and dereliction.

Following a spectacular refurbishment by the Arrowcraft Group in partnership with Merseyside Development Corporation, the Albert Dock was restored to its former

glory and is now a centrepiece of the renowned Merseyside waterfront (Figure 4.32). One of the first priorities of the regeneration was the restoration of the dock system, which had deteriorated rapidly since the Brunswick Dock gates had been left open. Contaminated silt was removed from the dock basin, dock gates were replaced, bridges restored and the dock walls were repaired.

Figure 4.32 Albert Dock, Liverpool

Today the Albert Dock is one of Liverpool's most important tourist attractions and a vital component of the city's UNESCO World Heritage Maritime Mercantile City. As well as being the number one tourist attraction in Liverpool, the Albert Dock is also the most visited multi-use attraction in the United Kingdom outside of London, with in excess of 4 million visitors per year (see Figure 4.33).

Amongst the many attractions at the Albert Dock are the Merseyside Maritime Museum, the Beatles Story and the Tate Liverpool. There are also two hotels within the Albert Dock: a Holiday Inn and Premier Lodge both located in the Britannia Pavilion.

On a site adjacent to the Albert Dock complex, a new museum opened on 19 July 2011 in a purpose-built landmark building on Liverpool's famous waterfront.

The area has now been completely transformed and the destination illustrates the ways in which urban regeneration schemes can exert very positive socio-economic and environmental impacts on former areas of industrial dereliction, as indicated in Figure 4.34.

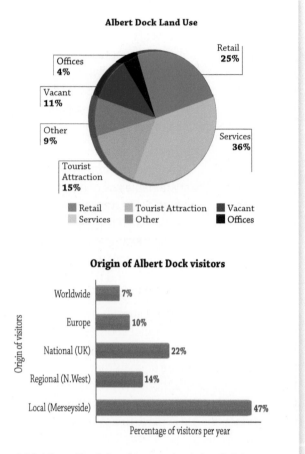

Figure 4.33 Albert Dock land use and origin of visitors

KEY CONCEPTS

Sustainability and responsibility

The earlier section highlights the importance of sustaining environmental regulations in order to protect natural resources by preventing overuse and destruction of natural wildlife.

ACTIVITY 11

Using the Dubai Desert Conservation Reserve and Albert Dock case studies, together with your own research, describe how tourism developments can bring about each of the following positive environmental impacts:

- an improved range of tourism assets
- improvements to the appearance of the landscape
- conservation of the natural and/or built environment
- regeneration of the natural and/or built environment
- improvement(s) due to the introduction of, and/or compliance with, building regulations.

The negative environmental impacts of tourism

Negative impacts from tourism occur when the level of visitor use is greater than the environment's ability to cope with this use within the acceptable limits of change. When tourism developments take place in an uncontrolled way they can easily bring about a range of negative environmental impacts such as:

- traffic congestion
- erosion of natural resources
- pollution of air and water
- litter
- increase in noise levels
- panoramic view damage
- destruction of natural wildlife systems and breeding patterns.

For example, when large numbers of tourists first started to visit Uluru (Ayres Rock) in the Northern Territories of Australia, the rise in visitor numbers started to create a

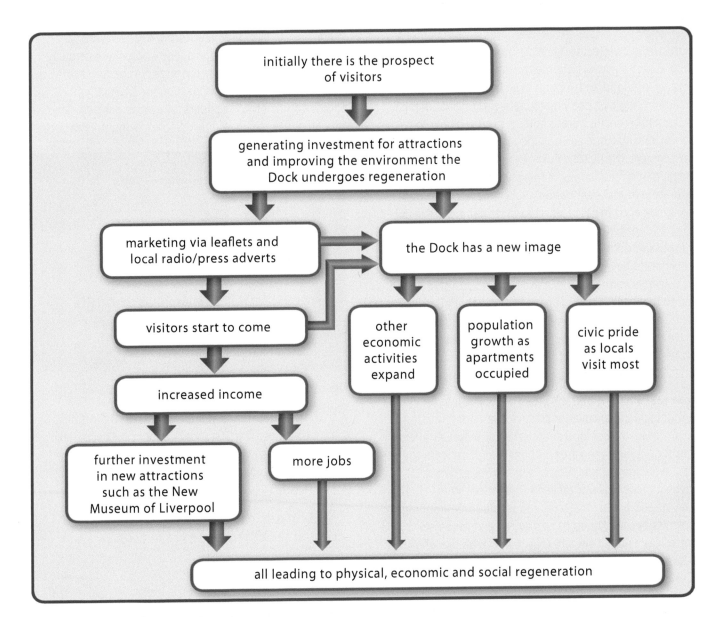

Figure 4.34 Impact of regeneration schemes

number of negative impacts. Aboriginal cultural sites and the local environment were damaged. An increasingly large amount of litter was being dropped and the local wildlife was being disturbed. Rare plants were picked and trampling by visitors caused additional erosion. Waterholes were polluted with soap and human waste, and the pressure of vehicles and people left the soil exposed to wind and water erosion.

However, as tourism takes place in both natural and built environments, the relative significance of such issues will depend on the nature and characteristics of the particular destination. The negative environmental impacts that may result from tourism development will thus vary with the type of destination. Uncontrolled conventional tourism

poses potential threats to many natural areas around the world. It can put enormous pressure on an area and lead to impacts such as:

- soil erosion
- increased pollution
- discharges into the sea
- natural habitat loss
- increased pressure on endangered species and heightened vulnerability to forest fires.

It also often puts a strain on water resources, and it can force local populations to compete for the use of critical resources. The growth of tourism inevitably brings pressure on the environment. Increasing amounts of litter and hotel waste are an internationally recognised problem, even in ecotourism destinations such as Costa Rica. Waste disposal becomes an issue as landfill takes up precious land and, if burnt in incinerators, adds to air pollution. Vehicles carrying tourists add to air and noise pollution in sensitive areas and unrestricted building scars the landscape as visual pollution. In recent years, for example, the historic European city of Bruges in Belgium has faced many of the environmental problems of mature tourist destinations, such as overcrowding, congestion, conflicts of land use and changes in the use of public spaces. Therefore, a systematic study of tourism supply and demand was carried out in order to gather information to improve tourism's benefits and to diminish its negative impacts. One of the main results of that study led to the establishment of a traffic plan that now diverts all traffic through a ring road and makes it impossible to drive through the centre of the city. Coaches bringing day visitors have no access at all to the centre and have to unload in special parking places around the ring.

New tourism developments may cause the loss of habitats due to excavations, and water contamination and the removal of food sources can all seriously affect the ecosystems of an area. Tourism developments such as the building or adapting of a wilderness space will involve the removal of soil and vegetation; however, this may be subject to local laws and regulations. Planning permissions may need to be granted and in some instances a public enquiry may ensue. With the influx of a large number of visitors to an area, congestion is sure to occur during peak times. Whether it is traffic or simply large numbers of people in one area, local people and infrastructures can suffer. The demands placed on roads, railways, bridges and local services (such as ambulance and police) can seriously create a negative impact for the local people and push up the costs to maintain services generally. Tourists visiting an area may also bring further issues of illegal trespass onto private land where disruption to the local community may not be considered or understood.

Adventure tourism is often associated with negative environmental impacts, for example with hard adventure tourism pursuits such as motocross (Figure 4.35). This is very popular in Spanish culture, however the sport takes place in the countryside creating large tracks and dust where tyres move through the earth. At Solmoto motocross there is a multitude of different motocross circuits, including the Alhama de Murcia, which is used for the motocross Grand Prix. The site is very popular as it caters for all levels of ability, with tracks ranging from world and national level to novices and beginners. The whole site is carefully managed to accommodate the large number of visitors. It arguably has a positive impact on the environment by encouraging motorcross riders to come to this dedicated site rather than riding in non-designated countryside areas.

Figure 4.35 Motocross in Puerto Lumbreras, Spain

With the growth of tourist numbers in many destinations, there is a very real fear that some locations are approaching visitor overcapacity. The World Tourism Organisation has defined the concept of tourism carrying capacity as being the:

maximum number of people that may visit a tourist destination at the same time, without causing destruction of the physical, economic, socio-cultural environment and an unacceptable decrease in the quality of visitors' satisfaction.

Therefore, the carrying capacity can be regarded as being the point at which a destination or attraction starts experiencing adverse conditions as a result of the number of visitors.

In order for it to be sustainable, any tourism development should attempt to make a low impact on both the local environment and local culture. However, all developments should help to generate income, employment and aid the conservation of local ecosystems.

ACTIVITY 12

Choose a tourism destination to research. Consider areas such as the coast, mountains or parks where environmental impacts of tourism can be assessed. Compare and contrast with other group members. Decide which area is most at risk and why.

CASE STUDY 10

Erosion in the English Lake District National Park

The Lake District was established as a National Park in 1951. The Lake District National Park Authority (LDNPA) is the local government body appointed to after look the Lake District National Park. It has two main purposes. The first is to conserve and enhance the natural beauty, wildlife and cultural heritage of the Lake District and the second is to promote opportunities for the understanding and enjoyment of the special qualities of the National Park. Furthermore, the LDNPA has a duty to foster the economic and social well-being of local communities within the Park.

With the growth in popularity of outdoor recreational activities there is now an urgent need to protect the area, not only for future generations but also to maintain the area's intrinsic values. Increased accessibility has resulted in increased visitor numbers and the park has a responsibility to conserve the environment. With over 14 million visitors each year, there is the danger that several areas will suffer overuse and it is vital that the area is managed properly.

The large number of tourists puts the environment under great pressure. One of the main problems is footpath erosion, which can create huge scars on the landscape. They are now so large that they can be seen on satellite pictures. To give an idea of the scale of the problem within the LDNPA area, a recent survey identified that some 41 690 man days of work were required at an estimated total cost of over £4.5 million to repair the damage along 180 footpath routes, such as the one shown in Figure 4.36.

Environment-related problems can be prevented in the future by a combination of good design, regular maintenance and managing the impact of visitors to the area. Measures which can be taken include the following:

Constructing hard-wearing, user-friendly paths
- Ensuring effective water drainage, which is fundamental to successful path management
- Carrying out regular maintenance tasks such as clearing water gullies, removing gravel and repairing minor damage
- Reducing grazing pressures
- Resting routes, such as temporarily changing the path, particularly in the early stages of erosion
- Fertilising and reseeding, which may be used on its own or in conjunction with the resting of routes
- Fencing is an extremely sensitive issue because of the access issue but it can be used on its own or in conjunction with other methods, making vegetation recovery possible
- Directing people along a preferred route using physical and psychological barriers, including walls, plants, stones and water (although re-routing people away from areas prone to erosion may be difficult if the path has very rigid boundaries or has been designated as a Right of Way)
- Educating mountain users through leaflets, talks and notices
- Managing visitor numbers through the limiting of car parking or re-channelling visitor publicity to areas less likely to suffer damage.

Figure 4.36 One of the Lake District footpath routes

187

By doing this, the tourism developments taking place within particular destinations will represent responsible tourism in that they are both ecologically and culturally sensitive. Furthermore, the destination as a whole is likely to be improved for both local people and visitors.

It is important that destinations attempt to manage these impacts in a sustainable way. It will make sense to try to maximise the positive effects of tourism within particular locations but it will be equally important to try to minimise the negative effects that can result from increasing tourist numbers. Tourism activities can take place in a range of locations throughout the world and each will have a different carrying capacity, that is, the number of visitors that can be managed without causing significant negative impacts.

Furthermore, these destinations can be at very different stages of development as indicated by the following types:

- High-density recreational areas: where a wide variety of uses and substantial development utilises all available resources. Such areas will be characterised by intensive development of resort hotels and facilities managed for maximum visitor usage (for example Disneyland and other purpose-built resort complexes).
- General outdoor recreational areas: which have a wide variety of use with substantial development. These areas offer a greater choice of activity and the resorts are some distance away from main population centres (for example, ski resorts and sailing centres).
- Natural environments or established wilderness areas: these allow multiple uses, with a variety of possible activities available according to the nature of the area (for example, National Parks).
- Unique areas of outstanding natural beauty or scenic grandeur: where the main activity was sightseeing, but where they are increasingly being exploited by different types of traveller (for example, the Grand Canyon).
- Primitive areas of undisturbed wilderness: areas with no roads where natural wild conditions can still be found (for example, areas such as trekking in the Himalayas or exploring Amazonia).

- Historic and cultural sites: which may be at a local, regional, national or international scale but they are significant attractions for travellers (for example the Inca Trail).

Destination management: developing sustainable practices

Successful destinations have developed strategies to help lay the foundations for a sustainable future and in many places attempts have been made to:

- maximise the retention of visitor spending at the destination
- invest tourism income in public and social projects for local communities
- widen access to the location's facilities and assets
- establish schemes for staff training and development
- expand training and employment of local people in tourism and related activities
- encourage tourism education.

To help illustrate some of the issues involved in the successful management of a destination we can now look at a small-scale case study from the UK and see what has happened to part of the South Sefton Coast in between Liverpool and Southport at Formby.

The Sefton Coast in North West England

The area around Formby is part of the Sefton Coast sand dune system. Figure 4.37 indicates that the landscape contains typical dune habitats and the wildlife found here is of national and European significance. Many visitors to the area are familiar with Formby's red squirrels, but the Formby dunes are also home to other rare and endangered wildlife. Two such inhabitants are the Natterjack Toad and the Northern Dune Tiger Beetle. The beetle is rare and can only be found at two sites in the whole of Britain.

The location is managed by the National Trust because Formby is also a site of major archaeological and historical importance. Not only is the area a stunning stretch of unspoiled coastline, offering visitors long sandy beaches intermixed with attractive and unspoilt pinewoods, it also has evidence of early human activity, including footprints that date back to the late Neolithic era (7000 years ago).

The National Trust has developed the site in a managed and sustainable way so that visitors can enjoy leisure and recreational activities without unduly damaging the natural environment. This has been achieved in the following ways.

The Formby site has been developed to preserve the three key components of the dune ecosystem:

- the beach area
- the sand dune belt
- the forest zone.

Figure 4.37 Sefton Coast sand dune

Visitor facilities such as picnic areas have been created and these have been constructed to blend in with the scenery as shown in Figure 4.39.

All paths are clearly signposted for visitors and different routes can be followed both through the sand dune area and through the forest zone as shown in Figures 4.40 and 4.41, with particular care being taken to avoid the more sensitive ecological areas.

To help minimise negative visitor impacts, waste bins (litter and dog) have been placed throughout the site. Furthermore, the National Trust uses the provision of waste bins as an additional opportunity to remind visitors of the importance of behaving in a responsible manner while they enjoy everything the site has to offer. This raising of impact awareness has an important part to play in educating the public about the significance of preserving the site for the future.

Figure 4.38 Car parking area

Figure 4.39 Forest trail picnic area

Figure 4.38 shows the car park that gives visitors direct access to the beach area. However, it has also been conveniently located for visitors wanting to walk through the whole site following the various paths that have been laid out.

Figure 4.40 Formby site map

189

Figure 4.41 Sand dune and woodland path

The National Trust uses the site to promote its aims and objectives by informing visitors about its work, offering membership and by the sale of guide books and related items.

In this way, the National Trust is able to share its **values and attitudes** to the development and management of sites under its protection with visitors more directly, and it also has the opportunity to receive feedback and comment about the service it provides. Such a dialogue can help inform the future development of the site and this may also benefit future visitors. With an understanding of **current issues and consumer trends**, the Trust can stage events and activities that will attract visitors and at Formby. A calendar of events is planned each year to meet a variety of visitor needs.

We can see how the National Trust has worked in partnership with the Sefton local authority to manage Formby in a sustainable and responsible way. The management of the destination has clearly minimised tourism's negative impacts by the introduction of a planned approach and the creation of zones (beach, dunes and forest) each with their particular visitor appeal. Access to the site has been carefully planned (car park, walks along signposted routes avoiding sensitive habitats) and visitor facilities blend in with the natural environment. Furthermore, the site is carefully monitored for signs of stress, and regular audits are taken to assess both tourist impact and to identify potential hazards to visitors. An example of this approach in action at the Formby site is shown in Figure 4.43.

4.12 Changes in the evolution of destinations

As we have already seen in Chapter 3 with the Butler Model, tourist destinations have a lifecycle. As part of their development destinations need to evolve in order to maintain their tourist appeal. Dubai is a particularly good example of this evolution.

The evolution of Dubai

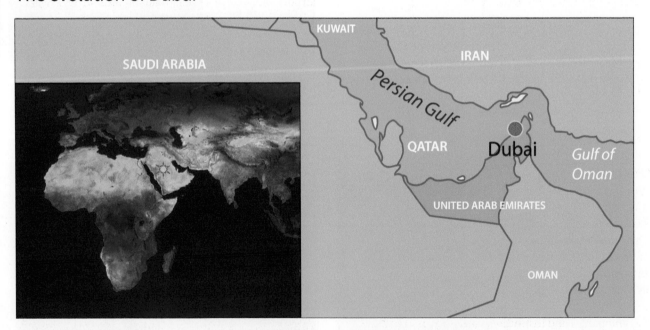

Figure 4.42 Map of Dubai

In the 18th century, Dubai was a small fishing and trading village inhabited by members of the Bani Yas tribe. Dubai was a transit point for caravans on the trade route from Iraq to Oman, and for dhows between India, East Africa and the Northern Gulf. This eventually led to the city's establishment as an international centre of commerce where many cultures and traditions mixed.

The emirate embraces a wide variety of scenery in a very small area. In a single day, the visitor can experience everything from rugged mountains and awe-inspiring sand dunes to sandy beaches. Along the Arabian Gulf coast, there are offshore islands, coral reefs and sabkha, or salt marshes. Stretches of gravel plain and sandy desert characterise the inland region.

However, the tourism industry in Dubai is relatively young. Until the late 1950s, there were no hotels in Dubai and so what few visitors there were had no choice but to stay with their hosts or with colleagues. The following decades saw Dubai start to develop basic facilities for travellers and an international airport was opened in 1959. In 1966, the Dubai Petroleum Company ('DPC') discovered four offshore fields and economic development of the area began to take place. Oil production peaked in 1991 at 410 000 barrels per day. It was during this period that a small number of hotels began to open to serve the needs of Dubai's growing economy.

In the 1970s, Sheikh Mohammed realised that Dubai would not be able to remain independent of Abu Dhabi's political and economic control if its economy relied on diminishing oil reserves alone. He therefore created a futuristic vision for Dubai as an international hub that keeps a delicate balance between modernity and the city's Arab and Islamic identity and deliberately redirected the oil revenues in a series of ventures designed to strengthen Dubai's position as a regional trading centre.

Taking advantage of Dubai's excellent location as a trans-shipment point between Asia and Europe, the government built major additions to the local infrastructure including:

- Port Rashid in 1971
- Port Jebel Ali in 1977
- Jebel Ali Free Zone in 1985
- Dubai International Financial Centre in 2002.

The mid-1980s saw the start of the creation of key institutions and activities that came to shape Dubai's development as a tourist destination. In 1985, the government founded Emirates Airlines, using Dubai airport as its main hub. In 1989, the Dubai Tourism Board was created. This was then transformed into the Department of Tourism and Commerce Marketing (DTCM) in 1997, allowing it to concentrate on international promotion and the positioning of Dubai as not just a commercial hub but also as a resort destination. The DTCM, along with the help of other key companies and institutions, held the first annual Dubai shopping festival in 1996. In 1997, the Jumeirah Group was established as a hotel management company. The company today has a portfolio of major hotels all around the world, including Dubai's iconic Burj Al Arab (the world's first 7-star hotel opened in 1999). These institutions generated Dubai's tourism growth. By 2000, 3.4 million tourists were coming to Dubai annually and the destination started to expand more rapidly.

The first decade of the 21st century saw Dubai develop at a phenomenal rate. The Palm Island projects, started in 2002, were the first of a series of 'mega-projects' aimed at expanding the destinations infrastructure. The main projects are shown in Figure 4.46.

Foreign investors poured into Dubai's development projects as wealthy tourists came to stay at the destination's ever-expanding range of hotels or to purchase some of its valuable waterfront properties. For example, as shown in Table 4.3, between 2006 and 2010, the number of hotel beds grew at an annual rate of close to 10%. In 2010, 6.5 million visitors stayed in Dubai hotels, bringing some US$3 billion in hotel revenues. In 2010, Dubai's hotels had the highest revenue per available room in the world at US$198 and Dubai was ranked 10th in the world in terms of occupancy (78.6%).

The capacity of Dubai's International Airport was extended in this period as well. The airport has developed to be the busiest airport in the Middle East and the 15th busiest airport in the world by passenger traffic. The airport serves over 130 airlines and 220 destinations in six continents. In 2010, Al Maktoum International Airport was opened and will become the world's largest airport with a capacity to handle 160 million passengers when it is fully operational. This means that the growth and development of Dubai as an international destination will continue, at least until 2020.

Cruising in the region is experiencing growth and is bringing a new segment of holidaymakers into Dubai.

Geographically, Dubai is well positioned as a cruise destination with its excellent flight network from around the world. Dubai hosted 390 000 passengers in 2010 and expects 625 000 by 2015. The Dubai cruise terminal can host up to 7000 passengers and three ships at one time.

Figure 4.43 Dubai's 'Mega-Projects'

1. Number of operating hotels

Hotel class	2001	2002	2003	2004	2005	2006	2007	2008	2009	2010
five star	27	29	32	34	38	42	43	51	52	57
four star	26	27	30	29	38	43	49	58	59	69
three star	32	35	39	41	36	40	42	42	55	59
two star	43	49	48	45	43	40	39	45	44	51
one star	52	63	76	85	106	123	125	136	126	128
listed/guest house	84	69	46	42	39	18	21	19	16	18
Total	264	272	271	276	300	306	319	351	352	382

2. Number of available rooms

Hotel class	2001	2002	2003	2004	2005	2006	2007	2008	2009	2010
five star	7 810	8 623	9 966	10 256	11 339	12 224	12 665	16 657	16 693	18 584
four star	3 529	3 686	4 261	4 386	5 739	6 503	7 541	9 920	10 817	13 251
three star	3 460	3 676	4 112	4 369	3 754	4 253	4 442	4 871	6 975	8 776
two star	2 524	2 962	3 164	2 930	3 813	3 741	3 074	4 129	3 807	5 154
one star	1 769	2 203	2 583	2 815	3 895	4 330	4 310	4 920	4 719	4 888
listed/guest house	2 336	2 020	1 485	1 399	1 294	594	585	484	408	462
Total	21 428	23 170	25 571	26 155	29 834	31 645	32 617	40 981	43 419	51 115

Table 4.3 Number of Dubai hotels and available rooms by class

Dubai has emerged as a major 21st-century city due to its rapid growth and many iconic structures. It has many world 'firsts' and there are numerous places to visit and see. Visitors can choose to go to a heritage site, the old Bastakia area, Dubai creek or to landmarks such as Burj Khalifa, Burj Al Arab or the Palm. They can visit purpose-built attraction such as Atlantis or Ski Dubai or go to beach parks or view the unique nature reserve. Dubai has been in the world's media time and again for its record-breaking achievements and landmarks or events. From the 'world's biggest', to 'world's highest' and 'world's first' and so on.

World records: here are some of them

- Burj Al Arab: the world's first seven star hotel
- Burj Khalifa: Formerly known as Burj Dubai: the world's tallest tower
- Dubai Mall: the world's biggest shopping mall
- Dubai Metro: the longest driverless network
- Ski Dubai: the first indoor ski resort in the Middle East
- Deira Gold Souq: the largest gold bazaar in the world
- Wild Wadi: has the highest and fastest water slide outside of North America
- Atlantis, the Palm: one of the largest open-air marine habitats in the world
- Dubai World Cup: the world's richest horse race
- Free Zones: the first free zones in the world for IT, outsourcing, media, biotechnology, among others
- Al Maktoum International Airport in Jebel Ali: will be the world's largest cargo and passenger hub with an annual cargo capacity of 12 million tonnes and a passenger capacity of 120–150 million passengers per year
- Floating Bridge: the longest floating bridge in the world
- Largest Flag: the world's largest flag at Union house.

ACTIVITY 13

You are now in a position to use Case study 11, and/or your own research into another destination of your choice, to help you consider the range of factors which determine how selected locations have evolved as tourism destinations. Now look at each section of table in turn.

Key features of the destination

Briefly describe how each of the following has had a positive influence on the development of tourism in the destination:

- weather and climate
- vegetation and wildlife
- modern built attractions

- accommodation options
- food/drink and entertainment
- scenery and landscape
- historical and cultural attractions
- indoor/outdoor activities
- events and festivals
- accessibility and gateways.

Tourist appeal by visitor type

Identify features of the destination that appeal to each of the following types of visitor. In each case give a brief explanation for your choices. You could present your findings in the form of a table such as the one shown below.

Visitor type	Destination features	Reason(s) for appeal
young people		
singles		
families		
DINKYs		
grey market		
special needs		
business tourists		

Table 4.4

Visitor statistics

Describe the recent trends in your destination's visitor numbers and offer a projection for the future based on current data. Using evidence from recent trends, suggest which stage of the Butler model the destination has reached giving reasons for your choice. What destination management activities might be implemented to bring about change for the future?

Factors influencing popularity

Briefly describe how each of the following might influence the number of tourists visiting your destination:

- cost of accommodation
- costs at destination

- destination promotional activity
- crime and social problems
- terrorism
- positive/negative tourism management
- growth in short breaks
- increased accessibility
- natural disasters
- cost of transport
- tour operator promotional activity
- over-commercialisation
- political instability and unrest
- positive/negative media coverage
- growth in independent travel
- exclusivity
- water/air/noise hazard

193

Change and development

The previous section details the enormous change in destinations that is ongoing. Dubai is an interesting example of how Butler's lifecycle model can be clearly demonstrated. Government, policy and imagination have conspired to create a destination that continues to inspire and appeal to a growing mass market.

Future development of tourist destinations and destination management

In the second decade of the 21st century, there are a variety of factors that will influence the future growth and development of tourist destinations around the world. In 2011, travel and tourism's total economic contribution, taking account of its direct impacts, was US$6.3 trillion in GDP, 255 million jobs, US$743 billion in investment and US$1.2 trillion in exports. This contribution represented 9% of GDP, 1 in 12 jobs, 5% of investment and 5% of exports. Over the medium term, the prospects of the industry are even more positive with average annual growth expected to be 4% through to 2022, by which time travel and tourism will employ 328 million people – or one in ten of all jobs on the planet.

The World Travel and Tourism Council (WTTC) predict that tourism development will experience the following trends:

- South and North-East Asia will be the fastest-growing tourism regions in 2012, growing by 6.7%, driven by countries such as India and China where rising incomes will generate an increase in domestic tourism spend and a sharp upturn in capital investment, and that there will be a tourism recovery in Japan.
- The mature economies of North America and Europe will continue to struggle in 2012. North America, which saw a slight upturn in the USA's economic situation at the end of 2011, should see growth of only 1.3% in travel and tourism direct GDP over the year.
- The prospects for travel and tourism growth in Europe in 2012 are precarious. Current forecasts suggest a 0.3% increase in direct GDP for the region overall, but this will be propped up by newer economies such as Poland and Russia. A decline of 0.3% is expected across the European Union. Consumer spending is set to tighten as austerity measures kick in, and there continues to be considerable uncertainty around the future of the Eurozone and peripheral economies of Greece, Spain, Italy and Portugal.

The WTTC makes these forecasts against a background of global uncertainty and, as we end this review of tourism development issues, we can consider what the future may hold for a country with a major tourism industry. We now look at the major issues influencing the future development of Thailand's tourism industry.

The tourism industry plays a crucial role in the Thai economy. It is the second largest source of revenue for the country. The Thai tourism industry has recently been facing the threat of a serious downturn due to a combination of unfavourable factors such as the worldwide economic recession, the H1N1 flu outbreak and domestic political instability. Key threats to the Thailand tourism industry are shown in Figure 4.47.

The Thai tourism industry was significantly affected by politics from late 2008 to mid-April 2009 when anti-government demonstrations led to riots in Bangkok. This was then followed by the crisis of May 2010 when the state used military forces to disperse a lengthy pro-democracy demonstration and killed scores of demonstrators. The number of international tourists to Thailand dropped sharply.

The presence of HIV/AIDS in Thailand has altered international tourist perceptions of what represents a safe and acceptable destination. Furthermore, Severe Acute Respiratory Syndrome (SARS) and avian influenza (bird flu) have both been significant factors in Thailand. As a clear example, SARS left behind the most negative impact in Thai tourism history, especially in 2003.

The current global economic situation is a strong factor that influences the Thai tourism industry. This can be seen with the fluctuation in the price of oil. If the Thai tourism industry is to maintain its current level of competitiveness then a government policy promoting stability will be required. The large proportion of GDP spent on importing oil and gas make the threat of inflation a constant one when oil prices are high, while this also has a negative impact on air fares and thus the willingness of international travellers to undertake long haul leisure journeys.

The 2004 tsunami had a major impact on Thailand and took 5395 lives, almost half of whom were international tourists. The tragedy affected the number of international tourists coming to Thailand for several years. It caused Thai tourism to decrease by 10% because international tourists were influenced by media reports and they were also worried about the state of the infrastructure and tourist facilities in affected resort areas.

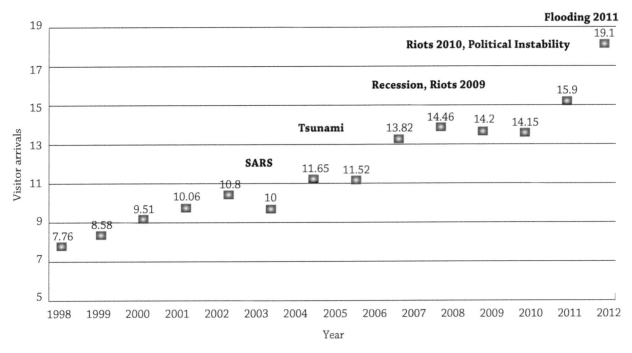

Figure 4.44 Factors influencing Thailand visitor arrivals 1998–2012

In spite of all these difficulties, the Tourism Authority of Thailand (TAT) announced that tourism arrival numbers for the Kingdom had returned to normal, following a slight decline at the end of 2011 due to the flooding. As the flooding started to recede, Thailand's tourism sector once again showed its resilience and returned to growth. With the co-operation of the public and private sectors, the TAT launched its 'Beautiful Thailand' campaign, which regained the confidence of international travellers and resulted in rapid growth in the number of tourist arrivals. By the end of 2011, Thailand welcomed a total of over 19 million international visitors, which represents annual growth of 20% compared to 2010.

Thailand started off 2012 strongly with over 300 000 international visitor arrivals during the first week of January. This is very close to the number of arrivals for the same period last year, demonstrating that Thailand's tourism sector has once again rebounded. However, for 2015, TAT targeted more than 30 million international arrivals, and hoped to increase this figure further in 2016.

Many other destinations in the world will be looking to mirror Thailand's experience. The future is uncertain, but there is no doubt that tourism will play a significant role in the continued growth and development of many MEDC and LEDC nations.

Summary

This chapter covers the variety of organisations that are involved in destination management. Their objectives are dependent upon to whom they are accountable, for example, a board of directors, the public or the government. Ultimately, this will dictate their priorities and activities. There are many activities that will be important to destination management, such as influencing policy and practice, working in partnership with other interested organisations and communicating with visitors and community members.

In understanding the objectives of tourism development and management it becomes clear that the process is one that has an overall aim of minimising the negative impacts of tourism whilst maximising the positive ones. Impacts are addressed by looking at economic, socio-cultural and environmental issues.

Exam-style questions

Question 1

Refer to Figure 4.45 for information about the redeveloped Victoria and Alfred Waterfront in Cape Town, South Africa.

The historic Victoria and Alfred Waterfront in Cape Town has been redeveloped as a mixed-use area with a focus on retail, tourism and residential development. The main purpose of the redevelopment scheme was to re-establish physical links between Cape Town and its waterfront area in order to create a quality environment that would become a desirable place to work, live and relax.

Cape Town's formerly declining old port area has now been transformed and the V&A Waterfront has become one of Africa's most visited destinations, with an average of over of 20 million people each year since 1997. Tour operators are being encouraged to market the area particularly to responsible tourists.

The building and restoration programme has introduced new land uses into previously derelict harbour warehouses, workshops and stores. Today, visitors are attracted to the waterfront area by the wide range of new facilities such as restaurants, taverns, speciality shops, the V&A Hotel, a theatre, an arts and crafts market, and the national Maritime Museum.

One of the more recent arrivals has been the Nautilus, a luxury 35-metre motor yacht permanently moored at Cape Town's V&A Waterfront. The yacht is licensed to carry 58 people at sea and can easily host a party of 110 people when moored at quayside. It offers customers lavish cruises as well as private hire for small conventions, cocktail parties and product launches.

Figure 4.45 Cape Town's V&A Waterfront

a Explain two positive social impacts that are likely to occur due to the redevelopment of urban areas for tourism purposes. **[4 marks]**

b Explain positive economic impacts that are likely to have resulted from the Waterfront's redevelopment. **[9 marks]**

c With reference to examples with which you are familiar, discuss how tour operators can encourage responsible tourism. **[12 marks]**

Question 2

Refer to for information about non-government organisation (NGO) – Tourism Concern. Tourism Concern works for ethical and fairly traded tourism wherever they can make a difference – campaigning, informing and supporting.

Figure 4.46 Tourism Concern action for ethical tourism logo

Different campaigns, same approach

Our campaigns are driven by the needs reported to us by the communities and organisations at destinations, or by travellers who have had problems on their holiday.

We consult with partners and stakeholders involved in tourism over issues such as water equity, land grab, international volunteering, work conditions and much more. We spend several months researching, investigating and collecting case studies. This enables us to find solutions.

Our campaigns require funding, and the search for support is an important part of our role. Our solutions are diverse. However, they always revolve around the following three areas:

1 Influencing
We aim to change the way that tourism is traded and developed through collaborative work with industry, government, development and human rights NGOs.

2 Creating alternatives
We create approaches to maximise tourism benefits to local communities through education and training.

3 Supporting communities
We help people and communities to be heard by supporting ethical tour operators such as Travel Indochina, who have been operating small group journeys and tailor-made holidays to Asia since 1993. Starting in Vietnam the company has grown to cover 11 destinations in Asia. They maintain a focus on cultural exchange and responsible local experiences. As well as offices in Australia, UK and the United States, Travel Indochina also has seven operations offices throughout Vietnam, Cambodia and Laos meaning they are able to control the content of their itineraries

and the actions of their suppliers. It also means they can employ local office staff wherever possible. They focus on responsible tourism and work with other social enterprises and NGOs. This includes the 'Streets International Training Restaurant' (provides a training programme for disadvantaged children) in the old port town of Hoi An in Vietnam; a deaf and blind workshop in Hue and a number of other socially minded organisations, including the Angkor Hospital for Children in Cambodia and Purkal Youth Society in India.

a   Tourism Concern is a non-governmental organisation (NGO). Describe **two** roles of a NGO. **[4 marks]**

b   Explain three principles of destination management. **[9 marks]**

c   Assess the ways in which ethical tour operators can support local communities. **[12 marks]**

Question 3

Refer to the information about tourism and its impacts on the Zambezi River.

Tourism needs careful planning to avoid impacts

The Zambezi River is recognised as a globally important wilderness tourism destination, with its major attractions including the Victoria Falls, the Batoka, Kariba, Mupata and Lupata Gorges, two man-made lakes as large as inland seas – Kariba and Cabora Bassa – and a combination of mountain habitats with abundant wildlife and spectacularly beautiful scenery. The river basin also incorporates two UNESCO World Heritage Sites (Victoria Falls/Mosi-oa-Tunya and Mana/Sapi/Chewore) and the Middle Zambezi Biosphere Reserve, as well as several of Africa's finest National Parks and safari areas. Its magnificent delta has, for centuries, been a focal point in the history and culture of the region.

With global tourism increasing annually, careful long-term planning is needed in order to prevent the pressure for tourism development and its associated impacts eroding the very wilderness values that make the Zambezi River such an attractive destination.

The effects of a growing tourism industry and pressure for more tourism development is most evident at Victoria Falls/Mosi-oa-/Tunya, the Zambezi River's most famous tourist destination. Lack of sensible planning and a tendency to ignore the wilderness and environmental factors in the rush for short-term profit, are in danger of reducing the quality of the visitor experience. After Zimbabwe's economic and political crisis years between 2000 and 2009, tourism has finally begun to return to the Zambezi Valley. There is now a clear policy to enhance the image and reputation of the destination over a long term. This requires working with other organisations such as the Zambezi Society and the Zimbabwe Parks & Wildlife Authority. These organisations are currently attempting to reduce tourism impacts in the Mana Pools area by:

- displaying its Respect the Wild Code of Conduct at tourist offices and encouraging visitors to read and understand its principles
- assisting with the introduction of a 'Carry-in-Carry-Out' policy for waste management in the Park
- assisting in the development of wilderness-sensitive tourism policies for incorporation into the Mana Pools Park Management Plan
- objecting to tourism development proposals that contradict the recommendations of the Park Management Plan.

a Outline **two** likely political objectives for developing tourism to the Zambezi Valley. **[4 marks]**

b With the return of tourism to the Zambezi Valley, assess the ways environmental impacts may be reduced. **[9 marks]**

c Evaluate the ways in which sustainable tourism development practices are likely to benefit destinations such as the Zambezi Valley. **[12 marks]**

Chapter 5
Planning and managing a travel and tourism event

In this section of the syllabus you will learn to:

- work as part of a team
- understand the processes for planning, managing and running a real-life event
- successfully complete an event
- produce a business plan and keep a record of your activities
- evaluate the whole programme of your chosen event
- make clear recommendations for the future.

Introduction

This chapter covers the coursework module for planning and managing a travel and tourism event. It gives a fantastic opportunity to work as part of a team to plan, carry out and evaluate a real project in the form of a travel or tourism event. The travel and tourism event market is huge and diverse. Events and event management companies can be found all over the world and they may specialise in specific events such as weddings or organise anything that a **client** desires, for instance fashion shows, business functions, music, holiday and sporting events (Figure 5.1). Their importance and worth within the industry should not be underestimated. Indeed, the UK events industry is said to be worth nearly £60 billion as it contributes £58.4 billion to the UK's gross domestic product (GDP).

Figure 5.1 Golf is a popular sport for event planners

> **KEY TERM**
>
> **Client:** individual or company booking an event.

Whilst the worldwide sports events market, (defined as all ticketing, media and marketing revenues for major sports), was worth €45 billion ($64 billion) in 2009. A country-by-country breakdown finds that the sports industry is growing faster than GDP both in fast-growing economies, such as the booming BRICS nations (Brazil, Russia, India, China and South Africa) and the MINT economies (Mexico, Indonesia, Nigeria and Turkey) and in more mature markets in Europe and North America. Football, the Olympics, swimming and golf remain some of the most popular sports for event planners.

Of significant interest is the strong, yet emerging market of the virtual event. Market research media shows that between the periods 2013 to 2018 the virtual event market will grow from nothing to $18.6 billion. This market is currently driven by corporate events however; it is believed that the evolution of event technology will soon incorporate the traditional conference and trade show.

For this chapter, the event organised must be set in a travel or tourism context, such as staging a conference, meeting or exhibition; the delivery of a guided tour or similar group activity; the running of a trip or other group venture. This coursework unit brings together prior learning from previous core elements of the course and candidates will be able to draw on experience in customer service, dealing with research and organising and maintaining records.

A detailed **business plan** should be produced. The plan should be developed as a group but presented individually.

The plan should cover:

- a description of the event
- objectives and timescales
- resources needed (physical, human and financial)
- legal aspects of the event (health and safety, security, insurance)
- methods to be used to evaluate the event.

A clear record of personal involvement in carrying out the team event must be included.

This can be in the form of a log book, personal notes (with dates of activities) and must include:

- details of their allocated task(s)
- details of any problems that arose and how individual team members responded to such difficulties
- details of deadlines and progress made towards each deadline
- an evaluation of their role of the event
- the effectiveness of the team in achieving the event's objectives.

This whole module culminates in the actual running and evaluation of the event, giving first-hand experience of a travel and tourism project in action.

201

5.1 Assessment

The work will be assessed through completion of a portfolio. Tutors will mark the coursework assignment and then forward the portfolio for external moderation.

Evidence should include:

- a business plan
- log book or other record of contributions through the planning of the project, including dealing with any problems
- details of research for the feasibility study and additional research during the management of the project
- an evaluation of personal performance, the team's performance and recommendations for both the organisational and personal improvement.

ACTIVITY 1

Look at your country and make a list of the top ten events that occur. Categorise them into:

- sport
- entertainment
- music, dance, arts
- business.

Latest IMEX America Index of Optimism results announced: Majority feel optimistic; meeting and event numbers plus budgets expected to increase slightly.

Keeping its finger on the pulse of the current mood and business potential within the North American meetings, events and incentive travel industry, IMEX America today announced results from its latest Index of Optimism survey. With the show's first principle being business generation, the Index of Optimism, which was conducted in March 2013, asked just over 400 North American respondents (70% buyers and 30% suppliers) to share how they felt about the meetings industry's business prospects over the coming months. **Result: Majority feeling positive and expecting to see some growth.**

Asked to compare their current levels of optimism to the same period (Q1) in 2012, 67% of respondents declared themselves 'more optimistic' than the same time in the previous year. Results also showed that just over 58% of respondents expected to see the number of meetings and events they organise increase slightly throughout 2013 and into the first quarter of 2014. Additionally 8.5% anticipate significant increases.

5.2 Stages in the event

Building a team

Before beginning to plan the event, candidates must gather into a small team. Suggested numbers are between four and six. This allows candidates to take responsibility for a specific role and to be able to share the workload.

Teamwork – the purpose of a team

There are plenty of definitions of teamwork. Teams are not simply a group of people without a purpose; they are a group of people who are jointly focused on a goal or product. The MIT Information Services and Technology definition of teamwork is:

> 'People working together in a committed way to achieve a common goal or mission. The work is interdependent and team members share responsibility and hold themselves accountable for attaining the results.'
>
> MIT Information Services and Technology

The success of the event depends on solid interaction of the team. Many travel and tourism projects hinge on the interaction of team members. A well-organised team can overcome problems and can help each other to devise innovative solutions and to work to their individual strengths.

The team structure

The event team will meet both informally and formally. Formal communication will be through planned meetings. These will give the opportunity to discuss specific tasks and allocate functions for individuals. The frequency and timing of these meetings will be dependent upon the timescale of the event. Formal meetings give the opportunity for feedback on tasks completed and for future actions. All formal meetings should be recorded. Each group member should retain a detailed log of what has been decided. The production of agendas and minutes should be integral to the formal meeting structure. Figure 5.2 provides an example of an agenda.

Understanding how teams work can be supported by the theories of Belbin or Tuckman. Teams need to meet regularly in order to fulfil the requirements for planning, working to deadline and monitoring targets. It is best that tutors teach candidates how to plan and run informal and formal meetings, including the use and production of agendas and minutes. Individual logs should be kept, recording activities undertaken and citing problems and how these were resolved.

Agenda

- welcome and introductions
- attendance
- apologies
- approval of the previous minutes
- matters arising
- update on event and dates
- specific agenda items to be discussed such as information on transport, venues, risks, legal issue, hospitality issues
- any other business
- date and time of next meeting.

Figure 5.2 Specimen of an agenda

Informal discussions may also take place on an *ad hoc* basis. These discussions may be the result of sudden changes in plans or decisions needing urgent attention.

Depending on the event organised, there may be a need to deal with outside agencies and external customers. If this is the case, good customer care skills, along with professional skills, must be employed. The event gives the opportunity to practise and mirror the skills required in the travel and tourism industry.

The following list could be useful:

- prioritising tasks
- the ability to discriminate between the trivial and the crucial
- knowing what resources to use and when
- working with a diary in order to accurately log activities
- employing communication skills: listening to each other
- keeping on task.

5.3 Forming – storming – norming – performing

One of the best-known theories of teambuilding was developed by Bruce Tuckman in 1965 and is known as the Forming – Storming – Norming – Performing model (Figure 5.3). Tuckman's theory of teambuilding looks at the way in which a team tackles a task from the initial formation of the team right through to the completion of the task. He also later added a fifth phase known as Adjourning and Transforming. Team challenges and teambuilding exercises are particularly relevant within this framework as teams are able to observe and assess behaviour within a determinate timeframe. As we have seen with the Olympics, events or team tasks can involve planning over many months or years and it can be difficult to understand or explain experiences in the context of completed tasks.

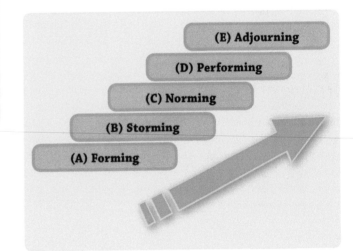

Figure 5.3 Tuckman's model of team building

Forming: is where the team is gathered together and tasks allocated. Team efforts involve planning, collecting information and bonding (forming good relationships between group members).

Storming: is where ideas are progressed. The team begins to look at the tasks in hand and bring different ideas and suggestions forward. This is a delicate stage of the proceedings as relationships between team members may become strained. This can create a negative imbalance and teams may become trapped in the Storming phase. Importantly, if a team settles on a consensus this may lead to a less effective completion of the tasks in hand. Careful guidance is needed and good leadership may well be the key.

Norming: is the stage where teams become harmonious and they are able to agree on the rules and standards on how they operate. The balance of working together leads to group members trusting each other as they begin to accept each other's contribution. The involvement and support of each member becomes the norm and the tasks become manageable as team members take on and complete roles. There may be risks involved with the norming stage where the team becomes complacent and the creative and proactive processes initially created in the storming stages are lost.

Performing: is where the team members are clearly aware of the task. They have shared visions for the event and are able to work without interference from others.

Figure 5.4 An event in progress

Adjourning: is seen as the completion of the group's event or tasks. Hopefully, these were completed successfully and group members are able to move on to new tasks.

Qualities of an effective team

The group dynamics are very important in all stages of planning an event. Should there be conflict or disharmony then there is a strong likelihood that the planning stages will be disrupted and the final event will be ruined. Therefore, it is important that team roles are made explicit in order that any misunderstandings or arguments can be ironed out in the very early stages of the event planning and do not hinder the working relationships between all parties. Good communication between group members is essential and it cannot be assumed that everyone possesses good communication skills at the outset. Good customer service skills may need to be employed.

Figure 5.5 A successful team requires appropriate leadership style

These involve:

*   listening skills
*   positive body language
*   verbal communication, including consideration of tone and intonation of speech
*   positive attitude and commitment to the project as a whole.

Within the context of a successful team, it may be useful to consider leadership styles. Different personalities and unusual personal characteristics may conflict and take up valuable time from the planning stages. A dynamic team should include individuals with diverse personalities. This should make for an interesting and exciting team and not one where there is constant conflict, which causes difficult working conditions. The following are well-documented leadership styles.

5.4 Autocratic leadership

Autocratic leadership is a classical leadership style. An autocratic leader usually likes to:

*   make as many decisions as possible
*   have the most authority and control in the decision-making process
*   retain responsibility rather than delegate
*   make decisions alone, with little consultation with work colleagues
*   work on the task in hand, with no interest in leadership development.

The autocratic leadership style is sometimes seen as a dated form of leadership and is not popular with other work colleagues. It is, however, still used as it often creates instant benefits and comes naturally to many leaders.

The benefits are said to include:

- A reduction in stress as the leader has responsibility for the project and therefore control of all decision-making.
- a belief that the team becomes more productive, as the leader is watching and controlling the amount of work that is produced
- improved operations, where the leader spots any problems in advance and all deadlines are strictly met
- quicker decision-making. When one person makes decisions with little consultation then the decisions can be made without dispute.

The disadvantages are said to include:

- work colleagues do not develop as they get no opportunity to expand their experience and lose the opportunity to gain new skills. This is said to lead to poorer decision-making and reduce the productivity in the long run
- autocratic leadership style is seen as easy but unpopular and creates an increased workload for the leader, who will then become overstretched and suffer ill health such as stress
- work colleagues dislike being told what to do all of the time. They become demotivated and may not be as productive.

Teams will become totally dependent on the leader and will have very little opportunity to make their own decisions and therefore their confidence and initiative are lost.

5.5 Democratic leadership

Democratic leadership is a style that promotes sharing of the responsibility by giving consideration to the views of all team members.

The main characteristics include:

- consultation with work colleagues on all major issues
- delegation of work tasks, giving the team members full control and responsibility
- the leader listens and responds to feedback from colleagues
- work colleagues are encouraged to become part of the leadership decision-making and to develop themselves.

 KEY TERM

Feedback: sharing of thoughts and observations following the completion of the event.

The benefits of democratic leadership style:

- There is a positive work environment where work colleagues are given the opportunity to have responsibility and to challenge themselves.

- There would be successful initiatives as consultation would be full, resulting in better decision-making.
- There is believed to be a greater degree of creative thinking as ideas are allowed to flourish and problems are solved in an atmosphere of positivity.
- There is a better working relationship between the team, and fewer conflicts result in lower staff turnover.

The disadvantages are said to include:

- lengthy consultations that hinder the decision-making process
- some colleagues feel that they are not really being listened to and that the leader will make their own decisions in the long run.

5.6 Bureaucratic leadership

Bureaucratic leadership is one where workers follow rules and procedures accurately and consistently. Leaders expect colleagues to have a business-like attitude to their work. Leaders gain power over decision-making and are ultimately able to exert their authority over work colleagues.

The benefits of bureaucratic leadership are:

- increased professional workplace where rules are enforced
- work quality is often meticulous as rules are followed
- work productivity can rise.

The disadvantages include:

- Some colleagues produce poor work as they become demotivated and suffer from low self-esteem by being told what to do all of the time.
- There is a lack of creativity.
- Poor communication results when colleagues have to go through a formal process to speak to their superiors.

KEY CONCEPTS

Change and development

The previous section details the importance of being able to work with others in order to effect a successful event. There are many thoughts on what a good team structure is and how leaders can be an important force for success. Personality traits will also play an integral role in the successful formation of any team, and being reactive and able to work in a variety of situations whilst remaining focused and calm are essential qualities for good results.

205

5.7 The team performance curve

It is often not straightforward for a group of individuals to come together to try to form a successful team. There may be confrontation and a person selected as the original leader may become unpopular and a change is enforced due to group dynamics and personality clashes. In 1993, Jon Katzenbach and Douglas Smith looked at the role of teams and they asserted that in order for a group to become a team they must pass a certain threshold. They devised five levels of teamwork which could be plotted onto a graph to form 'the team performance curve'. This curve takes on the appearance of a J-shape. Figure 5.6 shows the five stages. The Y (vertical) axis is the quality of performance by the team and the X (horizontal) axis is the team effectiveness over time. The five levels of teams are located along the curve.

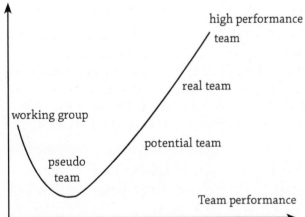

Figure 5.6 The team performance curve

The five stages are:

1   **Working group:** the members of the group come together. They are simply individuals with different skills and abilities. There is no solidity with the group having no common purpose or goals that require responsibility. At this stage, the group form roles for each member and divide the tasks.

2   **Pseudo team:** this team is located at the bottom of the curve and is therefore the weakest of the five levels. At this stage, there is no benefit to being within the team and members do not represent a working team; they are not interested in creating a common purpose or in achieving any final goals. There may be group disharmony and confusion over individual roles. This is perceived to be a dangerous stage of team development, as the team members believe that they are a real team but they produce inferior results.

3   **Potential team:** this type of team shows real gain in productivity and performance. Members work together on developing a clear purpose, including goals, and attempt to work towards solving problems and issues. This form of teamwork is common but may lack the discipline for working towards a common approach.

4   **Real team:** this consists of a small group of people who share a common purpose, goals and approach to work. They hold themselves mutually accountable for their results.

5   **High performance team:** this has all the same characteristics of the real team but the members are profoundly committed to each other and are mutually accountable. Team members form powerful relationships and work well together to exceed and achieve at a very high level.

5.8 Staffing for the event

Staffing for the event will be an important consideration. Within each group there will be members with differing skills and abilities and a strong group will play to each individual's strengths. Within the **feasibility study**, team roles and responsibilities will need to be identified. The business plan will dictate the actual roles and functions of each group member. The roles may include:

Chairperson or coordinator

This role is chiefly to ensure that tasks are completed. The person most likely to succeed in this role will be someone who has a personal record of being a consistent worker who has completed a job and is hard working. They should be able to make decisions, be fair and even-handed to all members of the group and persuasive. Ideal attributes include:

- to stimulate and inspire others
- enthusiastic, good-humoured
- able to work with all kinds of people
- help the group use all the abilities and experiences its members possess.

Marketing representative

- excellent spoken and written communication skills
- creative thinking
- good organisation and planning skills
- the ability to work well as part of a team
- drive, motivation and enthusiasm
- the ability to work under pressure and to deadlines
- the confidence to 'sell' your ideas
- attention to detail
- good business sense and budget awareness.

Finance representative

- good ability to work with figures
- able to safely calculate information regarding income and expenditure
- able to keep accurate records
- attention to detail
- able to keep details safe
- honest and hardworking.

Health and safety and security representative

- attention to detail
- able to work carefully within the given situation
- able to work through information and assess risks
- good at communication, and able to with people from all walks of life
- confidence
- sensible attitude towards working with others.

Administration representative

- good attention to detail
- able to stick to deadlines
- able to work well with others
- able to keep accurate and clear records
- honest and hardworking
- good computer skills
- clear handwriting and report writing skills.

KEY TERM

Feasibility study: assessment of the practicalities for running a proposed event.

Figure 5.7 Student visits require staffing assistance

These are only guidelines, but as a general rule, they are the main roles. Depending on the event chosen, there may be extra staffing to consider should an event involve younger children (Figure 5.7), charities, visits to local government sites and so on. Such events may also require staffing assistance outside of the small group, such as legal representatives, teachers and parents. In some instances, there will be clear guidelines regarding the ratio of children to adults and males to females. This will need to be carefully investigated in order for the event to run smoothly and have no legal or insurance complications.

The following case study shows an important and growing area in tourism known as 'team building'. Courses are offered to help organisations build strong working teams by helping to create trusting bonds between participants. These bonds can then relate back into the work place creating a strong team and highly effective workplace.

5.9 Investigate potential travel and tourism events and undertake feasibility studies

Before an event can be chosen, feasibility studies should be embarked upon. There are many different types of events – literary festivals, walking, food, sports, music and all manner of entertainments. Whatever event is planned, a detailed feasibility study must be conducted in the first instance. This is a thorough investigation into the viability of the event. This is to ensure that informed decisions

Welcome to Far and Wide Zimbabwe!

Figure 5.8

FAR and WIDE Zimbabwe is an outdoor adventure based team/leadership training school set in the beautiful wilderness areas of the Nyanga and Mutarazi Falls National Parks in Zimbabwe's Eastern Highlands.

In addition all our activities and wonderful accommodation options are available to families and tourists visiting the Nyanga and Honde Valley areas of Zimbabwe's Eastern Highlands.

See our exciting new TOP TEAMS Programme!

FAR and WIDE Extreme:

Canyoning adventures in the Nyanga National Park including 385 m abseil down Mutororo Falls... the highest commercial abseil in the world!

Turaco Trail... one of southern Africa's most beautiful multi day wilderness hiking trails.

FAR and WIDE MTB Trail... Single track mountain biking trail as well as free range trails throughout Nyanga National Park. Multi day trails with accommodation each night in exclusive villas and camps. Ride from FAR and WIDE to Aberfoyle Lodge.

Kayak Extreme... Guided white water kayaking expeditions on Pungwe, Gairezi Rivers and exclusive creeks in the Nyanga and Honde Valley areas of Zimbabwe's eastern Highlands.

Schools and Corporate

FAR and WIDE has been conducting team building and leadership training programmes for youth and company executives from Zimbabwe for over twenty years. Our mission is to teach leadership, team and life skills to young Zimbabwean school children and company executives whilst instilling in them an environmental awareness and social conscience. FAR and WIDE... if you are serious about outdoor based team building and leadership training for your organisation.

can be made and help to prevent mistakes and problems occurring when the event is running.

The feasibility study also forms the basis of the business plan. This sets out details of the proposal, including the operational management, marketing techniques, financial issues, staffing (including team roles) and the final method of evaluation.

Make as many suggestions for events as you possibly can. As soon as you have a good list, you can then begin to prioritise your preferences. For your event you must carry out a minimum of two, and a maximum of four, feasibility studies. Feasibility studies and selection of one event will be based on group discussions. Ideally, the final event chosen should involve both internal and external customers.

Whichever event is finally decided upon, it is vital that any discussion/decision making process is recorded on an individual basis.

ACTIVITY 3

Complete the following grid to assist with event planning.

Event suggestion	Pros	Cons
day trip to a visitor attraction		
exchange visit with students from another country		
overseas visit		
promoting an event for a travel or tourism product		
conference tourism		
tourism careers conference		
guided tour		

Table 5.1

5.10 Technology in the travel and tourism market

An exciting and emerging market is that of the virtual conference and trade show. Technology is a vital ingredient in the travel and tourism market. Traditionally it has been an area of skills shortage; however this picture is now changing thanks to the relentless availability of software and new applications. Today, social media forms an integral part of our leisure and business lives. Mobile phones, iPods, iPads and tablets are the new vocabulary.

Technology is also a driving force for shaping the future of events and cannot be ignored. Web-based conferences are seen to be a cheaper option than flying delegates around the world.

Figure 5.9 shows the influence of the electronic age in an area where gaming, social media and all forms of communication link strongly to the growth in technology.

It is believed that there will be a huge growth in virtual conferences and trade shows.

This includes:

- the software and licensing needed to support the growth
- the administration services of conference organisers
- and, of course, the sponsorship, media and training required to ensure virtual success.

It is thought that the virtual conference market will be worth over US$18 billion by 2018.

Figure 5.9 Virtual conference and trade market show

KEY CONCEPTS

Change and development

The growth of the event management sector is certainly on an upward trend. The use of technology is having an important impact on the way events are run. Many organisations do not need to travel around the globe but will use web based technology to meet and organise events with their teams.

CAGR (compound annual growth rate)

This refers to the year-over-year growth rate of an investment over a specified period of time. The compound annual growth rate is calculated by taking the nth root of the total percentage growth rate, where n is the number of years in the period being considered. This can be written as follows:

Discuss the feasibility studies and select one event

Here are the feasibility study questions to consider before preparing the business plan:

1 Who is in the group and what skills do they have?

2 How many group members are there/will there be? Remember, small groups are best.

3 What type of event suits the group and will not become dull to plan?

4 What might be the aims and objectives of the event?

5 What types of customers are going to be attracted to this event?

6 How much will the customers be willing to pay?

7 How much money is likely to be needed to run the event?

8 How do you tell people about the event?

9 Will you be able to get sponsorship or donations to run the event?

10 Will your school or college be happy that they are associated with such an event?

11 Are there likely to be any negative responses to running a particular event?

12 Will your income match your expenditure?

13 Are all in the group hard working and prepared to meet possible difficult deadlines?

14 What are the time frames for the event? Do you have a realistic amount of time to run it successfully?

15 Are there any legal constraints that might have an effect on the running and operation of the event?

16 Consider seasonality, tangibility and perishability of the travel and tourism event

17 Consider the SWOT analysis.

SWOT analysis

Following the answers to the initial questions regarding the proposed event, it will now be necessary to seriously consider a SWOT analysis to help with finally formulating a business plan. SWOT stands for Strengths, Weaknesses, Opportunities and Threats. SWOT analyses are used by businesses and marketing departments when they are planning a business venture or campaign. It aids in the consideration of all the issues that may affect a promotion, event or campaign – both positive and negative. Understanding these issues helps to strengthen subsequent steps and prevent failures. Strengths and Weaknesses are internal factors while Opportunities and Threats are external factors – those factors that are beyond the control of the organisation.

In the real world of travel and tourism a SWOT analysis (Figure 5.10) is an important tool to assist an organisation in its planning and promotion of certain goods or services.

For example, a tour operator may decide not to promote a particular holiday destination if the weaknesses and threats outweigh the strengths and opportunities. Travel and tourism products and services are set within a dynamic industry, one where trends and global issues can affect the success and stability of specific tourism products and services. Holiday destinations are certainly susceptible to this and may no longer be a viable option for a tour operator to promote should there be, for example, a war, civil unrest (Figure 5.11), natural disaster, acts of terrorism and so on.

Figure 5.10 SWOT analysis

Figure 5.11 Civil unrest in Egypt affected tourism

210

Research one of the most well-known events in the Scottish calendar: the Royal Edinburgh Military Tattoo. Follow the link to http://www.edintattoo.co.uk/the-experience/about-the-tattoo and read about the Tattoo and the plans that the organisers have.

Your event will not be as detailed and complicated as this, but you will appreciate the planning and importance of team roles in making and staging such spectacles. Mentioned here is a small excerpt.

Performers at the Tattoo come from over 48 countries and approximately 30% of the 220 000 audience each year are from overseas destinations. The Tattoo sees itself as a global gathering of musicians and performers, where they can showcase their singing, dancing, acting and musical talents. The Tattoo is televised in over 40 countries with an audience of 100 million people. The international flavour of the Tattoo has been deliberately developed in order to entertain audiences from every part of the globe.

The world is coming together for the 66th Tattoo

2015 saw the world's most spectacular military Tattoo host a parade of talent from four continents as the showpiece event celebrates 'East Meets West'.

East Meets West

Set against the stunning backdrop of Edinburgh Castle, a spine-tingling presentation included pipers, drummers, singers and dancers, as well as one of the world's most sensational percussion groups, Switzerland's Top Secret Drum Corps.

With state-of-the-art production technology including 21st-century surround sound, compelling graphic installations and ultra-modern lighting, the 90-minute show also celebrates Scotland's creative assets and will dazzle and enthrall a worldwide audience.

CASE STUDY 2

Spain to host World Tourism Day

The World Tourism Organisation (UNWTO) is the United Nations agency responsible for the promotion of responsible, sustainable and universally accessible tourism. Each year, they hold several conferences on tourism with a variety of relevant and up to date themes. The following is an extract highlighting World Tourism Day in Spain from 2012, with the theme of tourism and sustainable energy.

Spain to host World Tourism Day 2012 under the theme Tourism and Sustainable Energy

Madrid: The official World Tourism Day (WTD) celebrations will be held in Maspalomas, Gran Canaria, Spain (27 September). Under the theme 'Tourism and Sustainable Energy: Powering Sustainable Development', WTD highlights the need to bring the tourism sector and energy stakeholders closer together to spur tourism's contribution to sustainability.

'Tourism is at the forefront of many of the latest and most innovative sustainable energy initiatives,' said UNWTO Secretary-General, Taleb Rifai. 'One only has to think of the investments being poured into renewable energy sources for aviation, or the energy technology solutions implemented in hotels around the world, to know that sustainable energy is a major priority for the sector.'

About World Tourism Day

World Tourism Day is celebrated annually on 27 September. Its purpose is to foster awareness among the international community of the importance of tourism and its social, cultural, political and economic value. The event seeks to address global challenges outlined in the UN Millennium Development Goals (MDGs) and highlight the contribution the tourism sector can make in reaching these goals.

Planning and promoting an event such as this would provide the organisers with major considerations. They must first consider what their aims and objectives are, where they should hold the event, who they are trying to attract and at what costs. Their overall objectives appear in the form of a mission or vision statement:

to work in six main areas – competitiveness, sustainability, poverty reduction, capacity building, partnerships and mainstreaming – to achieve responsible, sustainable and universally accessible tourism.

5.11 Aims and objectives for the chosen event

For the planned event there should be a **mission and/ or vision statement**. That is a phrase or sentence that sums up exactly what is to be achieved and why. A mission statement can help to focus and make clear the intentions of the group and assist with clarifying overall aims and objectives. The mission statement of the Olympic Games is shown next.

The Olympic Games originated in Greece and dates back to the 4th century. The reintroduction of the Olympics in the modern era began in 1896. The now famous five Olympic rings were designed to symbolise each one of the world's inhabited continents at the time and they were first seen at the Antwerp games in 1920. The motto 'Citius, Altius, Fortius' (Faster, Higher, Stronger) was introduced at the outset of the International Olympic Committee (IOC). In 1924, the first Winter Olympic Games were held in Chamonix, France.

The IOC's mission statement was:

> ...to contribute to building a peaceful and better world by educating youth through sport practised without discrimination of any kind, in a spirit of friendship, solidarity and fair play.
>
> http://www.olympic.org/olympism-in-action

The Olympic Games must be one of the most difficult to arrange, but most popular and well known events in the world. Not only are there athletes to cater for, but there are the millions of people watching different events, **venues** to be prepared, health, safety and security to be considered, along with catering, accommodation and a network of support and coaching staff to look after. With all this in mind, the games must be a major headache for event planners. It is estimated that one billion people, or 15% of the world's population, watched the opening ceremony to the Beijing Olympics in 2008 (842 million people). The Beijing games were in preparation for nearly seven years. This preparation period is usually fairly lengthy as new facilities and venues need to be built. Researching, planning and building is often a complicated process. It may be necessary to apply for planning permissions, reclaim land and demolish current facilities. There may be extra consideration needed for potential hazards such as extreme climatic conditions, labour disharmony such as strikes and, of course, unexpected threats such as terrorism or political unrest.

KEY TERM

Venue: A place to hold meeting or event.

Figure 5.12 National Stadium during the Beijing Olympics opening ceremony, China

It is interesting to note that in 1896 in Athens, only 241 athletes from 14 countries took part in the games, while in 2008, more than 10 000 athletes from 204 nations took part in Beijing (Figure 5.12). In 2012, the Olympics moved to London. The media and marketing associated with the event had been in the planning and development stages since the destination was announced some four years previously. The BBC (British Broadcasting Corporation) estimated that 42 million people watched the BBC coverage of the Olympics, providing 2500 hours of live action for the TV viewers with 1233 cameras in place to host the broadcast coverage with 40 000 m of cable laid out within the Olympic Park. The logistics of putting together such an undertaking is difficult to comprehend, but the process of organising, planning and attention to detail ensured both the visual and economic success of the event. For 2016 the Olympic and Para Olympic Games will be in Rio de Janeiro, Brazil where they expect to see 10 500 athletes from 205 countries compete in 42 sports.

Aims and objectives for the event should become clearer when the mission statement is complete. Events may have more than one goal and may have a primary and several secondary purposes such as raising funds for a local charity and raising the profile of the school or college. Others include developing and working in a team, providing benefits for the group and local community, raising the awareness of the travel and tourism course and meeting the requirements of the budget set. Whatever is decided, all aims and objectives should follow the SMART criteria.

SMART is an acronym that stands for:

Specific — clearly applicable to the chosen event

Measurable — can be assessed for its effectiveness

Achievable — an event that can be easily completed within the time and deadlines

Realistic — can be achieved within the financial guidelines

Timed-framed — deadlines and the stages that are taken towards the finished event are achievable.

These aims and objectives should also take into consideration the target audience of the event. There must be a broad understanding of not only who it is aimed at but also why it should be aimed at a certain section of the population. Not knowing who your customers are makes the organisation and planning extremely difficult.

5.12 Marketing the event

Assuming that aims and objectives and the mission statement are in place, the marketing and promotion of the event can begin to take place. Marketing is a vital tool in aiding any business or event to gain success. Essentially, marketing is concerned with 'getting the right product to the right people at the right time in the right place and at the right cost'. This is a well known phrase, but one which all event organisers should remember.

There is simply no point in organising an event if the intended customers do not receive the information. Customer needs and expectations must be met, and deciding how to get the event message across will result in its ultimate success or failure. Event organisers should draw up a marketing plan. This includes the following:

- the mission statement
- aims and objectives
- proposed marketing strategy, including available budget
- a statement concerning the marketing mix, known as the 4Ps: Price, Product, Place and Promotion (see Figure 5.13).

Product
The event.

Price
The actual cost of planning and running the product (event) and the amount that the customers pay to attend (if appropriate).

Place
Two aspects for place: one is the physical location where the event is due to take place; the other is the chain of distribution used to get the product to the customers.

Promotion
The methods used to get the message across to the customers. Using advertising, press releases, broadcasting and the internet and so on.

Figure 5.13 Marketing mix

 KEY CONCEPTS

Customer focus

The previous section highlights the need to understand marketing and target effectively. The variety of methods available to event organisers are often linked to the use of technology and there must be careful consideration to the overall budget.

 KEY TERM

Questionnaire: a tool for gathering information by asking questions from a certain group of people. Answers can be written in person, spoken or online.

Market research

As part of the overall marketing strategy, market research may be required. Marketing research traditionally involves one of the following: **questionnaires** (postal), telephone or internet surveys and focus groups. Some form of market research will enable a clear understanding of the needs and wants of potential customers. In fact, a simple questionnaire could easily assist with identifying potential customers and if there is a demand for the intended event.

Questionnaire design can be a detailed and involved procedure. However, it can also be simplified in order to gain a reasonable outcome.

Generally the benefits of using a questionnaire are that it can:

- target a large number of people.
- reach respondents in many locations
- be relatively low cost in time and money
- be relatively easy to get information from people quickly
- provide standardised questions
- provide analysis that is straightforward and responses that are pre-coded.

Questionnaires should be made using the following points:

- Ask as many potential customers as possible.
- Keep the layout and design as simple as practical (Figure 5.14).
- Try not to include any distractions, such as unnecessary pictures or fonts.
- Offer yes/no responses or multiple choice style alternatives. This will help with analysing the results.
- Do not include any irrelevant questions, many people do not like completing questionnaires and a long, detailed affair will only serve to discourage completion.

Give a timeframe for completion of the questionnaire.

Figure 5.14 Questionnaires should have simple layout and design

Advertising and promotion

As soon as information has been gathered, it can then be clear whether or not the event has the potential to run. The next stage of the event can then proceed with the creation of an advertising and promotion strategy in order to get the message out to the customers. Then advertising through posters, newspapers and newsletters can go

ahead. It may be possible to contact the local radio station and the local press by issuing a press release and giving the necessary information. Within marketing strategies, the promotion aspect is seen to be an important feature for raising awareness of a product or service.

There are five main aspects to the promotional mix:

1 Advertising: printing of leaflets, brochures, advertisements on TV, radio, billboards, direct mail, signs, posters, displays, web pages, banners and emails.

2 Personal selling: persuading people to purchase certain aspects such as tickets, products or services. This can be done through sales meetings, presentations, selling face to face, internet and telephone.

3 Sales promotion: promotions done over a limited period of time to increase sales and demands. This usually helps to stimulate the market and most common methods include coupons, competitions, raffles or lotteries, trade shows and exhibitions.

4 **Public relations** (PR): supplying up to date and relevant news about the event or product in order to generate a favourable impression. This is usually done via the TV, radio and internet, and can also include contributions within speeches, seminars and presentations.

5 Direct marketing: a form of advertising that involves communication of a product or service direct to customer through mobile messaging, email, interactive websites, fliers, promotional letters and leaflets.

KEY TERM

Public relations: a promotional technique used by organisations to show their products or services in a positive light. This may include writing press releases, attending press conferences, lobbying and attending trade fairs.

Email marketing

Promoting facilities, products or services by email can be a powerful and flexible form of direct marketing. Messages can be sent quickly and are very cost effective. Messages can easily be tailor-made for your event. Email marketing is more successful if it focuses on people who you know are interested in what you are doing. Focus should be made on your USPs (unique selling points). Remember that email marketing is governed by laws on **data protection**, privacy and e-commerce.

Social media and the web

In the 21st century a second generation of internet users has developed. Customers are no longer satisfied with static websites, they want to engage with products and expect more dynamic and user generated content. Information must be honest, up to date, and in some instances there should be a way for customers to respond

and get involved such as through blogs, Twitter, Facebook and LinkedIn. There is also the possibility to do video sharing such as YouTube and **Podcasts**.

KEY TERMS

Podcast: digital audio file that can be downloaded from the internet.

Data Protection Act 1998: UK law covering the rights and responsibilities of dealing with personal data.

Promotion via press conference

Seychelles' first international Music Festival – a true brand of cultural tourism

April 26, 2012: With the increasing demand of unique destination experiences, Seychelles continues to shape its country's brand of cultural tourism by unveiling the first edition of the International Music Festival – strings vibration – to be held from 15–19 May, 2012.

In a joint press conference with the Organizing Committee of the Zikanzil International Music Festival, the Seychelles Minister for Tourism and Culture, Alain St. Ange, has highly praised the Zikanzil concept, saying that 'it appropriately falls within the strong branding of cultural tourism.'

'Zikanzil is one of a kind, an international music festival which showcases the artistic talents of the Seychelles and the Indian Ocean region. It's a pure and culturally untamed experience, which establishes bridges, mutual understanding, and creative cooperation between representatives from many countries. It has passed the test of time and the challenges it has faced, and all that remains is for this festival to become a major event of Seychelles' destination attractiveness.'

Initiated by 'Alliance Francaise', the Seychelles French-based institution promotes cultural diversity and French language. The five-day festival will feature a number of Seychelles music's biggest names with a multi-texture of sounds, namely: Jany de Letourdie, Ralf, David Andre, and Patrick Victor, appearing alongside Emmanuelle Peters and Rene Sida from the Reunion islands, Linda Volahasiniaina (alias Vola), and the masculine version

of Vola, Michel Rafaralahy from Madagascar, and Seychelles' own Jude Ally, Joel Manglou from Reunion, and Abaji from Lebanon.

The Seychelles Minister for Tourism and Culture said that 'the major reason that makes this festival special is its five-day music extravaganza involving some of the top, most well-known artists.'

The Vice President of Alliance Francaise, Mrs Marquise David, said that the annual International Music Festival is set to become a distinctive tourist attraction in Seychelles.

'The Music Festival has the potential to become one of Seychelles' niche cultural assets. The blend of cultural harmony, which constitutes this festival, showcases the dynamism of our culture. Zikanzil is a platform for cultural exchanges and that of universal language.'

Figure 5.15 Zikanzil International Music festival

Two other elements of promotional mix may also be added. These are:

- Corporate image: linked to the reputation of the organisation, for example, customers are more willing to buy a product from a company that has a good, strong image or one that is compatible with their own morals and beliefs, such as an eco-friendly company or one that has charitable links.
- Sponsorship: this is where an organisation may see fit to give some form of support or additional backing. This is not always given from a monetary perspective; it could also be through the provision of extra resources, such as free printing, assistance with advertising slots and advice.

ACTIVITY 5

Successful presentation tips

It may be useful to present ideas to customer groups or other team members regarding an event. Complete a checklist of items to be included in the preparation for a successful presentation.

The first one is done for you:

1   In advance of the presentation, check and confirm the facilities available.

2

3

4

5

Press release

Practise writing a press release for the chosen event. Include information that covers the following – who, what, where, when and why.

5.13 Use of appropriate resources

Venues, equipment and materials

Staging an event requires a variety of resources. These will include physical resources such as the venue. The venue may be as large as an arena, school hall, school field or an off-site venue such as a visitor attraction, national park or a small venue such as classroom or tent. There may be a need for portable equipment such as tables, chairs, flip charts, computers with PowerPoint. The connection and location of important utilities should also be considered. This may impact on the success of the event where electricity, gas and water supplies are needed. The preparation, sale and consumption of food and drink will

need to conform to regulations on health and hygiene and licence applications.

KEY CONCEPTS

Customer focus

The previous section sets out the importance of public relations as an essential tool in today's busy marketing world. Information is transferred immediately around the world and in order to effect a clear and up to date message, public relations must never be ignored.

ACTIVITY 6

The following poster is an advertisement for Brunei. It has been constructed using the 1 principle. Consideration has been given to colour, font, words used and imagery, and includes the reasons for the poster. This particular example is to promote the official Brunei Tourism App.

Study the design of the poster using the AIDA principle. How successful has it been? Would you make any improvements? Make notes on a poster design for your event. What information do you need to provide?

Figure 5.16 Advertisement for Brunei

KEY TERMS

AIDA: an acronym used in marketing to assist with the design and promotion of marketing material such as a poster, it is taken to mean: Attention, Interest, Desire and Action. It shows the process of how a consumer engages with certain products, for example, an advertisement must bring the product to the **Attention** of the customer, stimulate **Interest**, provoke **Desire** and then motivate the consumer into **Action** to buy the advertised product.

5.14 Finance

When considering the event through a feasibility study, the subject of finance will certainly have been considered. Whether there is a small budget or not, most events will incur some form of costs.

There may be an amount allotted to the event by college/school funds, or there may be a need to fund-raise in order to support the whole project. Start-up costs can be off-set by charging the customers a fee (entry or participation). There may be a delay in receiving payments and this may cause cash flow issues and can possibly affect the staging of an event. Therefore, timing and receipts should be carefully managed.

Essentially it is important to consider the start-up costs of the event such as basic materials, and venue hire. The basic running costs for the event could include providing paper, pens, tickets and food, and income can be raised through the sale of tickets, raffles, entry fees, charging to participate, sponsorships or donations. Payments will need to be administered to receive and bank monies received. In many schools and colleges, the handling of cash must be undertaken by staff and not students. The monitoring of funds and how they are apportioned must be tightly controlled otherwise inaccurate figures and projections can cause an event to fail.

ACTIVITY 7

Here is a suggested list for the equipment and venue for a conference style event.
Complete the opposite side of the table for your event.

Venue and equipment needed for a conference style event	Venue and equipment needed for the suggested event
conference room	
signing in area	
signs with routes clearly labelled	
paper	
pens and pencils	
computer with PowerPoint	
flipchart with pens	
appropriate sound acoustics	
interactive whiteboard	
windows with blinds	
flexible lighting with dimmable lights	
lectern	
microphones/speakers	
stage	
tiered seating that may offer flexibility to have breakout sessions if required	
good parking	
fire exits and fire escape	
accessible toilets	
tables	
chairs	
tablecloths	
water and glasses and other refreshments	
catering	
first aid provision	

Funding sources

Depending on the event, funding sources will vary greatly. It may be possible to ask the school or college for assistance. Parents and students may also be asked to contribute. Local sponsorship is also a useful source of funding. Running a cultural show could involve asking local retailers, hoteliers, travel agencies and so on for assistance. This assistance may not always come in the form of direct cash donations, but may be in the form of facilities, equipment, human resources, volunteers and other support in kind, such as providing free posters, leaflets and brochures or offering advice and guidance. Assistance can also come in the form of the provision of a useful list of local contacts that may be of benefit to an event for marketing purposes.

The event should be viewed as a small business where funds and responsibilities are clearly maintained in order to prevent any misappropriation of funds. Many events will involve receiving funds directly from participants and visitors. Entrance fees or participation fees must all be accounted for carefully and the following sections detail common financial procedures.

Funding allocation

Expenditure for each aspect of the event must be carefully recorded. Sufficient funds must be available in order that payments can be made. Contingency funds must also be considered should there be any unexpected costs. Many events that are organised for the first time can incur unforeseen requirements and costs. Some of these costs may not have been considered when the plans were discussed at the outset. It is not always easy or possible to predict fully for every eventuality, but some costs may be covered by appropriate insurance cover or contingency funds.

Income and expenditure

The event organised may not incur many costs but it is important that a budget for the event is produced. There are often extra costs incurred in events and changes to the income and expenditure budget need to be altered in the budget accordingly. Some events are planned to 'break even' where all income matches the expenditure. Some events may aim to make a profit. It may be that the event is organised to raise funds for a specific cause, such as a local charity or to fund prizes during the event. Figure 5.18 shows the budget sheet for cultural tourism day.

Figure 5.17 'Ponle Freno' charity race at El Retiro, Madrid, Spain

Income and expenditure budget

Costs	Expenditure (£)	Income (£)
funds from school tourism budget		50.00
income from entry fees (ticket sales) to cultural event 100 × £2.00	200.00	
income from sale of teas and coffees		50.00
hire of hall for cultural event 2 hours	50.00	
cost of buying tea, coffee	15.00	
hire of tables and chairs	25.00	
marketing costs	10.00	
hire of costumes for display	50.00	
stationery costs	5.00	
Profit		145.00

Figure 5.18 Budget sheet of cultural tourism day

Cash flow

Cash flow is linked to the event timescales. It tells an organisation or event manager how much money is in the bank at any one time. It will show the amount of surplus or deficit on received funds/income less expenditure made. A cash flow forecast reflects anticipated timings of income and expenditure and resulting balance figures. This is usually done on a month-by-month basis and is used to determine balance figures in the bank and to avoid cash flow difficulties.

Cash flow forecast						
	Month A	Month B	Month C	Month D	Month E	Totals
Opening balance	£ 0.00	£ 50.00	£ 25.00	£ 5.00	£ 95.00	
Income	£ 50.00	£ 50.00	£ 45.00	£ 105.00	£ 50.00	£ 300.00
Expenditure	£ 0.00	£ 75.00	£ 65.00	£ 15.00	£ 0.00	£ 155.00
Closing balance	£ 50.00	£ 25.00	£ 5.00	£ 95.00	£ 45.00	£ 145.00

Income and expenditure account						
	Month A	Month B	Month C	Month D	Month E	Totals
Date						
Income (£)						
Funds tourism	£ 50.00					£ 50.00
Ticket sales		£ 50.00	£ 45.00	£ 105.00	£ 00.00	£ 200.00
Sale teas/coffees					£ 50.00	£ 50.00
Total income						£ 300.00
Expenditure (£)						
Hall hire		£ 50.00				£ 50.00
Cost of tea/coffee				£ 15.00		£ 15.00
Hire tables/chairs		£ 25.00				£ 25.00
Marketing costs			£ 10.00			£ 10.00
Hire of costumes for display		£ 50.00				£ 50.00
Stationery costs			£ 5.00			£ 5.00
Total expenditure						£ 155.00

Table 5.2 Cash flow forecast and income and expenditure account for the cultural tourism show

An event organiser may have to buy goods in advance of the event before ticket sales are realised. A cash flow analysis would identify monies required for a possible (bank) loan (school fund) in order to be able to pay for the goods. Cash flow forecasting statements can be done manually or on a computer spreadsheet app. Table 5.2 shows the cash flow forecast as well as the income and expenditure account for the cultural tourism show.

5.15 Financial documents used whilst organising an event

Event organisers may consider giving themselves a trading name or title that seems appropriate to the event such as Sunshine Tours (for a guided trip) or Travel Bites (for a tourism cultural food day). Whatever is decided, it is important that all financial documents are kept up to date. These documents are used to support all evidence for the event or project. The most commonly used documents are given next and are used in business transactions throughout the world. It is important to keep a full 'audit trail' in order to show where all the monies have come from and what they have been spent on and to show 'transparency'.

It may be necessary to ask for quotations for certain goods or services, such as asking a local caterer to quote for providing lunches for 50 people. If the quote is acceptable, then a purchase order can be raised. This may be done through school or college or via a bank account that is set up specifically for the event through the school/college system. Most businesses keep purchase order forms in number order so that they can accurately record and trace expenditure and complete details easily. Invoices are sent from the supplier, such as from the caterer. The invoice can then be paid as soon as the goods are received and are accurate as to what had been ordered. Payment may be made by cheque or through an electronic system known as BACS (Banking Automatic Clearing System). This is where money is transferred from one organisation to another using given bank account details. Should a cheque or cash be used to pay an invoice, then a receipt must be given. This is an important record of payments made.

On occasion, payments or a **deposit** may be requested in advance of receiving goods/services.

- **Invoices:** an official document that requests payment for goods or services rendered. It contains supplier name and address, VAT registration number, if applicable, date of invoice, invoice number, tax point/date, payment terms (for example, to be paid within 28 days) and payment methods.
- **Purchase order statements:** provides details of goods or services requested.
- **Cheques:** a form of payment method instructing a transfer between accounts to a bank account.
- **Receipts:** written evidence of payments received.
- **Quotations:** written details of goods or services with anticipated costs for the stated goods or services, usually within or valid for a specified time limit.
- **Delivery notes:** evidence of goods received usually signed and dated.
- **Ticket stubs:** evidence of tickets sold, each stub corresponds to one particular ticket that has been issued, usually identified by a number and/or letter. This usually contains the name, title and date/time of event and may include row and seat number.
- **Bank statements:** these are issued by the bank and show the latest transactions that have occurred in the form of income and expenditure from a particular account over a stated period.

KEY TERM

Deposit: partial payment made in advance of the event to secure the booking.

5.16 Business plan

A business plan (Figure 5.19) should include the following:

- an event summary: an overview of the business you want to start
- a short description of the event: who you are, what you plan to do or offer, why and to whom
- your marketing and sales strategy: why you think people will buy into your event, what you want to sell, and to whom, and how you plan to sell to them
- the team: people you plan to work with (including yourself) and the roles they will be undertaking

- operations: where the event will take place, production facilities, your management information systems, staffing, resources, procedures and IT
- financial forecasts: this section translates everything you have said in the previous sections into numbers
- evaluation: methods to assess success or failure; this is from a personal perspective, team reflections and group interaction.

KEY CONCEPTS

Sustainability and responsibility

The previous business plan is an essential tool in the provision of a successful event. Consideration must be given to good practice and tourism theory in order that all elements are covered to a good standard. This ensures that good theory results in excellent practice.

Event timescales

Details of set times and events should be included in all planning in order to prevent mishaps and to ensure the fulfillment of both the event and the portfolio. Figure 5.19 is an example of a simple **Gantt chart**, which allows clear planning of all expected activities along a timeline. The chart helps to plan activities in sequence and show overlaps of activities going on at the same time. It shows how one activity depends on the successful completion of other activities in order for the next one to take place. Obviously different events will require different planning tasks. This must be taken into consideration when using a Gantt chart as a planning tool.

KEY TERMS

Gantt chart: an event management planning calendar, identifying tasks to be undertaken by whom and when.

Critical path analysis: a planning tool to assist with complex and time-sensitive events, helping to determine which activities are crucial.

KEY CONCEPTS

Change and development

The importance of understanding the need to keep to good time frames must not be underestimated. Planning tools are used in many organisations and an event is often made up of a complex set of workable tasks. Diaries, charts and working through a **critical path** of occurrences will all assist with the final execution of a successful event.

Event timescales	Custo	1 Sept	7 Sept	14 Sept	21 Sept	2 Oct	9 Oct	16 Oct	23 Oct	30 Oct	6 Nov
zone	Week commencing	█									
initial meeting		█									
feasibility study			█								
business plan			█								
marketing			█								
provisional bookings				█							
risk assessment				█							
legal documents					█						
confirm bookings						█					
collect monies							█				
parental consents if required							█				
itinerary or plan for the day							█				
rota for staff on the event day								█			
organise evaluation sheets								█			
day of the event									█		
evaluate event									█		
portfolio write-up completion										█	█

Figure 5.19 Gantt chart for planning event

ACTIVITY 8

Music festivals can be found around the world. One of the most important music festivals is the Umbria Jazz Festival. It has been running each year since 1973 in Perugia in Italy. There is also a Winter Jazz Festival that takes place in December in Orvieto. Research a music festival that takes place and look at the event timescales.

- Try to assess exactly when the event organisers begin to plan the event.
- What issues must they consider in order to ensure that the event actually takes place for when it is scheduled?

ACTIVITY 9

Use the following check list and make a note of the sources used for financial and staffing resources.

Budget	Sources
loan	
sponsorship	
donations	
grant	
income	

Staff resources	Sources
volunteers	
stewards	
vendors	
caterers	
security cover	
drivers	
emergency services	
clean up staff	

Materials and equipment	Sources
computers	
printing	
photocopying	
chairs	
rooms	
hall	
field	
car park	

Table 5.3

You will be able to add different resources to each of these sections as appropriate for your event.

KEY TERMS

Master of ceremonies (MC): organiser and caller of proceedings during the event itself.

VIP: important attendees at your event for example, local Mayor, head teacher, local MP.

Planning an event

The following information is based on a 'How to…' idea for an event. This study is suggestions for 'How to organise a cultural tourism show'. This is a popular event and can be easily linked to different travel and tourism themes.

1   Create a theme. This may be linked to a tourism destination, eco-tourism theme, tourism development charity or other good cause that you feel is appropriate. You may need to get the help of a local sponsor, for example a local retailer (clothing, food and drink at the local delicatessen and so on).

2   Build a knowledgeable team A successful cultural show requires the help of six key personnel:

    a   backstage manager

    b   show producer

    c   publicist

    d   sponsorship coordinator

    e   master of ceremonies

    f   marketing and sales manager.

3   The show producer is responsible for executing the theme of the show, creating a budget for the event and hiring all personnel. The backstage manager oversees the production of the cultural show. The publicist generates publicity for the event. The sponsorship coordinator liaises with all local sponsors and any other organisations that have donated products and services for the charity event. The marketing and sales manager is responsible for ticket sales, generating in-kind donations and managing the community links.

4   Select the venue. The venue determines the time of the show and the crowd capacity. When selecting the perfect cultural show venue, closely examine the venue's lighting and sound potential, backstage area, parking facilities, special needs access, insurance requirements and any hidden costs.

5   Select suitable products and services. All of the team is required to assist in this.

6   Sell tickets, invite VIPs and create excitement regarding the event. Invite journalists, editors and important charity donors to your cultural show. Send invitations a minimum of six weeks before the show. Submit press releases to media announcing the charity cultural show.

Objective

Devise ideas for a promotional campaign for an event.

Activity

Complete a chart to show two examples for each of the following promotional tools.

- advertising
- sales promotion
- direct marketing
- sponsorship
- public relations
- personal selling
- publicity material.

Resources

A3 paper or large sheet of paper for each group. Individuals to transfer to own coursework.

Risk assessments and contingency planning

Risk assessments and making a contingency plan or 'Plan B' are essential for the safe and realistic organisation of any event. Real contingency plans should be included to respond to problems that may arise with the actual event, such as bad weather preventing a trip going ahead or a power cut during a fashion show. The first part of a contingency is to assess all the possible problems that could arise for the actual event – many of these problems will be out of the control of the organisers and can occur at any stage of the event process.

Decisions should be made ahead of the actual event to overcome any potential difficulties. All contingency plans become part of the overall business plan.

Assessing any risk involved with an event is essential in order to reduce or eliminate any possible risks. This will help an organiser manage or highlight event risks and ultimately give consideration to whether or not an event is a safe and viable option.

Risk assessments look at:

- what the risks are
- how to improve the practices to reduce or eliminate risks
- help to decide whether the risks are worth taking at all (should the event be cancelled due to high risks involved).

 KEY TERM

Risk assessment: assessment of potential risks such as injury, loss or danger which may be encountered during the event.

Risk assessment involves the individual having to rate the chances of a particular risk or hazard occurring on a scale of 1–5. Consideration should then be assessed as to the severity of outcome and rate the worst probable consequence due to that risk or hazard on a scale of 1–5.

Likelihood of occurrence	Severity of outcome
1. highly unlikely to ever occur	1. slight inconvenience
2. may occur but very rarely	2. minor injury requiring first aid
3. does occur but only rarely	3. medical attention required
4. occurs from time to time	4. major injury needed hospitalisation
5. likely to occur	5. serious injury/disability/death

Table 5.4

Table 5.4 shows an indication of the rating of such risks. The score for the likelihood is then multiplied by the severity score to give the overall risk factor score. All risks can then be ranked in order from high to low and the assessor is able to identify the highest risks for priority attention. Risks assessments and contingency planning are not intended to be alarmist, but to help to reduce and highlight potential problems.

 KEY CONCEPTS

Global and growing

The previous section shows that there are many different types of events that are spreading across the globe. Events can be adrenalin charged or may be calm and quiet affairs, but the importance to the overall travel and tourism industry is not to be underestimated.

Contingency plans should be clear and appropriate. They should address the 'what if?' scenario: they should be realistic and achievable within the current environment. It is, therefore advisable that full consideration be given to the following health and safety questions.

1   What are the main objectives of the visit?

2   What is 'Plan B' if the main objectives cannot be achieved?

3   What could go wrong? Does the risk assessment cover:

- the main activity
- 'Plan B'
- travel arrangements
- emergency procedures
- staff numbers, gender and skill mixes
- generic and site-specific hazards and risks (including for Plan B)
- variable hazards (including environmental and participants' personal abilities and the 'cut off' points).

4   What information will be provided for parents?

5   What consents will be sought?

6   What opportunities will parents have to ask questions (including any arrangements for a parents' meeting)?

7   What assurances are there of the leader's competencies?

8   What are the communication arrangements?

9   What are the arrangements for supervision, both during activities and 'free time' – is there a code of conduct?

10 What are the arrangements for monitoring and reviewing the visit?

Insurance arrangements

Any event no matter how big or small must consider insurance. In the unlikely event of something going wrong during the event, it is vital that insurance policies are in place to cover all possible outcomes. In most instances, the event will be covered by the school/college insurance policy. However, should the event be conducted as a residential trip in an overseas destination, there may be a requirement for extra insurance coverage. Equipment and specialist apparatus may need to be included in extra policies. It is vital, therefore, that during the planning stages, insurance needs are discussed in detail and any extra policy requirements covered. It may be that a small charge is included in all participant fees in order to cover any extras that are required.

Carry out the event according to the plan

The event is expected to be real and should therefore actually take place. It may be useful to take photographs, DVD or video and complete a log of the event to help with the final evaluation. Case study 5 is a promotional advertisement for the Bavarian Garden and Flower Show in Bamberg, Germany. The event runs every year with the culmination of stunning floral displays set alongside open-air events. The show lasts for an incredible 165 days. It is difficult to imagine what pitfalls occur during the planning and execution of such an event, but it is interesting to see that the event links with cultural, eco and social benefits to the town, all set within the world heritage city of Bamberg.

ACTIVITY 10

Safari Adventures in Mauritius organise several different types of Big Cat tours on the beautiful island of Mauritius. Big Cat Encounters includes the exclusive Walking with Lion Experience, Walking with Tigers and the ever-popular Interaction with the Cats.

Look at their website to know about their activities and draw up a table to assess the likely risks that may occur during a visit to Safari Adventures. Start your information from leaving school or college.

Skyline Overseas is an event organiser specialising in charity events. They have organised 'Charity Bike Ride India': a ten day cycling event. Consider a contingency plan for the following:

- One of the participants becomes ill just before the event begins.
- There is a torrential downpour on day two of the event, which makes cycling very difficult for all participants.

Culture and nature at their best

The Bavarian Garden and Flower Show is staged in the world heritage city of Bamberg from April to October, creating a huge new recreational park for Bamberg. On the northern tip of the island district of Bamberg, where the two arms of the River Regnitz meet again after having flowed round the medieval old town of Bamberg, visitors can enjoy a garden party lasting the whole of the summer with colourful blossoms, plants of all sizes and kinds and great open-air events. Once the site of a textile factory, a huge area has been turned into a park. The floral planners have taken the theme of textiles to heart and there are many allusions to textile fabrics in the grounds and in the assembly of the plants and paths.

One of the main sights is the Fish Pass, the ecological top project. For about a mile, the fish creek winds its picturesque way through the grounds. Not only does it look wonderful, it also allows the local fish population to navigate the Regnitz River upstream again, after nearly a hundred years of a dead end at the lock of the textile factory. A patchwork garden, the pyramid meadows, a vast number of flower beds and perennials and lots of garden pavilions and information on gardening and plants are accompanied by more than 2000 cultural events during the 165 days of the show. All that amounts

to an incredibly attractive add-on for Bamberg visitors, just a few minutes away from the old town.

The garden show also finds its way into the city, thanks to the city-projects, like the new vineyard on the slopes of Michelsberg Hill, underneath St. Michael's Monastery, or the modern relaunch of the Gardener's museum in the Gardener's district of Bamberg and the new circular route taking visitors to the most important points of the district, explaining the history of gardening and wine growing in Bamberg.

Figure 5.20 The Englischer Garten in Munich

5.17 Evaluation

Event evaluation is an important part of the event process. Evaluation techniques should be considered at the early stages of the project. The business plan should contain assessment of evaluation methods. It is important that evaluation is made not only from a personal perspective but also considers the role of the other team members and the overall success or failure of the event itself. The evaluation may be conducted via questionnaires, interviewing group members or participants and the inclusion of a witness statement from the tutor, teacher or assessor.

Questionnaires

Questionnaires can be used to ask participants for their opinions on a variety of issues. This is often the easiest way of gaining good feedback and of gaining information regarding specific areas. An anonymous questionnaire often provides useful information that gives honest reactions to aspects of the event covering issues such as

the facilities, service, timing, catering (if used), success of the marketing, overall event success and suggestions for improvement.

Interim evaluation

To ensure the success of the event, an Interim Evaluation should be set in place. This is an ongoing procedure where checks are made throughout the planning stages. This may be done through formal or informal meetings. It helps to keep the event planning on track and be able to put in place any corrective measures or remedial action if needed. It prevents deadlines from slipping, targets from failing and keeps a check on group interaction and relationships.

Final evaluation

The final evaluation and report should be compiled through information gathered from participants, tutors and other team members. The following section lists some of the evidence that may be gathered for the event evaluation.

Witness statements

A witness statement(s) supplied by any or all of the following:

- employee of the attraction, event attended example, tour operator, guide and so on
- tutor, if the student is taking part in a Field Study residential trip
- teacher or lecturer accompanying the adventure trip.

These statements should provide comments about the following:

- an individual's contribution to the group activity
- demonstration of listening skills
- interaction with others
- skills development
- initiative shown/problem solving.

Personal evaluation

Personal evaluation should consider each of the following:

- comment about personal contribution to the activity and to highlight the role that was played within the group
- provide an appraisal about the group's performance during the activity and provide comment such as group behaviour and learning
- make reference to the teacher's assessment of the role in the planning of the group's chosen activity
- comment about what the employee (if appropriate) has said about skills development of the interaction of individuals with others
- the relationship between the group's objectives and the actual outcomes
- comment on the effectiveness of planning and the extent to which plans were actually adhered to
- appropriate recommendations about any future events
- a summary of what has been learnt through the whole event research, planning and execution.

To help them generate additional evidence for the evaluation, it is recommended that a questionnaire survey is administered amongst the various group members. Information to be considered might include any of the following. For example, participants might be asked to give some feedback based on their experience of the activity and to circle the most appropriate number on the scale below where 10 is best.

Quality of the activity as an experience:

1   2   3   4   5   6   7   8   9   10

How well the activity met your expectations:

1   2   3   4   5   6   7   8   9   10

Participants could then be asked:

- How would you summarise your experience of the event?
- What was most enjoyable?
- What was least enjoyable?
- What would have made it better?
- Any other comments or suggestions.

Quantitative and qualitative analysis

Questionnaire structure should allow for both quantitative and a qualitative analysis of participant opinion. The 'quality' and 'expectation' ideas allow for precise figures to illustrate evaluative analysis. Reliable feedback should be sought. This will provide details that will assist with future planning and recommendations of any subsequent event activity. It will also enable a reasoned self-evaluation of personal performance during participation in the chosen event.

Quantitative analysis is a formal, objective, systematic process in which numerical data are used to obtain data, it tries to quantify the problem and understand how prevalent it is by looking for projectable results to a larger population; such as data collection through surveys (online, phone, paper) and purchase transactions.

Qualitative analysis is data-gathering techniques that are focussed on the significance of observations made in a study, rather than the raw numbers themselves. Evidence is gathered through focus groups, interviews and observations.

Finally, the completion of your portfolio is essential to gain good grades. You should consider the following bullet points:

- Were the aims and objectives met?
- Were all the deadlines met?

- Was the planning workable and effective?
- Did all customers have a positive experience? If customer needs were not achieved, you should explain why.
- What went well and what was a disappointment?
- Did working in a team help with the event?
- Were my evaluation methods effective?
- How have my values changed since completing this event?
- What recommendations would I suggest for future events?

 KEY CONCEPTS

Customer focus

The previous section highlights the importance of good evaluation techniques. Without being able to assess the success of an event no future progress can be made. Learning from one's mistakes is a useful tool to develop good practice in the future. Evaluation tools such as questionnaires, surveys, quizzes, focus groups and so on are all useful. However, it is important that consideration is given to the correct type of technique.

Survey result of Singapore Airlines

The following details the results of surveys on Singapore Airlines from the general public, businesses and trade organisations. The success of their performance is seen through the various awards and tributes given.

Singapore airlines continues to receive accolades from around the world

08 January 2011 – Singapore Airlines again emerged on top in 2009 as the favourite airline among business and leisure travellers in numerous international rankings, highlighting its continued focus on product innovation and service excellence.

The repeat awards that Singapore Airlines has been winning over the years encompass categories such as in-flight entertainment, food and beverages, ground services, safety and company management. The awards reflect the Airline's philosophy to constantly innovate and keep pace with the changing tastes and preferences of consumers.

The Airline was recently named favourite for frequent business travellers in the annual global poll conducted by the respected Official Airline Guide organisation based in London. In the OAG Airline Industry Awards 2009, Singapore Airlines was voted 'OAG Airline of the Year' for the 7th time. In addition, the Airline earned top placing in the following categories: Best Airline based in Asia, Best Europe to Asia/Australasia Airline and Best Transpacific Airline.

Condé Nast Traveler (US), a leading travel publication, named Singapore Airlines 'Best Global Airline' for the 21st consecutive year in its 2009 Readers' Choice Awards.

The carrier also secured the 'Best International Airline Award' in the World's Best Awards survey conducted by the US-based travel magazine, Travel and Leisure, for the 14th consecutive year.

Singapore Airlines earned the 'Most-Admired Singapore Company' accolade in the Wall Street Journal Asia, Asia's 200 Most-Admired Companies survey in 2009, for the 17th consecutive year.

In the 2009 Zagat Airline Survey by the US-based Zagat organisation, Singapore Airlines was the Top-Rated International Airline for Premium and Economy Seating.

Readers of a leading regional travel magazine, Business Traveller Asia Pacific, voted Singapore Airlines the 'Best Airline' for the 18th consecutive year. In addition, readers rated the Airline as the 'Best Airline in the Asia Pacific' and the airline with the 'Best Business Class', 'Best First Class' and 'Best Economy Class'.

In the Swiss-based Bilanz Survey 2009, Singapore Airlines emerged as the winner in the following categories: Best Worldwide Business Airline (5th consecutive year), Best Airline for First Class and Business Class, Food, Service and In-flight Entertainment.

In AB Road magazine of Japan's Airlines Top 10 Ranking 2009, Singapore Airlines won in the Best Overall Airline (2nd consecutive year), Best In-flight Service (2nd consecutive year), Best Aircraft Products and Best In-flight Meals categories.

In Fortune magazine's The World's Most Admired Companies 2009 survey, the carrier was ranked 33rd.

In the Business Traveller UK Reader's Poll Awards 2009, readers rated Singapore Airlines as the Best Asian Airline. It was also voted the carrier with the 'Best Cabin Staff', 'Best Economy Class', 'Best Business Class' and 'Best Long Haul Airline'.

Readers of the Guardian and Observer newspapers voted the Company as the Best Long Haul Airline (for the 6th consecutive year) and with the Best Business Class.

Readers Choice Awards 2009 annual survey by another prestigious travel magazine, Jakarta-based DestinAsian, readers gave top marks to Singapore Airlines in the following categories: Best Overall Airline, Best Airline for Premium Class Travel, Best Airline for Economy Class Travel and Best In-flight Entertainment for the 5th consecutive year.

For the 8th consecutive year, Singapore Airlines was inducted into the Travel Hall of Fame in the TTG Travel Awards 2009. In the Skytrax World Airline Survey Awards 2009, it was named the airline with the 'Best First and Business Class'. In Aviation Week's Top Performing Companies 2009, it was ranked 1st in the Mainline Carriers category.

In the Readers Digest Trusted Brands (Singapore) survey, the Airline was awarded the 'Platinum Award – Airline Category in Singapore' and the 'Gold Award – Airline Category in Asia'. In the 2009 Global Reputation Pulse Survey, the Airline was ranked 10th in the 'The World's Most Reputable Companies' category.

At the Securities Investors Association of Singapore 10th Investors' Choice Awards 2009, Singapore Airlines received the 'Most Transparent Company Award 2009' for the 5th consecutive year, in the Transport/Storage/Communications Category.

Singapore Airlines (Figure 5.21) is grateful to its customers who have supported the airline through the years and consistently accorded it high ratings in the various surveys. In the midst of these challenging times, the Airline has upheld its commitment to invest in product and service development. The numerous awards therefore attest to the dedication of the Airline's staff, and serve as an encouragement to them to build upon their outstanding work.

Figure 5.21 A Singapore Airlines plane

ACTIVITY 10

The following is a suggested check list for organising a conference. After reading the list, create a computer or handwritten spread sheet that can be used as a working document for a conference event.

- How many delegates are likely to attend the event?
- What is your budget?
- What sort of conference or meeting facility do you need – theatre style, cabaret style, classroom style, boardroom style or a combination?
- Do you need any syndicate rooms?
- Do you need a display or exhibition area?
- What sort of audio-visual requirements do you need?
- What sort of technology do you want to use, if any, and what support do you need?
- How many coffee breaks do you require?
- Is social networking an important element of the event? You may wish to consider how refreshment breaks can help this process.
- Where are your delegates coming from and how will they arrive? Will they need car parking?
- Will your delegates need extra facilities such as a gym, swimming pool, satellite TV, internet access and restaurants?

- Is the venue acceptable for delegates with special needs? Are any special facilities or features required?
- Are you having any VIPs attending the event and do you need any special arrangements for them?
- Is there likely to be press interest in your event?
- Do you need to access support services such as photocopying and printing?
- Will you be webcasting or podcasting the event?

On a spread sheet, include a column for listing items and requirements on the day of the conference. You may wish to consider the following:

- meeting desk with someone to assist the signing in of delegates
- tick-sheet for names of delegates
- badges
- hand-outs
- computer software compatibility
- signage
- evaluation forms.

Summary

This chapter has covered all the main points to help you achieve a successful travel and tourism event. You should now understand the processes for planning, managing and running a real-life event. You will be able to form a small working group of between four and six members and work collaboratively as part of a team. This chapter shows you how to successfully complete your event by keeping detailed records of your involvement. It is essential that your work is completed on an individual basis. If work is included by other team members it must be made clear who has done the work, for example, a poster design.

Remember once the event is completed, you must complete an evaluation of the whole process from start to finish.

Finally, keep the syllabus and marking criteria handy. These will help to guide you to complete all the correct evidence needed.

Syllabus	Marks available
strand one Working in a team	12 marks
strand two Choosing the event (2–4 feasibility studies)	13 marks
strand three Business plan	12 marks
strand four Running and evaluating the event	13 marks
Total	50 marks

Table 5.5 Breakdown of the syllabus strands and marks available

Note: The letters 'f' and 't' following locators refer to figures and tables respectively

Ansoff matrix, 115

BACS. *See* Banking Automatic Clearing System (BACS)
Banking Automatic Clearing System (BACS), 231
brand health metrics, 155
branding destination, challenges
    delivering, 154
    effectiveness, 155
    lack of funding, 155
    marketing and promotion, 154
    social, economic and political factors, 155
    tourism offering, 153
    unique identity, 155
building destination brand
    appealing, 134
    awareness of, 133–134
    identity establishing, 131
    reasons, 131–132
    representation, 133
    stereotypes, 132
    tourist, 133
Butler 'Destination Lifecycle' model, 104f

coastal destinations, 17
Cohen's classification of tourists, 102t
commercial organisations
    and non-commercial, 180
    planning control, 180–181
competitor analysis, 114
competitor-based pricing, 126
countryside destinations, 17
creating brand identity
    corporate identity, 140
    distinctive packaging, 140
    logo, 138–139
    name, 138
    price with image, 139–140
    slogan/tagline, 138
    unique selling point (USP), 139
customer feedback
    comment cards, 92
    focus groups, 96
    informal, 91

market research, 94
mystery shoppers, 95–96
social media, 91
staff *vs.* customer, 96
suggestion box, 91–92
surveys, 95
customer service
    delivery of, 87–90
    external needs, 73–81
    feedback, 90–96
    global distribution of, 84f
    need of, 73
    organisational functional area, 85–87
    quality, 81–82
    tourism organisations, 82–85

dark tourism, 19
delivery of customer service
    benchmarking, 90
    individual performance, 88–89
desk research, 110
destination brand, marketing
    brand identity, 138–140
    challenges branding destination, 152–155
    communication methods, 146–149
    destination brand, 131–134
    difficulty in, 152
    effective, 134–138
    implementing, 144–146
    launching, 141–144
    media communication, 151–152
    selection communication methods, 150–151
destination brand identity, communication methods
    advertising, 148
    email marketing, 147
    environment, 149
    NTO, 147
    public relations (PR), 147–148
    publicity materials, 147
    sales promotion, 148
    signage, 149
    social media, 147
    websites, 147
    word of mouth, 148–149
destination lifecycle
    consolidation, 105
    decline *vs.* rejuvenation, 105

development, 105
exploration, 105
involvement, 105
stagnation, 105
destination management
activities, 175–177
branding and marketing, 180
commercial and non-commercial organisations, 180–181
community involvement, 183
education, 177–180
education training, 183
employment of locals, 183
environmental impact auditing, 181–183
environmental impacts of tourism, 194–202
evolution of destination, 202–207
organisations involvement, 165–171
socio-cultural impacts of tourism, 190–193
tourism development, 171–175, 184–189
destination management activities
carrying capacity, 176–177
tourism policies and practices, 175–176
Destination management companies (DMCs), 51
destination types, tourism, 16
coastal, 17–18
domestic, 15–16
independent, 16–17
island, 17–18
mass, 16
packaged, 16–17
resort, 17
rural, 17
town, city, country, 17
urban, 17
direct employment, 28
DMCs. See Destination management companies (DMCs)
domestic tourism, 15
dynamic sourcing, 140

earned media, destination brand identity, 152
ecological factors, tourism
attitudes and tastes, 43
budget polarisation, 43
cost/quality ratio of product, 45
environment protection, 40
global warming, 41–42
luxury products, 43
market driven, 43
natural conservation, 40
natural disasters, 41–42
new travel forms, 42–43
product differentiation, 45
product line extension, 45

specialised packages, 44
sustainable and responsible, 44–45
effective destination brand
accepted by stakeholders, 137–138
attractive, 135
attributes, 135–136
credible, 138
customer experience, 137
customer understanding, 136
existing customer, 137
memorable, 135
positioning, 136
promotional activities, 136
sustained period of time, 136–137
environmental impact auditing
encouraging tourist behavior, 183
monitoring and evaluation, 182
visitors and providers, 182
environmental impacts of tourism
adventure, 198
characteristics of destination, 195
destination management, 200–202
developments, 198–199
natural and built, 195
negative, 196
e-tourism, 39
evolution of destination, changes, 202–206

ferry services, 55
field research, 107
film tourism, 19
fine dining restaurant, 63
functional area customer service standards, 86

Gantt chart, 232
greenhouse gases, 41

high performance team, 218
hotel receptionist, 87

implementing destination brand
communicating, 144
interdependent stakeholders
commercial travel, 145
local community, 146
local tourism organisations, 145
National tourism organisations (NTOs), 144
non-commercial travel, 145
regional tourism organisations, 144–145
tourism organisations, 145
independent tourism, 16
innovators, 126

231

integrated resorts, 17
island destinations, 17

Jaguar executive coaches, 59

key performance indicators (KPIs)
    arrival numbers, 157
    brand awareness, 158
    destination popularity ranking, 156–157
    job creation, 157
    length of stay, 157
    market share, 158
    new/repeat business, 158
    occupancy rates, 157
    return on investments (ROIs), 158
    visitor spend, 157

launching brand
    agree timing for action, 141
    campaign, 144
    communication methods, 143
    costs and resources, 141
    guardians of, 141–142
    promotional materials, 143–144
    set objectives, 142–143
leakage, 186
LEDCs. See Less Economically Developed countries (LEDCs)
Less Economically Developed countries (LEDCs), 18
level of disposable income, 117

market analysis tools
    Ansoff matrix, 115
    Boston matrix, 115
    competition among destinations, 114–115
    destination life cycle, 115
    PEST, 113–114
    statistical analysis of data, 113
    SWOT, 113
    and techniques, 112
market research analysis
    competition, 100–101
    competition amongst destinations, 104
    customer behaviours
    allocentric, 102
    mid-centric, 103
    psychocentric, 102
    tourists classification, 102
    customer needs, 100
    destination lifecycle, 104–107
    market, 99–100
    popularity of destinations, 104

    preference for destination, 103
    travel trends, 101
market segmentation, 117
    demographic
        age, 118
        disposable income, 118
        ethnicity, 118
        gender, 118
    geographic, 119
    psychographic, 118
    travel motivation, 117
marketing
    key performance indicators (KPIs), 156–159
    monitoring costs, 155–156
    product positioning, 122–123
    research and analysis, 99–106
    research methods, 107–112
    reviewing mix, 124–130
    segmentation, 117–119
    tools and techniques, 112–116
    tourism, 99
    visitor profiling, 119–122
marketing communication, 129
marketing mix
    advertising, 129
    direct, 129
    place
        distribution channels, 128
        physical location, 127–128
        tourism distribution channels, 128–129
    price
        going rate, 126
        penetration, 126
        prestige, 127
        promotional, 126–127
        skimming, 126
        variable, 127
    product, 124–125
    promotion, 129
    public relations (PR), 129–130
    sales promotion, 130–131
Maslow's hierarchy of human needs, 73f, 75t
mass tourism, 16
MEDCs. See More Economically Developed countries (MEDCs)
Meetings, Incentives, Conferences and Exhibitions (MICE), 18
MICE. See Meetings, Incentives, Conferences and Exhibitions (MICE)
modern travel, affecting tourism
    currency exchange rates, 31
    disposable income, 30
    distribution of wealth, 30–31

employment opportunities, 31
infrastructure development and improvement, 32
national economy and GDP, 20–30
modes of transportation, 52*f*
monitoring costs
attendance, 156
marketing activities, 156
and marketing activities, 155
provider surveys, 156
resource invested, 155–156
search engine optimisation, 156
social media response rates, 156
visitor surveys, 156
website traffic, 156
More Economically Developed countries (MEDcs), 18

National tourism organisations (NTOs), 47
NTOs. *See* National tourism organisations (NTOs)

occupancy rates, 120
onatracom express, 59
organisation in destination management
commercial organisations, 168–171
destination management companies (DMCs), 166
government ministries, 165
national tourism organisations (NTOs), 165
non-governmental organisations (NGO), 167
organisational customer service standards, 85
owned media, destination brand identity, 152

packaged tourism, 16
paid media, destination brand identity, 152
performance management, 89
planning tourism event
adjourning, 216
aims and objectives, 224–225
appropriate resources, 228
assessment, 214
autocratic leadership, 216–217
bureaucratic leadership, 217
business plan, 232–236
democratic leadership, 217
evaluation, 237–240
feasibility study, 219–220
finance, 229–231
financial documents, 231–232
forming, 215
marketing, 225–228
norming, 216
performing, 216
staffing event, 218–219
stages, 214–215

storming, 215–216
team performance curve, 218
technology, 221–223
political factors, tourism
legislation changes, 37–38
security measures, 36–37
social harmony, 36
terrorism, war, civil unrest, crime, 36
visa regulations, 36–37
visa requirements and entry controls, 37
potential team, 218
premium pricing, 127
price discrimination, 127
price-matching, 126
product positioning
destination to competitors, 122–123
image and reputation, 122
image/position, 123
unique selling point (USP), 123
pseudo team, 218

quality customer service
for customers, 81
for employees, 82
for organisation, 82

recreational vehicles (RVs), 58
Regional and local tourism organisations (RTOs), 48
regional coach services, 59
research methods
primary
questionnaires, 107–109
surveys, 109–110
qualitative, 111
quantitative, 111–112
secondary
advantages, 110
disadvantages, 110
resort destinations, 140
RTOs. *See* Regional and local tourism organisations (RTOs)
rural destinations, 17

sales promotions, 148
seaports, 53*f*
selection communication methods
24 hour marketing, 150–151
costs, 150
global reach, 150
lead times, 151
options for personalisation, 151
track success/conversion rates, 151
service encounter, 85*t*

shared media, destination brand identity, 152
slum tourism, 19
social factors, tourism
    ageing population, 32–33
    declining in West, 34
    family structures, 34–35
    health awareness, 35–36
    leisure time, 33–34
    middle classes in East, 34
socio-cultural impacts of tourism
    local host population, 191
    negative, 191
    positive, 190
    slum tourism, 191–192
specialised markets, 43
specialised tourism, 16
subsectors of travel
    accommodation and catering
      food and beverages outlets, 62–63
      hotels, 60–62
    currency exchange
      car hire, 66
      guiding services, 68
      tourist information, 68
    tour operations and travel agencies
      and holiday representatives, 63–64
      travel agencies, 65
    transport
      air, 51–53
      rail, 57
      road, 58–60
      sea, 53–55
    visitor attractions, 65–66
SWOT analysis, 222f

target market, 117
team building, 219
technological developments
    information technology, 39–40
    transport, 38–39
tour guide, 68
tourism development
    economic, 172–173
    environmental, 174
    and management, 171
    political, 174–174
    socio-cultural, 173
tourism development impacts
    economic, 185
    and economic, 188

    negative, 186–188
    positive, 185–186
tourism developments, 198
tourism industry
    intangibility, 24
    perishability, 24
    seasonality, 22–24
tourism organisations, 82
tourism organisations of New Zealand, 49f
tourism participation rate, 29
tourist behavior education
    new products and services, 177–179
    visitor and traffic management, 179
tourist family lifecycle, 76t
travel scale
    areas and receiving areas, 27
    employee in industry, 28
    future predictions, 27
    key destinations, 27
    tourism, visitors, 28
    and tourism industry, 24
    transport, stay and rates, 28
travelling
    business, 18
    leisure, 18
    visiting friends and relatives (VFR), 18–19
travelling structure
    business ownership
      commercial organisations, 45
      non-commercial organisations, 45–47
    international
      consular service providers, 48
      Destination management companies (DMCs), 51
      industry groups, 50
      National tourism organisations (NTOs), 47–48
      Regional and local tourism organisations (RTOs), 48
      trade associations, 50
      world tourism organisation, 47
typical performance management process, 90f

UNWTO logo, 47f
urban destinations, 17

visitor profiling
    accommodation preference, 120
    booking methods, 122
    length of stay, 119–120
    media type, 121–122
    products and activities, 121
    spending power, 120–121

visitor destinations
   accessibility, 19
   accommodation, 22
   architecture, 21
   attractions, 19
   built and natural, 19–20
   climate, 20
   dress, 20
   events, 21
   gastronomy, 20

handicrafts, 20
history, 21
language, 20
leisure activities, 21
religion, 22
traditions, 20

Yahoo car express, 59

zones of customer experience, 84*t*